UNDERSTANDING LABOR LAW

Douglas E. Ray
Dean and Professor of Law
Widener University School of Law

Calvin William Sharpe
Professor of Law
Case Western Reserve University Law School

Robert N. Strassfeld
Professor of Law
Case Western Reserve University Law School

LEGAL TEXT SERIES

1999

MATTHEW BENDER

Outside the United States and Canada please call .... (212) 448-2000

For assistance with replacement pages, shipments, billing or other customer service matters, please call:

Customer Services Department at .... (800) 833-9844
Outside the United States and Canada, please call .... (518) 487-3000
Fax number .... (518) 487-3584

For information on other Matthew Bender publications, please call
Your account manager or .... (800) 223-1940
Outside the United States and Canada, please call .... (518) 487-3000

Library of Congress Catalog Card Number: 99-12362

ISBN 0-8205-4001-3

MATTHEW BENDER & CO., INC.
EDITORIAL OFFICES
2 Park Avenue, New York, NY 10016-5675 (212) 448-2000
201 Mission St., San Francisco, CA 94105-1831 (415) 908-3200

PREFACE

This book examines the multifaceted and complex law of private-sector labor law. It is a broad and interesting field. Labor legislation has shaped our country's labor relations system and labor law remains an important and evolving part of national policy and the framework of rights that defines our society. We think you will enjoy and benefit from its study.

Because the book focuses on relations between management and labor in the private sector, it deals primarily with the National Labor Relations Act, as amended, and its interpretation and application by the federal courts and the National Labor Relations Board. We have sought to include discussion of major cases found in standard casebooks on the subject and, where appropriate, bring in additional cases and other sources to help the reader reach a fuller understanding. We have especially sought to discuss the practical implications of doctrines as well as the interrelationships between them.

The treatise is organized in a format that is consistent with the organization of most Labor Law courses. At the end of each chapter is a section titled "Chapter Highlights." This section is intended to summarize some of the major doctrines discussed in the chapter and should be helpful for review and clarification purposes. Topics chosen for this treatment include matters which our combined teaching experience tells us are frequently misunderstood.

ACKNOWLEDGEMENTS

We wish to thank a number of people for the help they provided on this book. We are especially grateful to Aileen Jenner, Managing Editor, Mei Fung So, Legal Editor, and the composition and production staffs at Matthew Bender for their assistance and flexibility.

Dean Ray expresses his gratitude to Lin Whalen for her superb secretarial and organizational assistance and to Debra Baker, Josh Bills, and Judy Fornalik for the research and other assistance they provided while students at the University of Toledo College of Law. He especially thanks former Toledo colleagues William Richman, Roger Andersen and Marshall Leaffer for their advice and the example they set as authors of other volumes in the *Understanding* series. He is grateful, too, for the support provided by the Charles W. Fornoff Professorship in Law and Values at the University of Toledo which funded research, broadening his perspective into the many human and ethical issues raised in the practice of labor law. Finally, Dean Ray expresses his gratitude to his former labor law students who have added much to his understanding.

Professor Sharpe is grateful for the dedicated clerical assistance of Rebecca Wright, who coordinated the development of his chapters and consolidated the entire project. Professor Sharpe also benefitted from the excellent research assistance of Geoffrey Ashley and Phil Strzalka. Like Dean Ray, Professor Sharpe received generous financial support while he worked on this project. Case Western Reserve University Law School provided a grant for the completion of this project and the Chicago-Kent College of Law provided facilities and a stimulating intellectual environment during Professor Sharpe's sabbatical, when he commenced writing. For Professor Sharpe, any clarity in the presentation of this material reflects an ongoing effort to meet the intellectual demands of enthusiastic students during his years of teaching the subject at Case Western Reserve, the University of Virginia, Wake Forest, George Washington, Arizona State, DePaul, and the University of Minnesota law schools.

Professor Strassfeld wishes to thank Alice Hunt for her usual exceptional secretarial support and Carrie Nixon and Brian Wassom for their able research assistance. He also thanks Professor Douglas Leslie for nurturing his interest in labor law, while in law school and after, and Professor Calvin Sharpe, for his support and collegiality over the past decade. He is grateful, as well, to his past and current labor law students who have made labor law a gratifying subject to teach and who have in countless ways added to and influenced the story he has to tell. He thanks Case Western Reserve University School of Law, which has, in addition to providing an opportunity to teach labor law and advanced labor law, also provided summer research support for this project. Finally, at the risk of sounding trite, he thanks his wife Anne Strassfeld, and sons Jonathan and Daniel for their support and forbearance in the face of shirked household jobs and unplayed games of running bases.

We would appreciate your suggestions and reactions. Chapters 6, 8, 9, 10, 11 and 12 were the primary responsibility of Douglas Ray; Chapters 2, 3, 5, 7, 13 and 16 were the primary responsibility of Calvin Sharpe; and Robert Strassfeld was primarily responsible for Chapters 1, 4, 14, 15 and 17.

Douglas E. Ray
Calvin William Sharpe
Robert N. Strassfeld

DEDICATIONS

DER: With love to my wife, Caroline, my daughter, Katie, my son, Mike, and to my mother, Hazel Ray.

CWS: To my wife, Jan, my son, Kabral, and my daughters, Melanie and Stevie and now Nikki with love.

RNS: To my mother and father, Ruth and Meyer Strassfeld, who with their words and deeds taught me the importance of social justice; and in memory of my granduncle Tony, who, because he believed in One Big Union, would have greeted this project with kindhearted skepticism.

TABLE OF CONTENTS

Page

CHAPTER 1
INTRODUCTION

CHAPTER 2
THE NATIONAL LABOR RELATIONS BOARD

CHAPTER 3
THE AT-WILL DOCTRINE, EXCEPTIONS AND THEIR LIMITS

CHAPTER 4
SELECTING A BARGAINING REPRESENTATIVE: THE RIGHT TO ORGANIZE AND THE REPRESENTATION ELECTION

CHAPTER 5
EMPLOYER DOMINATION AND ASSISTANCE

CHAPTER 6
PICKETING AND STRIKING FOR RECOGNITION

CHAPTER 7
COLLECTIVE BARGAINING AND THE EXCLUSIVE REPRESENTATIVE

CHAPTER 8
DURATION OF UNION'S STATUS AS BARGAINING REPRESENTATIVE

CHAPTER 9
STRIKES

CHAPTER 10
LOCKOUTS

CHAPTER 11
SECONDARY BOYCOTTS

CHAPTER 12
CONSUMER PICKETING AND HANDBILLING

CHAPTER 13
ENFORCEMENT OF THE COLLECTIVE BARGAINING AGREEMENT

CHAPTER 14
FEDERAL PREEMPTION OF STATE REGULATION

CHAPTER 15
RECONCILING LABOR LAW AND THE ANTITRUST LAWS

CHAPTER 16
PROTECTING THE INDIVIDUAL IN A UNION AND NON-UNION ENVIRONMENT

Page

CHAPTER 17
NLRA REGULATION OF THE RELATIONSHIP BETWEEN THE INDIVIDUAL WORKER AND THE UNION

CHAPTER 1
INTRODUCTION

§ 1.1 Introduction: The Roots of American Labor Law

Law has regulated the work relationship in America since colonial times.[1] At first, American employment law was largely a transplant from its Old World sources, although, as was true of law more generally in the colonies, there was considerable local variation. Early colonial legislatures sought to regulate the prices of products and the wages paid to those who produced them by setting schedules of maximum prices and wages.

Much of the labor force in the 18th century was not free. This was obviously true of slaves, and because slavery was a social system, as well as a labor system, the role of law in maintaining that system was pervasive.[2] In addition to slaves there was a variety of other workers who, while clearly not slaves, were in a very real sense bound within a household economy.

Within the hierarchy of the crafts were master artisans, journeymen, apprentices, and indentured servants.[3] Masters were heads of households in a world where the household was the center of economic life as well as family life. Masters owned the workplace, typically a shed adjacent to the house, and the necessary tools and materials; they also sold the finished products, although toward the end of the 18th century, merchants, who did not participate in making the product, were beginning to appear.

Apprentices and indentured servants were legally bound to service for a specified number of years. Legally, they were dependent on their masters.

---

[1] On law relating to work in the colonies, see Stephen Innes, Labor in a New Land: Economy and Society in Seventeenth-Century Springfield (1983); Richard B. Morris, Government and Labor in Early America (1946); Robert J. Steinfeld, The Invention of Free Labor: The Employment Relation in English and American Law and Culture, 1350-1870 (1991); Christopher L. Tomlins, Law, Labor, and Ideology in the Early American Republic (1993).

[2] The literature on American slavery is vast. Good places to start, that are also sensitive to the law of slavery, include: Eugene D. Genovese, Roll, Jordan, Roll, The World the Slaves Made (1972); Eugene D. Genovese, The World the Slaveholders Made (1969); Winthrop D. Jordan, White Over Black: American Attitudes Toward the Negro 1550-1812 (1968); Kenneth M. Stampp, The Peculiar Institution: Slavery in the Ante-Bellum South (1956). On the law of slavery itself, see Mark Tushnet, The American Law of Slavery, 1810-1860: Considerations of Humanity and Interest (1981).

[3] There is a rich literature on the subject of household labor and the transformation from the household-centered economy to the economy of the 19th and 20th centuries. This discussion relies especially on Alan Dawley, Class and Community: The Industrial Revolution in Lynn (1976); Robert J. Steinfeld, *The Philadelphia Cordwainers' Case of 1806: The Struggle over Alternative Legal Constructions of a Free Market in Labor, in* Labor Law in America: Historical and Critical Essays 20 (Christopher L. Tomlins & Andrew King, eds. 1992); *see also* Bruce Laurie, Artisans into Workers: Labor in Nineteenth-Century America (1989).

They were obliged to respect their master's authority and to obey him, and he could lawfully punish their disobedience. He in turn, was responsible for their maintenance, as if they were his dependents. Like slaves, indentured servants and apprentices who ran away during their term of service were pursued and returned to their master if recaptured.

Journeymen were an important step up in the hierarchy. Skilled craftsmen, they owned their own tools but had not accumulated enough capital to become masters in their own right. They, too, lived and worked in the master's household, but they were not bound in the same manner as apprentices and indentured servants. But so long as they remained a part of the master's household, they were also subject to his command.

By the 18th century, the power to regulate prices and wages had largely passed from the state into the hands of the master artisans. Increasingly, journeymen's wages were set not by the legislature but by organized groups of master artisans. It seems inevitable that conflict between the two groups would occur.

§ 1.2 Regulation of Master-Servant Relations in Antebellum America

[A]—Beginnings of an American Labor Movement

During the early part of the 19th century, and to some extent, beyond, the conflict between wage earners and their employers generated legal intervention in the form of prosecutions for criminal conspiracy. These occurred against a backdrop of changes in the world of work. The old system of labor and social relations began to break down in the early decades of the American republic. There was a number of reasons why this happened. The American Revolution itself played an important role. Its message that social relationships and patterns of authority and dependency could be rethought and were up for grabs was not lost on the American people.[4] At the same time, household-centered production began to lose ground to other ways of organizing work. Gradually, indentured servitude disappeared.[5] In certain crafts, shoemaking, tailoring, and carpentry prominent among them, artisans found themselves forced to compete with shopkeepers and other merchants who sold cheaper, ready-made goods in place of the custom-made products of the artisans' households. These proto-manufacturers reorganized the work, often dividing the tasks into those that

---

[4] Steinfeld, *The Philadelphia Cordwainers' Case, supra* note 3, at 32-5.

[5] *See* Robert J. Steinfeld, The Invention of Free Labor: The Employment Relation in English and American Law and Culture, 1350-1870, 147-72 (1991).

required skilled craftsmen and those that could be given to less-skilled farmers on a seasonal basis. Both artisans and journeymen found themselves struggling in this changing economy. Increasingly, journeymen organized voluntary societies to help them in their clashes with masters over pay and conditions of work. Sometimes these clashes led to negotiated agreements on prices and wages and joint publication of price and wage schedules. Other times they led to the courts.

[B]—Criminal Conspiracy

In November 1805, the Philadelphia journeymen shoemakers (or cordwainers) struck for higher wages.[6] The strike was quickly broken when some of its leaders were arrested for the common law crime of conspiracy. In January 1806, they were prosecuted. On the instructions of the judge, they were found guilty and fined $8 each.

The trial of the Philadelphia cordwainers was but one of numerous similar prosecutions of early craft unions on the charge of conspiracy.[7] The conspiracy trials reflected a belief that the appropriate form of bargaining was between individuals; collective action to shore up a wage or to demand a higher one was both harmful to society and unlawful. Of course, not everyone saw it that way, and the *Cordwainers Case* was an occasion for the expression of two different views of labor relations and of the meaning of collective action by workers.

The prosecution protested that the cordwainers had not only set the price for their own work (something that each could do individually), but attempted to set it for everyone involved in the craft. According to the prosecution, this interfered with the rights of those who were willing to work for less. It also posed a threat to industry in Philadelphia and

---

[6] *The Philadelphia Cordwainers' Case (*Commonwealth v. Pullis*) (Mayor's Court of Philadelphia, 1806), in* 3 John R. Commons, Documentary History of American Industrial Society 59 (1910).

[7] The following discussion of the cordwainers' trial draws especially on Steinfeld, *The Philadelphia Cordwainers' Case, supra* note 3. For a discussion of the conspiracy cases and a list of cases, see Victoria C. Hattam, Labor Visions and State Power: The Origins of Business Unionism in the United States (1993). Other discussions of labor conspiracy include Wythe Holt, *Labour Conspiracy Cases in the United States, 1805-1842: Bias and Legitimation in Common Law Adjudication,* 22 Osgoode Hall L.J. 592 (1984); Alfred S. Konefsky, *"As Best to Subserve Their Own Interests": Lemuel Shaw, Labor Conspiracy, and Fellow Servants,* 7 Law and Hist. 219 (1989); Christopher L. Tomlins, *Criminal Conspiracy and Early Labor Combinations: Massachusetts, 1824-1840* 28 Labor Hist. 370 (1987).

undermined that city's ability to compete with other centers of industry; thus, it imperiled the welfare of the whole community by raising prices to artificial and uncompetitive rates. Further, this amounted to nothing less than an attempt to legislate—to act as a self-appointed government. To a generation that still remembered the Revolution, the prosecution raised the specter of a secret unelected group that would create and enforce law.

The cordwainers' lawyers also raised the specter of a private government, but the sinister force they identified was the masters. Unless journeymen were allowed to combine to demand a certain wage, argued the cordwainers, they would be powerless to influence the price of their labor. They, too, saw a threat to Republican government, but its source was the continued economic dependence of the journeymen, for, in a society that in many cases still limited suffrage to property owners, only the ability to earn a decent wage would allow them to acquire property and have the economic independence necessary to be equal citizens.

Most, but not all, labor conspiracy prosecutions ended in conviction. They represented a rejection of collective action in the marketplace in favor of individual bargains. The last reported conspiracy prosecution of the antebellum era, *Commonwealth v. Hunt*,[8] did not end in conviction. Instead, Chief Justice Lemuel Shaw found that the craftsmen in that case had not entered into a criminal conspiracy, but rather into a contract worthy of the same respect as any other lawful and enforceable contract. This decision proved to be something less than a *magna carta* for labor, but it appeared to have ended, at least for a while, the prosecution of workers for belonging to labor organizations.[9]

§ 1.3 Emergence of a National Labor Movement and the Expansion of Judicial Intervention

[A]—Rise of the Labor Movement

The period after the Civil War in the United States was one of tremendous economic growth that dictated the development of the national economy. All sorts of economic indicators reflect this rapid expansion. Between 1860 and 1920, the country's gross national product increased more than fivefold. Railroad track mileage increased from 30,000 to 240,000 miles between 1860 and 1910. By the mid-1890s, the U.S. had become the world's leading industrial power.

[8] 4 Met. (45 Mass.) 111 (1842).

[9] *See generally*, Konefsky, *supra* note 7.

The post-War growth was fueled by a tremendous expansion of manufacturing, unlike the country's earlier growth which was fueled predominantly by agriculture. The 1890 Census reported that industry had surpassed agriculture as the chief income producer in the U.S. Despite a depression in 1893, the distance between industry and agriculture had increased significantly by century's end.

Accompanying this growth were changes in the size and structure of companies and in how people earned their livings. In industry, there was a tendency toward bigness and concentration, fostered by technological changes that permitted increased industrial capacity and promised economies of scale, and a rapaciousness in business practices that earned many of the era's most successful businessmen the collective nickname "the Robber Barons." How Americans made their living was also changing. In 1860, most Americans were self-employed and engaged in agriculture. This was no longer true by 1890. By 1900, more than two-thirds of the workforce were wage workers. Industrial production bore little resemblance to the old system of household work, as workers were assembled in greater numbers first, in primitive factories, where the most important difference from earlier production methods was simply the mass of workers brought together under management's supervision; and, ultimately, in factories, where, to different degrees depending on the industry, crafts techniques and traditions were supplanted by a new organization of work. As Professor Alan Dawley notes of the shoe industry, "[t]he system of the factory was built on the twin foundations of mechanization and the division of labor."[10]

It is hard to tell what impact the criminal conspiracy doctrine had on labor unions, beyond the ones being prosecuted, during the first half of the century. We know that workers continued to organize themselves in trade unions, and sometimes organized local trade unions into city-wide federations of trade unions or combined with other local unions in the same trade to form national unions.[11]

Labor activity increased after the Civil War. In 1866, delegates from several unions representing twenty different trades and other labor reformers met to organize the National Labor Union.[12] This short-lived organization

---

10 Dawley, *supra* note 3, at 92.

11 *See generally,* Philip S. Foner, History of the Labor Movement in the United States, From Colonial Times to the Founding of the American Federation of Labor (1947).

12 David Montgomery, Beyond Equality: Labor and the Radical Republicans, 1862-1872, 176 (1967).

served as a forum for labor reformers and the union movement, as well as supported strikes and legislative activity in support of a shorter workday. Toward the end of the decade, the Knights of Labor emerged, first as a small group centered in Pennsylvania, but ultimately growing into a strong national organization, which, at its peak, could boast nearly 750,000 members.[13] Other unions not affiliated with the Knights also grew, and with them came increased strike activity. Strike activity bubbled over in 1877, most prominently on the railroads. Employers met it with a new counterweapon: the labor injunction.

[B]—The Labor Injunction

Increasingly, in the last decades of the 19th century and the first third of the 20th century, employers and their lawyers used the labor injunction as a means to end strikes.[14] Often initiated at an *ex parte* hearing for a temporary restraining order, and backed by the court's power to punish contempt, the injunction proved to be a powerful weapon. Perhaps the best known labor injunction case is *Vegelahn v. Guntner*,[15] in which the Massachusetts Supreme Court, over the dissent of Justice Oliver Wendell Holmes, appeared to hold that picketing is intrinsically intimidating and coercive and thus enjoinable. Consistent with that court's ruling over a half-century earlier in *Commonwealth v. Hunt* that the combination and agreement to strike were not in themselves criminal conduct, the court also followed the other teaching of *Hunt*: that the union must be pursuing lawful ends by lawful means. Strikes for any ends that a judge considered inappropriate or that used tactics that a judge considered inappropriate were tortious, and therefore enjoinable.

In the eyes of the judiciary of that era, many strikes failed either or both prongs of the ends/means test. Thus, in *Vegelahn,* a case involving a strike and picketing of a furniture manufacturer, the Massachusetts court enjoined all picketing, not merely picketing accompanied by force and threats, or picketing directed at workers under a contractual obligation to continue working for the employer. The court said that in addition to the use of

---

[13] Laurie, *supra* note 3, at 142.

[14] On the use of the labor injunction, see William E. Forbath, Law and the Shaping of the American Labor Movement (1991); Eileen Silverstein, *Collective Action, Property Rights and Law Reform: The Story of the Labor Injunction,* 11 Hofstra Lab. L.J. 97 (1993). On the common law courts' imposition of their views of valid and invalid objects and means, see also James B. Atleson, Values and Assumptions in American Labor Law (1983).

[15] 167 Mass. 92 (1896).

threats, it was also unlawful to make employment "unpleasant or intolerable" by the use of "moral intimidation."[16] The court seemed to imply that no matter how peaceful the picketing, if it might cause discomfort to strikebreakers or customers who saw it, the picketing was unlawful. Seemingly, no appeal to employees and customers would pass muster; and what the court may really have been saying was that while a joint decision to withhold their labor was permissible, no appeal to customers or employees would be.

Similarly, in *Plant v. Woods*,[17] a case growing out of a jurisdictional dispute between two unions, the court was quick to evaluate the worthiness of the union's ends and means and to enjoin the strike. In *Plant*, one of the two competing unions tried to enlist the employers on its side by enforcing a closed shop and by refusing to work for employers who would not. While the purpose of a closed shop was to enable a union to enforce its discipline on its members, and thereby collectively enforce a set of wage rates and other terms on their employers, the court judged that the union's purpose was too "remote" from the permissible purpose of seeking higher wages, and the union's conduct was therefore enjoinable.[18]

Ends as well as means were subject to the scrutiny and approval or disapproval of the courts. In a 1920 New York case, *Jaeckel v. Kaufman*,[19] defendant workers in the fur trade struck for a series of demands, many of them directed at the problem of layoffs and insufficient work. Among their demands were: a closed shop, limits on the workweek and hours and days of operation, grievance arbitration for discharge, work sharing in lieu of layoffs so that everyone bore the downturns in the industry equally, preference for hiring the unemployed before giving out overtime work, limits on apprentices, control of the supply of furriers, a fund for unemployment benefits, and a May Day holiday. While the court acknowledged that employees could strike for better wages or working conditions, it concluded that these demands constituted an attempt to interfere with the employers' prerogatives in running their businesses, and that the strike was therefore enjoinable.[20]

This sort of judicial intervention in labor disputes was widespread and increased dramatically in the 1920s during which time, according to

---

16 *Id.* at 97-98.

17 176 Mass. 492 (1900).

18 *Id.* at 505 (Holmes, J., concurring).

19 187 N.Y.S. 889 (Sup. Ct. 1920).

20 *Id.* at 899.

Professor William Forbath's estimate, 25% of all strikes prompted injunctions.[21]

[C]—Labor and the Sherman Act

In addition to the labor injunction, judicial hostility toward labor unions also manifested itself in the application of the antitrust laws. One of the nation's responses to the changes wrought by industrialization and concentration of industry was enactment of the Sherman Act in 1890. That Act prohibited "every contract, combination, in the form of trust or otherwise, or conspiracy in restraint of trade or commerce among the several States." There is no doubt that the framers of the law were thinking of industrial cartels and trusts and the danger they posed to smaller businesses. Nevertheless, the Act was enforced against labor unions more often than it was against businesses. Courts interpreted it as reaching various secondary boycott activity, including consumer boycotts of employers placed on union "unfair lists" and refusals to handle struck goods. The Supreme Court approved of this application of the Sherman Act in the *Danbury Hatters* case,[22] where the Court held that the Act reached a union boycott of retailers who sold hats manufactured by an employer who had resisted unionization. The case also gave birth to the American Anti-Boycott Association which vigorously pressed the use of the Sherman Act against secondary boycotts.[23]

Congress, on the prompting of organized labor, acted in the Clayton Act of 1914 to limit the application of the antitrust laws to union activity. Section 6 stated that labor was not an article of commerce, that labor organizations were not *per se* prohibited by the antitrust laws, and they did not prohibit unions from "lawfully carrying out" their "legitimate objectives." Section 20 sought to regulate the use of labor injunctions and specified various activities that were not enjoinable. Once again, however, the Supreme Court construed the Act unfavorably to union activity. In *Duplex Printing Press Co. v. Deering*,[24] the Court gave the Clayton Act's protections a narrow reading, emphasizing Section 6's requirement that the union activity be "lawful" and "legitimate," and then interpreting Section 20 to exclude boycott activity from the lawful activity that it protected. The Court, in effect, integrated the common law ends/means test into the application of the antitrust laws.

---

21 Forbath, *supra* note 14, at 197. *See also,* 187 N.Y.S. at 59-62.

22 Loewe v. Lawlor, 208 U.S. 274 (1908).

23 On the AABA and the application of the antitrust laws to unions, see Daniel Ernst, Lawyers Against Labor (1995).

24 254 U.S. 443 (1921).

[D]—Labor's Response to Judicial Intervention: The Triumph of Bread and Butter Unionism

The decline of the Knights of Labor in the late 1870s and the 1880s was followed by the creation of a new organization, the American Federation of Labor in 1886. That confederation of trade unions grew rapidly and successfully. Today, we associate the AF of L and its founder and long time President, Samuel Gompers, with "bread and butter" or "plain and simple" unionism. By that we mean that, unlike unions in other industrialized democracies, American unions focused on economic gains in the workplace and not on legislative gains, or on capturing the state through a labor party. Professor Forbath has persuasively shown, however, that both Gompers and the mainstream of the American labor movement were not initially hostile to a more political unionism. Rather, their experience with a hostile judiciary, which in addition to their use of the labor injunction and the Sherman Act also struck down hundreds of acts that labor had successfully lobbied for as violative of the due process clause, led them to see the state as hostile and to the belief that the best labor policy was government neutrality.[25]

§ 1.4 Early Labor Legislation

[A]—Railway Labor Act

Congress's first foray into labor legislation came in response to the paralyzing Pullman Strike in 1894. Upon the recommendation of the United States Strike Commission, in 1898, Congress enacted the Erdman Act which facilitated unionization in the railroad industry and provided for a mechanism for mediation of labor disputes. After part of the Act prohibiting discrimination against union members was struck down by the Supreme Court in *Adair v. United States*,[26] Congress eventually enacted the Railway Labor Act.[27]

The Railway Labor Act and the National Labor Relations Act resemble one another in some, but not all, of their features, and in some instances the courts have looked to doctrinal developments under one act for guidance in deciding the law under the other. Like the NLRA, the RLA is premised

---

25 *See generally*, Forbath, *supra* note 14. Forbath counts approximately 300 pro-labor statutes that were struck down by the courts by 1920.

26 208 U.S. 161 (1908).

27 45 U.S.C. §§ 151-63 (1994).

upon collective bargaining through representatives chosen by the employees to be their exclusive bargaining agents. It prohibits company unions imposed by the employer. It also guarantees the right to strike, although it creates a number of brakes to slow down or avert any movement toward a strike or lockout. It differs most importantly in this latter regard by creating dispute-resolution mechanisms designed to bring the parties to agreement without resort to economic weapons, although it also allows certain economic weapons, specifically certain secondary boycotts, that the NLRA, as amended, prohibits.

[B]—Norris-LaGuardia Act

Growing dissatisfaction with the use of labor injunctions led Congress to try once again to limit the power of courts (or at least federal courts) to intervene in labor disputes. In 1934, it enacted the Norris-LaGuardia Act.[28] Norris-LaGuardia prohibits federal courts from issuing injunctions in most "labor disputes." It broadens the definition of a labor dispute beyond what the Clayton Act had immunized. In response to the *ex parte* procedures that were so typical of the common law approach to labor injunctions, it also provides procedural safeguards in those instances where injunctions may be granted. Finally, it made quite explicit Congress's intention that the era of judicial oversight of labor disputes and labor policy should end.

§ 1.5 The National Labor Relations Act

[A]—Wagner Act

[1] The New Deal and the NIRA

The National Labor Relations Act, or NLRA,[29] was enacted by Congress in 1935. It did not spring from the head of its author, Senator Robert Wagner, without any antecedents. As noted above, the Railway Labor Act, though it establishes a somewhat different scheme of labor relations, was premised on the value of collective bargaining. Various commissions on

---

28 29 U.S.C. §§ 101-15 (1994).

29 29 U.S.C. §§ 151-69 (1994). As discussed below, Congress has made significant amendments to the Act in 1947 (the Labor Management Relations Act of 1947, or Taft-Hartley Act) and 1959 (the Labor-Management Reporting and Disclosure Act of 1959, or Landrum-Griffin Act). Throughout the text, we will refer to the Act, as amended, as "the Act," "the Labor Act," or the "NLRA." Where appropriate, we will refer to the amendments to the Act as such. Also, since portions of both the 1947 and the 1959 Acts did not amend existing parts of the NLRA, where we discuss those portions of either Act we will refer to the specific Act, for example "Title I of the Labor-Management Reporting and Disclosure Act of 1959."

industrial relations and the problems of strikes had recommended a scheme of collective bargaining as the solution.[30]

The NLRA was not part of President Roosevelt's New Deal agenda, although it has its origins in Section 7(a) of the ill-fated National Industrial Recovery Act. That Act, which would later be declared unconstitutional in the *Schechter Poultry Case*,[31] focused primarily on a strategy of creating industrial cartels as a means of fighting the Depression, and seemed to include Section 7(a)'s protection of the right to organize and bargain collectively in the National Recovery Administration codes of fair competition as an afterthought. Moreover, the Act provided no mechanism to guarantee these rights. Nevertheless, the Wagner Act was very much a product of its era, and the Senator's success in Congress (and his success in belatedly bringing President Roosevelt on board) reflected the growing distrust of market solutions to social and economic problems, as did another important piece of labor legislation, the Fair Labor Standards Act of 1938.[32]

[2] The Purposes of the Act

In their decisions interpreting the Act, the National Labor Relations Board and the courts tend to emphasize the Act's stated purpose of promoting industrial peace. Certainly, that was a motive behind the Act, but it is generally agreed by commentators, if not the bodies who interpret the Act, that the importance of that purpose has been overstated.[33] Rather, it appears that Senator Wagner primarily saw the Act as a weapon against the Depression, which he attributed to underconsumption caused by too unequal a distribution of wealth. Collective bargaining, he thought, would both restore an element of fairness and industrial democracy to the workplace, and redistribute wealth in such a way as to reinvigorate the economy.[34]

---

30 *See* David Brody, *Section 8(a)(2) and the Origins of the Wagner Act, in* Restoring the Promise of American Labor Law 29 (Sheldon Friedman et al. eds., 1994).

31 A.L.A. Schechter Poultry Corp. v. United States, 295 U.S. 495 (1935).

32 29 U.S.C. §§ 201-19. Amongst other provisions, the FLSA provided for a minimum wage and maximum hours, and restricted the employment of child labor.

33 On passage of the Act, see Irving Bernstein, Turbulent Years: A History of the American Worker, 1933-1941, at 318-51. On the overemphasis of industrial peace, see Kenneth Casebeer, *The Workers' Unemployment Insurance Bill, in* Labor Law in America 231, 253 (1992); Kenneth Casebeer, *Holder of the Pen: An Interview with Leon Keyserling on Drafting the Wagner Act,* 42 U. Miami L. Rev. 285, 320-22 (1987); Cynthia L. Estlund, *Economic Rationality and Union Avoidance: Misunderstanding the National Labor Relations Act,* 71 Tex. L. Rev. 921, 975-76 (1993).

34 In addition to the sources cited above, see Christopher L. Tomlins, The State and the Unions: Labor Relations, Law, and the Organized Labor Movement in America, 1880-1960, 103-40 (1985).

[3] Principle Features

Section 7 of the NLRA describes certain employee rights. In its original form (it was amended in 1947) Section 7 stated: "Employees shall have the right to self-organization, to form, join, or assist labor organizations, to bargain collectively through representatives of their own choosing, and to engage in other concerted activities for the purpose of collective bargaining or other mutual aid or protection."[35] Section 8 safeguarded these rights by prohibiting certain employer actions described as "unfair labor practices."[36] Section 8's overarching provision, Section 8(1) (Section 8(a)(1) in the amended Act) prohibited employer interference with the rights guaranteed by Section 7. Section 8(2) prohibited employer imposition of "representation plans," or company unions, and support or assistance to any labor organization. Section 8(3) prohibited discrimination in hiring or firing or terms of employment on account of union membership or activity. Section 8(4) shielded employees from retaliation for testifying or bringing charges before the NLRB. Section 8(5) required that employers bargain with the union chosen by the majority of its employees. Section 9 created the process by which the NLRB was to conduct representation proceedings.[37] Sections 3 and 4[38] created the National Labor Relations Board; and Section 10 both gave it its remedial powers and provided for judicial enforcement and review of Board orders.[39] Finally, Section 13 affirmed the right to strike, which was also encompassed in Section 7.[40]

On the heels of the Wagner Act, though questions of causation are more complicated, union membership grew dramatically.[41] The early Boards adopted the view that it was intended to aid and encourage organization of employees.[42] In *NLRB v. Jones & Laughlin Steel Corp.*,[43] the Supreme Court upheld thc constitutionality of the Act in response to a challenge on the grounds that the legislation went beyond Congress's powers to legislate under the Commerce Clause.

---

35 29 U.S.C. § 157 (1994).

36 29 U.S.C. § 158 (1994).

37 29 U.S.C. § 159 (1994).

38 29 U.S.C. §§ 153-54 (1994).

39 29 U.S.C. § 160 (1994).

40 29 U.S.C. § 163 (1994).

41 *See* Tomlins, The State and the Unions, *supra* note 34, at 148.

42 *See* R. Alton Lee, Eisenhower & Landrum-Griffin: A Study in Labor-Management Politics 4 (1990).

43 301 U.S. 1 (1937).

[B]—Labor Management Relations Act (Taft-Hartley)

The Wagner Act is properly seen as an attempt to encourage organization. It regulated employer behavior, but it did not similarly regulate union behavior. At the end of World War II, a series of strikes, which generated public hostility and led to labor being blamed for continued post-war shortages of various consumer goods, created an atmosphere in which business groups and New-Deal opponents saw an opportunity to restore "balance" to federal labor law.[44] There was also public concern about various union tactics, especially secondary boycotts and closed shops, that had been left unregulated by the Wagner Act. A coalition of Republicans (who had regained control of Congress in 1946) and Southern Democrats passed the Labor Management Relations Act, also known as Taft-Hartley over President Truman's veto.

The Taft-Hartley amendments inserted into Section 7 the right to refrain from the activities that the Wagner Act had protected. It also inserted a series of union unfair labor practices into Section 8. Amongst these were union interference with an employee's exercise of her Section 7 rights, secondary boycotts and strikes over jurisdictional disputes and pressuring an employer to discriminate against an employee because of her union membership or nonmembership under most circumstances. The Act prohibited the closed shop, but allowed for certain other union security agreements, which, in turn, it permitted the states to regulate or outlaw. It reorganized the NLRB to create the office of the General Counsel to separate the Board's prosecutorial and adjudicatory functions. Finally, it provided a forum in federal court for the enforcement of collective bargaining agreements.

[C]—Labor-Management Reporting and Disclosure Act of 1959 (Landrum-Griffin)

Congress's last major amendments to the NLRA came in 1959 after a congressional committee investigated and exposed corrupt practices in certain unions. The Labor-Management Reporting and Disclosure Act of 1959, or the Landrum-Griffin Act, primarily addressed matters relating to the operation of unions, including financial disclosure requirements, union elections, the fiduciary responsibility of union officers, and the rights of union members vis-à-vis their union. In addition, it included certain changes of the core provisions of the NLRA. Most notably, it inserted Section 8(b)(7) into the Act, which regulated organizational and recognitional picketing.[45]

---

[44] Lee, Eisenhower, *supra* note 42, 4-5. Lee reports that in late 1945 and 1946 nearly 5 million workers were involved in strikes.

[45] On the origins of the Act, see generally, Lee, *supra* note 42.

CHAPTER 2
THE NATIONAL LABOR RELATIONS BOARD

§ 2.1 NLRB Jurisdiction

The Board's jurisdiction broadly encompasses any private sector enterprise whose operations affect commerce.[1] In *NLRB v. Reliance Fuel Oil Corp.*,[2] the Supreme Court interpreted the breadth of the Board's jurisdiction as coextensive with the constitutional reach of the commerce clause. Generally, the Board is prevented from exercising jurisdiction only where the enterprise has a *de minimis* effect on interstate commerce.[3]

The Board's jurisdiction has been limited by the statute as well as the exercise of discretion, leaving millions of employees uncovered by the Act's provisions. Section 2(2) of the Act excludes the following categories of employers:

> the United States or any wholly owned Government corporation, or any Federal Reserve Bank, or any State or political subdivision thereof, or any person subject to the Railway Labor Act, as amended from time to time, or any labor organization (other than when acting as an employer), or anyone acting in the capacity of officer or agent of such labor organization.

In addition, because of First Amendment concerns, the Supreme Court in *NLRB v. Catholic Bishop of Chicago* held that the Act should not be construed to permit jurisdiction over secondary schools operated by the Catholic church.[4] The exclusion of public sector employers affects the largest number of employees, but many of them are covered by public sector

---

[1] Section 10 of the Act provides:

> (a) The Board is empowered, as hereinafter provided, to prevent any person from engaging in any unfair labor practice (listed in section 8) affecting commerce.

§ 2(6) defines "commerce" as follows:

> The term "commerce" means trade, traffic, commerce, transportation, or communication among the several States, or between the District of Columbia or any Territory of the United States and any State or other Territory or between any foreign country and any State, Territory, or the District of Columbia, or within the District of Columbia or any Territory, or between points in the same State but through any other State or any Territory or the District of Columbia or any foreign country.

"Affecting commerce" is defined in Section 2(7) as follows:

> (7) The term "affecting commerce" means in commerce or having led or tending to lead to a labor dispute burdening or obstructing commerce or the free flow of commerce.

[2] 371 U.S. 224 (1963).

[3] *See* NLRB v. Fainblatt, 306 U.S. 601 (1939).

[4] *See* 440 U.S. 490 (1979).

statutes that provide essentially the same rights as the NLRA with the important exception of the right to strike.[5] By contrast to the private sector, nearly three times the percentage of public sector employees are represented by unions as compared to private sector employees.[6]

Added to the employer exclusions are the following Section 2(3) employee exclusions:

> any individual employed as an agricultural laborer, or in the domestic service of any family or person at his home, or any individual employed by his parent or spouse, or any individual employed as a supervisor, or any individual employed by an employer subject to the Railway Labor Act, as amended from time to time, or by any other person who is not an employer as herein defined.

The agricultural exclusion deprives 1.9 million employees of the protection of the Act.[7] However, some states with a large agricultural presence—Arizona, California, Idaho and Kansas—have enacted laws patterned after the NLRA that create substantive rights and agricultural labor boards to protect such employees.[8]

The "independent contractor" category has been the subject of litigation dating back to before its inclusion in Section 2(3) under the Taft-Hartley amendments to the Act. Confronted with the question of whether newspaper vendors were employees within the meaning of the Act or independent contractors the Supreme Court in *NLRB v. Hearst Publications, Inc.*,[9] rejected the "right to control test." It examined the economic facts of the

---

[5] However, some states, such as Ohio, accord even the right to strike to most categories of public sector employees. *See* Ohio Revised Code 4117.01-23.

[6] *See* Archibald Cox, Derek Curtis Bok, Robert A. Gorman, and Matthew W. Finkin, Labor Law Cases And Materials 95 (12th ed. 1996).

[7] 1.9 million agricultural workers in 1992. *See* United States Census Bureau (visited 8/3/98) <http://www.census.gov/econ/www/ag0100.html>.

[8] *Arizona Agriculture Revisions Act, Arizona Revised Statutes Annotated, Title 23, Chapter 8, Article S, Sections 23-1381 to 23-1395 (1972).

*California Agricultural Labor Relations Act, Labor Code of the Deering's California Codes Annotated, Division 2, Part 3.5, Sections 1140-1166.3 (1975).

*Idaho Agricultural Labor Act, Idaho Code, Title 22, Chapter 41 Sections 22-4101 to 22-4113 (1980).

*Kansas Agricultural Labor Relations Act, Kansas Statutes Annotated, Chapter 44 Article 8, Sections 44-818 to 44-830 (1972).

[9] 322 U.S. 111 (1944).

relationship and the purpose of the statute to find that the vendors were closer to employees than independent businesses. The Court in *Hearst* affirmed the Board's holding that the vendors were "employees."

Following the *Hearst* decision Congress amended the Act to exclude independent contractors. Congress expressly criticized the Board and the *Hearst* decision for expanding the scope of the term "employee" to include independent contractors.[10] Thereafter, the Board began applying the "right to control" test to determine independent contractor status to the increased scrutiny of the courts. In *NLRB v. United Insurance Co.*,[11] the Supreme Court indicated that the heightened scrutiny by appellate courts of Board decisions regarding independent contractor status was inappropriate. Quoting from *Universal Camera Corp. v. NLRB*,[12] the Court said:

> Nor does it [the requirement for canvassing the whole record] mean that even as to matters not requiring expertise a court may displace the Board's choice between two fairly conflicting views, even though the court would justifiably have made a different choice had the matter been before it de novo.[13]

Even though the determination of independent contractor status did not require a special expertise, the Board's choice between two fairly conflicting views made it inappropriate for the Seventh Circuit to refuse to enforce the Board's order.

To further the interest of employers in the undivided loyalty of supervisors and the interest of employees in organizing free of supervisory interference, supervisors were excluded from coverage in the 1947 amendments to the Act.[14] They are defined in Section 2(11) of the Act as follows:

> [A]ny individual having authority, in the interest of the employer, to hire, transfer, suspend, lay off, recall, promote, discharge, assign, reward, or discipline other employees, or responsibly to direct them, or to adjust their grievances, or effectively to recommend such action, if in connection with the foregoing the exercise of such authority is not of a merely routine or clerical nature, but requires the use of independent judgment.

---

10 *See* H.R. Rep. No. 245, 80th Cong., 1st Sess. at 18 (1947).

11 390 U.S. 254 (1968).

12 340 U.S. 474 (1951).

13 390 U.S. at 260.

14 1 NLRB, Legislative History of the Labor Management Relations Act at 305 (1947).

This provision notes 12 supervisory activities and requires satisfaction of only one to qualify for supervisory status. As noted by the Supreme Court in *NLRB v. Health Care & Retirement Corporation Of America (HCR),*[15] Section 2(11) of the Act:

> requires the resolution of three questions; and each must be answered in the affirmative if an employee is to be deemed a supervisor. First, does the employee have authority to engage in 1 of 12 listed activities? Second, does the exercise of that authority require "the use of independent judgment"? Third, does the employee hold the authority "in the interest of the employer"?[16]

In *HCR,* where the issue was the supervisory status of licensed practical nurses (LPNs), the question was whether the nurses' supervisory tasks were exercised "in the interest of the employer." In that case staff nurses assured adequate staffing, made daily work assignments, monitored, evaluated, counseled and disciplined nurses' aides, and reported to management. The Board held that the LPNs were not supervisors, because their direction of the nurses aides was in the interest of patient care rather than the "interest of the employer." The Supreme Court upheld the Sixth Circuit's reversal drawing upon its reasoning in *NLRB v. Yeshiva Univ.,*[17] a case involving the classification of university faculty as "managerial" employees. The Court supported its conclusion with the following reasoning:

> As in *Yeshiva,* the Board has created a false dichotomy—in this case, a dichotomy between acts taken in connection with patient care and acts taken in the interest of the employer. That dichotomy makes no sense. Patient care is the business of a nursing home, and it follows that attending to the needs of the nursing home patients, who are the employer's customers, is in the interest of the employer . . . . We thus see no basis for the Board's blanket assertion that supervisory authority exercised in connection with patient care is somehow not in the interest of the employer.[18]

Justice Ginsburg writing for four dissenters disagreed with this analysis arguing that the Board's approach to resolving the tension between excluded supervisors and included professionals was both rational and consistent with

---

15 511 U.S. 571 (1994).

16 *Id.* at 573-74.

17 444 U.S. 672 (1980).

18 511 U.S. 571, 577-78 (1994).

the Act. The dissenters worried about the implications of the majority holding, saying:

> If any person who may use independent judgment to assign tasks to others or direct their work is a supervisor, then few professionals employed by organizations subject to the Act will receive its protections. The Board's endeavor to reconcile the inclusion of professionals with the exclusion of supervisors, in my view, is not just "rational and consistent with the Act," . . . it is required by the Act.[19]

The Board has distinguished from supervisors leadpersons, who are nonprofessional skilled employees having some authority to assign work or direct employees. These workers are deemed to be essentially rank-and-file employees.[20]

Though supervisors do not enjoy protection under the Act, the 1947 amendments also added Section 14(a), which disclaimed any prohibition against supervisory organizing and made explicit the implication that employers are not obligated to recognize supervisory unions.[21]

In some cases, an employer's treatment of supervisors may so affect the rights of "employees" such that supervisors are derivatively protected under the Act. For example, a supervisor discharged for refusing to comply with the employer's order to commit an unfair labor practice may be reinstated with back pay under Section 8(a)(1).[22]

Like supervisors, managerial and confidential employees are excluded from coverage, even though these categories are not listed among the employee exclusions. All managerial employees, defined "as those who 'formulate and effectuate management policies by expressing and making operative the decisions of their employer,' " are excluded from coverage

---

19 *Id.* at 598-99.

20 *See, e.g.,* Southern Bleacher & Print Works, Inc., 115 NLRB 787 (1956). *See* NLRB v. Bell Aerospace Co., 416 U.S. 267, 272 & 288 (1974) (for a summary of the legislative history reflecting Congress's intent to include "straw bosses, leadmen, set-up men, and other minor supervisory employees" as employees).

21 Section 14(a) reads:

> (a) Nothing herein shall prohibit any individual employed as a supervisor from becoming or remaining a member of a labor organization, but no employer subject to this Act shall be compelled to deem individuals defined herein as supervisors as employees for the purpose of any law, either national or local, relating to collective bargaining.

22 Parker-Robb Chevrolet, Inc. v. Automobile Salesmen's Union, 711 F.2d 383 (D.C. Cir. 1983).

and not only those "associated with the 'formulation and implementation of labor relations policies.' "[23] Confidential employees are "persons who exercise managerial functions in the field of labor relations."[24]

Even though the foregoing statutory exclusions leave it with very broad jurisdiction over private sector employers, the Board has exercised its discretion to limit its jurisdiction to those enterprises that have a substantial effect on interstate commerce.[25] Even where substantial effect is present, the Board, supported by the Supreme Court, has declined to exercise jurisdiction where it deemed the policies of the Act not served.[26]

To limit its exercise of jurisdiction to cases which involve a substantial effect on interstate commerce and serve the policies of the Act, the Board has created general and industry jurisdictional standards based on dollar volume.[27]

---

[23] 416 U.S. at 288 & 272 (1974).

[24] *See* Ford Motor Co., 66 NLRB 1317, 1322 (1946) and NLRB v. Hendricks County Rural Elec. Membership Corp., 454 U.S. 170 (1981) (upholding the Board's definition of "confidential employee" enunciated in *Ford Motor*).

[25] *See* NLRB v. Denver Bldg. & Const. Trades Council, 341 U.S. 675, 680-81, 683 & 684 (1951).

[26] *See* Guss v. Utah Labor Relations Board, 353 U.S. 1 (1957) (holding improperly Utah's assertion of jurisdiction in case where the Board declined to exercise jurisdiction but did not cede it to the state under Section 10(a) of the Act). In the 1959 amendments Congress endorsed the Board's jurisdictional caution in Section 14(c)(1) of the Act:

> (1) The Board, in its discretion, may, by rule of decision or by published rules adopted pursuant to the Administrative Procedure Act, decline to assert jurisdiction over any labor dispute involving any class or category of employers, where, in the opinion of the board, the effect of such labor dispute on commerce is not sufficiently substantial to warrant the exercise of its jurisdiction: Provided, That the board shall not decline to assert jurisdiction over any labor dispute over which it would assert jurisdiction under the standards prevailing upon August 1, 1959.

Congress also preserve the authority of states to fill the jurisdictional void in Section 14(c)(2):

> (2) Nothing in this Act shall be deemed to prevent or bar any agency or the courts of any State or territory (including the Commonwealth of Puerto Rico, Guam, and the Virgin Islands), from assuming and asserting jurisdiction over labor disputes over which the Board declines, pursuant to paragraph (1) of this subsection, to assert jurisdiction.

[27] The general standards are:

> **Nonretail Enterprise.* Sales of goods to consumers in other states, directly or indirectly (outflow), or purchases of goods from suppliers in other states, directly or indirectly (inflow), of at least $50,000 per year.

> **Retail Enterprises.* An annual volume of business of at least $500,000, including sales and excise taxes.

(Text continued on page 27)

**Retail and Manufacturing Enterprises Combined.* Either the retail or the nonretail standard, when a single, integrated enterprise manufactures a product as well as sells it directly to the public.

**Retail and Wholesale Enterprises Combined.* The nonretail standard, when a company is involved in both retail and wholesale operations.

**Instrumentalities, Links, and Channels of Interstate Commerce.* An annual income of at least $50,000 from furnishing interstate passenger and freight transportation services or performing services valued at $50,000 or more for enterprises that meet any of the standards except indirect outflow or indirect inflow established for nonretail enterprises.

**National Defense.* The enterprise has a substantial impact on national defense whether or not it satisfies any other jurisdictional standard.

**Territories and the District of Columbia.* The normal standards as applied in the states are applicable to the territories. Plenary jurisdiction is exercised in the District of Columbia.

**Multiemployer Bargaining Associations.* Regarded as a single employer in that the annual business of all members is totaled to determine whether any of the standards apply.

**Multistate Establishments.* The annual business of all establishments is totaled to determine whether any of the standards apply.

**Nonprofit Organizations.* The same standards as if the organization were operated for profit.

**Union Employers.* The appropriate nonretail standard.

Jurisdictional Standards for Specific Industries:

**Accounting Firms.* The Board has asserted jurisdiction over certified public accounting firms without specifying a precise jurisdictional standard. In the leading case, the firm received gross annual revenues in excess of $10 million.

**Arbitration Associations.* The Board has asserted jurisdiction over the American Arbitration Association, but has failed to establish a jurisdictional standard.

**Architects.* The Board has applied its nonretail business standards to architectural firms.

**Art Museums.* Gross annual revenues in excess of $1 million.

**Automobile Dealers.* Treated as retail operations, even if the dealer has a franchise from a national manufacturer.

**Building and Construction.* The appropriate jurisdictional standard in cases involving a single building trades employer, or the multiemployer bargaining association.

**Colleges, Universities, and Secondary Schools.* At least $1 million total annual income from all sources except those designated by the grantor as not available for operating costs. This applies to both profit and nonprofit institutions.

**Country Clubs.* Treated as retail concerns.

**Day Care Centers.* Gross annual revenues of at least $250,000.

**Entertainment and Amusement.* Treatment as retail concerns. The Board will not assert jurisdiction over horse and dog racing tracks.

**Federal Credit Unions.* At least $500,000 annual gross income from loans, deposits, investments, etc.

(Text continued on page 27)

**Gambling Casinos.* At least $500,000 gross annual revenue.

**Guard Services.* Companies furnishing plant guards to employers involved in interstate commerce are themselves subject to Board jurisdiction if the value of the services meets one of the Board's basic jurisdictional standards. The Board also has asserted jurisdiction over a company providing escort guard services where the nonretail standard was met.

**Health Care Institutions.* The Board's jurisdiction extends to any hospital, convalescent hospital, health maintenance organization, health clinic, nursing home, extended care facility, or other institution devoted to the care of sick, infirm, or aged person. Federal state, and municipal hospitals are exempt, as are administrative employers in the health field. The Board will assert jurisdiction over nursing homes, visiting nurse associations, and related facilities with gross revenues over $100,000 per year and over proprietary and nonprofit hospitals and other types of health care institutions with gross revenues over $250,000 per year.

**Hotels, Motels, Apartments, and Condominiums.* At least $500,000 total annual volume of business, whether an establishment is residential or nonresidential.

**Law Firms and Legal Aid Programs.* Gross annual revenues of at least $250,000.

**Office Buildings, Shopping Centers, and Parking Lots.* At least $100,000 total annual income, of which $25,000 or more is paid by other organizations which meet any of the standards, except the indirect outflow and indirect inflow nonretail standards.

**Postal Service.* Full jurisdiction as provided in the Postal Reorganization Act of 1970.

**Printing, Publishing, and Newspapers.* At least $200,000 total annual volume of business, and the employer must hold membership in or subscribe to interstate news services, publish nationally syndicated features, or advertise nationally sold products.

**Public Utilities.* At least $250,000 total annual volume of business or $50,000 outflow or inflow, direct or indirect. This standard applies to retail gas, power, and water companies, as well as to electric cooperatives. Wholesale utilities are subject to the general nonretail standards.

**Radio, Television, Telegraph, and Telephone Companies.* At least $200,000 total annual volume of business.

**Restaurants.* Treated as retail operations.

**Service Establishments.* Treated as retail operations.

**Sports, Professional.* The Board has refused to apply any specific jurisdictional standard to professional sports, but has regarded the industry as one affecting interstate commerce and has asserted jurisdiction in several cases.

**Symphony Orchestras.* At least $1 million total annual income, compiled from all sources except those designated by the donor as not available for operating costs.

**Taxicab Companies.* At least $500,000 total annual volume of business.

**Transit Companies.* At least $250,000 total annual volume of business.

**Union Employers.* The Supreme Court has held that the Board may not refuse to assert jurisdiction over unions as a class when they act in the capacity of employers. The Board generally asserts jurisdiction over local unions which are affiliated with national organizations and which remit to them dues or other fees across state lines.

See Kenneth C. McGuiness and Jeffrey A. Norris, How To Take A Case Before The NLRB 42-47 (BNA 6th ed.) (1992).

The Board declines jurisdiction over enterprises falling below the thresholds specified in these rules, and states may fill the void by asserting jurisdiction in those cases.[28]

§ 2.2 NLRB Organization

The NLRB enforces the NLRA.[29] The Board performs the two primary functions of conducting secret ballot elections to determine the representational status of labor organizations and preventing and remedying unfair labor practices committed by employers, unions and their agents.[30] The Board carries out this mission through two independent offices: the Board and the Office of the General Counsel.[31]

The Board is a five-member body, one member designated as Chair, where each member is appointed for a five-year term by the President with Senate approval.[32] It serves an adjudicative function, deciding appeals from the decisions of Administrative Law Judges (ALJ). Although the full Board renders decisions in some cases involving significant policy pronouncements, most of the Board's work is accomplished through panels of three Board members. Each Board member has a legal staff of approximately 20 lawyers headed by a Chief Counsel, which initiates the deliberation and resolution of cases.[33] The Board also is responsible for all representation matters, which it has delegated to Regional Directors.[34]

---

28 McGuiness and Norris, *supra* note 27, at 41-42. *See* Section 14(c)(2).

29 *See supra* Chapter 1, § 1.5.

30 *See* Sections 9(c) and (b) and 10(a) of the Act.

31 *See* Sections 3(a) and (d) of the Act.

32 Section 3(a) of the Act.

33 *See* Section 3(b) and 4(a), and *see generally*, McGuiness and Norris, *supra* note 27, at 33-34.

34 *See* discussion on the role of Regional Directors, *infra* § 2.3. The Board issued the following statement on May 4, 1961, effective May 15, 1961:

> Pursuant to section 3(b) of the National Labor Relations Act, as amended, and subject to the amendments to the Board's Statements of Procedure, Series 8, and to its Rules and Regulations, Series 8, effective May 15, 1961 and subject to such further amendments and instructions as may be issued by the Board from time to time, the Board delegates to its Regional Directors 'its powers under section 9 to determine the unit appropriate for the purpose of collective bargaining, to investigate and provide for hearings, and determine whether a question of representations exists, and to direct an election or take a secret ballot under subsection (c) or (e) of section 9 and certify the results thereof.'
>
> Such delegation shall be effective with respect to any petition filed under subsection (c) or (e) of section 9 of the Act on May 15, 1961.

McGuiness and Norris, *supra* note 27, at 831.

Though the Board has no authority over the investigation and prosecution of unfair labor practices (ULPs), it may veto the General Counsel's request for discretionary injunctions.[35]

The Board staff consists of an Executive Secretary who oversees case management agency communications, an Information Division that controls the release of agency information, a solicitor who is the agency's chief legal advisor, a division of judges that is independent of the Board whose members hear ULP cases de novo, and an Office of Representation Appeals—an adjunct to the Chair's office handling appeals of Regional Directors' decisions in representation cases.

The General Counsel (GC) of the Board, appointed for a four-year term by the President and approved by the Senate, supervises all Board attorneys except ALJs and Board member staffs. The GC supervises Regional office staff, has final authority over the investigation and prosecution of ULP complaints, and "such other duties as the Board may prescribe or as may be provided by law."[36] In a memorandum delegating powers to the GC, effective April 15, 1955, the GC assumed the authority to enforce Board orders in the United States Courts of Appeals and prosecute appeals before the Supreme Court, seek temporary restraining orders under Section 10(j), process election petitions and conduct elections under the national emergency provisions of Sections 206-209 of the Labor Management Relations Act, conduct 10(k) hearings in jurisdictional disputes, provide administrative and housekeeping services, and jointly with the Board, to formulate and execute budget requests.[37] The GC meets its statutory and delegated responsibilities through Regional Directors who head 34 regions and process all cases (representation and ULP) that arise in each region.[38]

The GC's office also has four divisions. The Enforcement Division enforces or defends the Board's orders in the Courts of Appeals and the Supreme Court, prosecutes contempt proceedings, and conducts any other

---

35 *See Memorandum Describing the Authority and Assigned Responsibilities of the General Counsel of the NLRB effective April 1, 1955, as last amended effective May 15, 1961*, McGuiness and Norris, *supra* note 27, at 826 (Section IB).

36 *See* Section 3(d) of the Act.

37 *See Memorandum, supra* note 35, and *see generally* McGuiness and Norris, *supra* note 27, at 36-37.

38 <http://www.nlrb.gov/fieldoff.htm>. In each regional office, the Regional Director presides over a regional attorney (the chief legal officer for the region), field examiners (investigators and election officers), and field attorneys (trial lawyers).

litigation in federal or state courts involving the Board's processes.[39] The Advice Division provides legal advice to the regional offices, supervises injunction litigation, and conducts legal research and special projects.[40] The Administration Division provides personnel, fiscal and administrative management. The Operations-Management Division manages all cases in the Washington GC divisions and supervises all field operations.[41]

§ 2.3 Procedure in Unfair Labor Practice Cases

Any person (Charging Party) may file a ULP charge with the Board in the region where the charge arose.[42] Section 102.10 requires the charge to be filed with the regional director for the region where the alleged ULP occurred. The Charging Party is responsible for proper service upon the opposing party (Charged Party). Even though the Regional Director will serve a copy of the charge on the Charged Party, the Charging Party retains responsibility for service. Section 10(b) of the Act contains a six-months statute of limitations that prevents the GC from issuing a complaint on any charge filed after this period, which begins when the ULP is committed.[43]

---

39 *See Memorandum, supra* note 35, at n.1, and *see generally* McGuiness and Norris, *supra* note 27, at 37-39.

40 *See* McGuiness and Norris, *supra* note 27, at 37.

41 *Id.* at 37.

42 McGuiness and Norris give the following examples from specific cases showing the breadth of this standing rule:

*An attorney, on behalf of individual employees;

*An individual, in effect a "stranger," who is not an employee;

*A discriminatorily discharged employee, on behalf of himself and other employees similarly discharged;

*An individual, on behalf of a labor organization, even though he is not authorized to file the charge;

*An employer who is not a member of an employer association in a case where rights of members of that association are involved;

*A labor organization which is not the majority representative;

*A labor organization which has no members in the employ of the charged company;

*A labor organization, against another labor organization, where both parties are affiliated with the same parent federation;

*A civil rights group, on behalf of individual employees;

*A party to a primary dispute, where the charge alleges an illegal secondary boycott. *Id.* at 314-315.

43 *See* United States Postal Serv. Marina Mail Processing Center, 271 NLRB 397 (1984) (holding that the period began with the date of the charging party's termination notice rather than its effective date). However, it is the charging party's notice of the ULP that starts

Filing occurs when the Board receives the charge.[44] The Charging Party may amend the charge to add, drop or modify allegations, and it may add completely new ULPs as long as it complies with the statute of limitations.[45]

At the time of filing the Charging Party must submit an affidavit setting forth the circumstances giving rise to the charge as well as the names and addresses of persons with information regarding the charge.[46] The Regional Director notifies the Charging Party of the receipt of the charge and the Charged Party of its filing, furnishes the Charged Party with a Statement of Procedures in Unfair Labor Practice Proceedings, and assigns the charge to a Board agent—field examiner or field attorney—for investigation.[47]

---

the clock. *See* Don Burgess Constr. Corp., 227 NLRB 765 (1977) (continuing violations will meet the Section 10(b) requirements as long as one or more in the series of violations occurs within the six-month period). *See, e.g.*, Campo Slacks, Inc., 266 NLRB 492 (1983) (each insurance fund debt and refusal to pay continued into the 10(b) limitations period). Evidence falling outside the 10(b) period may be admissible as relevant background evidence, even though it could constitute the basis for a separate violation. *See* Machinists Lodge 1424 v. NLRB (Bryan Mfg. Co.), 362 U.S. 411 (1960) (a complaint based on a ULP shall not be issued if it occurred more than six months prior to the complaining party's filing with the Board).

[44] Filing occurs when the Regional Director receives the charge as contrasted with service on the Respondent, which occurs when the charge is mailed. *See* 102.14 and 102.111(b)(1) and NLRB v. Preston H. Haskell Co., 616 F.2d 136 (5th Cir. 1980).

[45] *See* McGuiness and Norris, *supra* note 27, at 294-95, 324-25.

[46] NLRB Rules and Regulations, Series 8, as Amended, Section 102.12.

[47] The following statement from Form NLRB-4541 outlines ULP procedure:

Right to be represented by counsel - Any party has the right to be represented by counsel or other representative in any proceeding before the National Labor Relations Board and the courts. In the event you wish to have a representative appear on your behalf, please have your representative complete Form NLRB-4701, Notice of Appearance, and forward it to the respective regional office as soon as counsel is chosen.

Designation of representative as agent for service of documents - In the event you choose to have a representative appear on your behalf, you may also, if you so desire, use Form NLRB-4813 to designate that representative as your agent to receive exclusive service on your behalf of all formal documents and written communications in the proceeding, excepting charges and amended charges, and further excepting subpoenas which are served on the person to whom they are addressed. If this form is not filed, both you and your representative will receive copies of all formal documents, including complaints, orders and decisions. If it is filed, copies will be served only on your representative, and that service will be considered service on you under the statute. The designation, once filed, shall remain valid unless a written revocation is filed with the Regional Director.

Impartial investigation to determine whether charge has merit - Immediately upon receipt of a charge, the regional office conducts an Impartial investigation to obtain all the facts which are material and relevant to the charge. In order to determine whether

Generally, the Board agent commences the investigation within seven days and makes a determination regarding the disposition of the charge within 30 days.[48] The statute requires the Board to give priority to certain charges such as secondary boycotts,[49] hot cargo agreements,[50] strikes against the certification,[51] jurisdictional disputes,[52] recognitional picketing,[53] and discrimination.[54]

---

the charge has merit, the Region interviews the available witnesses. Your active cooperation in making witnesses available and stating your position will be most helpful to the Region.

The Region seeks evidence from all parties. Naturally, if only the charging party cooperates in the investigation, a situation results whereby the evidence presented by the charging party may warrant the issuance of a complaint, in the absence of any explanation from the party charged with having violated the law. Where evidence of meritorious defenses is made available, a number of cases are withdrawn or dismissed. Your active cooperation will result in disposing of the case at the earliest possible time, whether the case has merit or not.

If the charge lacks merit, charging party has opportunity to withdraw - If it is determined that the charge lacks merit, the charging party is offered the opportunity to withdraw it. Should the charging party refuse to withdraw the charge, the Regional Director dismisses the charge, advising the charging party of its right to appeal the dismissal to the General Counsel.

If the charge has merit, the matter may be voluntarily adjusted - If the Regional Director determines that the charge has merit, all parties are afforded an opportunity to settle the matter by voluntary adjustment. This is the policy of this office to explore and encourage voluntary adjustment before proceeding with litigation before the Board and courts, which is both costly and time consuming. The Regional Director and members of the staff are always available to discuss adjustment of the case at any stage and will be pleased to receive and act promptly upon any suggestions or comments concerning settlements.

Voluntary adjustments after issuance of complaint - If settlement is not obtained, the Regional Director will issue a complaint which is the basis for litigating the matter before the Board and courts. However, issuance of a complaint does not mean that the matter cannot still be disposed of through voluntary adjustment by the parties. On the contrary, at any stage of the proceeding the Regional Director and staff will be pleased to render any assistance in arriving at an appropriate settlement, thereby eliminating the necessity of costly and time-consuming litigation.

[48] *See* McGuiness and Norris, *supra* note 27, *citing* the Board's Casehandling Manual Par. 10051 Sections 12.10, FN 85, p. 331.

[49] Section 8(B)(4)(B).

[50] Sections 8(b)(4)(A), 8(e).

[51] Section 8(b)(4)(C).

[52] Section 8(b)(4)(D).

[53] Section 8(b)(7)(C).

[54] Sections 8(a)(3), 8(b)(2). *See* Sections 10(l) and (m).

As noted in the Statement of Procedures, the Board agent's investigation involves interviews with the parties and witnesses with or without the presence of counsel.[55] Generally, the agent takes the statements of the Charging Party and witnesses in the form of affidavits; however, the agent's interviews with the Charged Party and its witnesses are heavily influenced by the advice of counsel. The Charged Party's cooperation at this early stage of the ULP proceeding serves its interest, since many charges are dismissed or withdrawn based on the results of the investigation.

At the conclusion of the investigation, the Regional Director may dismiss or defer the charge, the Charging Party may withdraw the charge, the parties may settle the charge, or the Regional Director may issue a complaint.[56] The Complaint is written in sufficient detail to demonstrate the proper filing, service and amendment of the charge; the Board's jurisdiction; the identity and nature of the parties; the facts giving rise to the charge; the implicated statutory provisions; and the requested relief.[57] A notice of hearing is served along with the Complaint containing the date, time and place of hearing. Since the Complaint may be amended at any time before the Board issues an order, the Regional Director may amend the Complaint before the hearing, the ALJ at the hearing, and the Board after the record including after the ALJ's decision has been transferred to the Board.[58] Similarly, before the hearing the Regional Director may withdraw a complaint, during the hearing the ALJ must approve withdrawal, and after the ALJ's decision has issued the Board acts upon the GC's motion.[59]

Unless extended by the Regional Director, the Respondent's answer is due within 14 days from the service of the complaint.[60] It must "specifically admit, deny, or explain each of the facts alleged in the complaint, unless the respondent is without knowledge, in which case the respondent shall so state, such statement operating as a denial."[61]

---

[55] *See* Statement, McGuiness and Norris, *supra* note 27, at 331-33 (Section 12.10).

[56] *See id.* and discussion on deferral, *infra* Chapter 13, § 13.5.

[57] *See* McGuiness and Norris, *supra* note 27, *citing* the NLRB Casehandling Manual Par. 10262 Section 15.1, FN 6, p. 247.

[58] NLRB Rules and Regulations Section 102.17.

[59] *See* NLRB Rules and Regulations Section 102.18 and McGuiness and Norris, *supra* note 27, *citing* the NLRB Casehandling Manual at Pars. 10406.2, 19275.1, 10164-10174, 10275.3.

[60] NLRB Rules and Regulations, Sections 102.20 and 102.22.

[61] NLRB Rules and Regulations, Section 102.20, which also provides in part:

All allegations in the complaint, if no answer is filed, or any allegation in the complaint

Failure to answer constitutes an admission of the facts not answered, and the answer may be amended at any time before the hearing and in response to amendment of the Complaint or under parameters set by the ALJ or Board during the hearing.[62]

The Board entertains a variety of pre-trial motions from postponement of the hearing date to a Bill of Particulars and application for subpoenas.[63] Section 10(l) of the Act mandates petitioning the United States District Court for appropriate, pre-trial injunctive relief, when an investigation produces "reasonable cause" to believe that certain violations have occurred.[64] Under Section 10(j) of the Act, the Board may also, in its discretion, petition the appropriate United States District Court for temporary relief or a restraining order where warranted by the ULP.[65]

---

not specifically denied or explained in an answer filed, unless the respondent shall state in the answer that he is without knowledge, shall be deemed to be admitted to be true and shall be so found by the Board, unless good cause to the contrary is shown.

62 NLRB Rules and Regulations, Section 102.23.

63 *See generally* McGuiness and Norris, *supra* note 27, at 390-394.

64 *See* Section 10(l) of the Act.

65 Section 10(j) provides:

> (j) The Board shall have power, upon issuance of a complaint as provided in subsection (b) charging that any person has engaged in or is engaging in an unfair labor practice, to petition any United States district court within any district wherein the unfair labor practice in question is alleged to have occurred or wherein such person resides or transacts business, for appropriate temporary relief or restraining order. Upon the filing of any such petition the court shall cause notice thereof to be served upon such person, and thereupon shall have jurisdiction to grant the Board such temporary relief or restraining order as it deems just and proper.

Citing NLRB Casehandling Manual Par. 10310.2, McGuiness and Norris point to the following factors influencing the Board's exercise of Section 10(j) discretion:

> *The clarity of the alleged violations;
>
> *Whether the case involves the shutdown of important business operations which, because of their special nature, would have an extraordinary impact on the public interest;
>
> *Whether the alleged unfair labor practices involve an unusually wide geographic area, thus creating special problems of public concern;
>
> *Whether the unfair labor practices create special remedy problems that would make it impossible either to restore the status quo or to dissipate effectively the consequences of the unfair labor practices through use of the regular procedures provided in the Act for Board orders and subsequent enforcement proceedings;
>
> *Whether the unfair labor practices involve interference with the conduct of an election or constitute a clear and flagrant disregard of Board certification of a bargaining representative or other Board procedures;
>
> *Whether the continuation of the alleged unfair labor practices will result in exceptional hardship to the charging party;

The parties may also avoid a hearing in the case of agreement on the facts by waiving the hearing and stipulating the record to the ALJ or the Board.[66] Also preventing a full-blown hearing are such summary procedures as summary judgment, default judgment, and judgment on the pleadings.[67]

If the case goes to hearing, the ALJ administers the proceeding much like the trial court judge in a civil case. Section 102.35 of the NLRB Rules and Regulations details the duties and powers of the ALJ to develop the record at hearing and make a decision based on it.[68]

---

*Whether the current unfair labor practice is of a continuing or repetitious pattern;

*Whether, if violence is involved, it is out of control of local authorities or otherwise widespread and susceptible to control by Section 10(j) relief.

Additionally, McGuiness and Norris describe 14 categories of cases where the 10(j) injunction is appropriate:

(a) Interference With Union Organizational Campaign (No Majority);

(b) Interference With Union Organization Campaign (Majority);

(c) Subcontracting or Other Change to Avoid Bargaining Obligation;

(d) Withdrawal of Recognition From Incumbent Union;

(e) Undermining of Bargaining Representative;

(f) Minority Union Recognition;

(g) Successor Refusal to Recognize and Bargain;

(h) Conduct During Bargaining Negotiations;

(i) Mass Picketing and Violence;

(j) Notice Requirements for Strike or Picketing;

(k) Refusal to Permit Protected Activity on Private Property;

(l) Union Coercion to Achieve Unlawful Object;

(m) Interference With Access to Board Processes;

(n) Segregating Assets.

See McGuiness and Norris, *supra* note 27, at 397-98.

NLRB Acting General Counsel Fred Feinstein, reporting on the use of the 10(j) injunction from March 3, 1994 to March 2, 1998, stated that Regional Offices submitted 708 cases with a recommendation to seek a 10(j) injunction to the Injunction Litigation Branch of the Division of Advice and he sought injunctions in 313 (44%) of the cases. The Board authorized 10(j) proceedings in 292 cases (93%). Of the 292 authorized cases, 270 were pursued to conclusion, 133 (49%) were settled; and of the 137 resolved by court decision, 105 (88%) injunctions were granted. 144 Daily Lab. Rep. (BNA) d30.

[66] *See* McGuiness and Norris, *supra* note 27, *citing* NLRB Casehandling Manual Par. 10310.1.

[67] *Id.* at 394-400.

[68] Section 102.35 says:

It shall be the duty of the administrative law judge to inquire fully into the facts as

The GC, represented by an attorney in the regional office, becomes a prosecutor with the burden of proving the ULP case after the Complaint issues. Generally, the Federal Rules of Evidence apply in Board trials "so far as practicable."[69] The hearing itself proceeds in the sequence of a typical trial with Counsel for General Counsel having the burden of going forward with the evidence.[70]

---

to whether the respondent has engaged in or is engaging in an unfair labor practice affecting commerce as set forth in the complaint or amended complaint. The administrative law judge shall have authority, with respect to cases to the Board, subject to the rules and regulations of the Board and within its powers:

To administer oaths and affirmations;

To grant applications for subpoenas;

To rule upon petitions to revoke subpoenas;

To rule upon offers of proof and receive relevant evidence;

To take or cause depositions to be taken whenever the ends of justice would be served thereby;

To regulate the course of the hearing and, if appropriate or necessary, to exclude persons or counsel from the hearing for contemptuous conduct and to strike all related testimony of witnesses refusing to answer any proper question;

To hold conferences for the settlement or simplification of the issues by consent of the parties, but not to adjust cases;

To dispose of procedural requests, motions or similar matters, including motions referred to the administrative law judge by the regional director and motions for summary judgment or to amend pleadings; also to dismiss complaints or portions thereof; to order hearings reopened; and upon motion order proceedings consolidated or severed prior to issuance of administrative law judges decisions;

To approve a stipulation voluntarily entered into by all parties to the case which will dispense with a verbatim written transcript of record of the oral testimony adduced at the hearing, and which will also provide for the waiver by the respective parties of their right to file with the Board exceptions to the findings of fact (but not to conclusions of law or recommended orders) which the administrative law judge shall make in his decision;

To make and file decisions in conformity with Public Law 89-554, 5 U.S.C. section 557;

To call, examine, and cross-examine witnesses and to introduce into the record documentary or other evidence;

To request the parties at any time during the hearing to state their respective positions concerning any issue in the case or theory in support thereof;

To take any other action necessary under the foregoing and authorized by the published Rules and Regulations of the Board.

69 Section 10(b) of the Act.

70 *See generally* McGuiness and Norris, *supra* note 27, at 410-25.

The ALJ prepares a decision in the case after the close of the hearing and the receipt of the parties' briefs. The decision must contain "findings of fact, conclusions, and the reasons or basis therefor, upon all material issues of fact, law, or discretion presented on the record, and shall contain recommendations as to what disposition of the case should be made."[71] Any party may file exceptions to the ALJ's decision with supporting brief within 28 days of the decision or such additional time as the Board allows. The opposing party has 14 days to file a reply brief.[72] The Board then decides the matter "upon the record, or after oral argument, or [it] may reopen the record and receive further evidence before a member of the Board or other Board agent or agency, or may make other disposition of the case."[73] If the Board orders back pay and the parties cannot agree on the amount, the Regional Director may issue a back pay specification with a notice of hearing to resolve the controversy.[74]

If no exceptions are filed, the recommendations of the ALJ automatically become the decision and order of the Board.[75] The Board's order is not self-enforcing; therefore, the Board must petition a court of appeals for enforcement of its order in the absence of voluntary compliance.[76] Similarly:

> [a]ny person aggrieved by a final order of the Board granting or denying in whole or in part the relief sought may obtain a review of such order in any United States court of appeals in the circuit wherein the unfair labor practice in question was alleged to have been engaged in or wherein such person resides or transacts business, or in the United States Court of Appeals for the District of Columbia by filing in such court a written petition praying that the order of the Board be modified or set aside.[77]

Section 101.14 of NLRB Rules and Regulations nicely summarizes the procedural course of a Board case that reaches the Court of Appeals upon review:

> Upon such review or enforcement proceedings, the court reviews the record and the Board's findings and order and sustains them if they are

71 NLRB Rules and Regulations, Section 102.45.

72 NLRB Rules and Regulations, Section 102.46.

73 *Id.* Section 102.48.

74 *Id.* Section 102.52.

75 *Id.* Section 102.48.

76 Section 10(e) of the Act.

77 Section 10(f) of the Act.

in accordance with the requirements of law. The court may enforce, modify, or set aside in whole or in part the Board's findings and order, or it may remand the case to the Board for further proceedings as directed by the court. Following the court's decrees, either the Government or the private party may petition the Supreme Court for review upon writ of certiorari. Such applications for review to the Supreme Court are handled by the Board through the Solicitor General of the United States.

While noting the Court's authority to enforce, modify, enforce as so modified, or set aside in whole or in part a Board order, Section 10(e) requires the factual findings of the Board to be conclusive "if supported by **substantial** evidence **on the record considered as a whole**." The highlighted words were added to the section by the Taft-Hartley amendments of 1947. Interpreting this language, the Supreme Court in *Universal Camera Corp. v. NLRB*,[78] said that the 10(e) amendment requires the reviewing court to consider "whatever in the record fairly detracts from its weight."[79] Under this formulation, the ALJ's decision, which may have been reversed by the Board, is to be given increasing weight when credibility is important to the resolution of the issues.[80] The Court's view recognized the ALJ's advantages of living with the trial and observing witness demeanor. On the other hand, if the Board's reversal is due to matters within its special competence—matters of law and policy—Board decisions will not be reversed on the grounds of lack of "substantial evidence on the record considered as a whole." *Universal Camera* increases the importance of ALJ decisions that are based on objections to the ALJ's credibility findings.

It should be noted that *Universal Camera* dealt specifically with the court's posture in reviewing questions of fact. Courts will exercise a much greater scope of review with questions of law, mixed law and fact, and often policy.[81] The *Universal Camera* decision suggests continued deference to the Board in matters involving board expertise and the Board's choice between fairly supportable conflicting views.[82]

This suggestion gains full-blown judicial recognition in *Chevron, U.S.A., Inc. v. Natural Resources Defense Council, Inc.*,[83] where the Court

---

[78] 340 U.S. 474 (1951).

[79] *Id.* at 488.

[80] *Id.* at 496.

[81] *Id.* at 494.

[82] *Id.* at 490.

[83] 467 U.S. 837 (1984).

articulates a rule of deference to administrative agencies on matters of statutory interpretation. The rule is based on the understanding that Congress creates administrative agencies to implement legislative programs. With the creation of agencies for this purpose comes a delegation of power to fill in the statutory gaps through agency formulation of policy and promulgation of rules. The Court's role is to be limited to determining whether an agency's construction of the statute is reasonable—not contrary to clear congressional intent. The Court's rule of deference is best captured in the following language:

> When a court reviews an agency's construction of the statute which it administers, it is confronted with two questions. First, always, is the question whether Congress has directly spoken to the precise question at issue. If the intent of Congress is clear, that is the end of the matter; for the court, as well as the agency, must give effect to the unambiguously expressed intent of Congress. If, however, the court determines Congress has not directly addressed the precise question at issue, the court does not simply impose its own construction on the statute, as would be necessary in the absence of an administrative interpretation. Rather, if the statute is silent or ambiguous with respect to the specific issue, the question for the court is whether the agency's answer is based on a permissible construction of the statute. [Footnotes omitted.]
>
> The power of an administrative agency to administer a congressionally created . . . program necessarily requires the formulation of policy and the making of rules to fill any gap left, implicitly or explicitly, by Congress.
>
> . . .
>
> If Congress has explicitly left a gap for the agency to fill, there is an express delegation of authority to the agency to elucidate a specific provision of the statute by regulation. Such legislative regulations are given controlling weight unless they are arbitrary, capricious, or manifestly contrary to the statute. Sometimes the legislative delegation to an agency on a particular question is implicit rather than explicit. In such a case, a court may not substitute its own construction of a statutory provision for a reasonable interpretation made by the administrator of an agency. [Footnotes omitted.][84]

[84] 467 U.S. 837 at 842-44.

Notwithstanding the fairly clear statement of deference in *Chevron*, the guidelines are general enough to permit the exercise of considerable discretion among courts in applying them. This enhances the likelihood of significant variation among courts in enforcement actions.[85]

§ 2.4 Chapter Highlights

1. Though the Board's jurisdiction over private sector industry is as broad as the commerce clause itself, Congress has restricted the Board's jurisdiction through the exclusion of categories of employers and employees and the Board has exercised its discretion to exclude many others. (§ 2.1)

2. The Board's elaborate structure is designed to achieve government neutrality during the administration of representation cases and the investigation of ULP cases. Its structure also permits the Board to shift gears, becoming prosecutor as well as adjudicator, during the adversarial stage of ULP cases. (§ 2.2)

3. The Board's intricate network of procedures in ULP cases is designed to facilitate case processing while assuring maximum due process to the parties. (§ 2.3)

---

85 *See* Cox, Bok, Gorman and Finkin, *supra* note 6, at 108, noting the "significant disparity among circuit courts in affirmation rates" and saying:

> In exercising this discretion, courts will presumably be influenced to some degree by such other factors as the respect they hold for the capabilities and impartiality of the Board and the cogency and comprehensiveness of the arguments made by that agency in support of its conclusions. These factors are unavoidably subjective and may therefore cause considerable variation from one court to another concerning the nature of review.

CHAPTER 3
THE AT-WILL DOCTRINE, EXCEPTIONS AND THEIR LIMITS

§ 3.1 Introduction

The history of employee concerted activity, often unprotected and sometimes illegal, reveals a belief among employees that they can secure the greatest group and individual advantages when acting together.[1] Since World War II, agreements reached through collective bargaining, the most organized form of concerted activity, have included just cause provisions that are enforced through grievance-arbitration provisions.[2] The just cause standard requires an employer to prove that its discipline or discharge decision is justified by the employee's unsatisfactory performance or misconduct, threatening the employer's legitimate business interests.[3] Hence, just cause provides employees with a measure of job security by protecting them from termination for reasons that are unfair or arbitrary.

Just cause regimes under collective bargaining agreements displace a system of at-will employment that may prevail absent such agreements. The at-will rule is a default rule that governs the duration of the employment relationship without an agreement on the point by the employer and employee.

§ 3.2 Definition and History of the At-Will Doctrine

Unlike the earliest immutable rules in Anglo-American legislation governing the term of employment,[4] the at-will rule is a default rule. A default rule is more flexible, since it permits the parties to change the rule by agreement. The earliest default rule on the duration of employment was stated in the *Commentaries* of William Blackstone.[5] The Blackstone rule

---

1 *See* discussion of the background and history of the NLRA, *supra* Chapter 1, § 1.5.

2 *See* Roger I. Abrams and Dennis R. Nolan, *A Theory of Just Cause*, 85 Duke L.J. 594 (1985); Calvin William Sharpe, *Introduction* to Symposium, *An Oral History of the National War Labor Board and Critical Issues in the Development of Modern Grievance Arbitration*, 39 Case W. Res. L. Rev. 505 (1988 -1989).

3 *See* Abrams and Nolan, *supra* note 2.

4 *See* Statute of Labourers, 23 Edw. III (1439) (limiting the wages and mobility of employees who stood to gain from the labor shortage brought on by the plague of 1348) and the Statute of Artificers, 5 Eliz., c.4 (1562) (imposing a reciprocal obligation on the employer and employee to maintain the employment relationship for one year).

5 *See* 1 William Blackstone, Commentaries 413 (1765):

> If the hiring be general without any particular time limited, the law construes it to be a hiring for a year; upon a principle of natural equity, that the servant shall serve, and the master maintain him, throughout all the revolutions of the respective seasons, as well when there is work to be done, as when there is not: but the contract may be made for any larger or smaller term.

was designed to promote fairness in seasonal employment by obligating each party to continue the employment relationship throughout a full revolution of the seasons.[6]

Though cases in the United States applied the at-will rule two decades earlier, Horace Gay Wood is credited with having announced the at-will rule. In his treatise of 1877, he described the rule as follows:

> [T]he rule is inflexible that a general or indefinite hiring is prima facie a hiring at-will and if the servant seeks to make it out a yearly hiring, the burden is upon him to establish it by proof . . . . It is competent for either party to show what the mutual understanding of the parties was in reference to the matter; but unless their understanding was mutual that the service was to extend for a certain fixed and definite period, it is an indefinite hiring and is determinable at the will of either party, ...[7]

While controversy surrounds the origin and existence of the rule as well as the legitimacy of Woods' statement of it, that the rule has been well-entrenched since the early 20th century can be seen in *Skagerberg v. Blandin Paper Co.*[8] In that case the plaintiff, a consulting engineer with his own practice, turned down a teaching offer at Purdue University to take a job as consulting engineer with the company. What prompted this decision was a telephone conversation in which the plaintiff informed an officer of the company of Purdue's offer and the necessity to make an immediate decision. The officer agreed "that if plaintiff would reject the Purdue offer and also agree to purchase the home of defendant's power superintendent, it would give plaintiff permanent employment at a salary of $600 per month." After two years, the defendant terminated the plaintiff and the plaintiff sued alleging a breach of contract. The Minnesota Supreme Court upheld the dismissal of the plaintiff's claim saying:

> The words "permanent employment" have a well-established meaning in the law. The general rule is well stated in [the statute]: "In case the parties to a contract of service expressly agree that the employment shall be "permanent" the law implies, not that the engagement shall be continuous or for any definite period, but that the term being indefinite the hiring is merely at will."

---

[6] *See* Jay M. Feinman, *The Development of the Employment at Will Rule,* 20 Am. J. Legal Hist. 118 (1976).

[7] Horace Gay Wood, Master And Servant 283-284 (1877).

[8] 266 N.W. 872 (1936).

Moreover, the Court held that the plaintiff had not shown an appropriate exception to the at-will rule based on extra consideration. The *Skagerberg* court is typical of the majority of U.S. courts that treat terms such as "permanent," "annual," "yearly," "career," and "lifetime" standing alone as references to salary or other aspects of the job creating at-will employment relationships.[9]

The at-will employment rule governs over half of the total civilian non-agricultural workplace. According to 1988 United States Bureau of Census data, approximately 115 million employees worked in the civilian, non-agricultural workforce. Of those, approximately 19 million were represented by unions, and 22 million were government employees covered by civil service laws. Approximately 1.4 million employees are discharged each year.[10]

While the *Skagerberg* case shows that the at-will rule has been sufficiently robust to withstand the strong implications of seemingly clear language such as "permanent," a number of legal doctrines have seriously eroded the strength of the rule in recent decades. Contractual, tort, and good faith limitations on at-will employment have sprouted throughout the states. Other doctrines such as privacy and defamation have also undermined the employer's absolute sovereignty over the workplace. Given the broad application of the default rule, these developments have profound ramifications for the U.S. workplace.

§ 3.3 Common Law Erosions of the At-Will Doctrine

[A]—Contract Erosions

The very nature of the at-will rule as a default rule implies that it is superseded by the parties' contractual arrangement regarding the duration of employment. Even Horace Wood would acknowledge that one way to overcome the at-will presumption is expressly by contracting for a definite term of employment. Where the contractual arrangement is explicit, the issues are straightforward.

---

[9] *See* Robert A. Shearer, 42 Labor L. J. 214 (4/91). A countertrend is for courts to use a contextual approach to look at other evidence of the parties' intent. Also, statutes in some states, such as South Dakota and Georgia, may define the effect to be given to terms such as "permanent" and "annual."

[10] *See* Statistical Abstract of the United States, U.S. Bureau of the Census, Department of Commerce, 1990 at 378, 419; and Stieber & Murray, *Protection Against Unjust Discharge: The Need for a Federal Statute*, 16 U. Mich. J. L. Reform 319 (1983).

[1] Express Contracts

For example, in *Chiodo v. General Waterworks Corp.*,[11] the plaintiff had owned a telephone utility in northwest Utah during a period of industrial development. The plaintiff expanded the company and eventually sold it to the defendant. One of the terms of the sale was that the defendant would employ the plaintiff as manager of the utility for 10 years at an annual salary of $12,000.[12]

The defendant fired the plaintiff after three years, and the plaintiff sued for breach of contract. The Court characterized the agreement as a "contract of employment for a stated term" and held that it was "assumed that the parties intended that the employee would conform to the usual standards expected of an employee [to provide] honest, faithful and loyal service in accordance with his ability."

Employers can incur liability under a contract theory, even where no expression as clear and explicit as the one in *Chiodo* has been uttered. In *Hetes v. Schefman & Miler Law Office*,[13] the plaintiff was employed as a receptionist at a law firm for approximately 10 months. Before she was hired, plaintiff had at least two conversations with company officials who said she had a job "as long as [she] did a good job." Eight months later, the plaintiff was fired, and three months later, she sued the company claiming that it breached the employment contract by terminating her "in bad faith and without just cause." The Court of Appeals reversed the Trial Court's award of summary judgment to the defendant saying that the jury could find, based on the conversations between the plaintiff and defendant's representative, that the employer promised not to discharge the plaintiff except for just cause. Unlike *Chiodo*, the contract in *Hetes* was for an indefinite term. Yet the employee was protected by the just cause language of the agreement. The decision was based on the 1980 Michigan Supreme Court decision in *Toussaint v. Blue Cross & Blue Shield of Michigan*,[14] where the Court held that very similar statements made to a marketing director and an assistant to the company treasurer created a question for

---

[11] 413 P.2d 891 (1966).

[12] The pertinent contract provision in *Chiodo* read as follows:

> In accordance with the understanding and agreement, which we have arrived at, *your employment by Bear River is to continue for a period of ten years from the date hereof* . . . . Nothing in this letter agreement, however, shall be held to preclude your continuing employment by Bear River after such ten-year period.

[13] 393 N.W.2d 577 (1986).

[14] 292 N.W.2d 880 (1980).

the jury concerning discharge for cause. In 1991, the Michigan Supreme Court in *Rowe v. Montgomery Ward & Co.*,[15] appeared to retreat from the broad pronouncements of *Toussaint,* when it reversed a jury verdict of $86,500 in favor of an eight-year salesperson who was fired for being absent from the store without explanation for hours. The sales manager had told the salesperson at the time of her application:

> *[G]enerally,* as long as *they* generated sales and were honest [a salesperson in the plaintiff's position] had a job at Wards. *[A]bout* the only way that you could be terminated would be if you failed to make our draw.[16]

In distinguishing *Toussaint*, the court emphasized the executive positions and interviews with top company officials that included the topic of job security in that case contrasted with the general statements of the sales manager in *Rowe.* The *Rowe* decision leaves open the question of whether low level employees in Michigan like Hetes are as likely as high level employees to get to the jury with claims of for cause protection in indefinite contracts.[17] It might also be viewed as signaling a reversal of the pro-employee trend started in *Toussaint.*[18]

[2] Reliance and Implied-In-Fact Contracts

Except to the extent that weaker evidence of contract formation may establish the existence of a contract, explicit contractual arrangements cannot be said to erode the at-will employment rule. As a default rule, its viability depends on the parties not agreeing to an alternative arrangement. However, an erosion of the doctrine may well occur when contractual theories such as reliance and implied-in-fact successfully jettison the at-will rule. Thirty-two states permit such theories to trump the at-will rule.[19]

---

[15] 473 N.W.2d 268 (1991).

[16] *Id.* at 275.

[17] *See also* Ohanian v. Avis Rent A Car System, Inc., 779 F.2d 101 (1985) (where the Vice-President of Sales for the Northeast Region was able to establish a just cause contract based on the following statements: "there [was] no way [he was] going to get fired," "[he would] never get hurt here in this company," "his future was secure in the company, . . . unless he screwed up badly." Also, in *Ohanian*, the finding of a "just cause" instead of a good cause contract allowed the plaintiff to surmount the statute of frauds hurdle).

[18] *Cf.* Rood v. General Dynamics, 507 N.W.2d 591 (Mich. 1993) (where the Michigan Supreme Court held that an over-the-road driver established a genuine issue of material fact in his "just cause" claim, based on an employment handbook that provided a procedure for involuntary termination for "misconduct or unacceptable performance").

[19] *See infra* chart at § 3.6.

For example, in *Grouse v. Group Health Plan, Inc.*,[20] the employee was a pharmacist, who quit his job and turned down another job because he had accepted an offer with the defendant, a health clinic. After the plaintiff's acceptance of the offer and during his notice period with the current employer, the company hired another pharmacist, primarily because it was unable to secure references for the plaintiff. When the plaintiff reported to work as agreed, two weeks after his acceptance, he was informed that someone else had been hired. The plaintiff had difficulty regaining employment and lost wages as a result. The plaintiff sued to recover damages. In sustaining the plaintiff's cause of the action, the Minnesota Supreme Court said that the doctrine of promissory estoppel defined in the Restatement of Contracts as follows prevented the employer from refusing to employ the plaintiff:

> A promise which the promisor should reasonably expect to induce action or forbearance . . . on the part of the promisee and which does induce such action or forbearance is binding if injustice can be avoided only by enforcement of the promise.[21]

The court noted that Group Health knew that the plaintiff would have to resign his position in order to accept its offer and said that it would be "unjust not to hold Group Health to its promise."[22] The court emphasized that it was not announcing a new rule that assigned liability generally for the discharge of at-will employees. Rather, it said the following:

> What we hold is that under the facts of this case the appellant had a right to assume he would be given a good faith opportunity to perform his duties to the satisfaction of respondent once he was on the job. He was not only denied that opportunity but resigned the position he already held in reliance on the firm offer which respondent tendered him.[23]

---

20 306 N.W.2d 114 (1981).

21 *Id.* at 116.

22 *Id.*

23 *Id.* at 116. Other courts have used similar theories to correct the same kind of injustice. For example, see Pearson v. Simmonds Precision Products, Inc., 624 A.2d 1134 (1993) (where a senior test engineer on a design project for the B-2 bomber was discharged after cutbacks in the B-2 bomber project successfully sued on the theory of negligent failure to disclose and negligent misrepresentation based on the employer's assurance, during preemployment interviews, that there would be sufficient work for him even if the B-2 project failed) and Stewart v. Jackson & Nash, 976 F.2d 86 (2d Cir. 1992) (where a fraudulent inducement theory protected a young environmental lawyer with a successful practice, who was lured away from the practice on the promise of heading the employer's environmental law practice, that never materialized, and the young lawyer was terminated after two years).

The "reasonable length of time" that the employee was deemed entitled to in *Grouse* appeared as a standard in *Veno v. Meredith*,[24] where the question was whether the employee had given additional consideration to the employer to warrant insulation from discharge without just cause for a reasonable length of time. The court in *Veno* ruled that the plaintiff had not given additional consideration where he relinquished a job in Newark, New Jersey to move to Pennsylvania and turned down other job opportunities throughout his employment. The court express the standard as follows:

> [A] court will find "additional consideration" when an employee affords his employer a substantial benefit other than the services which the employee is hired to perform, or when the employee undergoes a substantial hardship other than the services which he is hired to perform. If the circumstances are such that a termination of the relation by one party will result in great hardship or loss to the other, as they must have known it would when they made the contract, this is a factor of great weight in inducing a holding that the parties agreed upon a specific period . . . .[25]

The managing editor of the Free Press, who had been fired for publishing a story critical of a local judge, had suffered no detriment different from any salaried professional, and his discharge after eight years of employment over a difference of opinion with the owner was "no great hardship or loss" in the court's view. The court also noted that the plaintiff had been employed eight years before his discharge, giving him a reasonable period of time on the job under the additional consideration standard.[26]

The circumstances of a person's employment might also give rise to an implied promise of continued employment. The most famous case demonstrating this point is *Pugh v. See's Candies, Inc.*[27] In that case, Pugh, a

---

[24] 515 A.2d 571 (1986).

[25] *Id.* at 580.

[26] Courts have used the "additional consideration" doctrine as a means of discerning the intent of the parties—additional consideration makes it less likely that the employee and employer failed to agree on contractual protection. *See* Darlington v. General Elec. Co., 504 A.2d 306 (Pa. Super. Ct. 1986); Miller v. Community Discount Centers, 228 N.E.2d 113 (Ill. App. Ct. 1967); Lanier v. Alenco, 459 F.2d 689 (5th Cir. 1972). Compare Romack v. Public Serv. Co., 499 N.E.2d 768 (Ind. Ct. App. 1986), and Ferreyra v. E. & J. Gallo Winery, 41 Cal. Rptr. 819 (Cal. Ct. App. 1964), where courts view hardships undertaken by employees as unreasonable, and therefore, as evidence defeating a plaintiff's attempt to show reasonable reliance.

[27] 171 Cal. Rptr. 917 (1981).

32-year employee with See's Candies, had dedicated his entire career to working for the Company. He started as a dishwasher and ended as Vice-President of Production and member of the Company's board of directors. Along the way, he took courses to increase his value to the Company, designed and facilitated the construction of new plants in the San Francisco area in 1950 and 1957, and generally was a pivotal employee in the life and success of the Company. Pugh took a trip to Europe in 1973, and upon his return to San Francisco, he was informed of his termination. At the time of Pugh's termination, See's had enjoyed a record-setting year in sales with increased production for which Pugh was largely responsible. The President of the Company discharged Pugh with the equivalent of saying "get out and don't come back," without so much as a "thank-you" and without giving a reason. At the time of Pugh's hire, the President told him that his "future was secure" "if [he was] loyal to See's and do a good job." The two succeeding presidents had followed the practice of retaining administrative personnel except for just cause. There had been no formal criticism of Pugh or indication of dissatisfaction with his work. The California Court of Appeals reversed the trial court's dismissal of Pugh's action saying that his evidence raised a question of fact about the existence of an implied-in-fact contract. About establishing such a contract, the Court said:

> In determining whether there exists an implied-in-fact promise for some form of continued employment courts have considered a variety of factors in addition to the existence of independent consideration. These have included, for example, the personnel policies or practices of the employer, the employee's longevity of service, actions or communications by the employer reflecting assurances of continued employment, and the practices of the industry in which the employee is engaged.
>
> . . .
>
> Here, . . . there were facts in evidence from which the jury could determine the existence of such an implied promise: the duration of appellant's employment, the commendations and promotions he received, the apparent lack of any direct criticism of his work, the assurances he was given, and the employer's acknowledged policies. While oblique language will not, standing alone, be sufficient to establish agreement, it is appropriate to consider the totality of the parties' relationship: Agreement may be "shown by the acts and conduct of the parties, interpreted in the light of the subject matter and the surrounding circumstances."[28]

---

[28] *Id.* at 925-926, 927.

Scholars argue that the most important factor in *Pugh* was the plaintiff's longevity of employment, since fairness concerns suggest that employees need protection in these cases.[29] The court noted that the plaintiff ultimately bears the burden of proving that he was wrongfully terminated, even though the "just cause" or "good cause" standard as applied to a high level employee such as Pugh in a contract of indefinite duration gives the company considerable latitude.

[3] Employment Manuals

In addition to explicit contractual and other bilateral theories of protection already discussed, the employment manual is a source of contractual obligation. The manual is a handy tool, because of its broad applicability to employees at minimal training costs.[30] Since the 1980's, courts have shown greater receptiveness to claims based on employment manuals, and a large majority of states now recognize manual-based claims of wrongful discharge.[31]

Woolley v. Hoffmann-La Roche, Inc.[32] is an example of the trend. The plaintiff was an engineer who had worked for the company for nine years and been promoted twice before his discharge. Approximately one month after starting work, he received an employment manual. The company touted the manual as "a practical operating tool in the equitable and efficient administration of our employee relations program."[33] It contained five pages on termination, and among the reasons for termination were disciplinary and performance problems constituting cause of termination. The termination section of the manual also contained procedures to be used before terminating an employee and a policy declaration that employees who perform "their duties efficiently and effectively" would be retained.[34] The question before the court was whether the company's employment manual could contractually bind the employer. The court held that an implied promise contained in an employment manual to fire employees only

---

[29] *See* Stewart J. Schwab, *Life-Cycle Justice: Accommodating Just Cause and Employment At Will*, 92 Mich. L. Rev. 8 (1993) (arguing that such protection is necessary because of an employer's incentive to terminate employees whose current rate of pay exceeds their productivity, unlike earlier stages of the employment life cycle).

[30] *See generally* Mark A. Rothstein, Charles B. Craver, Elinor P. Schroeder, Elaine W. Shoben, and Lea S. VanderVelde, Employment Law 525-532 (West 1994).

[31] *See id.*

[32] 491 A.2d 1257, *modified,* 499 A.2d 515 (1985).

[33] *Id.* at 1259.

[34] *Id.*

for cause is enforceable even in employment for an indefinite term, "absent a clear and prominent disclaimer."[35]

Functionally, employment manuals are much closer to collective bargaining agreements than individual contracts, since they purport to broadly order the workplace through generally applicable terms and conditions of employment. This affinity between collective agreements and manuals influenced the court's reasoning in *Woolley* as reflected in the following language:

> [Cases] holding that policy manual provisions do not give rise to any contractual obligation, have to some extent confused policy manuals with individual long-term employment contracts and have applied to the manuals rules appropriate only to the individual employment contracts.
>
> . . .
>
> Whatever [the worth of these rules] in dealing with individual long-term employment contracts, these requirements, over and above those ordinarily found in contract law, have no relevancy when a policy manual is involved. In that case, there is no individual lifetime employment contract involved, but rather, if there is a contract, it is one for a group of employees—sometimes all of them—for an indefinite term, and here, fairly read, one that may not be terminated by the employer without good cause.
>
> The trial court viewed the manual as an attempt by Hoffmann-La Roche to avoid a collective bargaining agreement. [Footnote omitted.] Implicit is the thought that while the employer viewed a collective bargaining agreement as an intrusion on management prerogatives, it recognized, in addition to the advantages of an employment manual to both sides, that unless this kind of company manual were given to the workforce, collective bargaining, and the agreements that result from collective bargaining, would more likely take place.[36]

The court in *Woolley* was unwilling to permit the employer to enjoy the advantages of union deterrence, improved morale, employee loyalty, and a heightened sense of cooperation among employees without incurring the cost of contractual commitment.

---

[35] *Id.* at 1257.

[36] *Id.* at 1262, 1263, & 1264.

[4] Disclaimers

The effect of the court's ruling in *Woolley* was not to place employers wishing to use employment manuals in an inextricable dilemma. Its holding was to bind employers "unless the language contained in the manual were such that no one could reasonably have thought it was intended to create a legally binding" obligation.[37] Indeed, the court takes great pains to explain the rationale of its decision and guide well-intentioned employers:

> All that this opinion requires of an employer is that it be fair. It would be unfair to allow an employer to distribute a policy manual that makes the workforce believe that certain promises have been made and then to allow the employer to renege on those promises. What is sought here is basic honesty: if the employer, for whatever reason, does not want the manual to be capable of being construed by the court as a binding contract, there are simple ways to attain that goal. All that need be done is the inclusion in a very prominent position of an appropriate statement that there is no promise of any kind by the employer contained in the manual; that regardless of what the manual says or provides, the employer promises nothing and remains free to change wages and all other working conditions without having to consult anyone and without anyone's agreement; and that the employer continues to have the absolute power to fire anyone with or without good cause.[38]

Consistent with the concern for honesty, disclaimers must give laypersons a clear explanation of the effect of the manual on the employment relationship. As noted by the court in *Woolley*, disclaimers must be conspicuous in their placement and visibility.[39] A disclaimer may be an acknowledgment in the job application of at-will status and of the ineffectiveness of any modification in that status.[40] Without an explicit limitation on modification, a disclaimer may be undermined by a later writing or inconsistent behavior.[41]

---

[37] *Id.* at 1266.

[38] *Id.* at 1271.

[39] *See* McDonald v. Mobil Coal Producing, Inc., 789 P.2d 866 (Wyo. 1990) (where disclaimer was ineffective, because contained in the general welcoming section and not in larger print, capitalized or set off by border) and Jones v. Central Peninsula General Hospital, 779 P.2d 783 (Alaska 1989) (a disclaimer of one sentence in an 85-page manual was not conspicuous).

[40] *See* Reid v. Sears, Roebuck & Co., 790 F.2d 453 (6th Cir. 1986).

[41] *See, e.g.*, Brown v. United Methodist Homes For The Aged, 815 P.2d 72 (1991) (disclaimer may have been modified by later policy expressed by supervisor at trial); Swanson

[B]—Tort Erosions

Scholars have suggested that the tort rationale of regulating parties in contractual relationships to protect third parties explains nicely the public policy cases.[42] A useful topology of public policy cases based on reasons for discharge is the following: (1) refusal to commit unlawful acts, (2) fulfilling a public obligation, (3) exercising a statutory right, and (4) reporting illegal activity.[43]

Under each of these categories, there may be a question about whether the existence of a public policy has been established. Public policy can come from a variety of sources, and the states vary on permissible sources. For example, Illinois gives public policy a broad identity—it concerns what is right and just—and provides that public policy can be found in the state constitution, state statutes and judicial decisions.[44] California more narrowly limits public policy sources to state statutes and the constitution. It explains that the narrow definition has the virtue of concreteness and reconciles the employer's interest in knowing that there might be exposure with the employee's interest in being protected by fundamental state policies and the pubic's interest in having fundamental policies served.[45] A broader definition of public policy creates more opportunities for successful claims than a more narrow definition.

An exceptionally broad reading of public policy that stretches the public policy rationale to its outer limit is found in *Novosel v. Nationwide Ins. Co.*[46] Novosel was a 15-year employee of Nationwide Insurance, who was a district claims manager at the time of his discharge. He was fired for refusing to lobby the Pennsylvania House of Representatives on behalf of Nationwide in support of no-fault insurance reform. Indeed, Novosel privately opposed the company's political position. The plaintiff sued seeking reinstatement, damages and declaratory relief. The employer filed a motion to dismiss that was granted in the District Court. The Third Circuit reversed and remanded saying that the complaint stated a cause of action

---

v. Liquid Air Corp., 826 P.2d 664 (1992) (where a memorandum may have modified disclaimer).

[42] *See* Steven L. Willborn, Stewart J. Schwab, and John F. Burton, Jr., Employment Law—Cases and Materials 125 & 128 (2d ed. 1998).

[43] *Id.* at 128.

[44] *See* Palmateer v. International Harvester Co., 421 N.E.2d 876, 878 (Ill. 1981).

[45] *See* Gantt v. Sentry Ins., 824 P.2d 680, 687-688 (Cal. 1992).

[46] 721 F.2d 894 (3d Cir. 1983).

for violation of the public policy of free political expression embodied in the Pennsylvania and United States constitutions. Though the court's decision manifests a valid concern about the potential distortion of the political process by powerful corporations, its ruling may be tantamount to creating a just cause rule for unorganized employees based, perhaps, on the Fifth and Fourteenth Amendments to the U.S. Constitution.

[1] Public Policy Violations

[a]—Refusal to Commit Unlawful Acts.

The more closely a plaintiff fits one of the categories in the topology, the more likely a plaintiff is to prevail. For example, in *Petermann v. Int'l Brotherhood of Teamsters, Local 396,*[47] where the employee was discharged for refusing to commit perjury at a legislative hearing, the court held that the firing violated public policy—the state's policy of encouraging truthful testimony. In this case, the third-party effect of undermining the factfinding process can clearly be seen in the employer's conduct.

Though most of the cases in this category involve criminal activity, most states also permit public policy claims for violations of civil laws such as anti-trust, consumer protection, FDA regulations, highway safety, and sometimes tort laws.[48] Even though a state permits a public policy claim for a discharge based on a refusal to perform an unlawful act, the success of the claim will depend upon the court's breadth of interpretation. For example, in *Sabine Pilot Serv. v. Hauck,*[49] the Texas Supreme Court recognized a public policy exception protecting employees fired for the sole reason of refusing to commit illegal criminal acts. Texas does not recognize a public policy exception for refusal to commit illegal acts carrying only civil penalties.[50]

A state's adoption of a narrow public policy approach can sometimes lead to distortions of the law to accommodate cases that obviously deserve public policy coverage. In *Lucas v. Brown & Root, Inc.,*[51] for example, the court upheld the wrongful discharge claim of an employee fired for

---

47 344 P.2d 25 (Cal. App. 2d 1959).

48 *See* Rothstein, Craver, Schroeder, Shoben, and VanderVelde, *supra* note 30, at 545-547. *See, e.g.,* Delaney v. Taco Time International, Inc., 681 P.2d 114 (Or. 1984) (where employee was fired for refusing to sign a false and defamatory statement).

49 687 S.W.2d 733 (Tex. 1985).

50 *See* Hancock v. Express One Int'l, 800 S.W.2d 634 (Tex. App. 1990).

51 736 F.2d 1202 (8th Cir. 1984).

resisting the sexual advances of her supervisor. The court found that the plaintiff was effectively refusing to violate the anti-prostitution laws. The Arizona Supreme Court rejected this cramped approach in *Wagenseller v. Scottsdale Mem. Hosp.*,[52] where the company discharged an employee for refusing to moon the audience along with other members of the group during a rafting trip. The plaintiff claimed that her actions amounted to a refusal to violate the indecent exposure statute prohibiting any exposure of genitalia, anus or breast that would be offensive to a reasonable person. Declaring the appropriate analytical emphasis to be on whether mooning would "contravene important public policy interests embodied in the law" rather than whether they technically violated the statute, the court said:

> We have little expertise in the techniques of mooning. We cannot say as a matter of law, therefore, whether mooning would always violate the statute by revealing the mooner's anus or genitalia. That question could only be determined, we suppose, by an examination of the facts of each case. We deem such an inquiry unseemly and unnecessary in a civil case. Compelled exposure of the bare buttocks, on pain of termination of employment, is a sufficient violation of the policy embodied in the statute to support the action, even if there would have been no technical violation of the statute.[53]

[*b*]—*Fulfilling a Public Obligation.*

A good example of a violation of public policy for fulfilling a public obligation is *Nees v. Hocks.*[54] In that case, the plaintiff had been terminated for essentially volunteering for service on a jury. The court considered the importance of jury service under the state constitution and laws and concluded that the community's interest in having its citizens serve on juries was sufficiently high to warrant protection against discharge for such service.

In *Nees*, the effect of the employer's actions on third parties figures prominently into the court's analysis.

[*c*]—*Exercising a Statutory Right.*

Cases dealing with the exercise of a right under state law involve a variety of statutes. Typically, these cases have involved worker's compensation

---

52 710 P.2d 1025 (Ariz. 1985).

53 *Id.* at 1035.

54 536 P.2d 512 (Or. 1975).

claims, but other statutes such as state occupational health and safety laws and minimum wage laws also underlie these claims.[55] Even though many statutes permit suits against retaliation for exercising statutory rights, common law actions may supplement legislative remedies. For example, in *Hodges v. S.C. Toof & Co.*,[56] the plaintiff was not limited to damages specified in the protective statute in suing for compensatory and punitive damages. Some statutes like the Nebraska law regulating employers' use of polygraph examinations provide for only criminal penalties; in those cases, the public policy tort may provide the only civil remedy.[57]

[*d*]—*Whistleblowing.*

Protecting the public's interest in health and safety are clearly appreciated third-party effects in protecting whistleblowers. For this reason, the overwhelming majority of states have passed legislation protecting employees reporting illegal activity. This protection typically extends to mistaken whistleblowers and efforts to determine the legality of an employer's action.[58] The public policy exception for whistleblowing also protects employees; however, courts often provide more protection for reports made to outside agencies (external) than those made with the employer (internal).[59] Courts choosing to protect only external whistleblowers may be concerned that they might be intruding into mere disagreements about company policy,[60] while those protecting internal whistleblowers may be concerned about the incentive "to bypass internal channels altogether and immediately summon the police."[61] Also, as with identifying the sources of public policy, courts and statutes may give broad or narrow whistleblower protection. Some provide protection only for reports of health and safety violations, while others cover state and federal statutes and regulations.[62]

55 *See, e.g.*, D'Angelo v. Gardner, 819 P.2d 206 (Nev. 1991) (firing employee for refusal to perform unreasonably dangerous work violated public policy contained in Nevada occupational safety and health laws); Amos v. Oakdale Knitting Co., 416 S.E. 2d 166 (N.C. 1992) (firing employee for refusal to work for less than state minimum wage violated public policy).

56 833 S.W.2d 896 (Tenn. 1992).

57 *See* Ambroz v. Cornhusker Square, Ltd., 416 N.W.2d 510 (Neb. 1987).

58 *See* Michigan statute protecting reports not knowingly false and Johnston v. Del Mar Distributing Co., 776 S.W.2d 768 (Tex. Ct. App. 1989).

59 *See, e.g.*, Adler v. American Standard Corp., 830 F.2d 1303 (4th Cir. 1987).

60 *See* Geary v. United States Steel Corp., 319 A.2d 174 (Pa. 1974).

61 *See* Belline v. K-Mart Corp., 940 F.2d 184, 187 (7th Cir. 1991).

62 *Compare* Cal. Lab. Code Section 1102.5 (protecting reports about violations of state or federal statute and state or federal regulations) *with* N.Y. Lab. Law Section 740 (protecting reports to supervisors or public bodies about substantial dangers to public health and safety).

In *Balla v. Gambro*,[63] the court upheld the trial court's dismissal of an action for retaliatory discharge brought by a company's in-house counsel. Even though the lawyer was discharged for threatening to report the company's health and safety violations to an outside agency, he was denied protection because the policy of protecting the lives and property of citizens was adequately safeguarded by the Illinois Rules of Professional Conduct.[64]

Thirty-seven states have whistleblower laws.[65] Whistleblower statutes typically protect the reporting of a wide variety of violations as distinguished from anti-retaliation provisions of discrete statutes. Though some states have whistleblower statutes that protect private sector employees, 27 of the 36 states and the federal government have laws protecting only public sector whistleblowers.[66] Statutes vary in their protection of external and internal whistleblowers, with a California Court, for example, interpreting the state's whistleblower statute as protecting only external whistleblowers and the Maine statute specifically requiring an initial internal report.[67] States also vary regarding available remedies and the relationship between common law and statutory causes of action.[68]

[2] Intentional Infliction of Emotional Distress

Still another genre of tort cases eroding the employment at-will doctrine involves intentional infliction of emotional distress. This tort focuses on the manner rather than the basis of discharge and is often termed "abusive discharge." Extreme mistreatment of employees characterizes abusive discharge cases.[69]

---

63 584 N.E.2d 104 (Ill. 1991).

64 In *Balla*, the plaintiff had threatened to "do whatever [was] necessary to stop the sale of [adulterated] dialyzers."

65 Rothstein, Craver, Schroeder, Shoben, and VanderVelde, *supra* note 30, at 561.

66 *See, e.g.*, Whistleblower Protection Act of 1989, Pub. L. No. 101-12, 103 Stat. 26 (protecting federal employees exposing government violations and creating an Office of Special Counsel to protect employee rights).

67 *Compare* Hejmadi v. AMFAC, Inc., 249 Cal. Rptr. 5 (Cal. Ct. App. 1988) *with* Me. Rev. Stat. Ann. tit. 26, Sec. 833.

68 *See generally* Steven L. Willborn, Steward J. Schwab, and John F. Burton Jr., Employment Law—Cases and Materials 157-160 (2d ed.).

69 In Agis v. Howard Johnson Co., 355 N.E.2d 315 (Mass. 1976), the Court said the following about this cause of action:

> [W]e hold that one who, by extreme and outrageous conduct and without privilege, causes severe emotional distress to another is subject to liability for such emotional distress even though no bodily harm may result. However, in order for a plaintiff to prevail in a case

Scholars who have surveyed this category of cases identify the following five stages of the dismissal process that may give rise to objectionable employer conduct: (1) investigative,[70] (2) disciplinary short of discharge,[71] (3) decisional,[72] (4) informational,[73] and (5) post-discharge.[74] One of the best examples of such outrageous treatment occurred in *Wilson v. Monarch Paper Co.*,[75] where the employer forced a 60-year-old Vice-President to quit by demoting him to the job of a warehouse janitor. He quit after four months in the humiliating job, which lead to respiratory problems and clinical depression. In rejecting the company's challenge to the trial judge's decision to send the case to jury, which awarded a $3.4 million judgment, the Fifth Circuit said:

> A reasonable jury could have found that this employer conduct was intentional and mean spirited . . . . Finally, the evidence supports the conclusion that this conduct was, indeed, so outrageous that civilized society should not tolerate it.[76]

---

for liability under this tort, four elements must be established. It must be shown that the actor intended to inflict emotional distress or that he knew or should have known that emotional distress was the likely result of his conduct, Restatement (Second) of Torts sec. 46, comment i (1965); (2) that the conduct was "extreme and outrageous," was "beyond all possible bounds of decency" and was "utterly intolerable in a civilized community," . . . (3) that the actions of the defendant were the cause of the plaintiff's distress; and (4) that the emotional distress sustained by the plaintiff was "severe" and of a nature "that no reasonable man could be expected to endure it." . . . These requirements are "aimed at limiting frivolous suits and avoiding litigation in situations where only bad manners and mere hurt feelings are involved," and we believe they are a "realistic safeguard against false claims . . . ."

[70] Rothstein, Craver, Schroeder, Shoben, and VanderVelde, *supra* note 30, at 556, cite overzealous surveillance, interviews, and interrogation as examples of abusive discharge, based on the manner of investigation.

[71] *See* Bodewig v. K-Mart, Inc., 635 P.2d 657 (Or. App. 1981) (where the employee was subjected to a humiliating strip search in front of the customer who persisted in accusing her of theft without reasonable foundation).

[72] *See* Agis v. Howard Johnson Co., 355 N.E.2d 315 (Mass. 1976) (where the employer informed employees that it would terminate employees in alphabetical order until the identity of a thief was uncovered and proceeded to terminate the plaintiff first).

[73] *See* Rothstein, Craver, Schroeder, Shoben, and VanderVelde, *supra* note 30, at 558 (citing assault and battery and yelling racial epithets).

[74] *See* Taiwo v. Vu, 822 P.2d 1024 (Kan. 1991) (where, upon the plaintiff's return to the employer to secure her paycheck, she was subjected to assault and battery and false police charges). *See generally* Rothstein, Craver, Schraeder, Shoben, VanderVelde, *supra* note 30, at 555-559.

[75] 939 F.2d 1138 (5th Cir. 1991).

[76] *Id.* at 1145.

[C]—Good Faith Limitations

The Uniform Commercial Code at Section 1-203 provides:

> Every contract or duty within this Act imposes an obligation of good faith in its performance or enforcement.

Similarly, the Restatement of Contracts Second, Section 205 says:

> Every contract imposes upon each party a duty of good faith and fair dealing in its performance and its enforcement.

Since the at-will employment arrangement is a contract of employment, some states have seized upon this covenant of good faith and fair dealing to impose limitations upon an employer's reasons for discharge.[77] The two main issues in applying this doctrine have been the potential scope of the concept of good faith and the remedies for breach of the covenant. Giving maximum scope to the notion of good faith might well amount to imposing a just cause requirement upon employers in at-will relationships, while tort damages could expose them to extraordinary damage awards.

Most states narrowly construe the covenant of good faith and fair dealing as preventing an employee's loss of the benefit of the bargain as the Supreme Judicial Court of Massachusetts did in *Fortune v. National Cash Register Co.*[78] Plaintiff Orville Fortune was a 61-year-old man who worked for The National Cash Register Company (NCR) under a written "salesman's contract." The contract was for at-will employment and provided for "a weekly salary in a fixed amount plus a bonus for sales made within the 'territory' (i.e., customer accounts or stores) assigned to him for 'coverage or supervision,' whether the sale was made by him or someone else." The contract also provided for the payment of bonus credits, computed as a percentage of the price of products sold, based on the timing of the territory assignment. A salesperson's interest in the bonus terminated within 18 months unless the territory was assigned to the sales representative at the time of delivery and installation or the delay was caused by special engineering requirements. After some cultivation, Fortune succeeded in signing a customer to the purchase on November 28, 1968, of 2,008 machines at a purchase price of approximately $5,000,000 and for a bonus credit of $92,079.99. NCR terminated Fortune in a letter dated the next business day, but later decided to keep Fortune on in a sales support position

---

[77] *See* Rothstein, Craver, Schroeder, Shoben and VanderVelde, *supra* note 30, at 537.

[78] 364 N.E.2d 1251 (Mass. 1977).

to coordinate and expedite the delivery of the machines. Fortune received approximately 75% of the bonus, and the company paid the other 25% to a system and installations person, contrary to the practice of only paying the salesperson. Approximately 18 months after receiving the termination notice the company asked Fortune to retire and, when he refused, fired him in June 1970. Fortune received no bonus payments on machines delivered to the customer after his termination. The trial judge denied the company's motion for a directed verdict on the grounds that Fortune could recover if his firing were in "bad faith" and sent the case to the jury. The jury returned a verdict for $45,649.62.

The court found that NCR's written contract with Fortune contained a covenant of good faith and fair dealing. It also found that the evidence permitted the jury to find bad faith—that NCR's termination of Fortune, a 25-year employee, "the next business day after NCR obtained a $5,000,000 order from First National was motivated by a desire to pay Fortune as little of the bonus credit as it could."[79]

California bucks the trend toward a narrow interpretation of the covenant of good faith and fair dealing by reading it more expansively as a requirement to deal fairly with at-will employees. In *Foley v. Interactive Data Corp.*,[80] the plaintiff, Wayne Foley, had worked his way up in the company's hierarchy starting as an Assistant Production Manager in 1976 at a salary of $18,500 and rising to become an award-winning manager and Branch Manager of the company's Los Angeles office in 1981 at a salary of $56,164, not counting a bonus of $6,772. In January of 1983, Foley reported in a private conversation with a company Vice-President that his recently-hired current supervisor was under investigation by the FBI for embezzlement at Bank of America, the supervisor's former employer. In March, the supervisor informed Foley that he had decided to replace him for "performance reasons" but would permit him to transfer to another division, an option that would allow him to avoid demotion. The supervisor also said that he would not fire Foley. One week after the transfer, the supervisor told Foley that he was not doing a good job; and six days later, told him that he could continue as branch manager if he would agree to a "performance plan." Although Foley agreed to the condition, the supervisor fired him the next day.

In his suit, one of Foley's allegations was breach of the implied covenant of good faith and fair dealing. The court held that Foley stated a claim for

[79] *Id.* at 1258.

[80] 765 P.2d 373 (Cal. 1988).

breach of the covenant of good faith and fair dealing. And since that claim amounted to the argument that he was fired for doing his job and not for being deprived of the benefit of the bargain, the California Court apparently adopted a broader definition of good faith.

However, significantly, the court held that contract and not tort (including punitive) damages were appropriate to remedy such breaches. Though the average award to successful plaintiffs has increased in California since the *Foley* decision, some scholars argue that *Foley*'s cap on damages creates a significant incentive not to bring such actions.

[D]—Other Issues Affecting Employer Sovereignty

The right to privacy is protected by common law tort actions against invasion of privacy and statutes like Title III of the Omnibus Crime Control and Safe Streets Act of 1968 that prohibits electronic surveillance and the interception of telephone calls. In addition, the Fourth Amendment of the United States Constitution protects against governmental intrusion upon the "right of the people to be secure in their persons, houses, papers, and effects, against unreasonable searches and seizures." Governmental employers as state actors are subject to this constitutional guarantee. The Supreme Court's decision in *O'Connor v. Ortega*,[81] shows that this Fourth Amendment protection hinges on the "reasonable expectation of privacy," which is affected by the employer's practices, procedures and regulations. It also points out that this privacy interest may be outweighed by the need for supervision, control and efficient operation.

Applying the privacy analysis contained in *Ortega*, the Texas Court of Appeals in *K-Mart Corp. Store No. 7441 v. Trotti*,[82] found that the plaintiff had a reasonable expectation of privacy against the invasion of her employee locker that had been secured by her personal lock.

Privacy issues often involve the off-duty conduct of employees. For example, in *Rulon-Miller v. International Business Machine Corp.*,[83] Virginia Rulon-Miller dated an employee of an IBM competitor. The relationship started when both the plaintiff and the employee worked for IBM and continued after his separation from IBM. The company knew of the plaintiff's relationship three years before her discharge, and her immediate supervisor acknowledged the year before that her dating the

---

81 480 U.S. 709 (1987).

82 677 S.W.2d 632 (1984).

83 208 Cal. Rptr. 524 (1984).

employee of a competitor raised no conflict of interest concerns. Then abruptly in 1979, after the plaintiff had received a $4,000 merit raise, her supervisor gave her a week to sever her relationship with the employee or lose her job and then forced her to make a decision the following day, saying "I'm making the decision for you." When the plaintiff protested, the supervisor terminated her. The plaintiff had been assured the right to privacy both by the California constitution and a memorandum by the former chair of IBM. The latter read in part:

> We have concern with an employee's off-the-job behavior only when it reduces his ability to perform regular job assignments, interferes with the job performance of other employees, or if his outside behavior affects the reputation of the company in a major way. When on-the-job performance is acceptable, I can think of few situations in which outside activities could result in disciplinary action or dismissal.

The plaintiff sued for invasion of privacy and intentional infliction of emotion distress and recovered $100,000 of compensatory damages and $200,000 of punitive damages. The court held that the jury could reasonably find based on the evidence that the plaintiff's dating practices did not interfere with her performance as a manager or the morale of employees.[84]

The basic privacy analysis focusing on employees' reasonable expectation of privacy and employers' interest in limiting or eliminating the right to privacy informs a number of testing issues in the employment setting. The privacy interests of employees limit but do not eliminate an employer's authority to subject employees to drug testing.[85]

Like the problem of drug abuse, theft in the workplace is a perceived national problem that might be controllable by an effective testing program. The Employee Polygraph Protection Act of 1988 regulates the use of the polygraph examination based on the twin concerns of employee privacy

---

[84] The off-duty misconduct issue is also frequently addressed in arbitrations where the standard, as articulated by Arbitrator Rimer in Indian Head, Inc., 71 LA 82, 85 (1985), is:

> [W]hat an employee does on his own time and off Company premises is not a proper basis for disciplinary action unless it can be shown that the employee's conduct has an adverse effect on the Company's business or reputation, the morale and well-being of other employees, or the employee's ability to perform his regular duties.

[85] *See* National Treasury Employees Union v. von Raab, 489 U.S. 65 (1989) and Skinner v. Railway Labor Executives Ass'n, 489 U.S. 602 (1989) (upholding the government's compelling interest in testing employees in limited circumstances). *Cf.* Feliciano v. City of Cleveland, 661 F.Supp. 578 (N.D. Ohio 1987), and Fed'n of Gov't Employees v. Weinberger, 651 F.Supp. 726 (S.D. Ga. 1986) (finding testing programs to be unreasonable).

and test reliability.[86] Even honesty tests, not covered by federal and state polygraph statutes, must submit to employee privacy concerns.[87]

Another type of privacy claim is the publication of embarrassing private facts.[88] Even if the facts are true, their revelation might violate the right to privacy.[89] The tort of defamation similarly involves a revelation that bears on privacy—the publication to others of statements harming someone's reputation. Defamation involves the following elements: (a) a false and defamatory statement concerning another; (b) an unprivileged publication to a third party; (c) fault amounting at least to negligence on the part of the publisher; and (d) either actionability of the statement irrespective of special harm or the existence of special harm caused by the publication.[90]

Defamation has a rich history as a tort, and in the last 25 years much scholarly discussion has centered around defamation law as applied to media defendants.[91] Also, today the workplace is a major arena for defamation claims. Between 1982 and 1987, employees filed one-third of all defamation claims.[92] Most of these cases involve negative references given by former employers.[93] Like other issues requiring privacy analysis the defamation

---

[86] *See* 29 U.S.C. Sections 2001-2009. Though the EPPA generally prohibits employers from conducting polygraph examinations except in conjunction with ongoing investigations of specific instances resulting in economic loss, it exempts employers whose compelling interests justify the use of such examinations.

[87] *See* Soroka v. Dayton Hudson Corp., 1 Cal. Rptr. 2d 77 (1991) (disallowing the inquiry into applicant's religious beliefs or sexual orientation using Psychscreen—a combination of the Minnesota Multiphasic Personality Inventory and the California Psychological Inventory—without demonstrating a compelling interest and job-related purpose; specifically that these aspects of employee privacy have a "bearing on the emotional stability or on the ability to perform . . . [the] job responsibilities").

[88] W. Page Keeton, Dan B. Dobbs, Robert E. Keeton, and David G. Owen, Prosser And Keeton On Torts 849-869 (5th ed., West 1984), identified the following four forms of invasion of privacy: (1) Appropriation, (2) Unreasonable Intrusion, (3) Public Disclosure of Private Facts, and (4) False Light in the Public Eye.

[89] *See, e.g.,* Bratt v. IBM Corp., 785 F.2d 352 (1st Cir. 1986) (upholding the employee's privacy claim against employer who disseminated the result of a psychiatric examination).

[90] The Restatement (Second) of Torts, Section 558.

[91] *See, e.g.*, Keeton, *Defamation and Freedom of the Press*, 54 Tex. L. Rev. 1221 (1976).

[92] According to a Wall Street Journal report of a study conducted by the Jury Verdict Research Inc., 8,000 such employee suits were filed. Wall St. J. 10/2/86, at 33. col 2. These results were consistent with a U.S. News & World Report survey. U.S. New & World Report, 10/16/89.

[93] *See generally* John Bruce Lewis, Bruce L. Ottley, and Gregory V. Merson, *Defamation And The Workplace: A Survey Of The Law and Proposals For Reform*, 54 Mo. L. Rev. 797 (1989).

cases attempt to balance the privacy concerns of employees concerning the harm to their employment prospects caused by negative information and the efficiency needs of employers in the flow of personnel information.[94]

§ 3.4 Legislative Erosions

A scholarly survey of the employment termination regimes of Canada, Great Britain, Germany, France, Italy and Japan reveals that these countries give greater than at-will protection to employees.[95] Protection is not universal in these countries, reinstatement is not a uniform remedy for wrongful dismissals, and monetary awards are modest by U.S. standards. By comparison United States coverage is small, but recoveries can be astronomical.

The American wrongful discharge situation is analogous to the recovery for workplace injuries before the onset of workers' compensation programs: a few injured workers did well, but most did not.[96] It is not surprising that the attention in the wrongful discharge field is turning to statutes that offer more protection while controlling recoveries.

The Montana Wrongful Discharge From Employment Act of 1987 and the Model Employment Termination Act both address the range of issues presented by the common law cases and scholarly commentary: (1) defining just cause; (2) allocating the burden of proof, (3) specifying the appropriate enforcement tribunal; (4) designing a remedial scheme; and defining the role of freedom of contract.[97] Both statutes adopt a "good faith" standard, generally interpreted as less exacting than a "just cause" standard; and both make it clear that general economic reasons would support termination without liability. Unlike META, the Montana statute sets forth specific grounds for a wrongful dismissal claim that may not include such well-settled bases as performing jury service.[98]

---

94 *See* Zinda v. Louisiana Pacific Corp., 440 N.W.2d 548 (Wis. 1989) (reversing a $50,000 judgment for defamation on the ground that the employer had a conditional privilege and a jury question existed as to whether the privilege was abused through excessive publication).

95 Samuel Estreicher, *Unjust Dismissal Laws: Some Cautionary Notes*, 33 Am. J. Comp. L. 310, 311-23 (1985).

96 *See* Theodore J. St. Antoine, *The Making of the Model Employment Termination Act*, 69 Wash. L. Rev. 361 (1994).

97 *See* Mont. Code Ann. Sections 39-2-901 to 39-2-914 and Model Emp. Term. Act (1991).

98 Section 4 of the Montana statute provides:

Elements of wrongful discharge. A discharge is wrongful only if:

(1) it was in retaliation for the employee's refusal to violate public policy or for reporting a violation of public policy;

Though META has not been adopted in any state, a three-year study by the American Civil Liberties Union National Taskforce on Civil Liberties in the Workplace suggests that adoption would benefit both employers and employees. Specifically, the study says that adoption would save employers over $300 million and slightly increase the money received by individual plaintiffs. While according to the study the number of annual complaints would rise, the average recovery would decrease along with attorneys' fees.[99]

Even though the at-will employment doctrine has eroded substantially in the last few decades, the resulting protections are uncertain and vary from state to state. Moreover, no groundswell of statutory protection for at-will employees has occurred, despite the economic incentives that support such a movement. Under these circumstances, recent common law and statutory developments do not approach the panoply of protections afforded under the typical collective bargaining agreement with its grievance-arbitration enforcement mechanism. Viewed in this light, the rights contained in the NLRA remain the principle vehicle for comprehensive regulation of the private sector workplace.

§ 3.5 Chapter Highlights

1. The at-will rule is a default rule that gained currency in the late 19th century and responded to the demands of the industrial revolution for mobile labor and capital. (§ 3.2)

2. As a default rule, the at-will doctrine yields to contractual arrangements agreed upon by the parties, express and implied contracts including employment manuals, and the covenant of good faith and fair dealing. (§§ 3.2, 3.3[A])

3. Tort theories concerned with the third-party effects of contracts have also limited the employment at-will rule by forbidding discharges that violate public policy, which vary in scope based on the sources of public policy and the kinds of public policy claims entertained. (§ 3.3[B])

---

(2) the discharge was not for good cause and the employee had completed the employer's probationary period of employment; or

(3) the employer violated the express provision of its own written personnel policy.

It should be noted that subsection (1) contains no reference to performing a public service. *Cf.* Nees v. Hocks, *supra* note 54.

[99] Individual Employment Rights, Vol. 10, No. 4 (BNA) (January 21, 1995).

4. The right to privacy also limits the employer's sovereignty over the workplace in a variety of ways. (§ 3.3[D])

5. Legislative developments have been stunted, giving no indication that uniform, predictable, rules governing wrongful discharge will gain currency in the near term. (§ 3.4)

§ 3.6 CHART

Common Law or Statutory Exceptions to the Employment At-Will Doctrine

State	Implied Contract	Public Policy	Emotional Distress	Good Faith & Fair Dealing
Alabama	X	–	X	–
Alaska	X(PE)	–	X	X(B)
Arizona	X	X	X	–
Arkansas	X	X	X	X(B)
California	X	X	X	X(B)
Colorado	X	X	X	–
Connecticut	X(PE)	X	X	X(N)
Delaware	–	X	X(NS)	X(N)
Dist. of Columbia	–	–	X	–
Florida	X	–	X	–
Georgia	–	–	X	–
Hawaii	X	X	X	–
Idaho	X	X	–	X(N)
Illinois	–	X	X	X(N)
Indiana	X(PE)	X	X	–
Iowa	X	X	X	–
Kansas	X	X	X	–
Kentucky	X(NS)	X	X	–
Louisiana	–	–	X	–
Maine	–	–(NS)	X	–
Maryland	X	X	X	–
Massachusetts	X(PE)	X	X	X(N)
Michigan	X(PE)	X	X	–
Minnesota	X(PE)	X	X	X(N)
Mississippi	X(NS)	X	X	–
Missouri	X(PE)	–(NS)	X	–
Montana	–	X	–	–
Nebraska	X	X	–	–
Nevada	–	X	X	–
New Hampshire	X(PE)	X	–	–
New Jersey	X	X	–	–(NS)
New Mexico	X	X	X	–
New York	–	–	–	–

State	Implied Contract	Public Policy	Emotional Distress	Good Faith & Fair Dealing
North Carolina	X	X	X	–
North Dakota	–	X	X	–
Ohio	X(PE)	X	X	–
Oklahoma	X	X	X	–
Oregon	–	X	X	–
Pennsylvania	–	X	X	X(NS)(B)
Rhode Island	–	X(NS)	X	–
South Carolina	–	X	X	–
South Dakota	X	X	X	–
Tennessee	X(PE)	X	X	–
Texas	X(NS)(PE)	X	X	–
Utah	X	X	X	–(NS)
Vermont	X	X	X	–
Virginia	–	X	X	–
Washington	X	X	X	–
West Virginia	–	X	X	–
Wisconsin	–	X	X	–
Wyoming	X	X	X	X(N)

(PE): Promissory Estoppel (N): Narrow
(NS): Not Settled (B): Broad

CHAPTER 4
SELECTING A BARGAINING REPRESENTATIVE: THE RIGHT TO ORGANIZE AND THE REPRESENTATION ELECTION

§ 4.1 Introduction

While Section 7 of the National Labor Relations Act[1] protects a variety of employee conduct, not all of which necessarily involves a union, at the core of the Act is its protection of workers' rights "to self-organization, to form, join, or assist labor organizations" and to "bargain collectively through representatives of their own choosing." The election process is only one way that employees may choose a bargaining representative and attain recognition for it. Employers can and do recognize unions without an election. But the election process is central to the framework, especially since 1947 when Congress amended the Act to increase the importance of the representation election.

This chapter focuses on the representation election. It looks first at the process by which employees, unions, or employers petition to initiate the election process and traces the Board's procedures from the earliest preelection stage through post-election objections. It then turns to the issues raised by the behavior of the parties during the campaign, and looks at what protections the Act affords to employee free choice in choosing a representative. It focuses, somewhat artificially, first on conduct that mostly implicates Section 8(a)(1) of the Act, as well as on conduct that while not violative of the Act may so undermine employee free choice that an election's results must be set aside and the election rerun. It then shifts its focus to conduct that implicates Section 8(a)(3)'s protection against discrimination intended to discourage union (or anti-union) activity or to punish those who engage in such activity. Finally, it turns to the remedies available for violations of these sections of the Act.

§ 4.2 Election Procedure

[A]—Initiation of the Process

Typically, the method by which employees select a union, or choose not to be represented by one, is by a majority vote in a secret ballot election in an appropriate bargaining unit. Since enactment of the Taft-Hartley Amendments in 1947, this has also been the Board's favored method,

---

[1] Section 7:

Employees shall have the right to self-organization, to form, join, or assist labor organizations, to bargain collectively through representatives of their own choosing, and to engage in other concerted activities for the purpose of collective bargaining or other mutual aid or protection.

although as will be discussed below, it is not the exclusive method.[2] The provisions governing the election process are found in Section 9, but the Act gives rather scant direction regarding the procedures the Board should follow in a representation election. Instead, one must look to the Board's rules and regulations for the details.[3]

As originally conceived, the task of certifying a representative for the employees in a bargaining unit and the accompanying decisionmaking authority for elections belonged to the Board. In 1961, however, the Board, pursuant to authority granted to it in the 1959 amendments to Section 3(b), delegated its powers in election cases to its regional directors.[4]

Under the Board's rules, its review of the Regional Director's decisions is discretionary and will only be granted under limited specified circumstances.[5]

Formally, the representation election process begins when a union (or an employee or group of employees, or, under some circumstances discussed below, an employer) files an election petition. In fact, a union may have begun its campaign long before it files an election petition, because once it files the petition it will almost immediately need to be able to show substantial support, amounting to 30%, among the workers in the unit it proposes to represent. Section 9(c)(1) of the Act provides for three types of representation petitions: (1) a petition for certification, known as an RC petition, filed by an individual or group of employees, or, much more commonly, by a union and alleging that a substantial number of employees want to be represented for collective bargaining and that their employer

---

[2] *See* NLRB v. Gissel Packing Co., 395 U.S. 575, 596 & nn.7 & 8 (1969).

[3] These can be found both within Title 29 of the CFR and in an NLRB publication, National Labor Relations Board, Rules and Regulations and Statements of Procedure §§ 102.60-102.72 (1996) [hereinafter NLRB Rules and Regulations].

[4] NLRB Rules and Regulations § 102.67.

[5] The Board will grant review only on one of the following grounds:

(1) That a substantial question of law or policy is raised because of (i) the absence of, or (ii) a departure from, officially reported Board precedent.

(2) That the Regional Director's decision on a substantial factual issue is clearly erroneous on the record and such error prejudicially affects the rights of a party.

(3) That the conduct of the hearing or any ruling made in connection with the proceeding has resulted in prejudicial error.

(4) That there are compelling reasons for reconsideration of an important Board rule or policy.

NLRB Rules and Regulations § 102.67(c).

refuses to recognize their desired representative; (2) a petition for decertification, known as an RD petition, filed by an individual or group of employees, or a union, alleging that the currently recognized bargaining agent no longer has the support of the majority of the employees in the unit; and (3) an employer's petition, known as an RM petition, seeking to resolve whether a union that has demanded recognition has majority support.[6] The employer petition poses a particular problem, the possibility that an employer will file before the union is ready for an election. The requirement that there be a prior demand for recognition made on the employer serves to blunt the employer's potential weapon of otherwise calling for a premature election in order to fend the union off. A demand for recognition can be made by a union in the course of an organizing campaign. It can also be made when an already recognized union makes a demand on the employer to bargain during, for example, the last days of a current collective bargaining agreement. An employer can, therefore, test whether an incumbent union has continued majority support through the filing of an election petition. But, to ensure that this mechanism by which an employer can force a vote would not be used either as an economic weapon by subjecting the union to the costs and risks of repeated elections, or to evade the employer's obligation to bargain in good faith, the employer must have a "good-faith" basis, founded on objective evidence, for its belief that the union no longer retains majority support.[7]

[B]—Grounds for Dismissing the Election Petition

After the petition is filed, a member of the regional staff will undertake a preliminary investigation mandated by Section 9(c)(1) to determine whether a "question of representation affecting commerce exists." If the petition has been filed by a union or an employee or group of employees, the petitioner must demonstrate that there is "sufficient probability" that the employees want the union in question to represent them. This "showing of interest" requires proof that at least 30% of the employees in the proposed unit support the named representative, proof typically supplied by turning over to the regional office signed and dated authorization cards, although

[6] 29 U.S.C. § 159(c)(1)(A)-(B) (1994); *see also,* NLRB Rules and Regulations § 102.60. The election process is also available for petitions requesting unit clarification, or an amendment of the current certification, or recission of the union's authorization to enter into a security agreement with the employer. *See* § 9(e); NLRB Rules and Regulations, *Statements of Procedure, Subpart C* [hereinafter, NLRB, *Statements of Procedure*].

[7] United States Gypsum Co., 157 NLRB 652 (1966). This subject is discussed further at *infra* § 8.6.

other indicators, such as a petition signed by the requisite number of employees or dues receipts may also satisfy this requirement.[8]

Any other union may intervene and participate in the representation proceedings with a showing of interest of 10% so long as it seeks to represent substantially the same bargaining unit; furthermore, it is entitled to a place on the ballot so long as it has the support of at least one unit employee.[9]

The showing of interest requirement, and the early moment in which it comes, places considerable pressure on a union's organizers to reach and have face-to-face contact with a large percentage of the unit's employees before the petition is filed, especially since unions typically prefer to file the petition with majority support rather than merely the 30% minimum.[10] This need underscores the importance of access that informs the issue of organizer access to employer property.

In addition to whether there is a sufficient showing of interest, the preliminary investigation conducted by the regional staff member will focus on: whether the employer falls within the Board's jurisdiction; whether the unit described is appropriate for collective bargaining; whether there is a bona fide question concerning representation; and whether the petition is timely.[11]

There are a number of reasons why a petition might be dismissed as untimely. First, from its early years the Board's practice was to shelter newly certified unions from challenges to their representative status by treating election petitions filed within a year of their certification as untimely. Congress extended this practice to all elections regardless of the

---

[8] NLRB, *Statements of Procedure,* § 101.18; *see also,* Robert A. Gorman, Basic Text on Labor Law: Unionization and Collective Bargaining 41 (1976); Robert E. Williams, NLRB Regulation of Election Conduct 9-10 (rev. ed. 1985). In the case of an expedited election triggered under Section 8(b)(7)(C), no showing of interest is required. For a discussion of expedited elections under that section, see *infra* § 6.7[C].

[9] Gorman, Basic Text on Labor Law, *supra* note 8, at 42.

[10] Unions recognize that they are likely to suffer some erosion of support during the election process. *See* Laura Cooper, *Authorization Cards and Union Representation Election Outcome: An Empirical Assessment of the Assumptions Underlying the Supreme Court's* Gissel *Decision,* 79 Nw. U. L. Rev. 87, 118-20 (1984). As discussed below, the ability to show prior majority support has become a prerequisite for a remedial bargaining order.

[11] NLRB, *Statements of Procedure,* § 101.18; *see also,* Gorman, Basic Text on Labor Law, *supra* note 8, at 42; Williams, NLRB Regulation of Election Conduct, *supra* note 8, at 9-10.

winner in 1947 when it added Section 9(c)(3), which states that "[n]o election shall be directed in any bargaining unit or subdivision within which, in the preceding twelve-month period, a valid election shall have been held." Note that this one-year "election-bar" rule only applies to valid elections, and therefore will not foreclose a Board-mandated rerun election.[12] Also, while it forecloses for a year the opportunity to have a second election within a unit or a subdivision thereof, it will not block an election in a bigger unit that also encompasses the one in which the earlier election was held.

In addition to the election-bar, the Board has, for similar reasons, adopted the practice of treating an election petition as untimely if it is filed within one year of the union's certification in those instances where there is a delay between the election and certification. Otherwise, the employer might be encouraged to raise post-election objections simply for the benefit of delay and the hope of dissipating support for the union. The Supreme Court approved the Board's practice in *Brooks v. NLRB.*[13] For similar reasons, the Board will also extend the certification-bar period if there is employer resistance to bargaining. In such cases it will count the one year period from the time that bargaining began.[14]

Where an employer has voluntarily recognized a union, the Board will provide the union protection from an election for a "reasonable period," which may be considerably shorter than a year, in order to give it an opportunity to bargain free from the pressure of a rival union's petition or a decertification petition.[15]

It has also long been the Board's practice to dismiss an election petition if there are substantial pending unfair labor practice charges affecting the unit, or, as they are typically referred to, "blocking charges."[16] The charging party may, nevertheless, request that the Board go forward with the election despite the pending unfair labor practice charge.[17] And because this is a

---

12 It will also not bar a runoff election, where more than one union sought to be certified and no one, including the ballot choice "neither" or "no union," received a majority of the votes cast. NLRB Rules and Regulations § 102.70.

13 348 U.S. 96 (1954). This case is discussed further in *infra* § 8.2.

14 Mar-Jac Poultry Co., 136 NLRB 785 (1962); *see also* Lamar Hotel, 137 NLRB 1271 (1962).

15 *See, e.g.*, Brennan's Cadillac, 231 NLRB 225 (1977) (affording the union a five-month sheltered period).

16 U.S. Coal & Coke, 3 NLRB 398 (1937) (dismissing decertification petition pending resolution of unfair labor practice charges against employer); *see also* NLRB, Casehandling Manual ¶ 11730 (1989) (describing Board practices regarding blocking charges).

17 *See, e.g.*, NLRB v. Tri-City Linen Supply, 579 F.2d 51 (9th Cir. 1978), *enforcing,*

matter of Board policy, rather than statutory mandate, the Board may, within its discretion, go forward with an election despite any unresolved unfair labor practice charges.[18]

Finally, in an effort to draw a balance between the goals of employee free choice and the stability of bargaining agreements, the Board has developed its contract-bar rules. Under these rules, a petition seeking an election among employees during the term of a valid collective bargaining agreement covering those employees will be treated as untimely if the bargaining agreement: is reduced to writing and executed by the contracting parties; grants exclusive representation for all unit employees to the contracting union; is for a fixed term; and contains substantial terms and conditions of employment beyond mere recognition of the union or a bare wage scale.[19] A collective bargaining agreement for a term beyond three years will only bar a rival union's petition for its first three years, but it will bar petitions from the contracting parties for the life of its term.[20] A collective bargaining agreement which, through the inclusion of a union-security provision (a provision requiring union membership or dues payment), violates the limits set out in Section 8(a)(3) on permissible union security provisions, will not create a contract bar because of the coercive effect such a provision would have on the unit members.[21] The contract bar will also not operate if the incumbent union is "defunct,"[22] is involved

226 NLRB 669 (1976) (Board did not abuse its discretion by proceeding with election on union's request despite pending charge against the employer, nor did it abuse its discretion by contacting an employee on the eve of the election in order to investigate the unfair labor practice charge); NLRB, Casehandling Manual ¶ 11730.4.

18 NLRB, Casehandling Manual ¶¶ 11730.4-.7 (stating exceptions to the blocking charge rule). The staleness of the unfair labor practice charges, for example, may militate in favor of going forward with the election. *Cf.* Templeton v. Dixie Color Printing Co., 444 F.2d 1064 (5th Cir. 1971) (Board abused its discretion when it dismissed a decertification petition seven years after alleged unfair labor practice and three years after filing of decertification petition).

19 Appalachian Shale Products Co., 121 NLRB 1160 (1958); Gorman, Basic Text on Labor Law, *supra* note 8, at 54-57.

20 General Cable Corp., 139 NLRB 1123 (1962). An uncertified incumbent union may, however, file a petition in order to have the benefits of certification, without running afoul of the contract-bar rule. General Box Co., 82 NLRB 678 (1949).

21 Pine Transp., Inc., 197 NLRB 256 (1972) (provision favoring union members over nonmembers regarding accrual of seniority). The Board has also held that a bargaining agreement that is racially discriminatory will not give rise to a contract bar. Pioneer Bus Co., 140 NLRB 54 (1962).

22 This essentially means what it sounds like. The union has ceased to operate in its day-to-day functions as a representative and a contract administrator. Hershey Chocolate Corp., 121 NLRB 901 (1958).

in a "schism,"[23] or the unit in question has undergone dramatic changes in circumstances due to significant expansion, the merger of operations, or changes in the employer's operations.[24]

The Board has special rules regarding the contract bar near the expiration of the contract term. In an effort to balance the need for employee free choice between incumbent and insurgent unions and the need for the employer and the incumbent union to be able to bargain for a new contract free of the distraction of an insurgent union's claims for recognition, the Board recognizes an "open" period beginning 90 days before the bargaining agreement expires and ending 60 days before expiration (or 90 to 60 days before the end of the third year of a contract whose term exceeds three years), at which point an "insulated" period begins. Petitions filed before or after this period are untimely.[25] Election petitions filed during this open period, however, are timely and will not be barred by the contract bar rule. If no one files a petition during the open period and the employer and union then negotiate a new contract or a contract extension during the insulated period, that new contract will operate once again as a contract bar.

If the investigation shows that the requirements for going forward with an election are met, the regional staff member will encourage the parties to resolve consensually all pre-election issues, including when and where the election will occur, the definition of the bargaining unit, and voter eligibility. If the parties are able to agree on these issues, as they most often do, they will enter into a consent election agreement, which is then subject to approval by the Regional Director.[26]

Otherwise, the staff member will schedule a hearing on these matters before a hearing officer in the regional office, who will take evidence in a trial-like hearing. The hearing officer makes no recommendation, but she forwards a transcript of the hearing and exhibits to the Regional Director.[27]

---

23 This occurs as the result of an open break between the local and its national or international parent union leaving in its wake instability. *Id.*

24 General Extrusion Corp., 121 NLRB 1165 (1958).

25 Deluxe Metal Furniture Co., 121 NLRB 995 (1958); Leonard Wholesale Meats, Inc., 136 NLRB 1000 (1962) (modifying the time periods for the "open" and "insulated" periods). Because of the Act's different treatment of the health care industry, the open period begins 120 days before the bargaining agreement expires and ends 90 days before its termination date. Trinity Lutheran Hospital, 218 NLRB 199 (1975).

26 On the rules for consent elections and a discussion of the two types of consent election agreements, see NLRB Rules and Regulations § 102.62; Williams, NLRB Regulation of Election Conduct, *supra* note 8, at 10-11.

27 NLRB Rules and Regulations §§ 102.64-66; Williams, NLRB Regulation of Election Conduct, *supra* note 8, at 11.

[C]—Bargaining Unit Determination

While the parties typically agree on the definition of the bargaining unit, when they do not, it is often a very contentious issue.[28] Moreover, when it is contested, it is usually very important because it can affect the outcome of the election. Indeed, it can determine whether there will be an election at all. If the unit is significantly different from the one that the union sought signatures for, the union may no longer have enough signed authorization cards to meet the showing of interest requirement, or it may conclude that the unit it first deemed appropriate is unorganizable and withdraw from pursuing an election.

Bargaining unit determinations are based on a list of factors. For all of its importance, like any multi-factor test, it yields little useful generalization. There are some things that we can say about them, however.

First, the term "bargaining unit" is something of a misnomer. A bargaining unit consists of the group of jobs that define the electorate for the representation election. A more accurate label would be "election unit."[29] While bargaining units often define the contours of the negotiating unit as well, bargaining units can evolve, or join together for negotiations, and negotiations can consequently cover many other employees who are not part of the original unit. As noted above, the unit is defined in terms of jobs or job categories, not individuals. This means that the comings and goings of individuals within the unit does not change the definition of the unit. New hires to jobs within a particular bargaining unit become members of the unit.

While the strategy of selecting a bargaining unit will vary from situation to situation, it is commonly thought that employers favor large (for instance plant-wide) units on the theory that they are more difficult to organize than smaller ones and more difficult to represent once a union is chosen because of the likelihood of greater diversity within the unit. Employers also worry about fragmented units, the existence of several units within one enterprise, because of their potential for inconsistent demands and a series of strikes. Unions, according to conventional wisdom, prefer smaller units, for the inverse of the employers' reasons for preferring large ones. Unions may, however, see advantages to larger units, including greater power and

---

[28] The best resources on bargaining units are John E. Abodeely et al., The NLRB and the Appropriate Bargaining Unit (rev. ed. 1981); Douglas L. Leslie, *Labor Bargaining Units,* 70 Va. L. Rev. 353 (1984).

[29] Gorman, Basic Text on Labor Law, *supra* note 8, at 66.

prestige, more members and dues, and possible economies of scale in administering the unit.[30]

The Act itself is not especially helpful in making unit determinations. It requires that the unit be appropriate, and it specifically prohibits certain combinations of jobs in a unit.[31] There are some additional things that we can say, however, about unit determinations. First, the petitioner (typically a union) gets first shot, and frames the debate. Further, as the statutory language suggests, the unit does not have to be *the most* appropriate unit, but rather *an* appropriate unit.[32] This means that it is possible that a particular enterprise could support several different appropriate bargaining unit configurations.

As noted above, the Board bases its determination on a multi-factor test. The critical question is whether the employees share a community of interest.[33]

Various commentators have compiled lists of factors considered by the Board. Professor Leslie offers the following composite list:

1. Similarity of pay and method of computing pay (e.g., weekly salary, hourly, piece-work).

2. Similarity of benefits (e.g., common pension plan, vacation schedule).

3. Similarity of hours of work.

4. Similarity of kind of work performed.

5. Similarity of qualifications, skills, and training.

6. Physical proximity and frequency of contact and transfers.

---

30 *Id.* at 67-68. For a more subtle discussion of the strategies that underlie bargaining unit preferences, see generally Leslie, *Labor Bargaining Units, supra* note 28.

31 Plant guards charged with the duty of enforcing property and safety rules may not be included in a unit with other employees. § 9(b)(3). Section 9(b)(1) provides that professional employees can only be included in a unit with nonprofessional employees if a majority of the professionals vote to be included.

32 Morand Bros. Beverage Co., 91 NLRB 409 (1950), *enforced in part,* 190 F.2d 576 (7th Cir. 1951).

33 This has long been the Board's keystone. 3 NLRB Annual Report 174 (1938).

7. Functional integration of the firm.

8. The firm's supervisory structure (common supervision) and organizational structure, especially as it relates to setting and applying labor relations policies.

9. Bargaining history.

10. Employee desires.

11. Extent of union organization within the firm.[34]

For the most part, they can be categorized under 3 headings: a) similarities among the would-be unit members (in pay, benefits, skills etc.); b) connections among the would-be unit members (mainly of physical proximity); and c) functional integration, by which the Board seems to be focusing on whether a strike by the smaller of the proposed units could shut down production for other parts of firm as well. The bargaining unit question can be critical, yet the decisions are very fact-specific, and the factors highly manipulable. The Board seems to write these decisions in such a way as to make them as factually bound as possible, thereby making them impervious to judicial reversal, and leaving Board discretion as unbounded as possible. And courts have tended to show the Board great deference in this regard.

The Board will approve multi-location units, but its history has been somewhat tortuous on this issue. The presumption is against multi-location units. As noted above, the bargaining unit does not necessarily define the negotiating unit. Both multi-employer bargaining and coordinated bargaining are quite common.[35]

Bargaining unit issues can come up in other settings besides a new organizing campaign. Accretion cases involve new job categories and the question of whether or not they should be added to an existing unit. The opposite issue, craft severance, was quite important in the days that the American Federation of Labor craft unions were engaged in competition with the Congress of Industrial Organizations' industrial unions. The Board has a long and changing history in its treatment of craft severance cases. The Board's last word on the standard for craft severance cases is *Mallinckrodt Chemical Works*[36] where it announced that it would apply a

[34] Leslie, *Labor Bargaining Units*, *supra* note 28, at 383.

[35] These issues are discussed at *infra* § 7.3[C].

[36] 162 NLRB 387 (1966).

multi-factor test in making craft severance determinations, rather than its prior craft-friendly approach. In fact, however, despite the Board's purported dedication to multi-factor analysis it appears that it will seldom allow craft severance since *Mallinckrodt.*[37]

[D]—Conduct of Elections

Upon review of the hearing record and any post-hearing briefs, the Regional Director will issue findings and conclusions on the contested questions and either order an election or dismiss the election petition. As previously noted, the Regional Director's decision is subject to the Board's discretionary review under limited circumstances. The Regional Director will typically schedule the election for a date between 25 and 30 days from the date of the election order. The Board requires an employer to provide it with a list of the names and addresses of eligible voters within seven days after the Regional Director has either approved a consent election agreement or issued her decision ordering an election. This *Excelsior* list, so-called for the *Excelsior Underwear*[38] decision, is then given to the petitioning union (or unions) to facilitate its contact with the employees in the bargaining unit. Because of restrictions on the union's right of access to the employer's property for campaigning purposes, the *Excelsior* list is an important tool in the union's campaign, and the Board strictly enforces the requirement that the employer timely produce an accurate list.

The election itself is generally held at the place of employment. It is by secret manual ballot vote under the supervision of the Board. Parties are permitted to supply observers. Any voter whose eligibility is challenged is permitted to vote, but his ballot is separated from the others. If challenged ballots cannot affect the outcome of the election, they are not counted. Otherwise, the Regional Director must rule on the challenges and they are then tallied along with the other ballots.[39] The Board's rules permit any party to file objections to the election under a quick timetable for objection and review. If no objections are filed, or once they are resolved, and if no run-off election is necessary, the Regional Director will issue a certification of representative if the union has won, or a certification of the results of the election if it has not. If, however, the Regional Director finds that a valid objection has been raised, she will order a rerun election, except in those instances where, because unfair labor practices have made it

37 *See* Gorman, Basic Text on Labor Law, *supra* note 8, at 84-86.

38 Excelsior Underwear, Inc., 156 NLRB 1236 (1966).

39 NLRB Rules and Regulations § 102.69; NLRB, *Statements of Procedure* § 101.19.

impossible to hold a rerun election, an order to the employer to bargain with the union (a *Gissel bargaining order*) is appropriate.[40]

[E]—Judicial Review of Representation Elections

The NLRA provides for review of final orders of the Board in an appropriate federal circuit court in unfair labor practice cases, either on the petition of "any person aggrieved" by the final order, or on the Board's petition seeking enforcement of its order.[41] The Supreme Court held in *AFL v. NLRB*[42] that Board determinations in representation cases were not final orders and, therefore, not amenable to review under these provisions. Instead, representation issues must be raised parasitically in unfair labor practice cases. In other words, the aggrieved party in a representation decision, such as on the configuration of the bargaining unit or the eligibility of certain voters, will commit an unfair labor practice, typically by violating the duty to bargain, and will be allowed to raise the representation issue in federal circuit court on review of the finding that it has committed an unfair labor practice. Note that this path to review is really opened only to employers. The union has no similarly easy trigger to get a representation issue before the appellate court, although Professor Douglas Leslie has suggested that a union might be able to bring representation issues before a federal circuit court by violating Section 8(b)(7)(B)'s prohibition of picketing for an organizational or recognitional purpose within twelve months of a valid election in the unit at question. Professor Leslie has found at least two cases where unions achieved appellate review through that mechanism.[43]

The Supreme Court opened the door a crack for federal court review of representation issues in *Leedom v. Kyne*.[44] There the Court held that a federal district court has jurisdiction to determine whether the Board was acting within its jurisdiction or beyond statutory boundaries. In that case, the Board approved a bargaining unit that seemed prohibited on the face of the Act.

---

[40] NLRB Rules and Regulations § 102.69. *Gissel* bargaining orders are discussed below at § 4.5[B].

[41] §§ 10(e)-(f), 29 U.S.C. §§ 160(e)-(f) (1994).

[42] 308 U.S. 401 (1940).

[43] Douglas L. Leslie, Cases and Materials on Labor Law: Process and Policy 371 (3d ed. 1992). The two cases are American Bread Co. v. NLRB, 411 F.2d 147 (6th Cir. 1969) and NLRB v. Teamsters Local 182, 314 F.2d 53 (2d Cir. 1963). Recognitional picketing and the intricacies of Section 8(b)(7) are discussed at *infra* Chapter 6.

[44] 358 U.S. 184 (1958).

Six years later, however, the Court indicated that little would be able to pass through the opening it had created in *Leedom.* In denying district court jurisdiction in *Boire v. Greyhound Corp.*,[45] the Court limited the *Leedom* exception to instances where the issue was purely a question of law and did not require review of the Board's factual determinations. Consequently, *Leedom* has had limited continuing significance.

[F]—Construction Industry Prehire Agreements

In 1959, Congress added Section 8(f) to the Act, which permits an employer primarily involved in the building and construction industry to enter into an agreement with a union representing workers in that industry before the employer hires its employees, and, therefore, before it would be possible to demonstrate the union's majority status by an election. Such a prehire agreement allows the union and the employer to forego the election process to accommodate the fact that the usual election process would often be unworkable in the construction industry because employment is often short-term and based on hiring hall referrals. The section also allows the prehire agreement to contain union security agreements that differ from those otherwise permitted under Section 8(a)(3), although they are subject to Section 8(a)(3)'s final proviso protecting against union discrimination on grounds other than failure to pay fees and dues.[46] The section does not permit, however, any prehire agreement with a union that has been dominated or assisted by the employer in violation of Section 8(a)(2). A prehire agreement also does not act as a contract-bar to an election under the provisions of Section 9.

§ 4.3 Safeguarding the Right of Self-Organization

[A]—Introduction

The Board not only oversees representation elections but it is also charged with the obligation to enforce Sections 7 and 8 of the Act. Violations of Section 8 are unfortunately commonplace in representation elections. The focus of the next sections will be on the major areas of unlawfulness in election campaigns, mostly involving Sections 8(a)(1) and 8(a)(3) of the Act, along with conduct that, while not unlawful, tends to impede a free and reasoned choice in elections.

---

45 376 U.S. 473 (1964).

46 For a discussion of union security agreements, see *infra* § 17.1[A].

[B]—Access to The Employer's Property For Campaign Purposes

Section 7 speaks unqualifiedly about employee rights "to self-organization and to form, join, or assist labor organizations . . . ." Section 8(a)(1) appears to be equally unqualified in its prohibition of employer interference with, and restraint or coercion of employees engaged in the exercise of their Section 7 rights. By contrast, nowhere does the Act speak of employer property rights. One might assume, therefore, that the Act had abrogated an employer's property rights insofar as they conflicted with the employees' Section 7 rights, and that an employer who sought to restrict union solicitation and distribution of literature on her property had violated Section 8(a)(1) at the very least. Yet it is hard to picture a scheme under which Section 7 rights are truly unqualified regardless of when, where, and how employees choose to exercise them. And it is similarly hard to imagine that Congress intended Section 7 to trump all of an employer's preexisting rights, and Section 8(a)(1) to disallow any employer response to employees' protected concerted activity. Indeed, shortly after enactment of the NLRA, the Supreme Court trumpeted the continuing viability of employer property rights in *NLRB v. Fansteel Metallurgical Corp.*[47] In that case, employees responded to Fansteel's pattern of unfair labor practices by engaging in a sit-down strike in the workplace. Judging the sit-down strike to have been prompted by Fansteel's misconduct, the Board ordered the reinstatement of discharged sit-down strikers. In rejecting this remedy, the Supreme Court stated that regardless of employer provocation, it was still entitled to "its legal rights to the possession and protection of its property."[48]

Thus, from the earliest moments of the NLRA, the Supreme Court assumed that Section 7 rights and employer property rights must in some way be reconciled when they clashed. Because the statute gives no guidance on how to reconcile these two sets of rights, the task has fallen on the Board and the courts to divine a proper balance. The result has been a somewhat zig-zagged doctrinal history.

[1] Employer Restrictions on Access by Non-employee Union Organizers

The Board and the courts have treated employer restrictions on nonemployee organizer access and on the organizational activities of employees in the workplace as doctrinally distinct. Indeed, the Supreme Court rejected

[47] 306 U.S. 240 (1939).

[48] *Id.* at 253.

the idea that the latter category of cases involved property rights at all.[49] This section examines the law related to nonemployee access. The next section looks at permissible and impermissible restrictions on employee organizational activity in the workplace.

While union organization campaigns may rely heavily on in-plant solicitation by employees, there are important practical reasons why a union might choose to have its own organizers solicit as well, or instead. First, there are the obvious advantages of using professional union organizers who both know the union and are experienced organizers, and may be fluent in several languages native to the employees the union is trying to reach. Further, it is widely believed that, increasingly, in-plant activists run the risk of employer retaliation and discharge.[50] A widespread belief that visible union support, let alone a more activist role, may result in job loss or other punitive consequences that chills the behavior of employees of law-abiding employers as well as those whose employers are willing to flaunt the protections and prohibitions of the Act. Consequently, a union may be hard-pressed to find employees willing to solicit on its behalf.

The leading case on nonemployee access to an employer's property is *Lechmere, Inc. v. NLRB.*[51] It comes at the end of a series of cases beginning with *NLRB v. Babcock & Wilcox Co.*[52] In *Babcock & Wilcox,* the employer

---

[49] *See* Republic Aviation v. NLRB, 324 U.S. 793, 798 (1945) (framing the employer interest in terms of maintenance of discipline in the workplace rather than in terms of property rights). *But see* Cynthia Estlund, *Labor, Property, and Sovereignty After* Lechmere, 46 Stan. L. Rev. 305, 312-15 (1984) (arguing that against the backdrop of the common law of trespass of the time, which recognized a property owner's power to limit the license of people coming onto his property, *Republic Aviation* involved an unacknowledged, but subsequently recognized by the Board, partial abrogation of property rights).

[50] *See, e.g.,* Thomas Geoghegan, Which Side Are You On?, 251-59. In a widely discussed and often-cited article, Professor Paul Weiler traced the great increase in Section 8(a)(3) charges filed between the 1950s and 1980. Professor Weiler concluded that in 1980 on average one union supporter would be fired for every twenty union voters in a representation election. Paul C. Weiler, *Promises to Keep: Securing Workers' Rights to Self-Organization Under the NLRA,* 96 Harv. L. Rev. 1769, 1781 (1983). According to Weiler, by 1985 the ratio had changed to one in ten union supporters. Paul C. Weiler, Governing the Workplace: The Future of Labor and Employment Law 112 (1990). For a critical appraisal of what they call Weiler's "rogue employer thesis," see Robert J. Lalonde & Bernard D. Meltzer, *Hard Times for Unions: Another Look at the Significance of Employer Illegalities,* 58 U. Chi. L. Rev. 953 (1991). Professor Weiler's rebuttal is found at Paul C. Weiler, *Hard Times for Unions: Challenging Times for Scholars,* 58 U. Chi. L. Rev. 1015 (1991).

[51] 502 U.S. 527 (1992).

[52] 351 U.S. 105 (1956).

denied access to its parking lot to nonemployee union organizers who sought to distribute union literature. The employer's plant was near Paris, a small town in Texas. Babcock's employees lived within a thirty mile radius of the plant, 40% of them in the neighboring town. Employees drove to work, and parked in Babcock's lot, which was reached by a driveway off of a highway. Consequently, there was no safe place to distribute the literature to employees as they came to work other than on the employer's property. Babcock, which had consistently applied its no distribution rule to non-labor groups as well as the union, justified its denial of access on the grounds of litter prevention and the need to apply its rule consistently.

The Board found that the parking lot and the walkway from it to the plant's gatehouse were the only "safe and practicable" places to distribute literature and that denial of access thereto violated Section 8(a)(1) by interfering with Section 7 rights, specifically the rights to self-organize and to form or join a labor organization. It ordered Babcock to rescind its no-solicitation rule.

The Supreme Court concluded that the case required a balancing of the employees' Section 7 right to hear the message of the union organizers against the property rights of the employer. In describing the conflicting rights in these terms, the Supreme Court rejected the Board's reliance on the line of cases, discussed in the next section, involving the rights of employees to engage in organizational activity during non-work time.[53] Stating, without more, that the difference between employee and nonemployee solicitation was "one of substance," the Court substituted its approach for the Board's.[54] Perhaps because the company had asserted that the basis for its no-solicitation rule was concern with litter on its property, the Court did not explore further the nature of Babcock's property right. One is left to wonder, however, if the property right does not often amount to nothing more than a right to exclude the union and impede an organizational campaign.

---

[53] The leading case in this line is Republic Aviation v. NLRB, 324 U.S. 793 (1945) (framing the employer interest in terms of maintenance of discipline in the workplace rather than in terms of property rights and not distinguishing between solicitor's and solicitee's rights). Prior to the Supreme Court's decision in *Babcock & Wilcox*, the Board did not distinguish between employee and nonemployee solicitation. *Babcock & Wilcox*, 351 U.S. at 110-113; Sarah Korn, *Property Rights and Job Security: Workplace Solicitation by Nonemployee Union Organizers*, 94 Yale L.J. 374, 378 (1985) (tracing the history of the Board's pre-*Babcock & Wilcox* decisions); Alan L. Zmija, *Union Organizing After* Lechmere, Inc. v. NLRB—*A Time to Reexamine the Rule of* Babcock & Wilcox, 12 Hofstra Lab. L.J. 65, 80-83 (1994) (discussing differences between the Board's and the Court's approaches).

[54] *Babcock & Wilcox*, 351 U.S. at 113.

What standard did the Court adopt? It said that an accommodation of the Section 7 right and an employer's property right "must be obtained with as little destruction of one as is consistent with the maintenance of the other." Therefore, an employer may exclude "nonemployee distribution of union literature if reasonable efforts by the union through other available channels of communication will enable it to reach the employees with its message."[55] In the particular instance of *Babcock*, where union organizers had other opportunities for contact with the company's employees and the company had not singled out union solicitors to eject from its property, the no-solicitation rule did not violate Section 8(a)(1).

In addition to saying that an employer would not be able to engage in discriminatory applications of the no-solicitation rule by singling out union organizers to eject from its property, the Court spoke in terms of requiring access where other reasonable union efforts would not enable nonemployee organizers to reach employees. The Board might have read this latter exception fairly broadly given the Court's invitation to evaluate whether "reasonable" alternatives to access were available, and its admonition that the rights on both sides of the balance should be preserved with "as little destruction of one as is consistent with the maintenance of the other." Subsequent Board rulings, however, interpreted this exception quite narrowly and essentially limited it to instances, such as remote lumber or mining camps and resorts, where the employees live on the employer's property and would therefore be completely inaccessible without access for the organizer to the property.[56] In *Monogram Models, Inc.*,[57] for example, a divided Board acknowledged that a union would find it more difficult and expensive in a large city than in a small town like Paris, Texas to use such alternative means of communication as home visits, but refused to adopt a "big city rule" for access cases in major metropolitan areas.

Further, in those rare instances where the Board concluded that reasonable alternative means to granting access to employer's property did not exist, it was likely to find courts unwilling to enforce its access order. A striking example of this is *NLRB v. Sioux City and New Orleans Barge Lines, Inc.*,[58]

---

55 *Id.* at 112.

56 *See, e.g.*, S & H Grossinger's Inc., 156 NLRB 233 (1965), *order modified & enforced*, 372 F.2d 26 (2d Cir. 1967) (ordering access to remote resort, where most employees also lived); NLRB v. Lake Superior Lumber Corp., 167 F.2d 147 (6th Cir. 1948), *enforcing* 70 NLRB 178 (1946) (ordering access to lumber camp).

57 192 NLRB 705 (1971).

58 472 F.2d 753 (8th Cir. 1973).

where three unions sought to represent towboat crews. The crews worked 30- to 60-day shifts, during which time they were almost always on their boats and their boats were almost always in motion, followed by extended vacations during which they dispersed to 118 separate residences in 15 different states. One union, the Inland Boatman's Union, hired 10 organizers to contact vacationing employees by phone or home visit. They also hired speedboats in order to approach the towboats and toss union literature on deck. At the end of this campaign, they had only succeeded in meeting 35 of the 118 employees face-to-face. The Eighth Circuit refused to enforce the Board's order allowing union access to the employer's boats.[59]

While the standard became one of no access except under narrow exceptions for nonemployee union organizers, a second strand of cases emerged involving nonemployee assertions of a right to access outside of the organizing context.

[2] The Shopping Center Cases

For a brief period, the Supreme Court analyzed union access cases that took place in shopping malls under First Amendment principles. The prototypical case involves union area standards, or recognitional picketing or consumer picketing in support of a strike in a shopping mall, or its parking lot. The First Amendment does not generally protect union or worker speech against employer restrictions since it only protects against government infringement of free speech. Shortly after World War II, however, the Supreme Court began to define "state action" more broadly to reach instances where an otherwise non-governmental entity or person performed a state function.[60] In *Amalgamated Food Employees Union, Local 590 v. Logan Valley Plaza, Inc.*,[61] the Court applied this approach

[59] In its opinion, the court emphasized its disagreement with the Board's conclusions both that granting access would not interfere significantly with the employer's operations and that the alternatives to access were inadequate. *See also* Kutsher's Hotel & Country Club, Inc., 175 NLRB 1114 (1969), *enforcement denied,* 427 F.2d 200 (2d Cir. 1970) (distinguishing the *Grossinger's* case, and refusing to apply remote resort exception to another Catskills resort).

[60] Early examples of this were Marsh v. Alabama, 326 U.S. 501 (1946) (holding that Chickasaw, Alabama, a company town wholly owned and administered by the Gulf Shipbuilding Corporation, could not impose a license requirement on a Jehovah's Witness distributing literature on its sidewalks, nor arrest him for failing to attain a license, because private owner of the town was the functional equivalent of a city government and, thus, subject to First Amendment) and Shelley v. Kraemer, 334 U.S. 1 (1948) (judicial enforcement of private racially discriminatory housing covenants constitutes state action and therefore violates the equal protection clause of the Fourteenth Amendment).

[61] 391 U.S. 308 (1968).

to union area standards picketing of a store within a shopping center. It held that the picketing could not be enjoined as trespass on private property, because the mall had been opened to the public and privately-owned malls have become the functional equivalent of the public streets of downtown districts, the site of many of the earlier landmark First Amendment cases.

The ascension of the Burger Court, however, was marked by a quick retreat from an expansive view of state action and from analogizing privately-owned shopping centers to downtown public streets. Eight years after its *Logan Valley* decision, the Court announced its complete repudiation of its First Amendment approach to shopping center picketing cases in *Hudgens v. NLRB.*[62] In *Hudgens,* a shoe company's striking warehouse workers decided to picket the employer's retail outlets, one of which was located in Scott Hudgens's North DeKalb Shopping Center. After Hudgens threatened the pickets with arrest, the union filed an unfair labor practice charge. While the Supreme Court overruled *Logan Valley,* it also ruled that the union might have access rights under the NLRA. The *Hudgens* Court reaffirmed the *Babcock* accommodation principle.[63] It added, however, that there is a "spectrum" of Section 7 rights and private property rights, and that the place of a particular right in that spectrum might affect the outcome of a case. On remand, the Board concluded that the threatened arrest restrained protected activity in violation of Section (8)(a)(1).[64] It focused not only on the relatively strong Section 7 interest in economic strike activity and the relatively weak property interest of the mall owner given that the property is open to the public, but also on the comparative difficulty relative to organizational access to reach the intended audience (potential customers of one store within a large mall) through alternative means without the message becoming greatly diluted. *Hudgens* seemed to mean that the intended audience and the relative ease or difficulty of reaching them through alternative means would often be dispositive. Rather anomalously, this meant that employer interference with nonemployee access for organizational activity, which certainly is at the core of Section 7 rights and necessary to enable employees to exercise many of their other Section 7 rights, was generally permissible because the Board analyzed those cases under its narrow interpretation of *Babcock & Wilcox*; while in other

62 424 U.S. 507 (1976). In two earlier cases, Lloyd Corp. v. Tanner, 407 U.S. 551 (1972) (anti-war protestors), and Central Hardware Co. v. NLRB, 407 U.S. 539 (1972) (labor picketing in the parking lot of a large store), the Court had signalled a change in direction from *Logan Valley.*

63 *See Hudgens,* 424 U.S. at 521, 522.

64 Scott Hudgens, 230 NLRB 414 (1977).

scenarios where the intended audience was consumers, denial of access was more likely to be impermissible even if the Section 7 activity was more peripheral. The combination of these two lines of analysis created a strong incentive for a union with an organizational purpose to disguise its activity to look like informational picketing directed at consumers.

In the aftermath of *Hudgens*, the Board's approach to the access question took on a variety of formulations until its decision in *Jean Country.*[65] In *Jean Country,* a non-union store, Jean Country, competed with a number of unionized stores selling similar merchandise in the same shopping mall. After an unsuccessful attempt to interest the employees in joining the union and to persuade the Jean Country management to recognize the union, the union engaged in what it called "informational picketing." There was some question whether the picketing qualified as area standards picketing or whether it was done with a recognitional purpose, making it subject to Section 8(b)(7)(C) of the Act. The mall management called the police to evict the pickets and threatened arrest. The union then filed unfair labor practice charges.

The Board, among other things, followed *Hudgens*'s suggestion that it makes a difference what kind of Section 7 right is implicated, and that it makes a difference what kind of property right is implicated. It also made clear that the availability of alternatives and the reasonableness of those alternatives are always factors to consider.[66] The Board identified a number of factors to consider in determining the weight of the Section 7 and property rights and the effectiveness of alternative nontrespassory means for the union to communicate to its audience:

> Factors that may be relevant to assessing the weight of property rights include, but are not limited to, the use to which the property is put, the restrictions, if any, that are imposed on public access to the property, and the property's relative size and openness . . . . Factors that may be relevant to the consideration of a Section 7 right in any given case include, but are not limited to, the nature of the right, the identity of the employer to which the right is directly related (e.g., the employer with whom a union has a primary dispute), the relationship of the employer or other target to the property to which assess is sought, the identity of the

[65] 291 NLRB 11 (1988).

[66] Prior to *Jean Country,* the Board followed a rule that alternative means became a consideration only if the property and Section 7 interests were of equal weight. Fairmont Hotel Co., 282 NLRB 139 (1986). *Jean Country* overruled that part of *Fairmont Hotel.*

> audience to which the communications concerning the Section 7 right are directed, and the manner in which the activity related to that right is carried out. Factors that may be relevant to the assessment of alternative means include, but are not limited to, the desirability of avoiding the enmeshment of neutrals in labor disputes, the safety of attempting communications at alternative public sites, the burden and expense of nontrespassory communication alternatives, and most significantly, the extent to which exclusive use of the nontrespassory alternative would dilute the effectiveness of the message.[67]

Jean Country possessed all of the strengths and weaknesses of a multifactor test. On the one hand, it recognized that not all assertions of property interests or of Section 7 interests are equally strong, and conformed to the *Hudgens* Court's admonition to consider the relative strengths of each interest. It also recognized that context and audience mattered, that in some settings and with some audiences a nontrespassory method of communication could be ineffective, dangerous, or harmful to neutrals. On the other hand, it gave little guidance regarding the weights to assign to different Section 7 activities or property rights, and consequently was manipulable and gave uncertain guidance to those trying to conform their behavior to the rules. Moreover, the demand that the Board evaluate the relative worthiness of various Section 7 activities rings of the old common law approach where judges would evaluate, seemingly on the basis of their notions of a good and orderly society and their personal preferences regarding labor relations, whether employees or unions were pursuing "lawful" objectives.[68]

---

67 *Jean Country*, 291 NLRB at 13. In *Jean Country*, the Board concluded that denial of access violated Section 8(a)(1). Because the property was a shopping mall, with a broad invitation to the public to enter, and had other "quasi-public characteristics," the Board found that the property right was "quite weak." *Id.* at 16-17. Regarding the picketing, it determined that the purpose was organizational and recognitional. It also concluded, however, that a second purpose was to further the interests of unionized employees at other stores. It also noted that picketing occurred at the situs of the dispute. It concluded, "that the protected picketing that took place is not on the stronger end of the spectrum of Section 7 rights . . . . However, it is a right that is certainly worthy of protection against substantial impairment." *Id.* at 18. Turning to alternative means of communication, it noted the difficulty of trying to reach potential Jean Country customers through nontrespassory means in a large shopping mall, including the difficult task of identifying them and of communicating to them without diluting the message, as well as the potential for enmeshing neutrals in the dispute because of the strong possibility that mall shoppers who received the union's message elsewhere than outside of Jean Country's doors might confuse it with one of the other mall clothing stores. *Id.*

68 *See supra* § 1.3[B].

[3] *Babcock & Wilcox* Revisited: *Lechmere Inc. v. NLRB*

After *Jean Country*, the Board seemed to liberalize its approach in access cases generally, including organizer access cases.[69] This came to a head in *Lechmere Inc. v. NLRB.*[70] *Lechmere* seemed to be a classic mall case, except that the intended audience were Lechmere employees and the purpose for nonemployee access was organizational. The store and various satellite stores were located in a strip mall, Lechmere Shopping Plaza, situated along a four-lane divided highway. The United Food and Commercial Workers Union, seeking to represent the Lechmere employees, generated little employee response to a local newspaper advertisement. When union organizers tried to put handbills on the windshields of Lechmere employees' cars, they were ordered off of the parking lot by a Lechmere manager. The union, resorting to various alternative means, had little success reaching employees and obtaining signed authorization cards. The Board found that denial of access to the mall parking lot violated Section 8(a)(1), and the Court of Appeals for the First Circuit affirmed.

The *Lechmere* Court reversed. Writing for the majority, Justice Thomas read *Jean Country* as inconsistent with *Babcock,* which he argued was controlling authority. In so doing he gave greater weight to the property right, which he argued should not be impaired unless reasonable access to employees outside of the employer's property is "infeasible."[71] Only in such rare cases involving totally inaccessible workers, such as remote lumber and mining camps, should the Board balance the competing statutory and property rights. In other words, there need be no accommodation of property rights to Section 7 rights, unless you would otherwise have a total destruction of Section 7 rights.

Justice White wrote a vigorous dissent, criticizing the majority for misreading *Babcock.*[72] That case, Justice White argued, was full of balancing and accommodation language, but the majority, instead, derived

[69] *See, e.g.*, Sentry Mkts., 296 NLRB 40 (1989), *enforced* 914 F.2d 113 (7th Cir. 1990); Lechmere, Inc., 295 NLRB 92 (1989); Chugach Alaska Fisheries, 295 NLRB 44 (1989); Tecumseh Foodland, 294 NLRB 486 (1989). Indeed, the Board stated in *Jean Country* that its approach applies to "all access cases." 291 NLRB at 14.

[70] 502 U.S. 527 (1992).

[71] *Id.* at 538.

[72] The decision also provoked considerable academic criticism. In addition to Estlund, *supra* note 49, and Zmija, *supra* note 53, see, for example, Robert A. Gorman, *Union Access to Private Property: A Critical Assessment of* Lechmere, Inc. v. NLRB, 9 Hofstra Lab. L.J. 1 (1991).

a rigid rule that seems to say access will only be granted if employees are barracked on the employer's premises. He attributed this misreading partly to the majority's seizing on the remote resort, and lumber and mining camp cases not as examples of instances where the accommodation of rights required that the property right give way, but as defining the boundaries of the universe of cases where any balancing and accommodation need be done at all. This misreading was compounded, he argued by Justice Thomas's interpretation of subsequent cases, such as *Hudgens,* as reaffirmations of a narrow reading of *Babcock* rather than of the balancing of rights principle. Finally, he argued that the Court need not slavishly adhere to *Babcock* because it was born of an era before the Court's modern approach of "deference to an administrative agency charged with administering a statute" when the agency's rule is a permissible interpretation of the statute, and Congress has left its meaning unclear.[73] The *Babcock* Court, by contrast, had nondeferentially brushed aside the Board's approach to this Section 7 and Section 8(a)(1) question and substituted its own construction of the statute. In conclusion, he wrote, "Under the law that governs today, it is *Babcock* that rests on questionable legal foundations."[74]

Lechmere clearly establishes the rule regarding employer restrictions on nonemployee organizer access to its property: unless it would be infeasible for the union to reach the employees by other reasonable nontrespassory means, or the employer applied its no-access rule discriminatorily, the employer may oust the union organizer.[75] *Lechmere* clearly overrules that application of *Jean Country.* More uncertain is whether there is anything left to *Jean Country* after *Lechmere.* Because the decision appeared to embrace both *Babcock & Wilcox* and *Hudgens,* there was reason to assume that *Jean Country* still had vitality outside of the organizational context, consistent with *Hudgens.* However, in a series of decisions[76] the Board

[73] *Id.* at 541, 545 (White, J., dissenting). The modern rule is stated in Chevron U.S.A. Inc. v. Natural Resources Defense Council, Inc., 467 U.S. 837 (1984).

[74] *Lechmere,* 507 U.S. at 548 (White, J., dissenting).

[75] Of course, access may still be available in those instances where the employer's property right is more limited than the full bundle of rights that we typically associate with property ownership. Where, for instance, the employer's right is limited to a nonexclusive easement, an employer may not exclude nonemployee organizers or pickets without running afoul of Section 8(a)(1). *See* O'Neils Markets, Inc., 318 NLRB 646 (1995), *aff'd in part and rev'd in part,* 95 F.3d 733 (8th Cir. 1996); Johnson & Hardin Co., 305 NLRB 690 (1991), *enforced in part and vacated in part,* 49 F.3d 237 (6th Cir. 1995).

[76] Leslie Homes, Inc., 316 NLRB 123 (1995) (*Lechmere* governs instances of area standards picketing); L'Enfant Plaza Properties, 316 NLRB 1111 (1995) (same); Oakland Mall, 316 NLRB 1160 (1995) (*Lechmere* permits mall property owner to bar nonemployees from

has extended *Lechmere*'s approach, and hostility to access, to access questions involving area standards picketing, and to secondary consumer boycott handbilling. In doing so, it has highlighted the paradox that the old access rules were friendlier to the often less highly valued Section 7 activity of the shopping center cases than to the core organizational activity that ran afoul of the *Babcock & Wilcox* rule. That result occurred in the earlier cases because of the greater difficulty in effectively reaching the mall's customers than the employees of a Lechmere or Babcock & Wilcox through nontrespassory means. But that notion of inacessability in the prior shopping center decisions had depended on the Board's acceptance of the idea that unions need not resort to advertising in mass media to reach its audience.[77] In one recent decision, the Board, with the subsequent approval of the D.C. Circuit, repudiated its prior approach to mass media campaigning, "at least where the Section 7 right is as attenuated as [consumer boycott handbilling] in question here."[78]

[C]—Employer Restrictions on Organizational Activity on Its Property

[1] Restrictions on Solicitation by Employees: *Republic Aviation*

The rules regarding employer restrictions on employee organizational activity in the workplace have been more stable than the rules relating to outsiders' access. The core rules are that: an employer may make and enforce a rule prohibiting union solicitation by employees during working time, and any such rule is presumptively valid, absent evidence of a discriminatory purpose. However, an employer may not generally enforce such rules to prohibit employee solicitation during non-work times, such as lunch or break periods, even though the employee is on the employer's property, and any rule that prohibits solicitation during non-working time is presumptively invalid, absent evidence of special circumstances requiring such a rule in order to maintain production or discipline. The basic foundation for these rules received its blessing from the Supreme Court more than half a century ago in *Republic Aviation Corp. v. NLRB.*[79]

---

handbilling on private property in support of secondary consumer boycott), *review denied sub nom.* United Food and Commercial Workers, Local 880 v. NLRB, 74 F.3d 292 (1996), *cert. denied sub nom.* Teamsters Local 243 v. NLRB, 117 S. Ct. 52 (1996). This issue is discussed further at *infra* §§ 6.8[C] and 12.5.

[77] *See, e.g., Jean Country,* 291 NLRB at 13.

[78] *Oakland Mall,* 316 NLRB at 1163.

[79] 324 U.S. 793 (1945).

Republic Aviation and its companion case, *NLRB v. Le Tourneau Co. of Georgia*, involved the permissibility of applying company anti-solicitation and anti-handbilling rules to soliciting employees. In *Republic Aviation,* the employer had a longstanding rule that prohibited all solicitation in its facilities. The company discharged an employee who defied the rule to solicit union memberships during lunch periods. Three other employees were asked to remove union-steward buttons they were wearing. When they refused, the company discharged them also. The company stated that it asked them to take off the buttons because it believed that tolerating the buttons would give the false appearance that it approved of the particular union, which was not then the designated bargaining representative of the company's employees though it was pursuing that role. The appearance of approval, it argued, could undermine both the company's policy of neutrality in union affairs and its then-existing grievance system.

The Board ruled that the no-solicitation rule interfered with Section 7 rights in violation of Section 8(1), and that the discharge for violation of the rule violated Section 8(3).[80] It similarly found that the discharge of the employees wearing union steward buttons also violated those two provisions.

The Supreme Court upheld the Board rulings. The Court did not perceive the question in terms of conflicting property and statutory rights. Rather, it construed the conflict as one between the Section 7 right of self-organization and the employers' right to maintain discipline in their workplaces. As is true of the employer's property right, the Act nowhere expressly protects an employer's right to maintain discipline. Nor did the Court cite any authority for this proposition; it was, instead, assumed to be part of the preexisting backdrop for the Act.

The Board had found that the company had not acted out of an anti-union or a discriminatory motivation. Nevertheless, the Court approved of the Board's ruling that the Act had been violated. With regard to violations of Section 8(a)(1), no showing of anti-union motive was necessary. Section 8(a)(3), however, speaks in terms of it being unlawful for an employer "by discrimination . . . to encourage or discourage membership in any labor organization," suggesting that there must be an anti- (or pro-) union motive behind the employer's conduct, and we will see in other contexts just such

[80] Prior to the adoption of the Taft-Hartley amendments which added, amongst other things, Section 8(b) to the Act, what is now Section 8(a) and its subparts were numbered Section 8(1)-(5). For consistency's sake (though not historical accuracy's), I will hereinafter refer to pre-Taft-Hartley sections as if Sections 8(1)-(5) had already become Sections 8(a)(1)-(5).

a requirement.[81] Here, however, the Court held that a discharge for union solicitation for violation of a no-solicitation rule that is invalidly applied to union solicitation, violates Section 8(a)(3) regardless of the employer's motive.[82]

The Court rejected Republic Aviation's argument that the Board must first show that its solicitation rule had demonstrable adverse effects on employee organization efforts before it can find a Section 8(a)(1) violation. Nor, in contrast to what the Court would say in the nonemployee access cases, need the Board consider whether reasonable alternative means of communication were available. Instead, the Court stated that an agency is entitled to deference within its area of expertise regarding the inferences that it draws from the facts established through its adversarial proceedings.[83] The Court then endorsed the Board's application of a set of presumptions from another decision, *Peyton Packing Company,*[84] in *Republic Aviation,* which stated, in part:

> The Act, of course, does not prevent an employer from making and enforcing reasonable rules covering the conduct of employees on company time. Working time is for work. It is therefore within the province of an employer to promulgate and enforce a rule prohibiting union solicitation during working hours. Such a rule must be presumed to be valid in the absence of evidence that it was adopted for a discriminatory purpose. It is no less true that time outside working hours, whether before or after work, or during luncheon or rest periods, is an employee's time to use as he wishes without unreasonable restraint, although the employee is on company property. It is therefore not within the province of an employer to promulgate and enforce a rule prohibiting union solicitation by an employee outside of working hours, although on company property. Such a rule must be presumed to be an unreasonable impediment to self-organization and therefore discriminatory in the absence of evidence that special circumstances make the rule necessary in order to maintain production and discipline.

In addition to, and sometimes as further elaboration of, the basic rule that employer prohibitions of solicitation during work time are presumptively valid, and that similar prohibitions of solicitation that cover non-work

---

81 For further discussion *see infra* § 4.4[C].

82 *Republic Aviation,* 324 U.S. at 805.

83 *Id.* at 798-800.

84 49 NLRB 828, 843-44 (1943) *quoted in* Republic Aviation v. NLRB, 324 U.S. 793, 803 n.10 (1945).

time are presumptively invalid, the Board had developed other rules regarding employee solicitation and distribution of literature. Often, the employee solicitor will also want to distribute literature about the union and the benefits of unionizing, and, perhaps, about the employer. *Le Tourneau,* the companion case to *Republic Aviation*, was such a case.[85] Such literature may play an important role in the election campaign, but it also can present problems of litter and possible interference with production. The Board has reconciled the competing interests by concluding that in addition to prohibiting distribution of literature during work time, an employer's rule that also prohibits distribution of literature in *work areas,* regardless of whether it is work or non-work time, is presumptively valid.[86] The Board has also consistently said that a request that a fellow employee sign a union authorization card should be governed by its more generous solicitation rule than by the more taxing distribution rule.[87]

More stringent restraints on solicitation are permissible in certain special locations because of its potential disruptive effect. Thus, retail department stores have been permitted to prohibit solicitation in selling areas even during break times.[88] Hospitals may similarly prohibit such solicitation in patient care areas, but not in other public areas where solicitation would not disturb patients or undermine the provision of healthcare.[89]

Also at issue in *Republic Aviation* was the employer's power to regulate the wearing of union buttons and insignia in the workplace. There the Court approved of the Board's conclusion that wearing such union emblems is a protected activity; therefore, the discharge of three employees for wearing union steward buttons violated Sections 8(a)(1) and (3).[90] In keeping with this holding, the *Board* has repeatedly reiterated the right of employees to wear union badges, buttons, and T-shirts while working.[91] This right is subject, however, to instances where, because of "special circumstances," the Section 7 right must give way.[92] Examples include cases where the

---

85 324 U.S. at 796-97.

86 Stoddard-Quirk Mfg. Co., 138 NLRB 615 (1962).

87 *Id.* at 619 n.5; Rose Co., 154 NLRB 228, 229 n.1 (1965).

88 Goldblatt Bros., 77 NLRB 1262 (1948).

89 NLRB v. Baptist Hospital, Inc., 442 U.S. 773 (1979); Beth Israel Hospital v. NLRB, 434 U.S. 1033 (1978).

90 *Republic Aviation*, 324 U.S. at 803-04.

91 *See, e.g.,* West Lawrence Care Ctr., 308 NLRB 1011 (1992); Woonsocket Health Ctr., 245 NLRB 652 (1979).

92 *Republic Aviation,* 324 U.S. at 803-04.

insignia might interfere with the employer's need to maintain production and discipline,[93] or, though there are decisions both ways, might alienate customers,[94] or might lead to friction or violence between groups within the workplace because of preexisting factionalism.[95]

The Board has long taken the position that employee solicitation rights are nontradeable. In other words, they cannot be bargained away in the collective bargaining agreement, regardless of how willing the union and the employer are to make the deal. That a union should not be able to agree with the employer to foreclose the solicitation rights of its dissident members and of any potential insurgent union, seems obvious.[96] Less clear is why a union and employer should not be allowed to trade the union's right to speak through solicitations and distributions otherwise permitted under *Republic Aviation* and the related rules. In *NLRB v. Magnavox*,[97] a divided Court approved of the Board's ruling that a union not only may not waive the solicitation rights of its critics and rivals, but it also may not waive its own solicitation rights (in this case while maintaining the right to post notices on a company bulletin board). It is less clear why this rule should apply to the union's gagging itself, and Justice Stewart, writing for himself and two others, would have permitted the union to do that. *Magnavox* reminds us how seriously the Court takes elections, and the flow of information necessary for an informed electorate, although that sentiment is belied in some of the cases discussed above. The Court's position may

---

93 *See, e.g.*, Fabric-Tek, Inc. v. NLRB, 352 F.2d 577 (8th Cir. 1965) (employer may prohibit wearing of oversized buttons and badges, or normal size ones worn in unusual and distracting ways in plant where production process requires constant concentration).

94 While the Board has generally held that concern about customer reaction falls short of special circumstances that would allow the employer to interfere with the right to wear union insignia, the circuit courts are divided in their willingness to enforce Board orders in such cases. *Compare* Burger King Corp. v. NLRB, 725 F.2d 1053, 1055 (6th Cir. 1984) (declining to enforce Board's order); *and* NLRB v. Harrah's Club, 337 F.2d 177, 178-89 (9th Cir. 1964) (same) *with* Meijer, Inc. v. NLRB, 130 F.3d 1209, 1214-17 (6th Cir. 1997) (rejecting circuit's prior *Burger King* rule, noting that right to wear union insignia is "near-absolute," and enforcing Board's order).

95 *See, e.g.*, Virginia Electric & Power Co. v. NLRB, 703 F.2d 79, 82-83 (4th Cir. 1983) (conflict between competing unions justifies requirement that pins be small and not "gaudy"); Caterpillar Tractor Co. v. NLRB, 230 F.2d 357 (7th Cir. 1956) (wearing buttons with slogan "Don't be a Scab" in a volatile work environment because of provocative nature of the message).

96 The Board adopted that rule in Gale Products, 142 NLRB 1246 (1963), *enforcement denied*, 337 F.2d 390 (7th Cir. 1964).

97 415 U.S. 322 (1974).

also be grounded in the notion that the Section 7 rights at issue belong to the employees and not the union, and their need to hear therefore trumps.

[2] The Content of Union Literature and the Protection of Section 8(a)(1)

Do these solicitation and distribution rules apply equally to any union (or, for that matter, anti-union) materials or speech? *Eastex, Inc. v. NLRB*,[98] a case whose principal importance relates to the definition of protected concerted activities, and is therefore discussed more fully elsewhere,[99] suggests that content might matter. In *Eastex*, employees in a unionized paper products plant in Texas sought to distribute a union newsletter in nonwork areas on nonwork time in order to generate greater support for the union, but were barred from doing so by the employer.[100] While two sections of the newsletter clearly pertained to labor-management relations in that plant and sought to promote the union specifically and unionization more generally, the other two sections only did so in an indirect manner. One urged resistance to an effort to add a right-to-work provision to the Texas Constitution, while the other deplored President Nixon's veto of a bill raising the minimum wage and urged employees to register to vote so they could support labor's friends and defeat its enemies. The Board rejected the employer's argument that because the latter two subjects were not about labor relations issues at Eastex and not about matters over which the employer had any power it was not required under the Act to permit distribution, and the Fifth Circuit enforced its order. The Supreme Court approved of the Board's analysis of the protected activity and the scope of *Republic Aviation*'s coverage questions. In dictum, in which Justice Powell took pains to state his reluctance to impose a solution on the Board rather than to let any fine-tuning of the *Republic Aviation* rule occur by an "evolutionary process," he suggested that some literature might be pertinent to matters affecting employees as employees yet be "so removed from the central concerns of the Act as to tip the *Republic Aviation* balance of employee and employer interests towards greater solicitude for employer control of protected activity on its property.[101]

---

98 437 U.S. 556 (1978).

99 *See infra* § 16.4.

100 As a right-to-work state, Texas had statutorily barred unions and employers from entering into union security agreements that would require employees to become union members. Thus many, but not all, employees were not union members, and the union produced the newsletter partly in the hope of attracting these nonmembers.

101 The Board's practice has been to treat distribution of "purely political tracts" as unprotected even though election outcomes may ultimately be relevant to working conditions. Ford Motor Co., 221 NLRB 663, 666 (1975), *enforced*, 546 F.2d 418 (3d Cir. 1976).

The Fifth Circuit subsequently concluded it had spotted such a case in *NLRB v. Motorola, Inc.*[102] *Motorola* involved a variety of employee reactions to the company's adoption of a mandatory random drug testing program, including, most importantly, the attempt to post and distribute materials from a community organization committed to electing city council candidates who would vote to enact an ordinance that would limit a company's ability to implement such testing.[103] The Board, on its reading of *Eastex,* ruled that because the literature directly related to a matter at issue between Motorola and its employees, the company could not ban its distribution under a blanket rule.[104] The Fifth Circuit declined to enforce this part of the Board's order, because the literature was that of a political organization, not of the employees' bargaining representative, which sought to distribute within Motorola's plant to advance its interests. Quoting Justice Powell's dictum in *Eastex*, the court stated: "We believe that the facts in this case reach that 'point of attenuation' posited by the Supreme Court in *Eastex.* Employees acting as members of outside political organizations cannot demand the same Section 7 rights as employees engaged in self-organization, collective bargaining, or in self-representation in disputes with management . . . . The Act is not intended to protect entities so far removed from the normal employer-employee relationship."[105]

[3] Captive Audience Speeches and the Right of Equal Access

An employer who prohibits solicitation under a facially valid rule might choose to exempt itself from such a rule. This might be done by permitting, or requiring, supervisors to engage in anti-union solicitation during work-time, or by requiring its employees to listen to the employer's anti-union speech. Such employer speech, if noncoercive, is protected by Section 8(c) of the Act, which was added in the 1947 Taft-Hartley amendments. Coercive employer speech raises additional issues, which are discussed below.

In the face of employer "captive audience" speeches, unions have demanded equal time. After some vacillating by the Board on this

102 991 F.2d 278 (5th Cir. 1993).

103 In addition to prohibiting distribution of the organization's materials on company property, Motorola briefly prohibited the wearing of "Just Say No to Drug Testing" T-shirts, but it quickly conceded that employees had a Section 7 right to wear such shirts to work.

104 Motorola, Inc., 305 NLRB 580 (1991).

105 *Motorola,* 991 F.2d at 285.

question,[106] the Supreme Court addressed the issue in *NLRB v. United Steelworkers (NuTone and Avondale Mills).*[107]

While it is clear that the Court held that the Board may not presume simply on the fact that the employer has violated his own otherwise concededly valid rule that the employer must afford the union equal access, the Court was less clear about the standard it was applying to determine whether denial of equal access would violate Section 8(a)(1). At one point, Justice Frankfurter suggested that the General Counsel is required to "make a showing that the no-solicitation rules truly diminished the ability of the labor organizations involved to carry their messages to the employees."[108] In other words, the Court seems to be imposing an adverse effects test—how adverse, seems to be defined by the phrase "truly diminished." This stands in stark contrast to *Republic Aviation*'s homage to the Board's capacity to draw categorical inferences from its experience and expertise regarding labor relations, and its rejection of the employer's argument that it could not be presumed to have violated the Act absent a showing of specific adverse effects.[109] Elsewhere, the Court said, "If, by virtue of the location of the plant and of the facilities and resources available to the union, the opportunities for effectively reaching the employees with a pro-union message, in spite of a no solicitation rule, are at least as great as the employer's ability to promote the legally authorized expression of his anti-union views, there is no basis for invalidating these otherwise valid rules."[110] Here the Court appears to direct a reasonable alternative means test similar to that in *Babcock & Wilcox*, but it does not address the question whether the distinction between employee and nonemployee speech should matter in this context, although it found that distinction fundamental in *Babcock.*

The result has been that captive audience speeches have remained an important tool in the employer's campaign without an opportunity for equal

---

106 *Compare* Bonwit Teller, Inc., 96 NLRB 608 (1951) (employer's denial of union request for equal access is an unfair labor practice because it discriminatorily applies no-solicitation rule), *remanded on other grounds,* 197 F.2d 640 (2d Cir. 1952), *cert. denied,* 345 U.S. 905 (1953) *with* Livingston Shirt Corp., 107 NLRB 400 (1953) (employer's right to deny equal access is protected by Section 8(c) and is therefore not an unfair labor practice).

107 357 U.S. 357 (1958).

108 *Id.* at 363.

109 Indeed, the Court cites *Republic Aviation* as if it stands as authority for the proposition that the Board must do case-specific fact-finding regarding adverse effects. *Id.* This contrast was noted and criticized by Chief Justice Warren in his partly dissenting and partly concurring opinion. *Id.* at 365, 366-68.

110 *Id.* at 364.

access. Contemporaneous with its abandonment of an equal access rule in 1953, the Board also established a rule, in *Peerless Plywood*, that prohibits captive audience speeches on company time within 24 hours of the election because of the risk they pose of undermining careful thought and free choice and the potentially great advantage that they offer to the last speaker.[111] The Board continues to enforce the *Peerless Plywood* rule strictly.

[D]—Wrap Up on Access and Solicitation

Both anecdotal evidence and empirical studies have emphasized the importance of union contact with the bargaining unit employees to the chances of union success in an organizing campaign.[112] Consequently, in the wake of *Lechmere*, the availability of alternative means for unions to reach the rank-and-file is critical for union organizing efforts. One important tool that pre-dates both *Lechmere* and *Jean Country* is the *Excelsior* list, which makes home visits by professional organizers and rank-and-file organizers alike easier to implement. In *National Labor Relations Board v. Town & Country Electric, Inc.*,[113] the Supreme Court left available to unions another means of access: sending its organizers to target companies as job applicants who can then campaign from within. Rejecting Town & Country's argument that full-time union organizer job applicants are not "employees" as that term is defined by the Act, the Court unanimously held that such union "salts" are entitled to protection under the Act. Consequently, an employer who refuses to hire such applicants or to retain them because of their union activity does so in violation of Section 8(a)(3).[114]

---

[111] Peerless Plywood Co., 107 NLRB 427 (1953).

[112] *See, e.g.*, Julius G. Getman et al., Union Representation Elections: Law And Reality (1976) (emphasizing effect of captive audience speeches and elimination of equal access); Kate Bronfenbrenner, *The Role of Union Strategies in NLRB Certification Elections*, 50 Indus. & Lab. Rel. Rev. 195 (1997) (emphasizing importance of person-to-person contacts, typically in home visits and small group meetings, and at the early stages, "underground" to escape notice of employer, as well as development of rank-and-file leadership to engage in campaigning). As these two examples suggest, such contact may be made in a variety of ways beside the traditional parking lot solicitation. *See also* Marion Crain, *Feminism, Labor, and Power*, 65 S. Cal. L. Rev. 1819, 1837-43, 1871-75 (1992) (contrasting traditional "patriarchal" approach to union organizing to "woman-centered" approach used recently with success in some university clerical worker campaigns that deemphasized distribution of literature in favor of face-to-face contact and use of organizers from within rank-and-file).

[113] 516 U.S. 85 (1995).

[114] For a discussion of *Town & Country* and its relationship to *Babcock* and *Lechmere*, see Michael H. Gottesman, *Union Summer: A Reawakened Interest in the Law of Labor?*, 1996 Sup. Ct. Rev. 285, 298-318.

Time will tell whether unions find salting to be an effective means for organization.

Confronted with an access case, how should you analyze it? First, ask: Who is the intended audience? If it is the employer's employees, ask: Who is doing the talking? If it is nonemployee organizers, *Lechmere* will govern, and unless the employer is applying its prohibition on outsider solicitation discriminatorily or fits into the rare exception for lumber and mining camps and similarly inaccessible settings, the employer's denial of access will be lawful. If, on the other hand, the person talking is an employee of the employer, *Republic Aviation* and its related rules will govern, and some solicitation and distribution rights will typically be available. Finally, if in answer to the first question you identify the audience as customers or suppliers of the employer, or other employers' employees, the current temper of the Board and the courts seem to be to deny access, whether by extension of *Lechmere* or by altering the *Jean Country* analysis to devalue the Section 7 activity that has created the access problem and to expect the union to shoulder more burdensome alternative nontrespassory means of communication than prior Boards have typically expected.

[E]—Election Propaganda: Employer and Union Speech

In the early years of the Labor Act, the NLRB took the position that the Act required that employers remain neutral in union elections. This practice reflected both the Board's belief that because of employees' economic dependence, employer participation was inherently coercive and would interfere with employee free choice, and its conclusion that as a nonvoter and noncandidate in the election the employer had no valid claim to participate.[115] Addressing the inherent coerciveness of employer campaigning, the *American Tube* Board wrote that "[i]t was impossible for the employees to distinguish between the [employer] *qua* candidate and the [employer] *qua* employer[]."[116] But the Board met with limited success in persuading the courts to enforce its orders in employer speech cases.[117]

---

115 American Tube Bending, 44 NLRB 121 (1942), *enforcement denied*, 134 F.2d 993 (2d Cir.) (1943), *cert. denied*, 320 U.S. 768 (1943). For a critical discussion of the premises of representation elections and the evolution of a role for employers in them, see generally, Craig Becker, *Democracy in the Workplace: Union Representation Elections and Federal Labor Law*, 77 Minn L. Rev. 495 (1993).

116 44 NLRB at 133.

117 *See, e.g.*, Midland Steel Prods. Co. v. NLRB, 113 F.2d 800, 804 (6th Cir 1940) (interpreting statute as prohibiting coercive employer speech, but not noncoercive speech, and arguing that the Board's reading would raise serious First Amendment questions).

Advocates of an employer's right to participate in representation elections argued not only that such a right was guaranteed by the First Amendment, but that employer participation was necessary to better inform the electorate about the arguments for and against unionization.[118]

Congress responded to the Board's effort to regulate employer speech by enacting Section 8(c) as part of the 1947 Taft-Hartley Amendments. Section 8(c) provides:

> The expressing of any views, argument, or opinion, or the dissemination thereof, whether in written, printed, graphic, or visual form, shall not constitute or be evidence of an unfair labor practice under any of the provisions of this Act, if such expression contains no threat of reprisal or force or promise of benefit.[119]

Accordingly, the fact of employer anti-union speech alone could not constitute an unfair labor practice (or, for that matter, stand as evidence of an unfair labor practice). The Board quickly responded in *General Shoe Corp.*[120] by developing the notion of "laboratory conditions." In *General Shoe*, the employer engaged in a vigorous anti-union campaign, which included home visits by supervisors and election-eve speeches delivered by the company President to small groups of employees brought to his office. Prior to enactment of Section 8(c), the Board would have treated this campaign as interference with employee free choice in choosing a bargaining representative and, therefore, a violation of Section 8(a)(1) (which, of course, was then Section 8(1)), and the hearing examiner, who made his findings before enactment of Section 8(c), so found. With the enactment of Section 8(c), the Board could no longer treat the employer's speech as an unfair labor practice unless it threatened reprisal or promised a benefit. Instead, the Board distinguished between representation cases and unfair labor practice cases and ruled that Section 8(c)'s protection of employer speech only applied to the latter. In other words, employer speech might give reason to set aside an election even if it had not violated Section 8(a)(1), if it failed to meet the Board's more demanding standard for a fair election. In *General Shoe*, the Board described that standard in terms of maintaining "laboratory conditions" under which to investigate employee choice. In likening the representation election to a scientific investigation the Board wrote:

---

118 *See* Becker, *Democracy, supra* note 115, at 541-45.

119 29 U.S.C. § 158(c) (1994).

120 77 NLRB 124 (1948), *enforced,* 192 F.2d 504 (6th Cir. 1951), *cert. denied,* 343 U.S. 904 (1952).

> In election proceedings, it is the Board's function to provide a laboratory in which an experiment may be conducted, under conditions as nearly ideal as possible to determine the uninhibited desires of the employees. It is our duty to establish those conditions; it is also our duty to determine whether they have been fulfilled. When, in the rare extreme case, the standard drops too low, because of our fault or that of others, the requisite laboratory conditions are not present and the experiment must be conducted over again.[121]

[1] Predictions and Threats of Reprisal

If speech that falls within the protection of Section 8(c) may, nonetheless, upset laboratory conditions, speech that falls outside Section 8(c) and violates Section 8(a)(1) almost certainly is ground for setting aside an election. But when does speech cross the line and become coercive? The Supreme Court has given some guidance to that issue in *NLRB v. Gissel Packing Company*,[122] although it is, perhaps, easier to state the Court's rules than to implement them consistently. *Gissel* was a consolidation of four cases involving many unfair labor practices and raising important questions about Board remedies.[123] Additionally, in one of the four cases, the Court was confronted with the question of how to distinguish a permissible prediction or statement of opinion from an implied threat. In approving of the Board's order and affirming the First Circuit's ruling enforcing that order, the Court acknowledged the tension between the employer's First Amendment right to express its opinions regarding unions generally and the union seeking recognition more particularly (which by that point was widely accepted), and the employees' First Amendment right of free association, as well as their statutory rights under Section 7. It also recognized that any balance drawn between these rights must be done with an understanding that because of their economic dependence on the employer, workers will have a keener ear and heightened sensitivity to an implied threat to their economic well-being. That position of economic dependence makes it difficult for employees to distinguish between mere "predictions" and "threats" of retaliation or "promises" of benefits for supporting the employer against the union, because, often, the employer can make her prediction a reality.[124] The possibility of the subtly implied

121 *Id.* at 127 (footnote omitted).

122 395 U.S. 575 (1969).

123 These are discussed below in *infra* § 4.5[B].

124 For this reason, most of the election cases involving threats or promises of benefits involve employers. While a union can run afoul of Section 8(b)(1)(A)'s prohibition of

threat also requires that the statements at issue be viewed in the context of overall election conduct.

What does the Court say the employer is allowed to say to his employees during the representation campaign? He can "communicate . . . his general views about unionism or any of his specific views about a particular union," but he may not make a "threat of reprisal or force or promise of benefit."[125] That alone seems to add nothing to the statute, but the Court then spoke to a framework for distinguishing between those employer statements about the future after a union victory that, permissibly, describe what the employer can reasonably believe is inevitable (for reasons external to him) and those that, impermissibly, convey a future punitive course of action that is within the employer's volition. Chief Justice Warren wrote that an employer may predict "the precise effects he believes unionization will have on his company," so long as they are based on "objective fact . . . as to demonstrably probable consequences beyond his control or . . . a management decision already arrived at to close the plant in case of unionization."[126] Critical to this distinction is the question of employer control over the predicted harmful course:

> If there is any implication that an employer may or may not take action solely on his own initiative for reasons unrelated to economic necessities and known only to him, the statement is no longer a reasonable prediction based on available facts but a threat of retaliation based on misrepresentation and coercion, and as such without the protection of the First Amendment.[127]

Given the subtlety of the distinction between predictions and threats, and the importance of context, it is not hard to find inconsistent NLRB decisions, and inconsistent treatment of those decisions within the circuit courts. Some recurrent patterns of campaign speech reveals how evasive the line between prediction and threat can be. An employer may disagree with election decisions regarding, for instance, the configuration of the bargaining unit and the eligibility of certain voters, and it is entitled to put the Board's determination of these issues to the test by a refusal to bargain. May an

---

restraining or coercing employees in the exercise of their Section 7 rights, the union's lack of economic power symmetrical to the employer's means that its promises and predictions are heard differently from the employer's.

125 395 U.S. at 618.

126 *Id.* (citation omitted).

127 *Id.*

employer warn its employees of its intent to refuse to bargain and to litigate these issues should the union win? A comment to that effect was deemed non-coercive by the Board in *Esquire, Inc.*,[128] but, in the context of various other statements, a similar comment was deemed coercive in *Dal-Tex Optical Co.*[129]

A common scenario involves various employer statements to the effect that the obligation to bargain with the union does not include a obligation to agree on any particular term, nor to start from any particular baseline. Typical statements include: "bargaining begins from scratch,"[130] "everything is up for grabs,"[131] "the company is legally entitled to bargain from ground zero,"[132] and "You bargain from minimum wage up."[133] For dramatic emphasis, the employer spokesperson might wave the Employee Handbook while explaining that many of the currently provided benefits may be lost through collective bargaining.[134] By looking at the statements, the context in which they were made, and whether the employer made any accompanying assurances that it would bargain in good faith, the Board has tried to tease out of these and similar cases whether the message conveyed is the factual one that in the process of collective bargaining one may lose, as well as gain, benefits, or the threat to act punitively, and, perhaps, to take away benefits unilaterally. Appellate courts have sometimes regarded skeptically these efforts at divining whether these and similar statements are threats or predictions.[135]

The Board has shown greater consistency in cases involving predictions of job losses or plant closings in the event that the union won. Employers understand that perhaps no threat is more troubling to employees in the course of a representation election, and cases involving predictions or threats of plant closings are common. Generally, statements to the effect that a union victory will make the company uncompetitive and force it to close,

---

128 107 NLRB 1238 (1954) (employer states disagreement with bargaining unit determination and describes the delay that will occur when he litigates it).

129 137 NLRB 1782 (1962).

130 Campbell Soup Co., 225 NLRB 222 (and countless others) (1976).

131 *Id.* at 225.

132 Histacount Corp., 278 NLRB 681 (1986).

133 Taylor-Dunn Mfg. Co., 252 NLRB 799 (1980).

134 Beverly Enterprises-Indiana, Inc., 281 NLRB 26 (1986). The Board was not especially receptive to this latter approach, at least in the context of various additional unfair labor practices.

135 *See, e.g.*, Shaw's Supermarkets, Inc. v. NLRB, 884 F.2d 34 (1st Cir. 1989), *enforcement denied*, 289 NLRB 844 (1988).

or to go elsewhere where labor costs are cheaper, and more dramatic presentations of the same idea will be viewed as coercive in violation of Section 8(a)(1), and as grounds to set aside an election.[136] Chief Justice Warren's statement that employer speech which conveyed "a management decision already arrived at to close the plant in case of unionization," is permissible has been given a narrow reading by the Seventh Circuit in *Wiljef Transportation Inc. v. NLRB.*[137] In that case, the employer read to its employees an old company by-law that said that it was corporate policy that "operations will cease and the corporation will be dissolved in the event of unionization of its employees."[138] The court enforced the Board's order finding that the company had violated Section 8(a)(1). It held that the same standard of objective evidence had to be met regarding any such by-law and resolution to establish that it was indeed a policy that the company would abide by and not a sham declaration intended to coerce the employees. Because in this case there was no proof offered beyond the old by-law that the company was prepared to commit corporate suicide, and no evidence of any plans having been drawn up for dissolution, the statement was coercive in violation of Section 8(a)(1).

[2] False Statements and Forgeries

This has been a rather volatile area in the Board's history, as it has vacillated between greater regulation of the content of campaign propaganda and a more laissez-faire approach to content, although not necessarily to the manner of presentation, with the expectation that employees will be sufficiently skeptical that they will be able to distinguish between truth and falsehood. Under its laboratory conditions standard for representation

---

[136] *Gissel* was such a case. There, the President of the company emphasized how an earlier strike had almost put the company out of business, how the union's only weapon was a strike to which the parent company may respond by closing the company, and how many other local companies had supposedly closed because of union demands. *Gissel,* 395 U.S. at 587-89. For other examples, see Reeves Bros., Inc., 320 NLRB 1082 (1996) (company violated Section 8(a)(1) where at captive-audience meetings, company read letters from two of its customers in which customers said they might reduce or eliminate their business if company went union, and presented them as saying they would pull their business resulting in reduced hours, and in other conversations, supervisors predicted job losses and plant closure); Be-Lo Stores, 318 NLRB 1 (1995) (coupled with many other violations, mock pink-slips sent to employees days before the election with the message that this is what the union has gotten for its members at other grocery stores violates Section 8(a)(1)), *aff'd in part and rev'd in part,* 126 F.3d 268 (4th Cir. 1997) (remarkably finding that pink-slip mailing was a permissible prediction and not a threat).

[137] 946 F.2d 1308 (7th Cir. 1991).

[138] *Id.* at 1310.

elections adopted in *General Shoe,* the Board began to look at election propaganda.[139] The Board's approach continued to evolve during the 1950s, and was eventually crystallized in its 1962 decision, *Hollywood Ceramics.*[140] There it said that misrepresentations made by the election winner, whether intentionally or inadvertently, would be grounds for setting aside the election if they involved a "substantial departure from the truth," were made too close to the election to allow for an effective reply, and they might "reasonably be expected to have a significant impact on the election."[141] The Board added that it would also consider whether the party making the statement was cloaked with expertise or knowledge about the subject of its statement, thereby giving employees reason to give added weight to its statement, and that it would not set aside an election if the employees "possessed independent knowledge with which to evaluate the statements."[142] This standard, which required determinations of the substantiality and materiality of the misrepresentation, as well as difficult questions of causation expressed in terms of whether a curative reply was possible, and whether it was likely that employees relied on the statement or knew enough to dismiss it, led, not surprisingly, to much litigation and inconsistent applications, as well as battles between the Board and the federal circuit courts.

After growing murmurs of dissatisfaction with the *Hollywood Ceramics* approach, the Board abandoned *Hollywood Ceramics* in *Shopping Kart Food Market, Inc.*[143] a decision of a fractured Board, that required a concurring opinion that appeared to be only partly committed to the majority's approach to form a majority of the entire Board. There the Board announced that it would no longer "probe into the truth or falsity of the parties' campaign statements," but would, instead, assume that employees would and could recognize campaign propaganda for what it was and discount claims accordingly.[144] It added that it would continue to overturn elections where the winning party had misleadingly misused or altered Board documents or had used forged documents, which by their nature conceal the fact that they are false.[145] In repudiating the *Hollywood*

139 *See, e.g.,* Gummed Products Co., 112 NLRB 1092 (1955) (repeated union misstatements of wage rates it negotiated elsewhere); United Aircraft Corp., 103 NLRB 102 (1953) (union sends employees forged letter purportedly from President of rival union).

140 140 NLRB 221 (1962).

141 *Id.* at 224.

142 *Id.* at 224 & n.10.

143 228 NLRB 1311 (1977).

144 *Id.* at 1311 & 1313.

145 *Id.* at 1313.

Ceramics rule, the majority argued that it was difficult to administer, led to unpredictable results because of its dependence on subjective judgments about such issues as materiality and substantiality of the misrepresentations, cluttered the Board's docket and involved it in continuing disputes with the courts, and undermined the finality of election results. Noting that these drawbacks might be worth incurring if the rule was an appropriate solution to a major problem, the majority pointed to a contemporary empirical study of representation elections by Professors Getman, Goldberg, and Herman.[146] Their controversial study of 31 elections concluded that many of the Board's campaign rules were based on unexamined and incorrect assumptions, that both lawful and unlawful campaigning bore little on how employees voted, that employee pre-campaign attitudes were the biggest determinant of how they would vote, and that campaign propaganda apparently had little impact on the election since voters had difficulty remembering it after the election.[147] On the basis of their data, the authors proposed that the Board "cease regulating speech and, for election purposes, nearly all conduct,"[148] and that it should stop setting aside elections because of campaign misrepresentations, threats, promises, or discriminatory discharges, while vigorously remedying the latter.[149]

---

[146] Julius G. Getman et al., Union Representation Elections: Law And Reality (1976).

[147] The study has spurred considerable criticism. *See* Richard B. Freeman & James L. Medoff, What Do Unions Do? 233-39 (1984); William T. Dickens, *The Effect of Company Campaigns on Certification Elections: Law and Reality Once Again,* 36 Indus. & Lab. Rel. Rev. 560 (1983); Patricia Eames, *An Analysis of the Union Voting Study From a Trade-Unionist's Point of View,* 28 Stan. L. Rev. 1181 (1976); Robert J. Flanagan, *The Behavioral Foundations of Union Election Regulation,* 28 Stan. L. Rev. 1195 (1976); Thomas A. Kochan, *Legal Nonsense, Empirical Examination and Policy Evaluation,* 29 Stan. L. Rev. 1115 (1976) (book review); James E. Martin, *Employee Characteristics and Representation Election Outcomes,* 38 Indus. & Lab. Rel. Rev. 365 (1985); Thomas F. Phalen, Jr., *The Demise of* Hollywood Ceramics*: Facts and Fantasy,* 46 U. Cin. L. Rev. 450 (1977); Paul Weiler, *Promises to Keep: Securing Workers' Right to Self-Organization Under the NLRA,* 96 Harv. L. Rev. 1769, 1784-85 (1983); Raymond Goetz & Edward L. Wike, *Book Review,* 25 Kan. L. Rev. 375 (1977); Cornelius Peck, *Book Review,* 53 Wash. L. Rev. 197 (1977). Getman, Goldberg, and Herman have defended their study in Stephen B. Goldberg et al., *Union Representation Elections: Law and Reality: The Authors Respond to the Critics,* 79 Mich. L. Rev. 564 (1981); Stephen B. Goldberg, et al., *The Relationship Between Free Choice and Labor Board Doctrine: Differing Empirical Approaches,* 79 Nw. U. L. Rev. 721 (1984). A study by Professor Laura Cooper supports some of the Getman, Goldberg, Herman conclusions. *See* Laura Cooper, *Authorization Cards and Union Representation Election Outcome: An Empirical Assessment of the Assumption Underlying the Supreme Court's* Gissel *Decision,* 79 Nw. U. L. Rev. 87 (1974).

[148] Getman et al., *supra* note 112, at 159.

[149] *Id.* at 146-63.

In less than two years, the Board's majority had shifted once again, and in *General Knit of California, Inc.*,[150] it reversed course, overruling *Shopping Kart,* and reinstating the *Hollywood Ceramics* standard. Four years later, a once-again divided Board redeemed *Shopping Kart,* overruling *General Knit* in *Midland National Life Insurance Co.*[151] In *Midland,* the Board again announced that it would not probe campaign propaganda in search of important misrepresentations. Rather, it would rely on the free flow of ideas and the intelligence of the voters to cure any misrepresentations and half-truths. As in *Shopping Kart,* the Board said that it would continue to set aside elections where the winning party had engaged in forgery to disguise propaganda and falsehoods.

While *Midland* has ushered in a period of relative stability, and most federal circuit courts appear to have accepted the Board's approach, the First[152] and Sixth[153] Circuits have expressed unwillingness to follow *Midland* in egregious cases, or where "the misrepresentation is so pervasive and the deception so artful that employees will be unable to separate truth from untruth and where their right to a free and fair choice will be affected."[154]

Doubts and a call for modification of the rule have also come from within the Board. In *AWB Metal*,[155] Member Raudabaugh failed to convince his fellow Board members to adopt an exception to *Midland* for misrepresentations that occur within 24 hours of the election.

[3] Appeals to Racist Sentiments and Bigotry

A variety of doctrines reveal a high tolerance for free-wheeling, hyperbolic, reckless, and, at times, downright obnoxious talk in the midst of labor disputes, union meetings, and union election campaigns.[156] The Board has

150 239 NLRB 619 (1978).

151 263 NLRB 127 (1982).

152 NLRB v. New Columbus Nursing Home, Inc., 720 F.2d 726, 730 (1st Cir. 1983) (dictum).

153 Van Dorn Plastic Machinery Co. v. NLRB, 736 F.2d 343 (1984).

154 *Id.* at 348. While the statement in *Van Dorn* was dictum, the Sixth Circuit has subsequently followed its rule and in cases where it judged the misrepresentation to be especially pervasive and artful, it has rejected application of *Midland* and remanded the case to the Board. *See, e.g.,* NLRB v. Hub Plastics, Inc., 52 F.3d 608 (6th Cir. 1995); Dayton Hudson Dept. Store Co. v. NLRB, 987 F.2d 359 (6th Cir. 1993).

155 306 NLRB 109 (1992), *affirmed,* 4 F.3d 993 (6th Cir. 1993) (mem.).

156 Examples include: the assumption that campaign falsehoods are taken for what they

generally been similarly reluctant to set aside an election on the basis of occasional instances of bigoted statements or arguments that play on prejudice. In 1962, however, during the height of the civil rights struggle, the Board set limits on the use of racist appeals as election propaganda in *Sewell Manufacturing Co.*,[157] where it set aside an election in rural Georgia that had been deeply infected by the employer's willingness to play off of the community's hostility toward African Americans and the civil rights movement and its fears of what was then called "race mixing." While the Board said that the union's position on civil rights issues was legitimately a subject for discussion in the campaign, any discussion of such issues must be "temperate in tone, germane, and correct factually." When, however, propaganda "exacerbate[s] racial feelings by irrelevant, inflammatory appeals," the laboratory conditions may have been upset.[158] The Board continues to apply *Sewell* to bigoted campaign rhetoric, and will set aside an election in an occasional case where it characterizes the appeal as inflammatory.[159]

[F]—Other Interference With the Right to Self-Organization

[1] Polling, Interrogation, and Surveillance

An employer might wish to poll her employees for a variety of reasons ranging from the benign to the malign. Presented with a demand for recognition, an employer might be willing to grant recognition if assured that the union really has majority support. But the employer should be aware that should she grant recognition out of a mistaken belief that the majority of her employees wish to be represented by the union, she is guilty of

---

are worth in Midland National Life Insurance Co., 263 NLRB 127 (1982), discussed above in § 4.3[D][2]; the high threshold for defamation in state actions arising out of union elections or other labor disputes established in Linn v. Plant Guard Workers, 383 U.S. 53 (1966), discussed in *infra* § 14.2[C]; and the shield provided by Title I of the LMRDA against union discipline for insulting and reckless speech regarding internal union matters articulated in Salzhandler v. Caputo, 316 F.2d 445 (2d Cir.), *cert. denied,* 375 U.S. 946 (1963). This is not universally true of labor law. For one important counterexample, see the discussion of loss of protection for disparaging the employer or her product at *infra* § 16.4.

[157] 138 NLRB 66 (1962).

[158] *Id.* at 71 & 72.

[159] *See, e.g.,* Zartic, Inc., 315 NLRB 495 (1994) (union effort to tar management as racist to inflame Hispanic employees); YKK(U.S.A.), 269 NLRB 82 (1984) (union appeal to anti-Japanese sentiment in campaign in Japanese-owned company); *see generally,* Daniel H. Pollitt, *The National Labor Relations Board and Race Hate Propaganda in Union Organization Drives,* 17 Stan. L. Rev. 373 (1965).

violating Section 8(a)(2) which, among other things, prohibits support or assistance to a union by imposing a minority union on employees.[160] On the other hand, an employer might engage in polling, including polling by such methods as handing out "Union No" buttons or T-shirts for its employees to wear, for the purpose of identifying union supporters and intimidating its workforce, or to try to preempt a scheduled representation election.

For a long time the Board's approach to employer polling was unsettled, sometimes to the annoyance of the federal circuit courts.[161] After a remand from the D.C. Circuit in the *Struksnes Construction Co.* case,[162] the Board announced the following prerequisites for acceptable polling absent "unusual circumstances":

> (1) the purpose of the poll is to determine the truth of a union's claim of majority, (2) this purpose is communicated to the employees, (3) assurances against reprisal are given, (4) the employees are polled by secret ballot, and (5) the employer has not engaged in unfair labor practices or otherwise created a coercive atmosphere.[163]

The Board continues to adhere to these criteria in determining whether or not an employer has polled in violation of Section 8(a)(1). In contrast, pre-election polling done by the union is not generally considered grounds for setting aside an election or a violation of Section 8(b)(1)(A) because the relationship between the employees and their employer is different from their relationship to the union.[164]

Polling is characterized by a systematic attempt to gauge the sentiments of all of the bargaining unit employees. Interrogation refers to investigation of an individual employee's or a small group of employees' attitudes toward

---

160 29 U.S.C. § 158(a)(2) (1994). In ILGWU (Bernhard-Altmann Corp.) v. NLRB, 366 U.S. 731 (1961), the Supreme Court determined that Section 8(a)(2) is a strict liability offense; that is, even if an employer recognizes a union in the good-faith mistaken belief that it has majority support, it has violated the Act. For a discussion of voluntary recognition and Section 8(a)(2)'s prohibitions of interference and assistance, see *infra* § 5.4.

161 *See, e.g.*, International Union of Operating Engineers, Local 49 v. NLRB (Struksnes Construction Co.), 353 F.2d 852 (D.C. Cir. 1965), *on remand*, 165 NLRB 1062 (1967); NLRB v. Lorben Corp., 345 F.2d 346 (2d Cir. 1965).

162 *See supra* note 161.

163 165 NLRB 1062, 1063.

164 NLRB v. Springfield Discount, Inc., 82 L.R.R.M. 2173 (7th Cir. 1972). Union interrogation coupled with an explicit or implied threat to punish its enemies, would, of course, constitute unlawful coercion.

the union. Again, both benign and malign motives may be at work, from the casual, passing-the-time conversation between a lower level supervisor and an employee friend or neighbor to a highly coercive grilling in a supervisor's office. The latter communicates with little ambiguity how strongly the employer opposes the union and may signal the lengths to which the employer may go to resist the union. Moreover, whether or not the employer so intends this message, employees understand that the first step toward firing strong union supporters is identifying them. The Board has vacillated between a rule that interrogation is inherently coercive absent special circumstances[165] and a totality of the circumstances approach.[166] In embracing a totality of the circumstances approach in *Rossmore House,* a majority of the Board noted that factors to be considered included "(1) the background; (2) the nature of the information sought; (3) the identity of the questioner; and (4) the place and method of interrogation," although it seemed to focus narrowly on the circumstances of an employer putting questions to an avowed union supporter uncoupled with threats or promises.[167]

Not long after *Rossmore House,* the Board again found interrogation noncoercive under circumstances quite different from those of *Rossmore.* In *Sunnyvale Medical Center,*[168] the Board found interrogation of an employee who had not self-identified as a strong union supporter that took place in a supervisor's office, in the context of a decertification election, and in which the supervisor stated the employer's strong desire to get rid of the union was not coercive. Here the Board relied heavily on the friendship between the employee and the supervisor and the employee's characterization of their conversation as friendly. *Sunnyvale* suggested that the Board might permit most interrogations, but subsequent decisions have been more balanced.

---

165 *See* PPG Industries, 251 NLRB 1146 (1980); Paceco, 237 NLRB 399 (1978), *vacated in part and remanded in part,* 601 F.2d 180 (5th Cir. 1979).

166 *See* Rossmore House, 269 NLRB 1176 (1984), *enforced,* 760 F.2d 1006 (9th Cir. 1985); Blue Flash Express, 109 NLRB 591 (1954).

167 *Id.* at 1178 n.20. In *Rossmore House*, the interrogatee had sent a mailgram to his employer stating that he and another employee were forming a union organizing committee and were aware of the protection offered them by the Act. There was conflicting testimony about what was said and the employee's version could be read to include an implied threat. Interrogation of a self-identified union supporter can be understood in more than one way. The Board concluded that it was unlikely to be coercive, because the employee had already announced his disposition. Yet, questioning someone whose position on the union the employer already knows may signal to the employee and her compatriots the strength of the employer's anti-union feeling and willingness to engage in reprisals.

168 277 NLRB No. 131 (1985).

Surveillance of employee activity is invariably held to violate Section 8(a)(1). This is true even when the employees remain unaware that they are being watched or monitored.[169] It is also a violation to create the impression of surveillance because of the chilling effect on protected activities that such an impression will have.[170]

[2] Promises and Inducements

In addition to "threats of reprisal or force," Section 8(c) excludes from its protection any "promise of benefit." In the course of an election campaign, an employer may not promise or confer a benefit conditioned on the employees rejecting a union. It also may not eliminate benefits in retribution for the election campaign, nor, at least under certain circumstances, confer a benefit unconditionally or solicit employee grievances if, by implication, it appears to promise a benefit.

Some of this is self-explanatory. If in response to an organizing campaign the employer decides to punish her workforce by eliminating various benefits, the employer is both interfering with the employees' exercise of their Section 7 rights in violation of Section 8(a)(1), and discriminating regarding certain terms of employment to discourage union membership in violation of Section 8(a)(3). The purpose of such punishment is obviously to deter continued union activity and is clearly coercive. A conditional promise also contains an inherent measure of coercion. To say to a neighbor, "I will let you borrow my riding-mower if you let me borrow your leaf blower" contains the implicit negative: "and if you do not lend it to me, don't count on ever borrowing my mower." But whereas your neighbor may be able to borrow an equally good mower from some other neighbor, the employer who conditions a benefit on the employees' rejection of a union is the exclusive source of their benefits. When she says, "do what I say, and you'll get something good (say, greater flexibility in scheduling vacation time)," they cannot help but hear, "unless you obey me, I'll withhold the vacation flexibility that you want."

NLRB v. Exchange Parts, Inc.,[171] deals with a different scenario: an unconditional conferral of benefits by the employer during the representation campaign. *Exchange Parts* is a perplexing case, less because of the rule it announced, which can, perhaps, be justified, than for the explanation

---

169 *See, e.g.*, NLRB v. J.P. Stevens & Co., 563 F.2d 8 (2d Cir. 1977), *cert. denied*, 434 U.S. 1064 (1978).

170 *See, e.g.*, P.E. Guerin, Inc., 309 NLRB 666 (1992).

171 375 U.S. 405 (1964).

that Justice Harlan offered for the rule. In *Exchange Parts,* there was little doubt that the employer's purpose in granting certain benefits during the election campaign was to avoid a union victory. When it announced these benefits the company took pains to relate them to the election campaign and to remind its employees that it, not the union, was their source.

The Board ruled that the company had violated Section 8(a)(1), but the Fifth Circuit disagreed and denied enforcement. The Supreme Court reversed. Comparing benefits granted by an employer during a campaign, seemingly with no strings attached, to a "fist inside the velvet glove," Justice Harlan argued that: "Employees are not likely to miss the inference that the source of benefits now conferred is also the source from which future benefits must flow and which may dry up if it is not obliged."[172] In other words, the grant of benefits serves as a reminder of who has managerial prerogative and who controls the assets of the firm and, therefore, as a reminder that she who giveth might taketh away if the employees displease her.

Doubtless, this is true, but, given any number of other reminders of who controls the assets of the firm and makes managerial decisions, is this really coercive?[173] Rather, it seems that Judge Wisdom, writing for the Fifth Circuit had the better of the argument when he wrote:

> It is impressive logomachy to turn "allurements" into "coercion" by divining a secret purpose. It is good, homey, country-lawyer advocacy to argue that a carrot on a stick may have the same effect on a donkey as a club. But a carrot is not a club. Labor is not a donkey. Persuasion is not coercion.[174]

---

172 *Id.* at 409.

173 Within the campaign context, for instance, the employer is allowed to compel its employees to listen to its anti-union campaigning in the workplace at captive audience speeches, certainly an effective reminder of the employer's authority within the firm; where it is permitted to remind them that it will bargain from scratch and is not compelled to give on any particular term. Given a choice, I suspect that most people would rather be "coerced" through unconditioned benefits.

174 NLRB v. Exchange Parts Co., 304 F.2d 368, 376 (5th Cir. 1962). For additional skepticism regarding the Board's and Justice Harlan's analysis, see Gorman, Basic Text on Labor Law, *supra* note 8, at 164-65; Derek C. Bok, *The Regulation of Campaign Tactics in Representation Elections Under the National Labor Relations Act,* 78 Harv. L. Rev. 38, 112-4 (1964); Charles C. Jackson & Jeffrey S. Heller, *Promises and Grants of Benefits Under the National Labor Relations Act,* 131 U. Pa. L. Rev. 1 (1982).

Perhaps, the case is better understood as expressing our distaste for bribes, for what Exchange Parts did seems closer to a bribe than a threat. And even if we do not think of bribes as being coercive, a bribe might be sufficient grounds to say that the laboratory conditions have been contaminated and a rerun election is necessary. Yet we ought to be clear on why we disapprove of bribes and what sort we will not allow. An especially pernicious sort of bribe would be one that is given discriminatorily to divide the employees. That would directly challenge the notion of collective action and collective strength that underlies the Act. *Exchange Parts* did not involve discrimination of this sort, however. The company made its benefits available universally. Perhaps we think that allowing an employer to grant wage increases and other benefits in the midst of an election campaign will muddle the thinking of the employees. Temporarily gratified by the wage or benefit increase, the employees will see little need for a union. This gives an unfair advantage to the employer in the campaign not only because the union has no ability to match the employer's "generosity," but because the employer can distort the union's reaction to the wage increase by depicting the union as the obstacle standing between the employees and the increase.[175] Indeed, there is some empirical support for this notion. One study of 261 certification elections in 1986-87 found that in 30% of the elections employers granted wage increases and in 56% of the elections they promised to do so, or to otherwise improve working conditions.[176] Obviously, the employers in question thought that these promises and benefits could influence the outcome of union elections, and the study's author concludes that "we can predict that the probability of the union winning the election would decline by 9 percent in units in which the company gave wage increases and by 13 percent in units in which the company made promises during the election campaign."[177]

Yet, it is hard to reconcile the Court's position on promises and the Board's less paternalistic approach in *Midland Insurance*. Clearly, there are consequences for the employer who, as Justice Harlan suggests she might, grants a pay increase before the election only to rescind it after the union

---

[175] In NLRB v. Gotham Indus. Inc., 406 F.2d 1306 (1st Cir. 1969) (denying enforcement of the Board's order on other grounds), the employer announced a wage increase before a representation election and soon thereafter told its employees that it could not implement it because of the union.

[176] Kate L. Bronfenbrenner, *Employer Behavior in Certification Elections and First-Contract Campaigns: Implications for Labor Law Reform, in* Restoring the Promise of American Labor Law 75, 82 (Sheldon Friedman et al. eds., 1994).

[177] *Id.*

has been defeated. Moreover, some anecdotal evidence suggests that the employer is not the only party capable of manipulative behavior in these cases.[178] Perhaps, ultimately, what is at stake is our notion of elections and our sense that free, untainted elections, whether they be for Cook County alderman, or selection of an exclusive bargaining representative, is what defines us as a society. *Exchange Parts* might best be explained as reflecting an intuition that the public interest in an untainted election process outweighs the interests of the employer and employees, for whom offering and accepting a bribe might be a rational decision. There are some bargains that we will not allow.[179]

Justice Harlan does one other curious thing in *Exchange Parts.* He writes that the employer has violated Section 8(a)(1) if she had an anti-union motive for extending the benefit. As Professor Gorman notes, this is inconsistent with the general approach to Section 8(a)(1), where an anti-union motive is not a prerequisite for liability.[180] While the Board nominally adheres to this prerequisite, it will presume an anti-union motive from the timing and size of the benefit and place the burden on the employer to rebut this presumption with a legitimate reason for the timing of the benefit.[181] Moreover, while *Exchange Parts* teaches that motive plays a role in determining unfair labor practice liability, there seems to be no reason why it should matter for purposes of finding that the laboratory conditions have been destroyed and setting aside an election.

Theorizing aside, there is a body of law relating to promises, inducements, and the withholding of benefits that the Board and the courts have developed in light of *Exchange Parts.* First, employer generosity that is motivated by a general, but abstract, desire to make her company unorganizable, and not in response to an ongoing organization campaign, does not violate the Act. In *NLRB v. Gotham Industries, Inc.*, the First Circuit wrote:

> Passing the exceptional employer who may raise wages out of fraternal generosity, we suppose that most nonunion employers give raises for one or both of two reasons: to keep employees, old and new, in the plant, and to keep unions out. As to the latter it cannot be that every time it can be shown that an employer was seeking to stay one step ahead of unionization he was guilty of an unfair labor practice; the situation must

[178] *See,* Bok, *The Regulation of Campaign Tactics, supra* note 174, at 114-16.

[179] Recall the *Magnavox* decision discussed at *supra* § 4.3[C][1].

[180] Gorman, Basic Text on Labor Law, *supra* note 8, at 165.

[181] *See, e.g.,* Speco Corp., 298 NLRB 439 (1990).

> have sufficiently crystallized so that some specific orientation exists. It would be a sorry consequence if the Labor Relations Act were to be construed as causing every nonunionized employer to think twice before initiating a wage increase lest some union should appear and claim that it had been frustrated.[182]

Because an employer cannot give new benefits to its employees during the representation campaign, it follows that the employer cannot promise to confer benefits either. Indeed, the employer may even get into trouble if during the campaign it solicits employee complaints, if in doing so the employer impliedly promises future benefits or other corrective measures.[183] This rule follows from *Exchange Parts,* because it eliminates the possibility that the employer will do on the cheap what *Exchange Parts* prohibits. But it also can be a trap for the employer who genuinely wishes to know more about the employees' grievances.

Can an employer who routinely gives a cost-of-living payraise every year-and-a-half, or who gives merit pay increases every Fall, continue to do so on the eve of an election? Such an employer faces a dilemma. If she gives the traditional increases, the Board may perceive her act as an inducement, and if she withholds them until after the election, it may conclude that she has acted coercively. The Board's approach to this issue is to require the employer to behave in the same way that it would have had there been no union and representation election in the picture. Thus, if either economic circumstance or past practice dictates a grant of benefits, the employer who fails to grant the benefits does so at the risk of Section 8(a)(1) liability.[184]

Section 8(b)(1)(A), which was added to the Act in the Taft-Hartley amendments, says in part that it is an unfair labor practice for a labor organization to restrain or coerce "employees in the exercise of the rights guaranteed in section 7 . . . ." Of course, these Section 7 rights include the right not to self-organize and the right to prefer a rival union. Under Section 8(b)(1)(A), union threats and violence are clearly prohibited. The issue of union promises is more tricky. *Exchange Parts* limits employer behavior during a representation campaign, but it has not had nearly as restrictive an impact on union conduct. For one thing, much of what a union

---

182 406 F.2d 1306, 1310 (1st Cir. 1969).

183 Montgomery Ward & Co., 225 NLRB 112 (1976); Hadbar, Div. of Pur O Sil, Inc., 211 NLRB 333 (1974).

184 *See, e.g.,* Great Atlantic & Pacific Tea Co., 166 NLRB 27, 29 (1967); McCormick Longmeadow Stone Co., 158 NLRB 1237 (1966).

has to offer in the campaign is its promise that it will obtain better wages and working conditions for the employees. To deny the union the ability to make such "promises" would essentially gag it and disable it from trying to persuade the employees of the benefits of union representation. Further, there is an essential difference between the employer's promise and the union's promise, and employees understand that the two are not equivalent. The employer, of course, has the power to implement its promises, while the union is really saying nothing more than that it will use its best efforts to obtain these benefits for the employee, and this is how it has done elsewhere, or how unions have done in this industry. In those instances where the union does have the power to carry out its promises, they bear similar treatment as an employer's promises or inducements. Thus, in *NLRB v. Savair*,[185] the Supreme Court held that the Board should have set aside an election in which the union promised to waive the initiation fee only of employees who signed "recognition slips" before the election. The Court did not, however, decide whether the union's conduct constituted a violation of Section 8(b)(1)(A).[186] A promise to waive dues nondiscriminately, however, is permissible.

§ 4.4 Retaliation in Response to Organization and the Exercise of Section 7 Rights

[A]—Protection Under Section 8(a)(3) Against Discrimination

The most frequently filed unfair labor practice charges are those for discrimination in employment in violation of Section 8(a)(3). Section 8(a)(3) prohibits "discrimination in regard to hire or tenure of employment or any term or condition of employment to encourage or discourage membership in any labor organization . . . ."[187] This section has long been understood to encompass acts of discrimination directed not merely toward "membership" in a union per se, but also toward participation in union activities.[188] The prototypical case is a decision to fire an employee because of her union activism, or because of her perceived pro-union sympathies.[189] But Section

---

185 414 U.S. 270 (1973).

186 The recognition slips were not legally binding, but the Court was concerned about the psychological impact of an equivalent of a preelection poll that had been influenced by the union's inducement and the moral constraint that some employees might feel having signed the recognition slips.

187 29 U.S.C. 158(a)(3) (1994).

188 *See* Radio Officers' Union v. NLRB, 347 U.S. 17, 39-40 (1954).

189 *See, e.g.*, Edward G. Budd Mfg. Co. v. NLRB, 138 F.2d 86 (3d Cir. 1943).

8(a)(3) protects against other forms of discrimination based on union activity also, including unequal meting out of benefits or discipline, discrimination regarding the terms of employment, or favoring one group of employees over another because of union activity on reinstatement of economic strikers or recall from layoffs.[190]

Early on, the Supreme Court determined that Section 8(a)(3) protects job applicants, as well as those who are already employed.[191] More recently it decided that this is also true in the case of job applicants who are also paid union organizers intent on organizing the employer.[192]

Proof of a violation of Section 8(a)(3) requires proof of discrimination and of an anti-union motive for the discrimination. Consequently, as Professor Cynthia Estlund notes: "The paradigmatic Section 8(a)(3) case—the discharge of a union activist—is almost invariably litigated as a simple factual dispute: was the discharge motivated by the employee's union activity or by the entirely different legitimate reason proffered by the employer, such as tardiness or poor production?"[193] While the language of the section speaks in terms of "discrimination . . . to encourage or discourage membership . . ." it is sufficient to show that encouragement or discouragement could be a natural and foreseeable consequence of the discrimination, rather than to show actual effects.

---

190 *See, e.g.*, Metropolitan Edison Co. v. NLRB, 460 U.S. 693 (1983) (more severe discipline meted out to union officials); NLRB v. Erie Resistor Corp., 373 U.S. 221 (1963) (grant of 20 years' superseniority to permanent replacement workers and crossovers); NLRB v. Mackay Radio & Tel. Co., 304 U.S. 333 (1938) (discrimination based on union activism in calling back to work economic strikers); NLRB v. Jakel Motors, Inc., 875 F.2d 644 (1989) (in addition to discharges, retaliatory transfers, less desirable work assignments, and unfavorable employment references).

191 Phelps Dodge Corp. v. NLRB, 313 U.S. 177 (1941). The Board has distinguished this protection, which is necessary to prevent blacklisting and make the protection of Section 8(a)(3) meaningful, from its analysis of who is an employee for purposes of Section 8(a)(5)'s duty to bargain and protection against some nonconsensual midterm modifications of the collective bargaining agreement. *Compare* Johnson-Bateman Co., 295 NLRB 180 (1989) (employer cannot unilaterally impose mandatory drug and alcohol testing of employees during term of collective bargaining agreement) *with* Star Tribune v. Newspaper Guild, 295 NLRB 543 (1989) (drug and alcohol tests for job applicants not a mandatory subject of bargaining, and can therefore be unilaterally imposed by the employer). These issues are discussed further at *infra* § 7.5[C].

192 NLRB v. Town & Country Electric, Inc., 516 U.S. 85 (1995).

193 Cynthia L. Estlund, *Economic Rationality and Union Avoidance: Misunderstanding the National Labor Relations Act*, 71 Tex. L. Rev. 921, 935-36 (1993).

As the above suggests, sometimes the employer's proffered reason for discharge or discipline is pretextual, and sometimes the employee's claim of discrimination is a rationalization to cover for poor work performance. We expect the administrative law judge who hears the unfair labor practice case to hear testimony, consider exhibits, make credibility determinations and sort it all out. Sometimes, however, the employer has more than ample reason, both lawful and unlawful, to discharge an employee; she may be both a union activist and a habitual violator of the bus company's rules against unauthorized breaks and against leaving one's keys in an unattended bus.[194] In these mixed-motive cases is the employer's anti-union animus enough to justify finding a Section 8(a)(3) violation? In its *Wright Line*[195] decision, the Board established its method for dealing with mixed-motive cases. Under the Board's rule, the General Counsel has the burden of showing that anti-union animus was a substantial or motivating factor in the discharge decision. At that point, if the employer cannot rebut the General Counsel's evidence, it has available an affirmative defense that it would have fired the employee anyway for permissible reasons relating to her unprotected conduct. Because this is an affirmative defense, the employer bears the burden of proof. In *NLRB v. Transportation Management Corp.*,[196] the Supreme Court held that the *Wright Line* approach was a permissible allocation of the burden of proof under the Act.

[B]—Going Out of Business, Partial Shutdowns, and Runaway Shops

Retaliation for union membership or activity or discrimination to discourage the same can take a collective form, as well as the individual form of discriminatory discharge or discipline of a particularly vocal union supporter. Probably the most potent threat in the arsenal of an employer who is inclined to threaten to stave off a union is the threat to close down or relocate. Capital restructuring decisions, such as the decision to close part of an operation, to subcontract out a department's work, to move one's business to a less unionized state, or abroad, or the decision to cease operations entirely, all can be motivated by the desire to punish or chill union activity. Of course, purer, and lawful, motives can underlie each of these decisions as well. And each implicates what outside the context of

---

194 *Cf.* NLRB v. Transportation Management Corp., 462 U.S. 393 (1983). The *Edward G. Budd Mfg.* case cited above, *supra* note 189, is a classic example of the employee who supplied ample reason for discharge; however, there it was clear that the employer was solely motivated by the employee Weigand's recent enlistment with the union.

195 251 NLRB 1083 (1980), *enforced* 662 F.2d 899 (1st Cir. 1981), *cert. denied*, 455 U.S. 989 (1982).

196 462 U.S. 393 (1983).

union activity or other protected activity, the courts tend to regard as matters at the core of managerial prerogative.

The Supreme Court dealt with a subset of these issues in *Textile Workers Union v. Darlington Manufacturing Co.*,[197] one of the Court's most troubling labor law decisions. *Darlington* at its core dealt with the question of when can an employer close shop in retaliation for the employees' decision to be represented by a union. Darlington was a textile company that operated one mill. Darlington was owned in turn by Deering Milliken, a textile manufacturer and marketer, which was controlled by Darlington's President, Roger Milliken, and his family. When a union organizing drive began at Darlington in 1956, the company vigorously resisted and threatened to close should the union win. Shortly after the Textile Workers Union won the election, Milliken called a meeting of Darlington's Board of Directors and they voted to close the mill. The union filed unfair labor practice charges alleging violations of Sections 8(a)(1) and (3), along with a violation of Section 8(a)(5)'s duty to bargain. A divided Board ruled that Darlington had violated Sections 8(a)(1) and (3), and that because Darlington was part of an integrated employer group controlled by the Millikens, Deering Milliken could therefore be held liable for the unfair labor practices. It ordered a back pay remedy. The Fourth Circuit denied enforcement, reasoning that irrespective of anti-union motive, a company had an unqualified right to close all or part of its business. The case came to the Supreme Court on certiorari.

Writing for the Court, Justice Harlan first made short shrift of the Section 8(a)(1) charge. Section 8(a)(1), he noted, does not require a showing of union animus. It does, however, require drawing a balance between the employer's business justification for its action and the affected Section 7 rights of the employees. Here, he saw only one way to draw the balance, writing that the decision to close one's business is "so peculiarly [a] matter[] of management prerogative," that it could never constitute a violation of Section 8(a)(1), unless it did so derivatively from a finding that Section 8(a)(3) was violated.[198]

---

197 380 U.S. 263 (1965).

198 *Id.* at 269. Because Section 8(a)(1) is the general statement of Section 8(a)'s protection of Section 7 rights under which the other four subsections are subsumed, a violation of any of the four also is derivatively a violation of Section 8(a)(1) because it interferes with the exercise of Section 7 rights. Additionally, however, Section 8(a)(1) captures various behavior that is not governed by any of the other subsections. Here, however, Justice Harlan argued that any vitality that the section has is derivative of Section 8(a)(3).

Turning to Section 8(a)(3), Justice Harlan rejected the union's argument that an employer cannot close completely if motivated by anti-union animus. He wrote that nowhere does the Act suggest that an employer who wants to go out of business can be restrained from doing so. So what is the measure of whether or not there is a violation? It is not whether the employer punished the employees for their union activity and acted to avoid operating with a union. Justice Harlan argued that the conduct must be motivated by a desire for future economic benefit. Since there can be no future economic benefit in a complete closing, it can never be a violation of the Act. Justice Harlan wrote: "A proposition that a single businessman cannot choose to go out of business if he wants to would represent such a startling innovation that it should not be entertained without the clearest manifestation of legislative intent or unequivocal judicial precedent. . . . We find neither."[199]

As to partial closings, Justice Harlan wrote: "a partial closing is an unfair labor practice under Section 8(a)(3) if motivated by a purpose to chill unionism in any of the remaining plants of the single employer and if the employer may reasonably have foreseen that such closing would likely have that effect."[200] The Court vacated the Fourth Circuit's Judgment and remanded so that the Board could make its findings guided by the Court's rule.

Justice Harlan's analysis seems compelling until one recognizes that he has misstated the question and has taken a leap in his analysis of the statutory language for which he cites no authority—because there is none to cite. Indeed, the decision has been much criticized.[201] Professor James Atleson has described its analysis as "bizarre,"[202] and Professor Clyde Summers has described the decision as "startling," "puzzling," and "inherently incredible."[203]

---

199 *Id.* at 270.

200 *Id.* at 275.

201 James B. Atleson, Values and Assumptions in American Labor Law 136-42 (1983); Estlund, *Economic Rationality*, *supra* note 193, at 936-38; Thomas G.S. Christensen & Andrea H. Svanoe, *Motive and Intent in the Commission of Unfair Labor Practices: The Supreme Court and the Fictive Formality,* 77 Yale L.J., 1269, 1323-24 (1968); Julius G. Getman, *Section 8(a)(3) of the NLRA and the Effort to Insulate Free Employee Choice,* 32 U. Chi. L. Rev. 735, 752-56 (1965); Clyde W. Summers, *Labor Law in the Supreme Court: 1964 Term,* 75 Yale L.J. 59, 64-67 (1965).

202 Atleson, Values and Assumptions, *supra* note 201, at 138.

203 Summers, *supra* note 201, at 64-67.

Justice Harlan asks the wrong question, it is not whether the employer has a right to close down her plant, but whether her employees are entitled to a damages remedy if she closes for retaliatory purposes. The Board had not ordered Darlington to reopen, but had ordered it to compensate its employees who had been subject to a mass retaliatory firing. Moreover, Justice Harlan's future benefit standard comes out of thin air. He cites no authority for his test; there is none to cite. And this test is applied nowhere else in analyzing Section 8(a) violations. As Clyde Summers points out, this test ignores the people who were harmed because of their exercise of Section 7 rights, and looks instead to see if other employees might be affected. The *Darlington* test shifts the focus from protecting employees in the exercise of their Section 7 rights to an inquiry into whether the employer stands to be unjustly enriched by the shutdown, a remarkable stretch of the statutory language and purpose.

Given the costs of committing corporate suicide, complete closings in response to union election victories do not happen often. Partial closings do happen, however, and as to them *Darlington* remains good law. Runaway shops, relocations to cheaper labor and less union-friendly states also are common, but the Board analyzes them under the traditional Section 8(a)(3) approach. The outcome will turn on whether the employer has articulated a business purpose for her conduct—whether the employer states an economic necessity as a reason for moving. The trouble with this approach, of course, is that a runaway employer's beliefs about unions and about business necessity are inextricably bound, and the rule rewards those who are crafty enough or lucky enough to emphasize the business costs part of the equation.

[C]—A Brief Note on Intent

The question of the intent necessary to support a Section 8(a)(1) and a Section 8(a)(3) violation can be vexing. For the most part we have seen that Section 8(a)(1) is a strict liability offense. In *Republic Aviation*, the rule was simply if the conduct interferes with, restrains, or coerces employees in the exercise of their Section 7 rights it violates the section, so long as employee interests outweigh employer interests. While Section 8(a)(1) did require a balancing of the employer's and the employees' interests, no showing of anti-union animus was necessary. This seems consistent with the statute which does not use language suggesting intent is an element. To be sure, we noted that a discriminatory application of an otherwise valid no-solicitation rule would be grounds for finding that its enforcement violated Section 8(a)(1), but in that case it is not clear whether the critical factor is that discriminatory enforcement reflects an anti-union motive or that it reveals that the employer herself does not think she has a strong business interest in enforcing the rule leaving the Section 7 interests to trump.

By contrast, to make out a violation of Section 8(a)(3), the General Counsel must show anti-union animus. In this regard, there is the problem of mixed-motive cases and the Board's solution to that problem in *Wright Line* (which subsequently won Supreme Court approval in *National Transportation Management Corp.*) where it said that the General Counsel had the burden of proving that conduct was at least partially motivated by anti-union animus, and that once she did, the burden shifted to the employer to prove that the employee would have been treated the same way absent union activity.

But remember that we have seen one case that deviated from this pattern: *Republic Aviation,* where no showing of anti-union animus was required. There, it was sufficient that the discharge was pursuant to a rule that violated Section 8(a)(1). This is still good law but has no application outside of the solicitation cases.

Darlington, as discussed above, adds its own idiosyncratic rules to the mix. It said that certain management decisions would not be subjected to the broader interest-balancing scrutiny of Section 8(a)(1) at all, and could only violate that section derivatively if they also violated Section 8(a)(3). Moreover, turning to Section 8(a)(3), the Court said that a complete shutdown was not violative of the Act irrespective of bad motive. It further stated that the purpose of Section 8(a)(3) is to prohibit discriminatory use of economic weapons in an effort to obtain "future benefits." It consequently held that a partial closing violates the section only if done in order to chill unionism in any of the employer's remaining plants. Like *Republic Aviation, Darlington* states a rule that seems to have no application outside of its special case, but that remains good law for that case.

All of this has gotten more complicated in the cases involving the employer's use of economic weapons where the Section 8(a)(1) analysis appears to be subsumed by the analysis of Section 8(a)(3), and where anti-union motive appears to be a critical element, but one that can sometimes be proven by demonstrating the inherently destructive nature of the employer's act, even if she offers a business justification.[204]

---

[204] Much of this development occurred in the lockout cases that were contemporaneous to *Darlington.* For a further discussion of this issue, see *infra* Chapters 9 and 10.

§ 4.5 Remedies for Interference With Organizational and Other Section 7 Rights

[A]—Remedies for Sections 8(a)(1) and 8(a)(3) Violations

Section 10 of the NLRA grants the Board broad remedial powers. In addition to its power to nullify an election and order a new one, which is technically not a remedy, the Board uses various remedies for violations of Sections 8(a)(1) and (3). Most important are its power to issue cease and desist orders and to order reinstatement and/or back pay for victims of discriminatory discharge. In some instances, discussed in the next section, the NLRB will use a bargaining order to cure employer misconduct. Any back pay award is subject to the traditional damages rule of mitigation.

Critics have noted that employer lawlessness in representation campaigns has grown exponentially and that the current sanctions, which focus on making the victim whole (minus what the discharged employee should have earned under his duty to mitigate) rather than on deterring violations do little to deter such lawlessness.[205] Moreover, there is reason to think that the remedies deliver less than they promise. First, the time between the commission of the unfair labor practice and the federal circuit court enforcement of the Board's remedial order has increased to several years. Moreover, the remedies do little to curb continued discrimination on the part of employers who are inclined to discriminate. Professor Paul Weiler describes two studies of the reinstatement remedy. They found that only 40% of employees accepted reinstatement when it was offered. Of those who did return to work, 80% were gone by the end of the second year, most of them blaming employer vindictiveness.[206]

These problems have led to proposals to forego the election process, which is where a major portion of violations occur, in favor of reliance on signed authorization cards to establish majority support, as is done in some parts of Canada, and to strengthen the remedies available to the Board. No such change is likely to be adopted in the foreseeable future.

---

205 *See generally*, Paul C. Weiler, Governing the Workplace 233-41 (1990); Paul C. Weiler, *Promises to Keep: Securing Workers' Rights to Self-Organization Under the NLRA*, 96 Harv. L. Rev. 1769 (1983). Also see the debate between Professor Weiler and Professors Robert LaLonde and Bernard Meltzer. Robert J. Lalonde & Bernard D. Meltzer, *Hard Times for Unions: Another Look at the Significance of Employer Illegalities*, 58 U. Chi. L. Rev. 953 (1991); Paul C. Weiler, *Hard Times for Unions: Challenging Times for Scholars*, 58 U. Chi. L. Rev. 1015 (1991).

206 Weiler, Governing the Workplace, *supra* note 205, at 234-37; Weiler, *Promises, supra* note 205, at 1791-93.

[B]—Bargaining Orders as a Remedy for Employer Misconduct

In *NLRB v. Gissel Packing Co.*,[207] the Court considered when, if ever, the Board might order an employer to bargain with a union on the basis of signed authorization cards from a majority, or perhaps less, of the employees in a bargaining unit. For a long time the Board awarded bargaining rights to a union on the basis of signed cards from over 50% of the employees in the bargaining unit if the cards authorized it to bargain on behalf of the employee who had signed. Over time, the Board gradually retreated from this approach. Initially, the Board held that the employer could refuse to bargain with a union having a card majority only if the she had a good faith doubt about the union's majority status. The Board in *Joy Silk Mills, Inc.*[208] said that lack of good faith was shown if the employer had engaged in unfair labor practices, or if she could articulate no good reason for her doubt. The Board in *Aaron Brothers*[209] shifted the burden of proof to the General Counsel to show lack of good faith.

Many courts of appeals, however, were wary of authorization cards and were reluctant to grant bargaining rights on the basis of a card majority. These courts doubted the validity of card majorities because cards could be fraudulently obtained through a misrepresentation of what their legal consequences were, or obtained through peer pressure, or simply forged. Moreover, with the growing concern about the employer's right to speak in a representation campaign, courts were dissatisfied with the authorization card route to recognition because it preempted the employer's opportunity to argue the other side to the employees.

In *Gissel*, because of employer unfair labor practices the unions wanted either to set aside an election with unfavorable results or to avoid an election altogether. In either case, they sought recognition through an order from the Board requiring that the employer bargain with them. The *Gissel* Court, in approving the bargaining order remedy for certain cases of pre-election unfair labor practices, rejected the idea that single-purpose authorization cards, those that unambiguously designated the union as the representative of the signing employee, were inherently unreliable.[210] The Supreme Court would hold, however, in the subsequent case of *Linden Lumber Div. v.*

---

207 395 U.S. 575 (1969). This case is discussed above in *supra* § 4.3[E][1].

208 85 NLRB 1263 (1949), *enforced*, 185 F.2d 732 (D.C. Cir. 1950), *cert. denied*, 341 U.S. 914 (1951).

209 158 NLRB 1077 (1966)

210 395 U.S. at 601-09.

NLRB[211] that an employer in the ordinary case need not bargain with the union merely on the basis of a card majority.

The Court further held that while an election was the preferred method of establishing a union's representative status, it was not the only permissible route. Only an election, however, would get the union the benefits of certification, such as one year's protection against rival unions or employees filing decertification petitions.[212]

Finally, the Court followed the Board, which had abandoned its prior approach that focused on whether the employer's doubt was in good faith, in favor of a focus on whether or not the employer had committed unfair labor practices, and, if so, whether they were so egregious as to make a free and fair election impossible. The Court described three categories of unfair labor practices and explained the permissible response of the Board in each case. First, a bargaining order would never be appropriate where the unfair labor practices were "minor or less extensive," because of the "minimal impact" they would have on the election. Second, bargaining orders were inappropriate in cases like those in *Gissel.* In such cases, the unfair labor practices were more significant and would tend to undermine the union's majority and taint the election, while the union could demonstrate a prior majority. The Court stated that "[i]f the Board finds that the possibility of erasing the effects of past practices and of ensuring a fair election . . . is slight and that employee sentiment once expressed through cards would, on balance, be better protected by a bargaining order, then such an order should issue." Finally, in what was clearly dicta, the Court said that in some "exceptional" cases the unfair labor practices might be so "outrageous" and "pervasive" that the only suitable remedy would be a bargaining order even if the union cannot show that it ever had majority support.[213]

The Board has vacillated on whether it will issue a *Gissel* bargaining order without a showing of prior majority support for the union. Since 1984, its position has been that it neither has the authority under the Act to issue such order, nor would it if it had the authority because it would be bad policy to do so.[214]

---

211 419 U.S. 301 (1974).

212 395 U.S. at 597-99 & n.14.

213 *Id.* at 610-15.

214 Gourmet Foods, Inc., 270 NLRB 578 (1984). Were the Board to change its mind, it seems unlikely that a court would enforce a minority bargaining order.

While *Gissel* establishes an important remedy, the Board is finding increasing resistance on the part of the circuit courts to enforce *Gissel* bargaining orders. The remedy represents a compromise between sacrificing current employee choice (which is presumed to be heavily influence by the employer's unfair labor practices), and using bargaining orders as a club to deter employer lawlessness and interference with a free election, thereby preserving the values of Section 9's election system. It attempts to put the world where it would have been but for the impact of the unfair labor practices. It is not the only instance where we sacrifice current employee desires for the stability of giving force to their desires at some other time, as our treatment of the presumption of majority support for a union during its certification year, and our approach to successorship demonstrates.[215]

Of course, there is reason to doubt how often a bargaining order is really efficacious. As Professor Weiler has noted:

> If a decent employment package is to be extracted from a recalcitrant employer, it must come through the efforts of the workers themselves—that is, through the threat of strike action. Here lies the catch-22 of *Gissel.* The bargaining order has been issued because the employer's behavior is thought to have so thoroughly cowed the employees that they cannot express their true desires about collective bargaining even within the secrecy of the voting booth. But all the order can do is license the union to bring negotiations to the point at which its leadership must ask those same employees to put their jobs on the line by going on strike.[216]

Indeed, he reports one study of 38 *Gissel* orders that showed how difficult it was for the unions in those cases to achieve a first contract. In each of the 38 units the union had over 50% support, and in 14 they had over 70% support. Nevertheless, a preliminary collective agreement was only reached

---

215 The courts have been especially critical of the Board's failure to demonstrate that a fair rerun election is not possible and to account to their satisfaction with the effects of the passage of time. Significant passage of time and turnover among employees raises a concern in these courts that either the effects of the unfair labor practices have been dissipated, or that because of turnover, the union never had support of the majority of the current members of the bargaining unit. *See, e.g.,* NLRB v. Pace Oldsmobile, Inc., 739 F.2d 108 (2d Cir. 1984). For a study of the practice of several courts, see Terry A. Bethel & Catherine A. Melfi, *Judicial Enforcement of NLRB Bargaining Orders: What Influences the Courts?,* 22 U.C. Davis L. Rev. 139 (1988). For a highly critical assessment of how the courts have sacrificed collective rights to individual rights in these cases, see James J. Brudney, *A Famous Victory: Collective Bargaining Protections and the Statutory Aging Process,* 74 N.C. L. Rev. 939 (1996).

216 Weiler, *Promises, supra* note 205, at 1794-95.

in 14 (37%) of the units in contrast to the normal rate of 63% of certifications that later resulted in first contracts.[217]

§ 4.6 Chapter Highlights

1. The typical and preferred method for establishing a union's representative status is through a Board-supervised election, a process that can be initiated by employees, unions, or, under certain circumstances, an employer. (§ 4.2[A])

2. On the heels of *Lechmere* there is little chance that a nonemployee organizer can gain access to the employer's property for purposes of organizing without the employer's permission. (§ 4.3)

3. Employer prohibitions of solicitation during work time are presumptively valid, while similar prohibitions of solicitation that cover non-work time are presumptively invalid. (§ 4.3[C][1])

4. The Board has reconciled competing employer and employee interests by concluding that in addition to prohibiting distribution of literature during work time, an employer's rule that also prohibits distribution of literature in *work areas,* regardless of whether it is during work or non-work time, is presumptively valid. The Board also has special rules for the selling areas of retail stores and for patient care areas of hospitals. (§ 4.3[C][1])

5. A union is not entitled to equal time and equal access to address an audience of employees simply because the employer has delivered a captive audience speech, and indeed, rarely will a union be accorded equal access. (§ 4.3[C][3])

6. An employer may "communicate . . . his general views about unionism or any of his specific views about a particular union," but he may not make a "threat of reprisal or force or promise of benefit." The employer may predict "the precise effects he believes unionization will have on his company," so long as they are based on "objective fact . . . as to demonstrably probable consequences beyond his control or . . . a management decision already arrived at to close the plant in case of unionization." (§ 4.3[E][1])

7. The Board will not probe campaign propaganda in search of important misrepresentations, but it will set aside elections where the winning party

---

217 *Id.* at 1795 n.94, *citing* R. O'Shea *Gissel* Bargaining Orders (May 1982) (unpublished LL.M. thesis).

had engaged in forgery to disguise propaganda and falsehoods. It will also set aside elections tainted by especially inflammatory racist appeals. (§ 4.3[E][2]-[3])

8. The Board applies the *Strucksnes* guidelines to systematic polling cases, but will review cases involving individual interrogation on a case-by-case basis. (§ 4.3[F][1])

9. An employer cannot give new benefits to its employees during the representation campaign, nor can it promise to confer benefits. Indeed, the employer may even open itself to accusations of violating the Act if during the campaign it solicits employee complaints, if in doing so the employer impliedly promises future benefits or other corrective measures. Unions have a freer hand, but not unlimited, because of the employee understanding that they do not have the same control over benefits as employers do. (§ 4.3 [F][2])

10. Section 8(a)(3) protects the individual employee against discharge or other differentially negative treatment relating to work conditions that is caused by the employer's union animus regarding the employee's membership or nonmembership in the union, or participation or nonparticipation in its activities. (§ 4.5[A])

11. An employer's decision to shut-down its operations completely, even if motivated by anti-union sentiment, never violates Sections 8(a)(1) and (3), because it is a matter of "management prerogative" and because the employer stands to gain no "future economic benefit" from closing. A partial closing, however, does violate Section 8(a)(3), and derivatively Section 8(a)(1), if the employer is "motivated by a purpose to chill unionism in any of the remaining plants of the single employer and if the employer may reasonably have foreseen that such closings would likely have that effect." (§ 4.4[B])

12. Runaway shops, and decisions to subcontract a portion of the work are analyzed under the traditional Section 8(a)(3) approach to determine whether the employer had a business justification or was acting with an anti-union motive. (§ 4.4[B])

13. The Board will issue an order to the employer to bargain with a union, despite the adverse election result for the union or the Board's decision to forego an election at all, if the union can demonstrate (usually by signed authorization cards) prior majority support, and if the chances of undoing

the effects of the unfair labor practices and holding a fair and free election are slight. Courts are increasingly hostile to such bargaining orders, however, and demand a strong showing that a fair election is impossible and that the passage of time has not made a bargaining order inappropriate. (§ 4.5[B])

CHAPTER 5
EMPLOYER DOMINATION AND ASSISTANCE

§ 5.1 Introduction

Among the most prevalent employer practices designed to control employee organization at the time of the Wagner Act's passage was a phenomenon known as the company union. These organizations ranged from joint labor-management committees, whose institution, meetings and agenda were management initiated and controlled, to employee committees that functioned more independently of management while remaining under its control.[1] A company's control of an employee organization results in something less than the arms-length collective bargaining envisioned by the Act and affects the quality of employee representation.

When the Wagner Act was under consideration, company unions represented approximately 2.5 million union members, 60% of total union membership, and company unions were growing faster than trade unions.[2] It was in this context that Congress enacted Section 8(a)(2) of the Act, a provision essentially outlawing the company union. Section 8(a)(2) makes it an unfair labor practice for an employer "to dominate or interfere with the formation or administration of any labor organization or to contribute financial or other support to it." The application of this provision raises several recurring issues.

§ 5.2 Labor Organization

First, by its terms Section 8(a)(2) only proscribes dominating or interfering with a "labor organization." If the employer's actions are directed to something other than a labor organization, no liability can attach under Section 8(a)(2). Section 2(5) defines a labor organization as:

> any organization of any kind, or any agency or employee representation committee or plan, in which employees participate and which exists for the purpose, in whole or in part, of dealing with employers concerning

---

1 *See* Rafael Gely, *Whose Team Are You On? My Team Or My Team*, 49 Rutgers L.J. 323, 330-339 (1997) (giving a brief history of company unions and describing the various forms of workplace cooperative efforts). Also, see generally William B. Gould IV, *Reflections on Workers' Participation, Influence and Powersharing: The Future of Industrial Relations*, 58 U. Cin. L. Rev. 381 (1989); Thomas C. Kohler, *Models of Worker Participation: The Uncertain Significance of Section 8(a)(2)*, 27 B.C. L. Rev. 499 (1986); and Note, *Rethinking the Adversarial Model in Labor Relations: An Argument for Repeal of Section 8(a)(2)*, 96 Yale L.J. 2021 (1987).

2 Archibald Cox, Derek Curtis Bok, Robert A. Gorman, and Matthew W. Finkin, Labor Law—Cases and Materials 190 (12th ed. 1996).

grievances, labor disputes, wages, rates of pay, hours of employment, or conditions of work.

Analytically, this provision gives rise to three questions: (1) do employees participate in the organization, (2) does the organization exist at least partially to deal with employers, and (3) do the dealings concern conditions of work such as those specified in the section. Since the language makes it clear that a labor organization is "any organization of any kind" and the existence of employee participation is not likely to be controversial, the early issue under this provision was what constituted "dealing with." In *NLRB v. Cabot Carbon Co.*,[3] an employee committee, established to handle employee grievances, made and discussed proposals with the company on topics "covering nearly the whole scope of the employment relationship" such as seniority, hours, job bidding, vacation and sick leave. Management implemented a number of the committee's proposals. Finding that "dealing with" in Section 2(5) was synonymous with "bargaining" and that the committee by-laws gave it no authority to bargain with the employer, the Fifth Circuit Court of Appeals held that the committee was not a labor organization. Even though no bargaining agreement was sought, the Supreme Court reversed, finding that the committee's proposals and requests on matters related to working conditions, and management's participation in discussions with the committee regarding those requests and its attempts to resolve them constituted "dealing with." To reach this decision, the Court drew upon the legislative history of the Secretary of Labor's unsuccessful attempt to amend Section 2(5) by substituting "bargaining collectively" for "dealing with."[4]

Despite the potential breadth of the Court's decision in *Cabot Carbon,* the Sixth Circuit and the Board have attempted to limit the broader implications of the decision. In *NLRB v. Streamway Div. Of Scott & Fetzer Co.*,[5] the employer, a producer and seller of water faucets and valves, established the In-Plant Representation Committee (Committee) "to provide an informal yet orderly process for communicating Company plans and programs; defining and identifying problem areas and eliciting suggestions and ideas for improving operations." The Committee had eight employee members who served rotating terms of three months after an initial term of three to six months in order to maximize employee participation. The Sixth Circuit rejected the Board's reading of *Cabot Carbon* as broad enough

[3] 360 U.S. 203 (1959).

[4] *Id.* at 211-214.

[5] 691 F.2d 288 (6th Cir. 1982).

"to call any group discussing issues related to employment a labor organization." In finding that the Committee was not a labor organization, the court cited such factors as the rotating of Committee members making the Committee more closely resemble groups speaking to management on an individual basis rather than as a representative, the absence of anti-union animus, and the non-existence of any perception by the employees that the Committee was a labor organization.

The Board has also held that an employer-employee grievance council served an adjudicatory rather than an advocacy function and did not deal with the employer.[6] Accepting the employer's argument, the Board found that a joint employer-employee committee making grievance determinations, having a right and obligation to recommend changes in regulations, rules and standards, and actually making recommendations regarding working conditions, did not exist to deal with the employer but to give employees a voice in settling grievances.[7] The Board also found no labor organization but work crews where a job enrichment program consisted of teams of employees that divided job assignments, assigned job rotations, assigned overtime, and held periodic meetings to discuss working conditions with the help of a company-paid consultant. Furthermore, supervisors attended and acted upon recommendations growing out of the meetings.[8]

The Board examined the parameters of Section 2(5) in *Electromation, Inc.*,[9] an important decision involving employer domination under 8(a)(2) and the role of labor-management cooperation in national labor policy. The employer was an electrical components manufacturer employing approximately 200 employees. Faced with financial losses, the employer decided to cut costs by eliminating an attendance bonus program and a wage increase, replacing the wage increase with lump sum payments based on seniority. The employees reacted negatively to these measures and about 35% of them signed a petition protesting the new attendance policy. After several meetings with supervisors and rank-and-file employees about wages, bonuses, incentive pay, attendance programs and leave policy, the employer decided that it was best to deal with these issues bilaterally through discussions with its employees rather than unilaterally. The employer then

[6] *See* Sparks Nugget, Inc., 230 NLRB 275 (1977).

[7] *See* Mercy-Memorial Hospital Corp., 231 NLRB 1108 (1977) (indicating some communication between management and committee possible without finding of labor organization).

[8] *See* General Foods Corp., 231 NLRB 1232 (1977) (program was simply a means of communication between the employees and management).

[9] 309 NLRB 990 (1992), *enf'd*, 35 F.3d 1148 (7th Cir. 1994).

met with a select group of eight employees and proposed the creation of Action Committees to deal with each of the issues. The employer established five action committees, each consisting of six rank-and-file employees, one or two management employees plus the employee benefits manager as the coordinator of the committees. The employer generated sign-up sheets, explained the goals and responsibilities of each committee, and determined the composition and size of the committees. Committee members were expected to canvas other employees for ideas on the relevant issues. The committees began meeting in late January and early February, 1989. They were scheduled to meet on a weekly basis, and the employer paid employees for their time spent doing committee work and supplied needed materials. On February 13, the Teamsters demanded recognition—apparently this was the employer's first knowledge of a union campaign. At the next scheduled meeting of each action committee the employer informed employees that it could no longer participate in their discussions but that they could continue to discuss the issues. Two committees decided to continue meeting, one disbanded, and the fourth decided to write up a report and discontinue meeting. One committee actually presented a proposal that was approved by the comptroller, although it was never presented to the president. On March 15, the employer announced that it could not participate in the committee process until after the election to be held on March 31.

Summarizing *Cabot Carbon, Mercy-Memorial Hospital,* and *General Foods Corp.,* the Board said that "dealing with" was broader than "collective bargaining but not broad enough to encompass organizations that perform essentially a managerial or an adjudicative function. The Board offered the following definition of "dealing with":

> Referring again to the abuses Congress meant to proscribe in enacting the Wagner Act, we view "dealing with" as a bilateral mechanism involving proposals from the employee committee concerning the subjects listed in Sec. 2(5), coupled with real or apparent consideration of those proposals by management. A unilateral mechanism, such as a "suggestion box" or "brainstorming" groups or meetings, or analogous information exchanges does not constitute "dealing with."[10]

Rejecting the suggestion that the action committees were limited to quality and efficiency concerns and designed to be a communication device to promote these concerns, the Board said:

[10] 309 NLRB 990, 995, n.21 (1992).

> The evidence thus overwhelmingly demonstrates that a purpose of the Action Committees, indeed their only purpose, was to address employees' disaffection concerning conditions of employment through the creation of a bilateral process involving employees and management in order to reach bilateral solutions on the basis of employee-initiated proposals. This is the essence of "dealing with" within the meaning of Section 2(5).[11]

Because the function of action committee members was to solicit the ideas of fellow employees in order to find solutions that would satisfy the full complement of employees—to act in a representational capacity—the Board also found that the action committees were an "employee representation committee or plan" under Section 2(5).

Electromation and *E.I. DuPont* make it clear that the Board will give full effect to the broad *Cabot Carbon* interpretation of labor organization in Section 2(5) of the Act.[12] Under that interpretation, with few exceptions, committees that give employers feedback on labor-management issues and provide a basis for making significant improvements will fit the definition of labor organization under Section 2(5).

§ 5.3 Domination

The Act contemplates union representatives with sufficient independence to serve the best interest of employees through arms-length negotiations with employers. This policy is reflected in Section 1's express goal of "protecting the exercise by workers of full freedom of association, self-organization, and designation of representatives of their own choosing for the purpose of negotiating the terms and conditions of their employment or other mutual aid or protection."[13]

---

[11] *Id.* at 997.

[12] E.I. DuPont, 311 NLRB 893 (1993) (six safety committees and a fitness committee discussed working conditions with management membership on the committees, held committees deal with management through committee process).

[13] Another part of Section 1 explains the necessity of this goal:

> The inequality of bargaining power between employees who do not possess full freedom of association or actual liberty of contract, and employers who are organized in the corporate or other forms of ownership association substantially burdens and affects the flow of commerce, and tends to aggravate recurrent business depressions, by depressing wage rates and the purchasing power of wage earners in industry and by preventing the stabilization of competitive wage rates and working conditions within and between industries.

Employer-controlled unions substantially undermine this goal by depriving employees of the choice of representatives and limiting the representative's advocacy to those positions that are palatable to the employer. The cases strive to identify the indicia of domination that lead to these untoward results. Because the impact of employer domination occurs whether the employer's motives are innocent or calculating, this and other 8(a)(2) violations receive *per se* treatment.[14]

The Board in *Electromation* offers the following definition of domination:

> [A] labor organization that is the creation of management, whose structure and function are essentially determined by management, . . . and whose continued existence depends on the fiat of management, is one whose formation or administration has been dominated under Section 8(a)(2).[15]

The Board also articulated a limit to the concept of domination:

> However, when the formulation and structure of the organization is determined by employees, domination is not established, even if the employer has the potential ability to influence the structure or effectiveness of the organization.[16]

For several reasons, the employer dominated the action committees in *Electromation.* The idea for the committees originated with the employer, and it essentially presented employees with the choice of the *status quo* or accepting the action committees. The employer determined the purpose, composition, and service terms of members of the committees without initial employee support for the idea. Having management and rank-and-file on the committees working on the issues before they were submitted to upper management allowed the employer to sit on both sides of the table.[17] The

[14] *See* NLRB v. Newport News Shipbuilding Co., 308 U.S. 241 (1939); International Ladies' Garment Workers' Union, AFL-CIO, v. NLRB, 366 U.S. 731 (1961); and Electromation, Inc., 309 NLRB 990 (1992). *See also* Note, *New Standards for Domination and Support Under Section 8(a)(2),* 82 Yale L.J. 510 (1973).

[15] 309 NLRB 990, 995.

[16] *Id.* at 995-996.

[17] Similarly, in the *DuPont* case, the following indicia of domination were present: (1) the employer made the decision to organize the committees then called and chaired the organizational meeting and determined who would serve; (2) the employer determined who and how many employees served on each committee; (3) a member of management served as either chair or advisor setting the agenda for each meeting; (4) decision-making was by consensus giving management veto power; (5) the employer could abolish the committees at will. The employees had no independent voice in determining the structure, composition or operation of the committees. 311 NLRB 893.

Board distinguished the action committees from organizations "where the impetus behind the organizations emanated from the employees themselves."[18]

Remedially, the Act calls generally for cease and desist orders as well as appropriate affirmative relief to cure unfair labor practices. The Board attempts to restore the *status quo ante* when it finds violations of Section 8(a)(2). When the employer has dominated the labor organization, the remedy is disestablishment.[19]

§ 5.4 Interference

By contrast, when the employer's conduct falls short of domination, the appropriate remedy will be less drastic than disestablishment. When the employer has improperly influenced or unlawfully assisted a labor organization without domination, the remedy will typically be a cease and desist and withdrawal of recognition order pending the demonstration of an uncoerced and unassisted majority.[20] Where the employer has merely given unlawful support to the labor organization, the cease and desist order may well stand alone.[21]

International Ladies' Garment Workers Union v. NLRB (Bernhard-Altmann Texas Corp.) supplies the best example of unlawful support.[22] In

---

[18] 309 NLRB at 996 n.25. In drawing this distinction the Board cited NLRB v. Northeastern University, 601 F.2d 1208 (1st Cir. 1979); Hertzka & Knowles v. NLRB, 503 F.2d 625 (9th Cir. 1974); and Chicago Rawhide Mfg. Co. v. NLRB, 221 F.2d 165 (7th Cir. 1955).

[19] *See* Carpenter Steel, 76 NLRB 670 (1948). In *Electromation*, the Board issued, in part, the following remedial order:

> The National Labor Relations Board orders that the Respondent, Electromation, . . . its officers, agents, successors, and assigns, shall
>
> 1. Cease and Desist from
>
> (a) Dominating, assisting, or otherwise supporting the Action Committees created in January 1989 at its Elkhart plant.
>
> (b) In any like or related manner interfering with, restraining, or coercing employees in the exercise of the rights guaranteed them by Section 7 of the Act.
>
> 2. Take the following affirmative action necessary to effectuate the policies of the Act.
>
> Immediately disestablish and cease giving assistance or any other support to the Action Committees.

[20] *See, e.g.*, International Ladies' Garment Workers v. NLRB (Bernhard-Altmann Texas Corp.), 366 U.S. 731 (1961).

[21] *See* A.M.A. Leasing Ltd., 283 NLRB 1017 (1987).

[22] 366 U.S. 731 (1961).

that case, the International Ladies' Garment Workers Union (ILGWU) started a campaign to organize employees at Bernhard-Altmann's San Antonio, Texas plant. On August 30, 1957, after some strike activity not related to the union campaign, the union and employer entered into an understanding that the employer would recognize the union as collective bargaining representative of the employer's production and shipping employees. Both the employer and the union believed at the time that the union represented a majority of the employees. It did not. Two and one-half months later, the employer and union signed a collective bargaining agreement; the union represented a majority of employees when the parties signed the agreement.

The employer's granting and the union's accepting of recognition before the union had secured majority support violated Sections 8(a)(2) and 8(b)(1)(A) of the Act. The Supreme Court noted that the employer's understanding with the union in August, 1957, "afforded [the union] a deceptive cloak of authority with which to persuasively elicit additional employee support," and explained the applicability of 8(a)(2) as follows:

> Section 8(a)(2) of the Act makes it an unfair labor practice for an employer to "contribute . . . support" to a labor organization. The law has long been settled that a grant of exclusive recognition to a minority union constitutes unlawful support in violation of that section, because the union so favored is given "a marked advantage over any other in securing the adherence of employees," . . . .[23]

Responding to the union's effort to assert a good faith defense, the Court said:

> The [union], while taking no issue with the fact of its minority status on the critical date, maintains that both [the employer's] and its own good faith beliefs in [the union's] majority status are a complete defense. To countenance such an excuse would place in permissibly careless employer and union hands the power to completely frustrate employee realization of the premise of the Act—that its prohibitions will go far to assure freedom of choice and majority rule in employee selection of representatives. We find nothing in the statutory language prescribing scienter as an element of the unfair labor practices here involved. The act made unlawful by 8(a)(2) is employer support of a minority union. Here that support is an accomplished fact. More need not be shown, for, even if

---

[23] *Id.* at 738

mistakenly, the employees' rights have been invaded. It follows that prohibited conduct cannot be excused by a showing of good faith.[24]

Other examples of unlawful support by employers include contributing financial and other support to the union,[25] assisting a union in its effort to organize employees,[26] soliciting employees to join a union,[27] permitting a union to conduct meetings during paid work time,[28] permitting use of company facilities,[29] and providing secretarial and clerical assistance.[30] Often these individual practices occur together or in a larger context of unlawful activity that results in a finding of illegality.

On the other hand, unlawful support is distinguishable from lawful cooperation. Where the employer and union have an arms-length relationship, some of the activities seen as violations in the preceding paragraph will be treated as lawful assistance.[31] For example, in *Baker Mine Services, Inc.*, the employer paid the labor organization's negotiating committee members for time spent negotiating a collective bargaining agreement, printed and provided ballots to the organization for conducting elections, provided ballots used to ratify the agreement negotiated with the organization, and paid employees for the time spent participating in the ratification vote.[32] The following excerpt reveals the Board's analytical approach to distinguishing cooperative efforts from unlawful assistance:

> As a general rule, the Board examines the aggregation of facts presented to it in assessing allegations of unlawful assistance . . . . We conclude that the facts in this case do not establish that the [employer] engaged in acts of unlawful assistance.

---

24 *Id.* at 738-739. It should be noted that the Act does permit some forms of minority union representation, e.g., "members only" agreements, *see* Retail Clerks Local 128 v. Lion Dry Goods, Inc., 369 U.S. 17 (1962), and pre-hire agreements, authorized in the construction industry by Section 8(f) of the Act.

25 *See, e.g.*, Kaiser Foundation Hospitals, Inc., 223 NLRB 322 (1976).

26 Tuschak/Jacobson, Inc., 223 NLRB 1298 (1976).

27 *See, e.g.*, Stoll Industries, Inc., 223 NLRB 51 (1976) and Brown Transport Corp., 296 NLRB No. 75 (1989).

28 *See, e.g.*, Hoover, Inc., 240 NLRB 593 (1979) and Schwab Foods Inc. d/b/a Mooresville IGA Foodliner, 284 NLRB 1055 (1987).

29 *See, e.g.*, Keeler Brass Automotive Group, div. of Keeler Brass Co., 317 NLRB 1110 (1995).

30 *Id.*

31 *See, e.g.*, Coamo Knitting Mills, Inc., 150 NLRB 579 (1964).

32 279 NLRB 609 (1986).

> The use of company time and property in connection with collective-bargaining negotiations does not per se establish unlawful assistance . . . . On the contrary, we have recognized generally that permitting the use of company time and property in such circumstances "serve[s] to permit an otherwise legitimate labor organization to perform its functions for the benefit of all concerned more effectively than otherwise might be the case.
>
> Similarly, we have held that permitting an employee committee to hold biweekly meetings on paid time and on company premises to prepare for meetings with management, to conduct steward classes on company property with partial pay for employees involved, and to conduct elections on paid time do not violate Section 8(a)(2). . . . It is also well settled that an employer, in addition to paying committee representatives for time spent on union committee business, permissibly may shoulder the cost of printing a collective-bargaining agreement . . . .
>
> Finally, we discern no impropriety under Section 8(a)(2) for an employer, as here, to meet with employees in cooperation with the employees' bargaining representative for the purpose of discussing the bargaining process, or to inform employees of impending union committee meetings.
>
> In short, in the absence of probative evidence demonstrating the absence of an arm's-length relationship between employer and union, . . . we can only construe the activities by the [employer] alleged to be unlawful as cooperation of a ministerial character growing out of an amicable labor-management relationship.[33]

Interference may also come in other forms of employer influence that do not rise to the level of domination. These cases often involve supervisory involvement in union activities. For example, in *Nassau & Suffolk Contractors' Ass'n*, the Board found that it was illegal for supervisors to vote in union elections or to serve as union officials or bargaining team members.[34]

---

[33] *Id.* at 610-611.

[34] 118 NLRB 174 (1957). *Cf.* Power Piping Co., 291 NLRB No. 80 (1988) (in examining all the circumstances, the Board concluded that the employer acted lawfully when its foreman voted in the internal union election—employees would not be reasonably led to believe that the foreman was acting on behalf on management).

§ 5.5 The *Midwest Piping* Doctrine

An employer's duty under Section 8(a)(2) to refrain from giving unlawful assistance or support to a labor organization has, perhaps, its greatest impact in the rival union situation. Where employee sentiment is divided before a competing union emerges with a clear mandate, an employer's support for one of the competitors may be devastating to employee free choice. The Board recognized this problem in *Midwest Piping & Supply Co.*[35] In that case, the Steamfitters Union petitioned the Board for an election among Midwest's employees. On September 30, 1944, the Steamfitters requested that the employer bargain with it regarding a new collective bargaining agreement. Also on September 30, 1944, the Steelworkers advised the employer that it represented a majority of the employees and requested a bargaining session. The Steelworkers also advised the employer not to execute an agreement with any other labor organization until the employees had exercised their rights under the Act. On the same day, the Steelworkers petitioned the Board for an election. The employer responded to the Steelworker's letter on October 2, 1944, and requested the Steelworkers to produce evidence of its majority status. The Steelworkers declined to produce the evidence. On October 12, the employer agreed to confer with the Steamfitters regarding a new agreement. On December 20, 1944, after the Steamfitters submitted authorization cards from a majority of the employees, the employer executed an agreement with the Steamfitters.

The Board held that the employer had an obligation to be neutral. By executing an agreement with the Steamfitters while representation proceedings were pending with the Board, the employer: (a) indicated its approval of the Steamfitters, (b) accorded the Steamfitters unwarranted prestige, (d) encouraged membership in the Steamfitters, (d) discouraged membership in the Steelworkers, (e) rendered unlawful assistance to the Steamfitters, and (f) interfered with, restrained, and coerced its employees in the exercise of Section 7 rights. The Board reasoned that employees should have the greatest possible freedom in selecting and retaining bargaining representatives when there is a question concerning representation as reflected in the election petitions. The Board rejected the argument that the employer's agreement based on the Steamfitters' demonstration of majority support should be a defense saying:

> [I]t is well known that membership cards obtained during the heat of rival organizing campaigns like those of the respondent's plants, do not

[35] 63 NLRB 1060 (1945).

necessarily reflect the ultimate choice of bargaining representative; indeed, the extent of dual membership among the employees during periods of intense organizing activity is an important unknown factor affecting a determination of majority status, which can best be resolved by a secret ballot among the employees.[36]

Following this decision, the Board extended the *Midwest Piping* doctrine to impose a duty of neutrality where the rival union raised a question concerning representation using authorization cards,[37] made a "colorable claim" based on an insubstantial number of cards,[38] or petitioned the Board for an election while the employer was bargaining with an incumbent union.[39]

Encountering resistance in the circuit courts on its extension of the *Midwest Piping* doctrine, the Board announced new rules in two cases.[40] In *Abraham Grossman d/b/a/ Bruckner Nursing Home*, Local 144 notified the employer in September, 1974, that it held authorization cards from a majority of its employees, and the parties set a date for a card count. Shortly afterwards, Local 1155 sent a mailgram to the employer saying that it was engaged in a campaign among the employees and that the employer should not extend recognition to any other organization. The card count was conducted on September 27, 1974; it supported Local 144's claim of majority support. Negotiations between Local 144 and the employer ensued, and the parties executed an agreement on December 18, 1974. At the time of the card check, Local 144 possessed authorization cards from 80-90% of the employees, while Local 1115 had two cards. Neither union had filed an election petition. Local 1115 filed charges under the *Midwest Piping* doctrine on March 7, 1995. The ALJ said that Local 1115 had a "colorable claim" to representation and held that the employer had given unlawful assistance to Local 144 in violation of Section 8(a)(2) of the Act. In reversing the ALJ, the Board announced a new rule to be applied in initial organizing rival union situations. Recounting the history of the doctrine as extended, including enforcement problems in the circuit courts, the Board said:

---

36 *Id.* at 1070 n.13.

37 *See* Novak Logging Co., 119 NLRB 1573 (1958).

38 Playskool, Inc., 195 NLRB 560 (1972).

39 *See* Peter Paul, Inc., 185 NLRB 281 (1970).

40 *See, e.g.*, Playskool, Inc. v. NLRB, 477 F.2D 66 (7th Cir. 1973); NLRB v. Inter-Island Resorts, Ltd., d/b/a Kona Surf Hotel, 507 F.2d 411 (9th Cir. 1974); and American Bread Company, 170 NLRB 85 (1968), *enforcement denied*, 411 F.2d 147 (6th Cir. 1969).

> [W]e will no longer find 8(a)(2) violations in rival union, initial organizing situations when an employer recognizes a labor organization which represents an uncoerced, unassisted majority, before a valid petition for an election has been filed with the Board. However, once notified of a valid petition, an employer must refrain from recognizing any of the rival unions. Of course, we will continue to process timely filed petitions and to conduct elections in the most expeditious manner possible, following our normal procedures with respect to intervention and placement of parties on the ballot.[41]

The Board saw the new rule as advancing both free choice and industrial stability. Unions securing at least the 30% support among employees necessary to demonstrate a showing of interest in support of an election petition can forestall recognition of a rival under the rule, while unions with a "colorable claim" of less than 30% will no longer be able to circumvent a legitimate collective bargaining relationship. Similarly, the rule removes the uncertainty for employers, since they need not be concerned with claims for recognition that are not accompanied by a petition for election. The election petition indicates a true contest for employee votes, and the election removes the doubt associated with dual authorization cards. The Board was also careful in *Bruckner* to point out the continuing liability of employers under 8(a)(2) for recognizing unions that have not secured majority status.[42]

In *RCA Del Caribe, Inc.*,[43] the Board announced a new rule to apply in situations where an incumbent union is challenged by an outside union. Under the new rule, the employer is not required or permitted to "withdraw from bargaining or executing a contract with an incumbent union," based on the mere filing of an election petition by an outside union. The employer will not violate 8(a)(2) by continuing to bargain with the incumbent, but it will violate 8(a)(5) by refusing to bargain solely because of the petition. It may, of course, withdraw recognition in good faith based on objective considerations.[44] The incumbent will be put to the test in the ensuing election. If the incumbent prevails in the election, any contract signed with the employer will be valid and binding. If the outside union prevails, any contract between the incumbent and the employer will be nullified.[45] The

---

[41] 262 NLRB 955, 957 (1982).

[42] *See Bernhard-Altmann, supra* note 22.

[43] 262 NLRB 963 (1982).

[44] *See infra* Chapter 8, § 8.4.

[45] Chairman Van de Water vigorously dissented in this case, claiming that *Linden Lumber* establishes a clear preferences for elections. In his view, the employer's continuing

Board majority thought that the new rule was necessary to produce a better balance between employee free choice and the stability concerns reflected in the presumption of continuing majority status.[46] The Board stated the following rationale:

> We have concluded that requiring an employer to withdraw from bargaining after a petition has been filed is not the best means of assuring employer neutrality, thereby facilitating employee free choice. Unlike initial organizing situations, an employer in an existing collective-bargaining relationship cannot observe strict neutrality. In many situations, as here, the incumbent challenged by an outside union is in the process of—perhaps close to completing—negotiation of a contract when the petition is filed. If an employer continues to bargain, employees may perceive a preference for the incumbent union, whether or not the employer holds that preference. On the other hand, if an employer withdraws from bargaining, particularly when agreement is imminent, this withdrawal may more emphatically signal repudiation of the incumbent and preference for the rival. Again, it may be of little practical consequence to the employees whether the employer actually intended this signal or was compelled by law to withdraw from bargaining. We further recognize that an employer may be faced with changing economic circumstances which could require immediate response and commensurate changes in working conditions. Put another way, the ebb and flow of economic conditions cannot be expected to subside merely because a representation petition has been filed. Thus, to prohibit negotiations until the Board has ruled on the results of a new election might work an undue hardship on employers, unions, and employees. Under the circumstances, we believe preservation of the status quo through an employer's continued bargaining with an incumbent is the better way to approximate employer neutrality.[47]

---

negotiations with an incumbent provided the latter with a "deceptive cloak of authority" in addition to the natural advantages of day-to-day presence of the steward and visibility already enjoyed by the incumbent. The rule, the Chairman argued, gives the employer an opportunity to manipulate the vote by bargaining hard, if it likes the challenger, or soft, if it prefers the incumbent. On the other hand, employers may be leery of bargaining seriously for fear it will be futile should the challenger win. Dissenting Member Jenkins viewed the new rule as effectively converting the representation election into a ratification vote.

[46] 262 NLRB 963, 976 (1982).

[47] 262 NLRB 963, 965.

§ 5.6 Labor-Management Cooperation Policy

Company unions are now subsumed under the more expansive concept of workplace cooperative efforts.[48] Though workplace cooperative efforts date back to the end of the 19th century and were prevalent during the Wagner Act debates, such programs have seen widespread experimentation among United States firms since the mid-1980's.[49] Workplace cooperative efforts that have come under the scrutiny of Section 8(a)(2) are employee participatory programs such as quality circles, quality of work life, and strategic participation and teams defined as "a small number of people with complementary skills who are committed to a common purpose, performance goals, and approach for which they hold themselves mutually accountable."[50] Teams have broader authority than employee participatory programs including "near-total responsibility for producing a product or service."[51]

Employers argue that these workplace cooperative efforts are increasingly indispensable to their global competitiveness, and the sanctions of Section 8(a)(2) leave them at a distinct disadvantage in the global market. Unions, on the other hand, remain suspicious that these efforts are primarily directed at union avoidance.[52] Because of the importance of this question, the Board, the Commission On The Future Of Worker-Management Relations appointed by President Clinton under the Chairmanship of John T. Dunlop, and Congress have all entertained the debate about the regulation of workplace cooperative efforts under Section 8(a)(2) of the Act.

Though the Board outlawed the action committees in *Electromation*,[53] three Board members wrote separate concurring decisions to respond to party and amici concerns about the permissibility of employee participation

---

48 *See* Gely, *supra* note 1 (suggesting an internal labor market approach to interpreting Section 8(a)(2)).

49 *Id.* at 333.

50 Gely, *supra* note 1, at 336, *citing* Jon R. Katzenbach & Douglas K. Smith, The Wisdom Of Teams 45 (1993).

51 *Id.* at 337, *citing* Cynthia D. Fisher et al., Human Resource Management 439-440 (2d ed. 1993). Autonomous groups are a kind of team. They are given authority to make significant logistic decisions concerning scheduling, work assignment, hiring, and compensation practices. They have the ability to alter production methods and make major logistical decisions concerning their work process. As in the case of quality circles, there is no additional direct compensation. *Id.*

52 *See* Gely, *supra* note 1, at 326.

53 *See* discussion of case, *supra* § 5.3.

programs under Section 8(a)(2). Member Devaney emphasized that certain enlightened forms of employer-employee communication are not outlawed by Section 8(a)(2), even if employer-initiated. Into this category he puts committees set up to deal with productivity, efficiency, conservation and safety concerns. He notes that the Wagner Act was concerned with sham unions, not employer-initiated programs dealing with such managerial issues. Member Devaney would also make representation a necessary element of a labor organization finding under Section 2(5).[54]

Member Oviatt expressed concern about the flexibility of American companies to respond appropriately to diverse competitive pressures in the world economy. He argued that the decision does not prevent employer-initiated committees designed to address efficiency and productivity concerns such as quality circles,[55] quality of work life programs,[56] and employer-employee committees established to facilitate better communication between employees and employer. In Member Oviatt's view, these programs present no problem under Section 8(a)(2), since they do not concern grievances, labor disputes, wages, rates of pay, hour of employment, or conditions of work under Section 2(5).[57]

Like Members Devaney and Oviatt, Member Raudabaugh was concerned that some forms of employee organization, particularly employee participation programs (EPPs) pass muster under Section 8(a)(2). Member Raudabaugh conceded that EPPs are labor organizations under Section 2(5), since employees participate and deal with employers about conditions of employment. He also believes that employers dominate EPPs under the *Newport News* decision, because they are not independent of the employer, even if they are supported by employees; that they bring about better labor relations, and that they are not unlawfully motivated. However, Member Raudabaugh argued that *Newport News* no long has vitality because of the intervention of the Taft-Hartley amendments to the Act and of changing industrial realities including labor-management cooperation since the 1939 decision.

---

54 309 NLRB 990, 998-1003 (1992).

55 Member Oviatt describes the purpose of quality circles to use employee expertise by having the group examine certain operational problems such as labor efficiency and material waste. *Id.* at 1004.

56 Member Oviatt offers the following description of quality of work life programs:

> These involve management's attempt to draw on the creativity of its employees by including them in decisions that affect their work lives. These decisions may go beyond improvements in productivity and efficiency to include issues involving worker self-fulfillment and self-enhancement.

57 *See id.* at 1003-1005.

Member Raudabaugh proposed a four-factor test as a reinterpretation of "domination" that would accommodate labor-management relations and Section 7 rights under 8(a)(2): (1) the extent of the employer's involvement in the structure and operation of the committees; (2) whether the employees, from an objective standpoint, reasonably perceive the EPP as a substitute for full collective bargaining through a traditional union; (3) whether employees have been assured of their Section 7 right to choose to be represented by a traditional union under a system of full collective bargaining, and (4) the employer's motive in establishing organization. Each of these factors would be considered in determining whether an EPP is lawful with none being necessarily dispositive.[58]

Following the *Electromation* decision on September 27, 1995, the U.S. House of Representatives passed a bill seeking to amend Section 8(a)(2). Its stated findings and purposes encompassed the demands of global competition, the necessity for enhanced employee involvement in workplace decisionmaking, the widespread operation of employee involvement programs in approximately 30,000 workplaces including over 80% of the largest employers, the positive impact of such programs on the lives of employees, the consistency of the legislation with existing joint efforts of Congress, business, labor and academics to encourage such programs, the distinction between efforts to interfere with Section 7 rights using company unions as in the 1930's and current employee involvement programs, and the current threat to such programs under Section 8(a)(2). The amendment reads:

> Section 8(a)(2) of the National Labor Relations Act is amended by striking the semicolon and inserting the following: *Provided further,* That it shall not constitute or be evidence of an unfair labor practice under the paragraph for an employer to establish, assist, maintain, or participate in any organization or entity of any kind, in which employees who participate to at least the same extent practicable as representatives of management participate, to address matters of mutual interest, including, but not limited to, issues of quality, productivity, efficiency, and safety and health, which does not have, claim, or seek authority to be the exclusive bargaining representative of the employees or to negotiate or enter into collective bargaining agreements with the employer or to amend existing collective bargaining agreements between the employer and any labor organization, except that in a case in which a labor

58 *See* 309 NLRB 990, 1013.

organization is the representative of such employees as provided in section 9(a), this proviso shall not apply.[59]

This amendment would have narrowed the reach of Section 8(a)(2) by changing the definition of a labor organization under Section 2(5). Under the amendment, an organization would only be a "labor organization" for purposes of establishing domination or interference, if it sought to engage in collective bargaining with the employer. Thus, the action committees in *Electromation* would not have violated Section 8(a)(2) since no collective bargaining agreement existed. The committees did not seek to become a collective bargaining representative, and any agreements reached probably would not have been deemed collective bargaining agreements. However, the amendment does not embrace Member Raudabaugh's proposal for a motive requirement. Though Congress ultimately passed the Team Act, President Clinton vetoed it on July 30, 1996.[60]

On March 24, 1993, the President announced the formation of a Commission on the Future of Worker-Management Relations (The Dunlop Commission) through the Secretaries of Labor and Commerce. Over a 12-month period the Commission held 11 national hearings in Washington, D.C. and six regional hearings taking testimony from 354 witness and amassing 3,858 pages of transcript plus scores of exhibits, letters, papers, articles and studies.[61] The Commission's charge was to: investigate the current state of worker-management relations in the United States and report back to the Secretaries in response to the following questions:

1. What (if any) new methods or institutions should be encouraged, or required, to enhance work-place productivity through labor-management cooperation and employee participation?

2. What (if any) changes should be made in the present legal framework and practices of collective bargaining to enhance cooperative behavior, improve productivity, and reduce conflict and delay?

3. What (if anything) should be done to increase the extent to which work-place problems are directly resolved by the parties themselves, rather than through recourse to state and federal courts and government regulatory bodies?[62]

---

59 H.R. 743, 104th Cong. Sec. 3 (1995).

60 *See* Daily Lab. Rep. (BNA) 147 (7/31/96).

61 *See* XI U.S. Dep't of Labor, Fact Finding Report: Commission on the Future of Worker-Management Relations (May 1994).

62 *See id.* xi.

The Commission found employee participation in a wide variety of forms to be a growing phenomenon and projected continued future growth, based on factors such as the improved education of the workforce, opportunities created by technology to share information and delegate decision-making, and the pro-participation sentiment of surveyed workers. The Commission also found labor representatives to favor employee participation as a means of enhancing both competitiveness and workplace democracy. It also found that management representatives viewed it as integral to the work process and workable in union and non-union settings. Though the Commission found evidence that sustained employee participation improves economic performance, it also found that labor-management cooperation is difficult "to sustain and diffuse in the American environment." While admitting a lack of clarity about the factors that limit the diffusion and sustainability of employee participation, the Commission did cite the following: insufficient trust, the inability of employees to initiate participation, economic pressures on employers, and government policies and legal issues.

Following the release of the Fact Finding Report, the Commission held four additional national hearings between July and September, receiving testimony from 57 additional persons. It also received correspondence, studies and articles from representatives of business groups, labor organizations, professional associations, academics, women's organizations, civil rights groups and other individuals. In December 1994, the Commission submitted its Report and Recommendations to the Secretaries of Labor and Commerce, which contained the following recommendations among others:

> (1) Facilitate the Growth of Employee Involvement
>
> The Commission recommends that non-union employee participation programs should not be unlawful simply because they involve discussion of terms and conditions of work or compensation where such discussion is incidental to the broad purposes of these programs.
>
> (2) Continue to Ban Company Unions
>
> The law should continue to prohibit companies from setting up company dominated labor organizations. It should be an unfair labor practice under NLRA Section 8(a)(1) for an employer to establish a new participation program or to use or manipulate an existing one with the purpose of frustrating employee efforts to obtain independent representation.[63]

---

63 *See* Report And Recommendations, Comm'n On The Future Of Worker-Management Relations 7 (1994).

Under the second proposal, the Commission noted that employees should be protected from retaliation for expressing their views on workplace issues. It noted such protection under current law for "concerted activities for the purpose of mutual aid and protection."[64]

The Commission proposal has encountered some academic criticism for failing to fully appreciate the need for the protection currently provided by Section 8(a)(2). Critics have recognized, however, that the Commission's recommendations differ from the Team Act, since they recognize the need for continue prevention of company unions and protection of employee expression.[65]

§ 5.7 Chapter Highlights

1. The 8(a)(2) violation is a *per se* violation that does not require a finding of bad faith. (§§ 5.3, 5.4, and 5.6)

2. The 8(a)(2) violation draws upon two parts of the Act—the definition of labor organization under Section 2(5) and the terms of the violation in 8(a)(2). The most significant issue under Section 2(5) is the definition of "dealing with," which has been litigated since 1959 and was the subject of a recent Congressional attempt to amend Section 8(a)(2). (§§ 5.2 and 5.6)

3. The domination prohibition in Section 8(a)(2) assures that the employer will maintain an arms-length relationship with any organization representing the employment interests of employees. Since employers tend to conceive and implement programs designed to address those interests, domination is easily shown once the existence of a labor organization has been shown. (§ 5.3)

4. Interference short of domination comes in a variety of forms from undue supervisory influence to improper financial and other assistance. However, it is important to distinguish between cooperation, which is permitted, and unlawful assistance. (§ 5.4)

5. A species of the prohibition against unlawful assistance is the employer's obligation to maintain neutrality where rival unions compete

---

64 *Id.* at 8.

65 *See* Gely, *supra* note 1, at 368-369 (arguing that the Commission failed to provide any protection against the opportunistic behavior that may result form the impact that workplace cooperative efforts have on the employment relationship).

for the sentiment of employees. Recent cases have altered the modified *Midwest Piping* doctrine that had been viewed by many circuit courts as particularly onerous. (§ 5.5)

6. Labor-management cooperation policy is influenced by the interpretation of Section 8(a)(2), and the national debate about the legal framework for workplace cooperative efforts continues. (§ 5.6)

CHAPTER 6
PICKETING AND STRIKING FOR RECOGNITION

§ 6.1 Introduction

Issues involving so-called recognition or organizational picketing and the provisions of Section 8(b)(7) of the National Labor Relations Act are among the most confusing in the field of labor law. This chapter will discuss the role and function of recognition picketing by a union and the limits imposed on it by law. It will begin with an overview of the statute's history. It will then provide a detailed discussion about what recognition picketing is, how it is distinguished from other forms of picketing and the limits imposed by Section 8(b)(7). Because peaceful picketing is a form of speech, legal limits on recognition picketing must be carefully applied.

Additional topics in this chapter include NLRB expedited election procedures available when a Section 8(b)(7) charge has been filed and the extent to which the law protects employees engaged in organizational picketing or recognition strikes.

It is important to note at the outset that the statute does not impose an absolute ban on all picketing with a recognitional or organizational objective. Section 8(b)(7) will only bar such picketing when another union has been lawfully recognized by the employer and contract-bar rules do not yet allow holding an election, when a valid election has been held within the preceding 12 months, or when no petition for election has been filed "within a reasonable period of time not to exceed thirty days from the commencement of such picketing."

Unions use recognition and organizational picketing for a variety of reasons. Generally, it involves picketing the premises of an employer, the employees of which the union is attempting to organize. Picketing may be conducted by employees of the targeted employer or, often, by non-employees. If the picketing causes employees of the targeted employer to refuse to come to work, it becomes a recognition strike.[1]

A union may use recognition picketing as an alternative to NLRB representation election procedures or concurrently with such procedures. In some settings, a union may use recognition picketing as a means to force the employer to voluntarily recognize the union without an election. The employer will be under substantial economic pressure to sign a recognition agreement if employees refuse to cross the picket line to work, if deliveries

---

[1] For a more detailed explanation of recognition picketing and problem areas associated with applying the statute, see Lee Modjeska, *Recognition Picketing Under the NLRA*, 35 U. Fla. L. Rev. 633 (1983).

or pickups are stopped or delayed because truck drivers refuse to cross the picket line, or if customers choose to go elsewhere because of the picket line. If the union is able to win voluntary recognition without an election, it can avoid the erosion of its support that can occur during a lengthy pre-election campaign.

As will be discussed, the statute and NLRB rules allow for an expedited election (without delays for unit determination hearings and other pre-election matters) in certain recognition picketing situations. Thus, a union seeking representative status might engage in recognition picketing in hopes of inducing an employer into making a request for an expedited election. Because pre-election delays often favor the employer, this type of election reduces the risk that a union will lose its majority support before the election is held.

Distinct from picketing with a recognitional objective is picketing to publicize the employer's non-union status and below union-standards wage scales. If such picketing is not for a recognitional objective, it may be beyond the reach of Section 8(b)(7) and may help the union to direct business to employers who have workforces represented by the union.

Finally, a union may seek to picket under the proviso to Section 8(b)(7)(C) which allows picketing, even for a recognitional objective, if such picketing is purely informational and does not have the effect of stopping deliveries or pickups or causing persons to refuse to perform services. This type of picketing allows the union to maintain economic pressure on the non-union employer beyond the time limits which Section 8(b)(7) otherwise imposes on recognition picketing.

Because recognition picketing and organizational strikes which comply with legal guidelines constitute protected activity under Section 7 of the Act,[2] employers are forbidden under Sections 8(a)(1)[3] and 8(a)(3)[4] from coercing, interfering with or discriminating against employees engaged in recognition or organizational picketing or strikes.[5] The rights of employees also are balanced against employers' property interests in cases involving access to property for organizational picketing or handbilling.[6]

---

[2] 29 U.S.C. § 157.

[3] 29 U.S.C. § 158(a)(1).

[4] 29 U.S.C. § 158(a)(3).

[5] *See infra* § 6.8.

[6] *See infra* § 6.8[C].

§ 6.2 Section 8(b)(7) and Its Origins

Prior to the 1959 Landrum-Griffin amendments, the issue of picketing and striking for recognition was governed solely by Section 8(b)(4)(C)[7] of the National Labor Relations Act, which had been added as part of the 1947 Taft-Hartley amendments. Section 8(b)(4)(C) forbids a union from picketing for recognition in situations where the employer already has a duty to bargain with another union certified by the National Labor Relations Board (NLRB). This provision, however, did not reach the situation in which no union had been recognized or certified. It also did not affect the case of an employer already bargaining with another union that had achieved recognition without benefit of a NLRB election or certification. Further, Section 8(b)(4)(C) did not necessarily reach peaceful organizational picketing directed at employees. Thus, in its 1960 *NLRB v. Drivers, Chauffeurs, Helpers, Local 639 Curtis Bros.*[8] decision, a case based on pre-Landrum-Griffin law, the Supreme Court held that peaceful picketing by a union to compel the employer to grant recognition is not union conduct which restrains or coerces employees under Section 8(b)(1)(A).[9] Congress had, prior to 1959, authorized the Board to regulate peaceful recognition picketing only to the extent that it violated Section 8(b)(4)[10] and had not barred such picketing in situations where there was no union or no certification.

In 1959, Congress enacted Section 8(b)(7)[11] as part of the Landrum-Griffin amendments to more specifically deal with the issue of recognition and organizational picketing. In debates leading up to the 1959 amendments, members of Congress expressed considerable concern over perceived abuses in recognition and organizational picketing. Under prior law, a union could threaten to picket and picket if an employer refused its request for recognition. Such picketing might, in addition to affecting employees, cause truck drivers employed by suppliers or customers of the picketed employer to refuse to cross the picket line to make pickups or deliveries. Some referred to such picketing as "blackmail recognition picketing,"[12] especially when conducted at times when the union represented few employees. Unless the employer complied with the recognition request, harm to its business

[7] 29 U.S.C. § 158(b)(4)(C).

[8] NLRB v. Drivers, Chauffeurs, Helpers, Local Union No. 639, 362 U.S. 274 (1960).

[9] 29 U.S.C. § 158(b)(1).

[10] 29 U.S.C. § 158(b)(4).

[11] 29 U.S.C. § 158(b)(7).

[12] 105 Cong. Rec. 14347 (1959) (Remarks of Cong. Griffin).

could result. Because it is illegal under Section 8(a)(2)[13] for an employer to voluntarily recognize a union which does not enjoy majority support,[14] this put the employer in a difficult position. Thus, there was an interest in limiting such picketing, although a total ban could have interfered with significant Section 7 rights to form, join or assist labor organizations and to strike. Section 8(b)(7) of the current National Labor Relations Act, as amended, limits, but does not eliminate, recognition or organizational picketing. The section provides that it is a union unfair labor practice:

> to picket or cause to be picketed, or threaten to picket or cause to be picketed, any employer where an object thereof is forcing or requiring an employer to recognize or bargain with a labor organization as the representatives of his employees, or forcing or requiring the employees of an employer to accept or select such labor organization as their collective bargaining representative, unless such labor organization is currently certified as the representative of such employees:
>
> (A) where the employer has lawfully recognized in accordance with this Act any other labor organization and a question concerning representation may not appropriately be raised under Section 9(c) of this Act.
>
> (B) where within the preceding twelve months a valid election under Section 9(c) of this Act has been conducted, or
>
> (C) where such picketing has been conducted without a petition under Section 9(c) being filed within a reasonable period of time not to exceed thirty days from the commencement of such picketing: Provided, that when such a petition has been filed the Board shall forthwith, without regard to the provisions of Section 9(c)(1) or the absence of a showing of a substantial interest on the part of the labor organization, direct an election in such unit as the Board finds to be appropriate and shall certify the results thereof:
>
> Provided further, That nothing in this subparagraph (C) shall be construed to prohibit any picketing or other publicity for the purpose of truthfully advising the public (including consumers) that an employer does not employ members of, or have a contract with, a labor organization, unless an effect of such picketing is to induce any individual

[13] 29 U.S.C. § 158(a)(2).

[14] *See generally* International Ladies' Garment Workers' Union, AFL CIO v. NLRB (Bernhard-Altmann), 366 U.S. 731 (1961).

employed by any other person in the course of his employment, not to pick up, deliver or transport any goods or not to perform any services.

Nothing in this paragraph shall be construed to permit any act which would otherwise be an unfair labor practice under this section 8(b).[15]

The section's language has led to litigation over the definition of most of its terms. Chief among the issues addressed was the definition of picketing,[16] the mode of analysis used to determine whether recognition is "an object" of picketing,[17] the specific application of the language of subsections (A),[18] (B),[19] and (C),[20] and the NLRB's application and interpretation of the unclear language of the expedited election[21] and publicity provisos[22] to subsection (C). Finally, employee participation in an organizational strike is a protected activity and the intersection of this protection with employer efforts to replace strikers must be explored.[23]

Under NLRB Statements of Procedure and Rules and Regulations, the NLRB is to give charges filed under Section 8(b)(7) priority treatment.[24] If neither the union nor the employer file an election petition and if the regional office finds reasonable cause to issue a complaint, the NLRB is to apply for injunctive relief in federal court under Section 10(1)[25] of the NLRA.[26] Violations of Section 8(b)(4)(C)[27] are subject to priority handling and federal court injunctive relief as well. In addition, violations of Section 8(b)(4) can be grounds for a damages suit under Section 303 of the NLRA.[28]

---

[15] 29 U.S.C. § 158(b)(7).

[16] *See infra* § 6.3.

[17] *See infra* § 6.4.

[18] *See infra* § 6.5.

[19] *See infra* § 6.6.

[20] *See infra* § 6.7.

[21] *See infra* § 6.7[C].

[22] *See infra* § 6.7[D].

[23] *See infra* § 6.8.

[24] *See* 29 CFR § 102.95.

[25] 29 U.S.C. § 160(1).

[26] *See* 29 CFR § 101.37.

[27] 29 U.S.C. § 158(b)(4)(C).

[28] 29 U.S.C. § 187.

§ 6.3 What Is Picketing

The statute makes it illegal for a union under certain specific circumstances to picket an employer, cause it to be picketed, or threaten to picket if an object of such picketing is recognition. The statute does not specifically define the term "picket."

The line between forbidden "picketing" and other activity is not usually an issue. Most often, when a union seeks to force the employer to grant recognition or to encourage support from employees, it sends its message by means of persons patrolling in front of a business entrance while carrying signs, thus meeting the generally understood definition of picketing. Issues of definition can arise, however, if there are signs but no patrolling, or if patrolling is carried out without signs. Legal analysis turns on the messages being sent and received. Generally, picketing is found where union representatives or striking employees place picket signs in a snowbank and wait nearby in a car, coming out to talk to persons seeking to enter the premises.[29]

A large group of strikers milling in front of an entrance also can send a message to customers and others to stay away from a business even if they do not carry or post signs. This can be held to be "picketing" as well.[30]

§ 6.4 What Constitutes an Object of Recognition or Organization

[A]—Generally

The most important question to be answered about picketing for purposes of this chapter concerns the object of such picketing. Section 8(b)(7) makes certain picketing illegal only "where an object thereof is forcing or requiring an employer to recognize or bargain with a labor organization as the representative of his employees, or forcing or requiring the employees of an employer to accept or select such labor organization as their collective bargaining representative."[31] Picketing for other purposes does not violate Section 8(b)(7).

---

[29] *See* Teamsters Local 182 (Woodward Motors Inc.), 135 NLRB 851 (1962), *enforced,* 314 F.2d 53 (2d Cir. 1963).

[30] *See, e.g.,* Mine Workers District 30 (Elkhorn Min. Co.), 163 NLRB 562 (1967); Stoltze Land & Lumber Co., 156 NLRB 388 (1965).

[31] 29 U.S.C. § 158(b)(7).

In its 1962 *International Hod Carriers, Local 840 (Blinne Constr.)*[32] decision, the National Labor Relations Board held that, because of its structure and language, Section 8(b)(7) prohibits picketing only where recognition or organization is established as an object. The Board stated that "subparagraphs (A), (B) and (C) are subordinate to and controlled by the opening phrases of Section 8(b)(7)."[33] It further stated that "the thrust of all the Section 8(b)(7) provisions is only upon picketing for an object of recognition or organization and not upon picketing for other objects."[34]

Thus, a union may picket despite the incumbency of another representative, may picket within 12 months of a valid election and may picket for more than 30 days without filing a petition for election so long as its picketing is *not* motivated by an organizational or recognitional object.

On the other hand, recognition or organization need only be *an* object of the picketing to bring it within the reach of Section 8(b)(7). It need not be the sole object. To determine if recognition or organization is an object of picketing, the Board looks at the totality of facts and circumstances.[35] The question of object is treated as a question of fact,[36] with the party alleging a violation bearing the burden of establishing a forbidden object.[37] To prove a violation, it need only be shown that one object of the picketing was recognition.[38] Language on picket signs can be relevant as can the union's prior actions. Statements of purpose by union officials and picketers, as well as disclaimers of recognitional objective made contemporaneously with the picketing can be important.[39] Questions as to the union's objectives in picketing arise most frequently in cases involving so-called "area standards" picketing and cases involving picketing which is allegedly for the purpose of protesting employer unfair labor practices.

[B]—Area Standards Picketing

Area standards picketing occurs when a union pickets a nonunion employer to protest that employer's paying its employees wages and

---

32 International Hod Carriers, Local 840 (Blinne Constr.), 135 NLRB 1153 (1962) (supplemental decision).

33 135 NLRB at 1159.

34 *Id.*

35 United Furniture Workers (Jamestown Sterling Corp.), 146 NLRB 474, 478 (1964).

36 Plumbers Local 741 (Keith Riggs Plumbing), 137 NLRB 1125 (1962).

37 Automobile Workers Local 259 (Fanelli Ford), 133 NLRB 1468 (1961).

38 Stage Employees, IATSE Local 15 (Albatross Productions), 275 NLRB 744 (1985).

39 Machinists Local 1173 (Alhambra Motors), 266 NLRB 91, 93 (1983).

benefits below the standard paid by unionized establishments. It is considered to be outside the reach of Section 8(b)(7) so long as the purpose of such picketing is to induce the picketed employer into raising its wage and benefits levels to those of unionized employers. Raising such wage and benefits levels can help eliminate any competitive advantage enjoyed by the nonunion employer and, thus, provides a motive other than recognition.

Such picketing may deter consumers from patronizing picketed retailers and can affect operations at a construction site. Even if the picketing continues for more than 30 days or causes persons to refuse to work or make deliveries, it is not illegal under Section 8(b)(7) in the absence of an organizational or recognitional objective.[40]

If Section 8(b)(7) charges are filed by the employer, the Board will look at the facts on a case-by-case basis to determine whether the asserted object, that of protesting wages and benefits falling below area standards, is a cloak for a recognitional or an organizational objective.

If union officials state that picketers will leave only if recognition is granted, or if the picket signs themselves disclose a recognitional objective, Section 8(b)(7) applies. In less obvious cases, the Board may consider relevant whether the union has picketed other below-standard employers,[41] whether the union has inquired of the employer as to its wage and benefits standards and whether the union is otherwise aware of the employer's standards. If the union does not even know the level of wages and benefits paid by the employer, it is unlikely that picketing is for the object of protesting such wages, and likely that a Section 8(b)(7) violation will be found.[42]

The union will want to establish that its claims of substandard wages and benefits are made in good faith[43] and based on reliable evidence[44] acquired from an investigation of conditions existing when the picketing was initiated.[45]

---

[40] *See, e.g.*, Houston Bldg. & Constr. Trades (Claude Everett Construction), 136 NLRB 321 (1962).

[41] Penny Constr. Co., 144 NLRB 1298 (1963).

[42] *See* Better Home Deliveries, 274 NLRB 164 (1985).

[43] San Francisco Local Joint Executive Board of Culinary Workers, 207 NLRB 199 (1973).

[44] Service Hospital Employees Union, Local 399 (Modern Maintenance Co.), 206 NLRB 889, (1973).

[45] Carpenters Local No. 1622 (Paul E. Iacona Structural Engineers, Inc.), 250 NLRB 416 (1980). The Court of Appeals for the Sixth Circuit has described this as a "heavy burden." NLRB v. Great Scot, 39 F.3d 678 (6th Cir. 1994).

The Board also will find relevant the question of whether the union has advised the employer that it disclaims any recognitional objective.[46] Finally, to avoid the label of recognition picketing, a union should limit its requests to asking the employer to bring its general wage and benefits costs up to area standards rather than asking the employer to bargain over specific terms. If the union demands specific allocations of wages and benefits or demands adoption of specific employment practices usually found in its collective bargaining agreements, its objectives can be found to be recognitional and, therefore, covered by Section 8(b)(7).[47]

Even if a recognitional objective is found, peaceful picketing not violating subsections (A) (incumbent representative and question of representation cannot be raised) or (B) (within 12 months of valid election) may continue under subsection (C) for a reasonable period not to exceed 30 days without filing a petition. Further, if the picketing meets the limitations of the second proviso to subsection (C) because it is merely informational picketing, it may continue indefinitely without filing a petition.[48]

[C]—Picketing to Protest Unfair Labor Practices

In its 1962 *International Hod Carriers, Local 840 (Blinne Constr.)*[49] decision, the Board dealt with the issue of picketing to protest employer unfair labor practices. This case, one of the first to interpret Section 8(b)(7), has set the tone for interpreting its scope and limits. The case addresses issues concerning picketing for the dual motive of recognition and protesting unfair labor practices, as well as picketing solely to protest unfair labor practices.

The facts in *Blinne* are straightforward. Three laborers at a jobsite, a majority of the workforce, signed union authorization cards. The union then demanded recognition. The employer refused to recognize the union and threatened to destroy the majority by transferring one of the laborers. The threat was carried out 5 days later. The union, which was not the certified representative, began and continued picketing for more than 30 days without

---

[46] *See* Hunts Point Elec. Wiring, 271 NLRB 1580 (1984).

[47] *See* NLRB v. Retail Clerks International Ass'n, Local Union No. 899, AFL CIO, 404 F.2d 855 (9th Cir. 1968), *enforcing* 166 NLRB 818 (1967); NLRB v. IBEW Local 265, 604 F.2d 1091 (8th Cir. 1979). *See also* Teamsters Local 456 (Construction City), 233 NLRB 418 (1977) (insistence on point-by-point contract terms shows recognitional objective).

[48] *See infra* § 6.7[D].

[49] International Hod Carriers, Local 840 (Blinne Constr.), 135 NLRB 1153 (1962) (supplemental decision).

filing a representation petition. Picketing was peaceful and conducted by one picketer carrying a sign which stated: "C.A. Blinne Construction Company, Unfair." The announced objectives of the picketing were recognition, payment of Davis-Bacon scale wages, and protest of unfair labor practices. Unfair labor practice charges were filed.

The General Counsel argued that the union violated Section 8(b)(7)(C) because an object of the picketing was recognition, the union was not certified, and no petition for representation had been filed within 30 days of commencing picketing. The union argued that Section 8(b)(7)(C) was not intended to apply to picketing by a majority union and, further, that the employer's unfair labor practices excused the union from filing a timely representation petition.

The Board disagreed with the union's first argument, that picketing by a majority union cannot be unlawful. It viewed the statutory scheme as one designed to resolve issues of majority status by election whenever possible, contrasting the difficulties of determining majority status by other means. The Board also noted that the statute, by its explicit terms, seemed to exempt only "currently certified" unions from its rules. Thus, even if a picketing but unrecognized union could prove support by a majority of unit employees, it could still violate Section 8(b)(7).

The Board also disagreed with the union's argument that employer unfair labor practices are a defense to a Section 8(b)(7)(C) violation. The Board first held that Congress meant to require a representation petition to be filed within a reasonable period, not to exceed 30 days, so that a prompt election could be held. Although the Board recognized that unremedied employer unfair labor practices can prevent a free and fair election from being held, it did not regard this as an unresolvable dilemma. Instead, the Board held it would continue to follow its usual practice of holding representation cases in abeyance pending resolution of serious unfair labor practice charges. Therefore, requiring a union to file a timely petition does not keep it from protesting the unfair labor practice. Once the union files a petition, further picketing would no longer violate the statutory injunction against continued picketing without filing a petition. Further, filing a prompt petition would not force the Board to hold an election tainted by unfair labor practices because, under its "blocking charge" practices, the NLRB will hold the petition in abeyance pending resolution of the charges. Groundless charges can be quickly dropped and an election held. More substantial charges can be resolved before any election is held.

The *Blinne Construction* opinion limits the reach of organizational picketing by encouraging resort to the election process. It holds, in effect, that a union seeking recognition continues to be obliged to file a representation petition even if it also seeks to protest alleged unfair labor practices. *Blinne Construction* also clarifies the statute with regard to the scope and meaning of its "object" limitation and its limitation of the subsection (C) provisos.[50]

Picketing solely for the purpose of protesting unfair labor practices and not with an object of recognition will not violate Section 8(b)(7).[51] With regard to the issue of picketing to protest unfair labor practices, the *Blinne Construction* Board clearly stated that had the charged union "confined its picketing to these objectives rather than, as it did, include a demand for recognition, we believe none of the provisions of Section 8(b)(7) would be applicable."[52] By footnote,[53] the Board noted legislative history indicating that Congress did not intend to outlaw picketing against unfair labor practices where there was no evidence of an organizational, recognition or bargaining purpose and disavowed its earlier *Lewis Food Co.*[54] analysis that a strike to compel reinstatement of a discharged employee was necessarily a strike to force recognition and bargaining. The Board acknowledged that "in the long view all union activity including strikes and picketing, has the ultimate economic objective of organization and bargaining"[55] but recognized that Congress had drawn a "sharp distinction"[56] between recognition and organizational picketing and other types of picketing. In the same footnote, the Board noted that a cease and desist order against picketing violating Section 8(b)(7) should enjoin "only picketing for recognition, bargaining or organization and will not be a bar to picketing against unfair labor practices."[57]

Thus, even a union which has lost a representation election and is within the proscribed 12-month period may theoretically continue picketing if its object is not one of recognition but, rather, to protest unfair labor practices.

---

[50] *See infra* § 6.7.

[51] *See* UAW, Local 259 (Fanelli Ford Sales, Inc.), 133 N.L.R.B. 1468 (1961) (protesting employee discharge does not violate Section 8(b)(7)(C)).

[52] 135 NLRB at 1167, 1168.

[53] 135 NLRB at 1168.

[54] Lewis Food Co., 115 NLRB 890 (1956).

[55] International Hod Carriers, Local 840 (Blinne Constr.), 135 NLRB at 1168.

[56] 135 NLRB at 1168 n.29.

[57] 135 NLRB at 1168.

The Board will look carefully, however, to determine whether such picketing is a subterfuge for recognition or organization. For example, even if the union files timely charges with the NLRB and even if picket signs clearly protest unfair labor practices, a recognitional objective may be found if it continues picketing after the Regional Office has dismissed the charges as without merit.[58]

§ 6.5 Applying Section 8(b)(7)(A)

Under subsection (A), picketing or threatening to picket with an object of organization or recognition is illegal "where the employer has lawfully recognized in accordance with this Act any other labor organization and a question concerning representation may not appropriately be raised under Section 9(c) of this Act."[59]

In effect, subsection (A) furthers the Act's policies of protecting labor stability and encouraging peaceful resolution of organizational issues through the NLRB's election mechanism. Employers in a bargaining relationship with an incumbent union are protected from recognition picketing whether the incumbent union was voluntarily recognized[60] or attained representative status through an election. Because a "question concerning representation" cannot be raised within one year after a certification[61] or during the term of a collective bargaining agreement of up to three years,[62] recognition picketing may not take place at these times either.

Even if the picketing does not violate subsection (A) because the employer's recognition of the incumbent was not lawful or because the picketing is conducted at times when an election petition can be filed, it will still be subject to the time limitations of subsection (C).

§ 6.6 Applying Section 8(b)(7)(B)

As noted above, an incumbent union relationship is protected from picketing during times when a petition cannot be filed, including times

[58] *See* Waiters Local 500 (Mission Valley Inn), 140 NLRB 433 (1963).

[59] 29 U.S.C. § 157(b)(7)(A).

[60] This assumes that the voluntary recognition was lawful. If the union did not have majority support at the time of recognition, such recognition would not be lawful even if the union later achieved the support of a majority. *See* International Ladies' Garment Workers' Union AFL-CIO NLRB (Bernhard-Altmann), 366 U.S. 731 (1961).

[61] 29 U.S.C. § 159(c)(3).

[62] *See* General Cable Corp., 139 NLRB 1123 (1962).

within the year following certification. Where the union has lost an election, the employer is protected by subsection (B) which forbids picketing or threats to picket for recognition or organizational purposes "where within the preceding twelve months a valid election under section 9(c) of this Act has been conducted."[63]

Through subsection (B), Congress provides the employer and employees a 12-month period during which they are insulated from recognition or organizational picketing and from further elections. Section 8(b)(7)(B) insulates the employer from picketing and furthers the policy behind Section 9(c)(3),[64] which provides that the National Labor Relations Board cannot conduct an election within 12 months of a valid election. As with subsection (A), this limitation allows picketing only at times when an election can be held. The 12-month period runs from the date of the certification of results of the election rather than the date of actual voting.[65]

The major limitation on this subsection is the same placed on Section 9(c)(3). It only applies to the period 12 months after a "valid" election, thus enabling a picketing union to defend its picketing based on the alleged invalidity of the election.

Section 8(b)(7)(B) also applies to picketing by former incumbent unions which have lost their representative status. In its 1991 decision in *Teamsters Local 812 v. NLRB*,[66] the Court of Appeals for the District of Columbia Circuit upheld a Board ruling that a former incumbent union which continued to engage in economic strike picketing after losing a decertification election violated Section 8(b)(7)(B). Although the union argued that Section 8(b)(7)(B) was not intended to reach picketing by a recognized union in support of a peaceful economic strike, the Board and the Court of Appeals rejected this argument. Citing *NLRB v. Lawrence Typographical Union No. 570*,[67] a Tenth Circuit case, the court noted that a union losing an election loses its status as incumbent. Further, to allow it to use picketing as a pressure tactic to help regain the status it lost at the ballot box would permit it to destabilize the situation at a time when Section 9(c)(3)[68] would not allow an election for 12 months. The court also rejected the union's

63 29 U.S.C. § 158(b)(7)(B).

64 29 U.S.C. § 159(c)(3).

65 *See* Retail Clerks, Local 692 (Irvins Inc.), 134 NLRB 686 (1961).

66 Teamsters Local 812 v. NLRB, 937 F.2d 684 (D.C. Cir. 1991).

67 402 F.2d 452 (10th Cir. 1968).

68 29 U.S.C. § 159(c)(3).

argument that application of Section 8(b)(7)(B) to the case violated the First Amendment.

The Board reached a similar result in its 1991 decision in *Graphic Communications Local I-M (Heinrich Envelope Corp.).*[69] The NLRB held that, although pre-election picketing was privileged by the union's then-incumbent status, post-election picketing violated Section 8(b)(7)(B) because it occurred within 12 months of a valid election. The Board held that, based on the failure to change the signs and the failure of the union to make any contemporaneous indication to the employer that its purpose in picketing had changed, the pre-election objective of forcing bargaining was carried over and, hence, was illegal. Thus, while it is theoretically possible for the purpose of picketing to change from economic strike picketing with a bargaining objective to picketing for the purpose of protesting employer unfair labor practices, such a shift in purpose is difficult to prove. Unless the union clearly communicates its new objective and disclaims a bargaining objective, and unless it takes steps consistent with a changed objective such as changing the wording of picket signs, its arguments will have little weight.

§ 6.7 Applying Section 8(b)(7)(C)

[A]—Generally

The major change implemented by the 1959 addition of Section 8(b)(7) to the National Labor Relations Act was the enactment of subsection (C). Subsection (C) substantially limits organizational and recognition picketing by making it illegal

> where such picketing has been conducted without a petition under Section 9(c) being filed within a reasonable period of time not to exceed thirty days from the commencement of such picketing: Provided, That when such a petition has been filed the Board shall forthwith, without regard to the provisions of section 9(c)(1) or the absence of a showing of a substantial interest on the part of the labor organization, direct an election

[69] Graphic Communications Local I-M (Heinrich Envelope Corp.), 305 NLRB 603 (1991). There, the union began an economic strike which included picketing on December 5, 1989. On January 9, 1991, it lost a decertification election and filed unfair labor practice charges. Picketing ceased on January 9 but picket signs were left in the ground. Union representatives then picketed from February 5 to February 8, 1991, at which time the union learned that its unfair labor practice charges would be dismissed. Picket signs continued to bear "strike" language.

in such unit as the Board finds to be appropriate and shall certify the results thereof: Provided further, That nothing in this subparagraph (C) shall be construed to prohibit any picketing or other publicity for the purpose of truthfully advising the public (including consumers) that an employer does not employ members of, or have a contract with, a labor organization, unless an effect of such picketing is to induce any individual employed by any other person in the course of his employment, not to pick up, deliver or transport any goods or not to perform any services.[70]

It is important to note that subsection (C) does not absolutely prohibit recognition picketing or recognition strikes. It limits only recognition picketing conducted for more than a reasonable period without an election petition having been filed. Once an election petition is filed, picketing may generally continue even if it continues for longer than 30 days.

A recent case applying subparagraph (C) is *Stadium Hotel Partners, Inc.*[71] There, the Board upheld a Section 8(b)(7)(C) charge filed by the purchaser of a hotel which had been picketed for more than 30 days. Although the union argued that it had resumed picketing after a hiatus solely to protest substandard wages and benefits, the Board found that its organizational objective carried over. The union's picket signs did not uniformly mention substandard wages, the union had not picketed other hotels over substandard wages or benefits, and other circumstantial evidence pointed to an organizational motive.

If a union pickets in violation of Section 8(b)(7)(C), the National Labor Relations Board may seek a federal court injunction under Section 10(1) of the Act.[72] To obtain an injunction, the Regional Director need only prove reasonable cause exists to believe that the elements of an unfair labor practice are present and that the legal theory upon which the case is based is "substantial and not frivolous."[73]

The federal district court is limited to determining whether the facts, taken in the light most favorable to petitioner, might support a conclusion that an unfair labor practice has occurred.[74] This standard was applied by the

---

[70] 29 U.S.C. § 158(b)(7)(C).

[71] Local Union No. 274, Hotel Employees Restaurant Employees International Union (Stadium Hotel Partners, Inc.), 314 NLRB 982 (1994).

[72] 29 U.S.C. § 160(l).

[73] *See* Hirsch Building Construction Trades Counsel of Philadelphia, 530 F.2d 298 (3d Cir. 1976).

[74] *See* Lewis ILA Local 1497, 724 F.2d 1109 (5th Cir. 1984).

U.S. District Court for the Eastern District of Pennsylvania in its 1993 *Hirsch v. Hotel Restaurant Employees* decision.[75] The judge issued an injunction based on evidence that union picketers of a nonunion hotel carried signs reading "scab-hotel" which made no mention of area wage standards and shouted slogans such as "union yes; scabs no." The court concluded that the union's picketing, which continued for more than 30 days without a petition being filed, had the purpose of forcing the hotel to recognize or bargain with the union.[76]

[B]—What is a "Reasonable Period"

The statute specifically limits the duration of recognition picketing where no petition has been filed to "a reasonable period of time not to exceed 30 days from the commencement of such picketing."[77] The union does not, however, have an absolute right to picket for 30 days without filing a petition. If the union has engaged in picket line violence, for example, the Board may hold picketing of less than 30 days duration to be unreasonably long due to the potential impact of the violence on the election process.[78] Such picketing could then be enjoined.[79] If, however, the employer has also committed numerous unfair labor practices during the same period, the NLRB may not always shorten the period considered reasonable for picketing.[80]

---

[75] Hirsch v. Local 274, Hotel Restaurant Employees, 144 LRRM (BMA) (2594 (E.D. Pa. 1993).

[76] The union then stopped picketing for 36 hours and resumed its picketing with signs explicitly referring only to area wage standards. In a subsequent NLRB suit for contempt based on the earlier injunction, the District Court ruled that the NLRB had failed to prove by clear and convincing evidence that the purpose of the continued picketing was to force recognition. Finding the standard for holding a party in contempt much higher than that for issuing an injunction under Section 10(l), the court did grant the Board injunctive relief, ordering a hiatus in all picketing for 45 days to allow any subsequent area standards picketing to be cleansed of the taint of the earlier unlawful conduct. Hirsch v. Local 274, Hotel & Restaurant Employees, 145 LRRM 2450 (E.D. Pa. 1994). For another perspective on whether area standards picketing is outside the proviso of 8(b)(7)(C), see Samuel D. Rosen, *Area Standards Picketing*, 23 Lab. L.J. 67 (1972).

[77] 29 U.S.C. § 158(b)(7)(C).

[78] *See* Eastern Camera, 141 NLRB 991 (1963); Laborers' Union Local 1184 (Cates Constr.), 296 NLRB 1325 (1989). In addition, unlawful actions by the union may diminish its chances of obtaining a bargaining order based on unlawful employer conduct. *See* Daniel Finley Allen & Co., 303 NLRB 123 (1991).

[79] *See* Cuneo v. United Shoe Workers, 181 F. Supp 324 (D. N.J. 1960).

[80] *See* Daniel Finley Allen & Co., 303 NLRB 846 (1991).

[C]—The Expedited Election Proviso

The first proviso to subsection (C) states:

> Provided, that when such a petition has been filed the Board shall forthwith, without regard to the provisions of section 9(c)(1) or the absence of a showing of a substantial interest on the part of the labor organization, direct an election in such unit as the Board finds to be appropriate and shall certify the results thereof.[81]

The National Labor Relations Board has interpreted this proviso to allow an employer faced with recognition picketing or the threat thereof to file a Section 8(b)(7)(C) charge and a petition for an expedited election. Thus, if the picketing union has filed a petition and the employer files a Section 8(b)(7)(C) charge, or if the employer files both a charge and its own petition, an expedited election may be held.

The NLRB Statements of Procedures and Rules and Regulations provide in Section 101.23[82] that a representation petition filed in connection with a Section 8(b)(7) charge will be handled under an expedited procedure when investigation of the charge reveals that the employer's operations affect commerce, picketing is being conducted for a proscribed object, subsection (C) applies to the picketing, and the petition has been filed within 30 days of the commencement of picketing. A member of the Regional Director's staff will investigate the petition to determine the appropriate unit and whether an election will further the policies of the National Labor Relations Act. If the Regional Director determines an election is warranted, the Regional Director may direct an election in an appropriate unit without conducting a hearing. The director will then set the place, date and hours of balloting as well as the basis for eligibility of voters. If the Regional Director believes a hearing necessary on issues raised by the petition, a hearing may be held but the parties will not file briefs. Under Sections 101.24[83] and 102.75,[84] the Section 8(b)(7) charge which was held in

---

[81] 29 U.S.C. § 158(b)(7)(C).

[82] 29 CFR § 101.23.

[83] 29 CFR § 101.24.

[84] 29 CFR § 102.75. Under 29 CFR Sec. 102.95, whenever a Section 8(b)(7) charge is filed, the regional office is to give the case priority treatment. The above provisions apply only where a petition for election has been filed. If no petition is filed, the NLRB investigation is to be conducted with priority and, if reasonable cause to issue a complaint is found, the NLRB will apply for injunctive relief in federal court under Section 10(l) of the NLRA, 29 U.S.C. § 160(l), unless a complaint-worthy Section 8(a)(2) charge has been filed. *See* 29 CFR § 101.37.

abeyance pending investigation of the petition will then be dismissed upon issuance of the direction of election. A complaint will not be issued.

Thus, if a union pickets for recognition, the employer may obtain an election by filing a charge under Section 8(b)(7) and by filing its own petition for representation. Under NLRB rules, the employer need not assert that the union has made a claim to be recognized as the exclusive representative of the employees in the unit claimed to be appropriate.[85] If the NLRB views the charge as having merit, an election can be conducted with the appropriateness of the unit and voter eligibility being determined by the Regional Director without a hearing. In addition, the union is not required to make a showing of substantial interest in the form of authorization cards.[86]

[D]—The Publicity Proviso

Even recognition picketing which continues beyond 30 days without a petition being filed may be legal if it complies with the provisions of subsection (C)'s publicity proviso. The proviso states:

> Provided further, That nothing in this subparagraph shall be construed to prohibit any picketing or other publicity for the purpose of truthfully advising the public (including consumers) that an employer does not employ members of, or have a contract with, a labor organization, unless an effect of such picketing is to induce any individual employed by any other person in the course of his employment, not to pick up, deliver or transport any goods or not to perform any services.[87]

The publicity proviso applies only to picketing which otherwise violates Section 8(b)(7)(C) and does not protect picketing forbidden by subparagraphs (A) and (B). The proviso permits picketing for an indefinite period so long as its message and its impact are limited.[88] This is so even if the

[85] 29 CFR §§ 101.23, 102.76.

[86] Thus, recognition picketing which causes the employer to file a charge and petition for an election can allow a union to obtain an election even though it could not have obtained one on its own for lack of sufficient authorization cards to show substantial interest.

[87] 29 U.S.C. § 158(b)(7)(C).

[88] In its NLRB v. Local 3, IBEW, 317 F.2d 193 (2d Cir. 1963), decision, the Court of Appeals for the Second Circuit reviewed a Board order finding that a union had violated Section 8(b)(7)(C) by picketing to protest the award of work to a non-union construction subcontractor and seeking to have the work awarded to a subcontractor which employed its members. In remanding the case to the Board, the court interpreted the publicity proviso. It determined that, under the "purpose" language in the publicity proviso to Section

union's object in picketing is to obtain recognition. (If the union did not have a recognitional object, Section 8(b)(7) would not apply at all and there would be no need to seek protection under the proviso.) This issue was addressed in *Smitley, d/b/a Crown Cafeteria v. NLRB.*[89] In that case, the court reviewed a Board finding involving a union that picketed a cafeteria for more than 30 days without filing a petition with an object of securing recognition. The picketing did not stop deliveries or services and was for the purpose of truthfully advising the public that the employer had no contract with the union and employed non-union employees. After reviewing legislative history, the court held that the proviso would be meaningless unless it protected picketing with an object of recognition because it would otherwise be referring to conduct not prohibited by Section 8(b)(7). What is protected is a truthful appeal to consumers that does not ask organized labor or other unionized employees for a response. If deliveries or pickups are stopped, the Board will apply a "substantial impact" test to determine whether informational picketing will fall outside the proviso. If refusals are few and isolated, they may not necessarily cause the picketing to be outside the proviso's protection if they do not disrupt, interfere with or curtail the employer's business.[90] To avoid problems, unions generally confine picketing to public or consumer entrances and to times when the picketed business is open to the public. To be within the proviso's protection, picket signs should address the public and not employees or delivery personnel. The signs will often be worded in the language of the proviso.

§ 6.8 Employee Rights and the Protected Status of Organizational Picketing and Strikes

[A]—In General

Employees engaged in recognition picketing or a strike for the purpose of obtaining recognition are engaged in protected concerted activity. Thus, an employer can violate Section 8(a)(1)[91] by interfering with, restraining or coercing employees engaged in a recognition strike.

8(b)(7)(C), most picketing for publicity is protected but that after the allowed reasonable period, signal picketing asking for an organized economic response from labor is barred as is publicity picketing which goes beyond the limited information specifically allowed by the proviso.

[89] 327 F.2d 351 (9th Cir. 1964).

[90] *See* Retail Clerks Local 324 (Barker Brothers), 138 NLRB 478 (1962), *enforced*, 328 F.2d 431 (9th Cir. 1964).

[91] 29 U.S.C. § 158(a)(1).

[B]—Rights of Organizational Strikers

Employees engaged in a legal recognition strike have the same rights as other strikers. In its 1991 *Fun Connection* decision,[92] the Board held that the employer violated the National Labor Relations Act by threatening to discharge strikers if they did not return to work and cease their demands for union recognition. It also violated the Act by later discharging them. Furthermore, the employer violated the Act by requiring temporarily replaced strikers to sign statements withdrawing their union authorization cards before they could return to work. These unfair labor practices warranted issuance of a bargaining order.

On the other hand, picketing which violates Section 8(b)(7) may not be protected. The employer may not legally be obliged to reinstate strikers engaged in an illegal recognition strike.[93]

A recognition strike generally is considered to be an economic strike, and the employer may be able to hire and retain permanent replacements for strikers in the absence of proof that the strike was really for the purpose of protesting employer unfair labor practices.[94] If the employees were only temporarily replaced, the employer must reinstate strikers upon their unconditional offer to return.[95] In its 1991 *Daniel Finley Allen*[96] decision, the Board decided that a union which had been neither certified nor recognized could make a valid offer to return to work on behalf of recognition strikers. Rejecting the employer's argument that the union had no representative status, the Board ruled that the union's offer to return to work on behalf of all striking employees was effective because employees had signed authorization cards and participated in a strike supervised by the union. This, in the Board's view, created an agency relationship which empowered the union to make the offer. The employer's refusal to accept the offer exposed it to back pay and reinstatement liability.

An employer can also violate the Act by filing retaliatory lawsuits against unions engaging in lawful recognitional picketing. In *Geske & Sons*,[97] for

---

[92] Fun Connection, 302 NLRB 740 (1991).

[93] *See* Claremont Polychemical Corp., 196 NLRB 613 (1972).

[94] *See infra* § 9.5.

[95] *See infra* § 9.5[B].

[96] Daniel Finley Allen Co., 303 NLRB 846 (1991).

[97] Geske & Sons, 317 NLRB 28 (1995) (the Board did not find it necessary to reach the issue of whether the suit was also groundless because it was preempted by federal law).

example, the Board held that an employer violated Section 8(a)(1) of the Act by filing a suit alleging trade libel and tortious interference with contractual relations against a union engaging in lawful recognition picketing. The Board viewed the suit against the union and its agents to be without a reasonable basis and motivated by a desire to retaliate against protected activity.

[C]—Access to Property Issues

A series of 1994 and 1995 Board cases address picketers' access to property in light of the Supreme Court's 1992 decision in *Lechmere, Inc. v. NLRB*[98] which upheld restrictions on union organizers' access to private property. In *Leslie Homes,*[99] union representatives sought to pass out area standards handbills in front of the employer's model homes. A Board majority held that *Lechmere,* a case involving union organizational activity, could be applied to area standards picketing and handbilling and that, absent unique obstacles that frustrate union access to employees or customers, the employer is entitled to bar union non-employees from its property.

In a similar case,[100] the Board held that the operator of a store and a mall owner did not violate the Act by restricting access to its property and barring non-employee area standards handbillers and picketers seeking to induce a consumer boycott.

The Board has also determined that the Supreme Court's *Lechmere* decision does not eliminate the "discrimination" exception to general rules for nonemployee access. If the employer or property owner discriminatorily applies its no-access rules against unions and their messages, such rules may not be enforceable. Thus, in *Riesbeck Food Markets,*[101] a Board majority held that the employer violated the law by filing state court actions to bar union Section 8(b)7(C) proviso informational picketing and handbilling from private property near its consumer entrances. The employer had permitted various charitable and civic solicitations in the past. The majority rejected the employer's argument that it could validly distinguish between

---

98 502 U.S. 527 (1992).

99 316 NLRB 123 (1995). *See* R. Wayne Estes and Adam M. Porter, Babcock/Lechmere *Revisited: Derivative Nature of Union Organizers' Right of Access to Employers' Property Should Impact Judicial Evaluation of Alternatives*, 48 SMU L. Rev. 349 (1995).

100 Makro Inc., 316 NLRB 109 (1995). *See also* Oakland Mall, 316 NLRB 1160 (1995); L'Enfant Plaza Properties, 316 NLRB 169 (1995).

101 314 NLRB 940 (1994).

charitable organization activity and activity which adversely affected its business.[102]

Finally, if the "area standards" picketing and handbilling violates Section 8(b)(7), it will not be a protected activity under Section 7 and the Board and courts will not have to reach the question of whether the employer's attempts to suppress it violate the Act.[103]

§ 6.9 Chapter Highlights

Section 8(b)(7) is one of the most difficult to understand provisions of the National Labor Relations Act, perhaps due to its origins as a compromise between those who wished to ban all picketing for recognition and those who wished to allow recognition picketing. Common misunderstandings can be avoided by keeping the following points in mind:

1. Section 8(b)(7) does not apply at all unless the picketing has an object of recognition or organization. Picketing purely to protest failure to observe area standards or to protest employer unfair labor practices is not reached by Section 8(b)(7) unless there is also an organizational objective. This is so even if the picketing stops deliveries or causes persons not to work. Unless, of course, the picketing constitutes a secondary boycott under Section 8(b)(4).[104] (§ 6.4)

2. Even a union seeking recognition may picket for a reasonable period of up to 30 days without filing a petition, so long as its picketing does not occur during the time lines of subsections (A) and (B), and so long as the picketing is not violent or otherwise in violation of the law. Once a petition for election is filed, the union may continue picketing up to election even when such picketing continues more than 30 days. (§§ 6.5, 6.6 and 6.7)

3. Even picketing with an organizational objective may continue indefinitely without a petition being filed if it is carefully tailored to fall within the publicity proviso to subsection 8(b)(7)(C). The proviso does not, however, protect picketing that violates 8(b)(7)(A) or 8(b)(7)(B). (§ 6.7[D])

---

102 In dissent, Members Stephens and Cohen disagreed, arguing that the employer had not discriminatorily enforced its ban on messages carrying a "do not patronize" theme.

103 *See* NLRB v. Great Scot, 39 F.3d 678 (6th Cir. 1994) (holding that picketing and handbilling at supermarket's entrance was not protected activity and that store operator could properly ask picketers to leave and request assistance of police and courts).

104 29 U.S.C. § 158(b)(4). *See infra* Chapter 11.

4. An employer faced with recognition or organizational picketing that does not violate 8(b)(7)(A) or 8(b)(7)(B) has three choices. First, it can voluntarily recognize the union after ascertaining that the union has the support of a majority of employees in the requested bargaining unit. Second, it can wait out the picketing. After a period of up to 30 days, the union must file a petition or cease picketing. Third, under the expedited election proviso to 8(b)(7)(C) and NLRB Regulations, the employer can file both an unfair labor practice charge alleging a violation of Section 8(b)(7)(C) and its own petition for election. The NLRB will conduct an expedited election which will be held much more quickly than a traditional election because there will not be delays caused by checking the level of union support or hearings to determine the appropriate unit. (§ 6.7[C])

CHAPTER 7
COLLECTIVE BARGAINING AND THE EXCLUSIVE REPRESENTATIVE

§ 7.1 Introduction

Once a collective bargaining representative has been designated or selected by the employees, the employer must recognize the representative and bargain in good faith.[1] This representative has the exclusive authority to negotiate on behalf of employees regarding wages, hours, and other terms and conditions of employment.[2]

§ 7.2 Designated or Selected

A labor organization may achieve recognition for purposes of collective bargaining in several ways. The most common way is through an election conducted by the National Labor Relations Board (Board) among employees in an appropriate unit.[3]

---

[1] Section 8(a)(5) of the Act makes it an unfair labor practice for an employer

> (5) to refuse to bargain collectively with the representatives of his employees, subject to the provisions of section 9(a).

[2] Section 8(d) of the Act provides in part as follows:

> For the purposes of this section, to bargain collectively is the performance of the mutual obligation of the employer and the representative of the employees to meet at reasonable times and confer in good faith with respect to wages, hours, and other terms and conditions of employment, or the negotiation of an agreement, or any question arising thereunder, and the execution of a written contract incorporating any agreement reached if requested by either party, but such obligation does not compel either party to agree to a proposal or require the making of a concession . . . .

[3] As the following provision shows, unit determination may be affected by a variety of factors:

> § 9
>
> . . .
>
> (b) The Board shall decide in each case whether, in order to assure to employees the fullest freedom in exercising the rights guaranteed by the Act, the unit appropriate for the purposes of collective bargaining shall be the employer unit, craft unit, plant unit, or subdivision thereof: Provided, That the Board shall not (1) decide that any unit is appropriate for such purposes if such unit includes both professional employees and employees who are not professional employees unless a majority of such professional employees vote for inclusion in such unit; or (2) decide that any craft unit is inappropriate for such purposes on the ground that a different unit has been established by a prior Board determination, unless a majority of the employees in the proposed craft unit vote against separate representation or (3) decide that any unit is appropriate for such purposes if it includes, together with other employees, any individual employed as a guard to enforce against employees and other persons rules to protect property of the employer or to protect the safety of persons on the employer's premises; but no labor organization shall be certified as the representative of employees in a bargaining unit of guards if such organization admits to membership, or is affiliated directly or indirectly with an organization which admits to membership, employees other than guards.

This method is initiated by a petition to the Board supported by at least 30% of the employees. It is the only method that leads to "certification" of the collective bargaining representative.[4] Protections against rival unions during and after the certification year,[5] and the freedom to dispute work assignments and engage in recognitional picketing distinguish the certified union.[6]

Also, as noted in Chapter 5, an employer may incur the bargaining obligation by voluntarily recognizing a union that demonstrates majority support among its employees.[7] This alternative means of establishing a legally recognized collective bargaining relationship is sanctioned under Section 9(a) of the Act giving exclusive bargaining authority to representatives "designated" or "selected" by a majority of employees in an appropriate unit.

A union may also achieve bargaining status in a third way—through a Board order. As noted in Chapter 4, the Supreme Court in *NLRB v. Gissel Packing Co.*,[8] approved the Board's use of a bargaining order to remedy pervasive unfair labor practices that have a tendency to undermine the union's majority strength and the election process. Under such an order the

---

[4] Section 9 of the Act provides:

> (c)(1) Whenever a petition shall have been filed, in accordance with such regulations as may be prescribed by the Board—
>
> (A) by an employee or group of employees or any individual or labor organization acting in their behalf alleging that a substantial number of employees (i) wish to be represented for collective bargaining and that their employer declines to recognize their representative as the representative defined in section 9(a), . . . the Board shall investigate such petition and if it has reasonable cause to believe that a question of representation affecting commerce exists shall provide for an appropriate hearing upon due notice. Such hearing may be conducted by an officer or employee or the regional office, who shall not make any recommendations with respect thereto. If the Board finds upon the record of such hearing that such a question of representation exists, it shall direct an election by secret ballot and shall certify the results thereof.

[5] *See* Section 9(c)(3) and Brooks v. NLRB, 348 U.S. 96 (1954), protecting certified unions from rival unions during the certification year. Section 8(b)(4)(C) protects the certified union from recognitional picketing by a rival union.

[6] Section 8(b)(4)(D) permits certified unions to bring economic pressure against employers who fail to comply with a Board certification in assigning work. Section 8(b)(7) permits certified unions to engage in recognitional or organizational picketing.

[7] *But see* International Ladies' Garment Workers v. NLRB (Bernhard-Altmann Texas Corp.), 366 U.S. 731 (1961) (where voluntary recognition was defeated because the union did not represent a majority of the employees at the time of recognition).

[8] 395 U.S. 575 (1969).

offending employer is required to bargain with a union demonstrating majority support, even where no election has been conducted or the union has lost the election. The Court articulated the following test for issuing a *Gissel* bargaining order:

> If the Board finds that the possibility of erasing the effects of past practices and of ensuring a fair election (or a fair rerun) by the use of traditional remedies, though present, is slight and that employee sentiment once expressed through cards would, on balance, be better protected by a bargaining order, then such an order should issue.[9]

Under any of these methods of securing recognition, the employer must bargain with the union in good faith for a reasonable time in an effort to reach an agreement. In the case of a certified union, "reasonable time" has a well-settled duration of one year, generally known as the certification year.[10] Where recognition has been voluntary or ordered, the duration of the bargaining obligation is less certain. Generally, the test is whether the bargaining process has had a fair chance to succeed, based on such factors as the good faith negotiations of the parties, the existence of an impasse, the number of issues agreed upon, whether the parties are negotiating their first agreement, and the union's conduct during negotiations.[11]

§ 7.3 Exclusivity

Recognition of a majority representative, whether voluntary or mandatory, excludes any other person or group seeking to represent the same employees regarding wages, hours, and other terms and conditions of employment.[12] This concept, known as "exclusivity," has been specifically incorporated into the Act at Section 9(a). However, before the language of that section became a part of the Act, the first Labor Board had ruled under the National Industrial Recovery Act (NIRA), the short-lived precursor to the Act, that language similar to Section 7 of the Act standing alone imposed an exclusive bargaining obligation on employers.[13] Since Section 7 essentially gives employees the right to bargain collectively through representatives of their own choosing, why was the old Labor Board moved to interpret the language as requiring exclusivity? The answer lies in the

[9] *Id.* at 614-615.

[10] *See* Brooks v. NLRB, 348 U.S. 96 (1954).

[11] *See* Brennan's Cadillac, Inc., 231 NLRB 225 (1977).

[12] *See* Section 9(a), *infra* note 42.

[13] *See* Houde Engineering Corp., 1 NLRB (old series) 35 (1934).

economics of collective bargaining. A pluralistic scheme would permit employers to use divide-and-conquer tactics, foment inter-union rivalry, and prevent the union from mounting a credible strike threat, all creating a downward pressure on wages and other conditions of employment or leading to differences between similarly-situated employees.[14] If the goal of the Act was to promote effective representation, exclusivity was a prerequisite.

Since the economics of pluralism favored employers, they tested the principles of exclusivity and majority rule early in the life of the Act. In *J.I. Case Co. v. National labor Relations Board*,[15] the manufacturer of farm machinery and war materials executed individual contracts with approximately 75% (450) of its 600 employees. The contracts contained one-year terms promising employment at a specific pay rate and hospital facilities in return for faithful and honest service, compliance with factory rules, and no payment for defective work. In 1941, a union petitioned the Board for an election among the company's production and maintenance employees. The company unsuccessfully asserted the individual contracts as a bar to the election. The union won the election, the Board certified the union as collective bargaining representative, and the company refused to bargain with the union while the individual contracts were in effect. The Board held that the company, by refusing to bargain with the union, violated Section 8(a)(5) and, derivatively, 8(a)(1) of the Act.[16]

The Supreme Court, in an essay on the relationship between individual contracts and collective bargaining agreements, likened collective agreements to overriding standards such as tariffs and utility rates governing individual entities. It also pointed out that individual contracts cannot detract from collective agreements and that individual advantages are contributed to the good of the whole under a collective bargaining regime.

---

[14] *See* Edwin G. Dolan, Basic Economics 591-598 (3d ed. 1983) (describing the impact of exclusive union representation on the competitive labor market as a matter of economic theory).

[15] 321 U.S. 332 (1944).

[16] Sections 8(a)(1) and (5) provides as follows:

§ 8(a) It shall be an unfair labor practice for an employer—

(1) to interfere with, restrain, or coerce employees in the exercise of the rights guaranteed in section 7;

. . .

(5) to refuse to bargain collectively with the representatives of his employees, subject to the provisions of section 9(a).

Following the principles laid down in *J.I. Case*, the Board and the courts have interpreted the exclusivity requirement to prevent employers from bypassing the union to negotiate directly with employees. The cases reveal the Board's primary concern to be whether the employer's conduct undermines the effectiveness of the union as representative.

For example, on the same day as *J.I. Case*, the Supreme Court decided *Order of Railroad Telegraphers v. Railway Express Agency, Inc.*[17] That case arose under the Railway Labor Act, which, like the NLRA, gives employees a right to bargaining collectively through their selected representative.[18] The union and the company had negotiated an agreement setting rates of pay for unit members. Following a restructuring of the business, a few employees received substantially greater compensation under the contractual scheme than under the old business structure. The company successfully rectified the discrepancy by negotiating directly with the individuals receiving the windfall rather than the union. Upholding the union's protest, the Court held that the terms of the individual agreements could not supersede those of the collective agreement. The Court worried that the company's interpretation would permit collective agreements to be promptly unmade by individual ones. It would also prevent the entire bargaining unit from benefitting from the union's exercise of the bargaining leverage supplied by the unintended windfall.[19]

Another important direct-dealing case was *Medo Photo Supply Corp. v. NLRB*.[20] The employer recognized a union that had been designated by a majority of the employees in an appropriate unit. Two days before the first negotiating session between the employer and the union, a majority of the employees approached the employer and offered to abandon the union if the employer would grant them a wage increase on their own. The employer agreed and the employees informed the union that they no longer wanted union representation. The Supreme Court affirmed the Board's finding of a violation, holding that bargaining directly with employees "would be subversive of the mode of collective bargaining which the statute has ordained" and granting a wage increase in exchange for abandonment of the union is obvious interference.[21] The kind of direct dealing found

[17] 321 U.S. 342 (1944).

[18] 45 U.S.C. § 152, Fourth.

[19] 321 U.S. 332, 346-347.

[20] 321 U.S. 678 (1944).

[21] *Id.* at 684-687.

in *Medo* would undermine the bargaining representative in several ways. First, competition between the employees who disavowed union representation and the union represented employees would reintroduce the downward pressure on wages and working conditions. Second, employees would lose the long-run benefits of union representation through the disadvantages of dealing face-to-face with the employer, including the lack of bargaining experience and unity of presentation and the fear of discharge or economic reprisal.[22] Third, by encouraging employees to abandon the union, the employer deprived the union of an opportunity to act upon its election mandate.

Together, *J.I. Case, Order of Railway Telegraphers,* and *Medo* show three different forms of undermining the union's exclusive agency through direct dealing: refusing to recognize the union's monopoly over the labor market; depriving the collective of the right to redistribute individual assets to benefit the collective; and not giving the union a chance to act upon its bargaining mandate. Subsequent Board cases involving direct dealing reveal the pivotal issue to be whether the employer's conduct undermines the union's exclusive agency.

For example, in *United Technologies v. International Association of Machinists,*[23] where the employer expressed his bargaining position to employees in individual discussions and letters urging them to inform the union of their preferences, the union's agency status was not threatened. The Board noted that the communications were non-coercive, the employer acknowledged the role of the union and did not suggest abandonment for the promise of better terms, the employer bargained lawfully, and the parties had a long and fruitful relationship with no employer effort to eliminate the union or change the bargaining relationship. In this context, the direct communications with employees were lawful. On the other hand, the Board in *Obie Pacific, Inc. v. Seattle Local 49,*[24] held that the employer's polling of the employees' sentiments regarding a contractual provision in order to secure a concession from the union in subsequent negotiations violated the principle of exclusivity. In explaining this holding the Board said the following:

> [The employer's] obligation to bargain with the employees' exclusive agent demands that [he] accept and respect the exclusivity of that agency.

---

[22] *See* Weyand, *Majority Rule in Collective Bargaining*, 45 Colum. L. Rev. 556 (1945).

[23] 274 NLRB 609 (1985).

[24] 196 NLRB 458 (1972).

> While, under appropriate circumstances, an employer may communicate to employees the reasons for his actions and even for his bargaining objective, he may not seek to determine for himself the degree of support, or lack thereof, which exists for the stated position of the employees' bargaining agent. If we were to sanction such efforts, we would impede effective bargaining.[25]

In *Obie*, the Board also nicely explains how the polling triggers the central concerns of the exclusivity doctrine:

> Part of the task facing a negotiator for either a union or a company is effectively to coalesce an admixture of views of various segments of his constituency, and to determine, in the light of that knowledge, which issues can be compromised and to what degree. A systematic effort by the other party to interfere with this process by either surreptitious espionage or open interrogation constitutes clear undercutting of this vital and necessarily confidential function of the negotiator. It is indeed designed to undermine the exclusive agency relationship between the agent and its collective principals.[26]

Considering the untoward economic effects that direct dealing is likely to have upon the terms and conditions of employment, the employer has, perhaps, a natural incentive to engage in such conduct. However, employees may also seek to bypass the union and deal directly with the employer. *Emporium Capwell Co. v. Western Addition Community Organization*[27] is an example. In that case, two minority employees sought to bypass the union and bargain with the employer over minority working conditions. Eventually, the employer fired the employees for seeking to force the employer through economic pressure (picketing, leafletting and publicity campaigning) to accede to their bargaining demands. The activists' concerns about racial discrimination were also an important aspect of national labor policy as reflected in Title VII of the 1964 Civil Rights Act,[28] and the Board is obliged to interpret the Act consistently with other labor legislation. Yet, the centrality of exclusivity to the collective bargaining scheme of the NLRA prevailed. The Supreme Court majority upheld the discharges, holding that Section 7 of the Act did not protect minority employee attempts

[25] *Id.* at 463.

[26] *Id.* at 463-64.

[27] 420 U.S. 50 (1975). *See generally* Calvin William Sharpe, *"Judging in Good Faith" — Seeing Justice Marshall's Legacy Through a Labor Case*, 26 Ariz. St. L.J. 479 (1994).

[28] 42 U.S.C. § 2000e-2.

to bypass the union and bargain with the employer. Speaking for the majority, Justice Marshall, whose anti-discrimination credentials cannot seriously be questioned, said:

> The policy of industrial self-determination as expressed in Section 7 does not require fragmentation of the bargaining unit along racial or other lines in order to consist with the national labor policy against discrimination. And in the fact of such fragmentation, whatever its effect on discriminatory practices, the bargaining process that the principle of exclusive representation is meant to lubricate could not endure unhampered.[29]

Though the reach of exclusivity may seem to produce harsh results as reflected in *Emporium Capwell,* the doctrine is held in check by the operation of other rules under the Act. At the threshold, the exclusivity principle only applies when a majority representative exists. The employer does not violate this principle when it negotiates a "members only" agreement with a non-majority representative. Though "members only" agreements have been the subject of some controversy,[30] the Board has condoned such agreements even as it rejects an interpretation of Section 8(a)(5) that would require an employer to bargain with such unions.[31] *Philadelphia Electric Co.*[32] presents an example of a "members only" agreement. There, the employer maintained a non-contractual arrangement with an employee group called the Independent Group Association (IGA). The IGA represented individual employees in presenting grievances under the employer's elaborate grievance system. The IGA met annually with the employer before it granted its annual wage and benefits package in order to inform the employer of the desires of IGA members. Thereafter, the employer unilaterally implemented wages and benefits. Adopting the Administrative Law Judge's decision, the Board held that the employer's conferral of "members only" recognition upon the IGA was perfectly valid. That decision also held that the employer's refusal to enter into a similar arrangement with another employee group did not violate the Act since the

---

[29] 420 U.S. 50, 70 (1975).

[30] *See* Douglas L. Leslie, Cases and Materials on Labor Law: Process and Policy 336 (3d ed. Little-Brown 1992).

[31] *See* Mooresville Cotton Mills, 2 NLRB 952, 955 (1937), *modified and enforced,* 94 F.2d 61 (4th Cir. 1938), *modified,* 97 F.2d 959 (1938), *modified and enforced,* 110 F.2d 179 (1940).

[32] 268 NLRB 830 (1984).

other group was not a majority representative under Section 9(a) of the Act.[33]

Even when a majority representative carries the mantle of exclusivity, other provisions of the Act are designed to contain the potential "tyranny of the Majority."[34] The union's duty of fair representation requires it to accord equal protection to all employee interests within the unit.[35] Employees have a right periodically to oust the union through a decertification vote.[36] Under the Landrum-Griffin Act bill of rights, union members have a right to speak out on all matters relating to union policy.[37] Employees need not join the union unless the employer and union make a union shop agreement,[38] and even under those agreements unit employees may opt to become financial core members of the union rather than full members subject to the union's constitution and by-laws.[39] Under Section 14(b) of the Act states, may even prohibit union shop agreements.[40]

Exclusivity only applies to mandatory subjects of bargaining—wages, hours, terms and conditions of employment.[41] Employers may bypass the exclusive representative and bargain with individuals or groups of employees over non-mandatory subjects. Regarding mandatory subjects, Section 9(a) gives individual employees the right to present and adjust grievances without union intervention.[42]

---

[33] *Id.* at 830 n.4 & 837.

[34] 420 U.S. 50, 64 (1979).

[35] *See infra* Chapter 16.

[36] *See* Section 9(c)(1) of the Act. Like any other valid election, a valid decertification election may not be held more frequently than once every 12 months.

[37] 29 U.S.C. § 411(a)(2).

[38] *See* Section 8(a)(3) of the NLRA.

[39] *See* NLRB v. General Motors Corp., 373 U.S. 734 (1963) and Communications Workers v. Beck, 487 U.S. 735 (1988).

[40] Section 14(b) states:

> (b) Nothing in this Act shall be construed as authorizing the execution or application of agreements requiring membership in a labor organization as a condition of employment in any State or Territory in which such execution or application is prohibited by State or Territorial law.

[41] *See* NLRB v. Wooster Division of Borg-Warner Corp., 356 U.S. 342 (1958).

[42] Section 9(a) of the Act reads as follows:

> Representatives designated or selected for the purposes of collective bargaining by the majority of the employees in a unit appropriate for such purposes, shall be the exclusive representatives of all the employees in such unit for the purposes of collective bargaining in respect to rates of pay, wages, hours of employment, or other conditions of employment:

Finally, distinct groups of individuals are protected from the expansive effect of exclusivity through unit determination, which narrowly defines the represented unit as employees who share a community.[43] This similarity of duties, skills, working conditions, job classifications, employee benefits, promotional ladders, degree of interchange and commonality of supervision among employees seeks to assure that what benefits one within the unit benefits all.[44] Because all of these safeguards against the abuse of exclusivity have a limited effect, some scholars have called for the elimination of exclusivity as the American model of collective bargaining.[45]

§ 7.4 Bargaining Before the Execution of the Agreement

[A]—The Duty to Bargain In Good Faith

Collective bargaining is a process characterized by power and rationality. Through the exercise of economic power and rational discussion, the parties are able to narrow their differences and reach settlement upon the range of issues that order the workplace. Sections 8(a)(5), 8(b)(3), 9(a), and 8(d) are the statutory vehicles that permit this process to work. Section 8(a)(5) defines as an employer unfair labor practice (ULP) the refusal to bargain collectively with the union subject to section 9(a),[46] which grants exclusive representational status to the majority representative to bargain on behalf of represented employees on questions of "wages, hours of employment, and other conditions of employment."[47] Section 8(b)(3) imposes a corresponding duty on the union subject to Section 9(a).[48] And Section 8(d)

Provided, That any individual employee or a group of employees shall have the right at any time to present grievances to their employer and to have such grievances adjusted, without the intervention of the bargaining representative, as long as the adjustment is not inconsistent with the terms of a collective-bargaining contract or agreement then in effect: *Provided further,* That the bargaining representative has been given opportunity to be present as such adjustment.

[43] *See* Section 9(b), *supra* note 3.

[44] Quaker City Life Insurance Co., 319 F.2d 690 (1961).

[45] *See, e.g.,* George Schatzki, *Majority Rule, Exclusive Representation, and the Interests of Individual Workers: Should Exclusivity Be Abolished,* 123 U. Pa. L. Rev. 897 (1975).

[46] Section 8(a)(5) provides:

(a) It shall be an unfair labor practice for an employer—

(5) to refuse to bargain collectively with the representatives of his employees, subject to the provisions of section 9(a).

[47] *See supra* note 42.

[48] Section 8(b)(3) provides:

(b) It shall be an unfair labor practice for a labor organization or its agents—

defines the elements of the duty to bargain including the obligation to confer in good faith; it specifically disavows any obligation on either party to agree to a proposal or make a concession.[49]

In erecting this framework for hammering out agreements, the Act seeks only to keep the parties faithful to attempting to reach an agreement by their own efforts; it does not seek to create a government imposed agreement on the parties. Rather, the agreement contemplated under the statute is a function of the parties' interests, bargaining skills and economic power. The Supreme Court reinforced this point in *NLRB v. Insurance Agents' International Union*[50] by striking down a Board finding that the union's use of unprotected economic pressure in a bargaining dispute violated its duty to bargain in good faith. In that decision the Court said:

> The scope of Section 8(b)(3) and the limitations on Board power which were the design of Section 8(d) are exceeded, we hold, by inferring a lack of good faith not from any deficiencies of the union's performance at the bargaining table by reason of its attempted use of economic pressure, but solely and simply because tactics designed to exert economic pressure were employed during the course of the good-faith negotiations. Thus the Board in the guise of determining good or bad faith in negotiations could regulate what economic weapons a party might summon to its aid. And if the Board could regulate the choice of economic weapons that may be used as part of collective bargaining, it would be in a position to exercise considerable influence upon the substantive terms on which the parties contract. As the parties' own devices became more limited, the Government might have to enter even more directly into the negotiation of collective agreements. Our labor policy is not presently erected on a foundation of government control of the results of negotiations . . . . Nor does it contain a charter for the National Labor Relations

---

(3) to refuse to bargain collectively with an employer, provided it is the representative of his employees subject to the provisions of section 9(a);

49 In part Section 8(d) provides:

> For the purposes of this section, to bargain collectively is the performance of the mutual obligation of the employer and the representative of the employees to meet at reasonable times and confer in good faith with respect to wages, hours, and other terms and conditions of employment, or the negotiation of an agreement, or any question arising thereunder, and the execution of a written contract incorporating any agreement reached it requested by either party, but such obligation does not compel either party to agree to a proposal or require the making of a concession . . . .

50 361 U.S. 477 (1960).

Board to act at large in equalizing disparities of bargaining power between employer and union.[51]

[1] Good Faith Violations

The parties' mutual obligation to bargain in good faith is the central component of the statutory framework. It contemplates a sincere desire—an open mind and sincere effort to find a basis—to reach an agreement. The problem that runs throughout the cases is how the Board and the courts should determine whether the parties have bargained in good faith. As usual, determining the state of mind of the parties is problematic. This determination is complicated in the context of collective bargaining because it involves a review of the entire process that often entails a close examination of all party behavior and communications at the bargaining table. The Board is forced to examine the procedures of bargaining as well as the content of party proposals. This complexity is further complicated by the deference to freedom of contract found in Section 8(d). Consequently, a party's refusal to agree to a proposal or make a concession will rarely be sufficient evidence of bad faith to justify a Section 8(a)(5) or 8(b)(3) finding.[52]

The Supreme Court reinforced this view in *NLRB v. American National Insurance Co.*[53] when it denied enforcement of a Board order finding a *per se* violation of Section 8(a)(5) based on the employer's insistence upon a broad management functions clause. The clause gave the company unreviewable discretion over many terms and conditions of employment. Noting that the Act does not compel any agreement between the parties, the Court said that the Board "may not, either directly or indirectly compel concessions or otherwise sit in judgment upon the substantive terms of collective bargaining agreements."[54]

Yet, as the Eleventh Circuit noted in *NLRB v. A-1 King Size Sandwiches, Inc.*,[55] in order to prevent surface bargaining, the Board must consider the

---

51 *Id.* at 490.

52 It should be noted that most refusal-to-bargain cases involve employers and not unions as respondents. It comes as no surprise because, in the collective bargaining situation, the union is attempting to wrest from the employer some of its sovereignty over the workplace. That sovereignty represents the employer's leverage in negotiations. The union's leverage, on the other hand, cannot be its inherent control over wages, hours, or terms and conditions of employment, since it is an outsider. Rather the union's leverage lies in its control over employees—its ability to lead employees into job action.

53 343 U.S. 395 (1952).

54 *Id.* at 404.

55 732 F.2d 872 (11th Cir. 1984).

substantive proposals of the parties, which might be the only indicia of bad faith where the parties are sophisticated. In *A-1*, the parties were only able to agree upon a few ancillary contractual provisions over 18 bargaining sessions during an 11-month period. The company had met at reasonable times and places with the union, bore no animus toward the union, and engaged in no conduct away from the bargaining table that would have suggested bad faith. The court stated the issue as follows:

> Whether the content of the Company's bargaining proposals together with the positions taken by the Company are sufficient to establish that it entered into bargaining with no real intention of concluding a collective bargaining agreement.[56]

After examining the details of the company's wage, management rights, zipper clause, no-strike clause, discharge and discipline, layoff and recall, dues checkoff, and non-discrimination clause proposals, the court said:

> Deciding when a party has reached the "point when hard bargaining ends and obstructionist intransigency begins," . . . is "an inescapably elusive inquiry." But it is clear from our extended recital of the proposals made over a ten-month period that the Company insisted on unilateral control over virtually all significant terms and conditions of employment, ...
>
> . . .
>
> The Board correctly inferred bad faith from the Company's insistence on proposals that are so unusually harsh and unreasonable that they are predictably unworkable . . . . They would have left the Union and the employees with substantially fewer rights and less protection than they would have had if they had relied solely upon the Union's certification.[57]

Testing the parties' good faith is one of two analytical approaches under the duty to bargain. The good faith analysis is subjective. It is contextual and considers whether the totality of a party's conduct demonstrates bad faith as indicated in *A-1*. The other approach is objective. It considers whether the procedures of collective bargaining such as meeting and conferring have been met and leads to a *per se* violation when they are

[56] 732 F.2d at 874.

[57] 732 F.2d 874, 876-877.

not. Procedural violations under the *per se* approach do not require a finding of bad faith.[58]

In a difficult test of the good faith doctrine,[59] Lemuel R. Boulware, the Vice-President of Labor Relations for General Electric, adopted and implemented a bargaining strategy known as Boulwareism in 1960. First, the employer ascertained the desires of its employees and then translated them into contract proposals. It denounced the traditional "give and take" approach to bargaining and arrived at what it would consider a final offer, which it called a "firm, fair offer" and presented it to the union on a take-it-or-leave-it basis. With this approach, the employer combined a comprehensive publicity campaign directed to its employees and the general public through a variety of media—plant newspaper, bulletins, letters, TV and radio announcements, and personal contacts. The campaign was designed to convince employees of the employer's intention to do right voluntarily without artificially overstating and understating proposals as in the typical collective bargaining process. The Company argued that it had not violated Section 8(a)(5), because it was willing to reach an agreement, could not be forced to make a concession, could make a "firm and fair" offer without submitting to the Board's judgment about the reasonableness of the proposals, and could communicate its views to its employees under Section 8(c).

The Board held and the Second Circuit confirmed that Boulwareism violated Section 8(a)(5). The employer's take-it-or-leave-it approach alone did not make the conduct unlawful; under Section 8(d), the employer could not be required to make a concession. However, the combination of the take-it-or-leave-it approach and the campaign of unbending firmness evidenced the employer's bad faith. The campaign painted the employer into a corner that prevented it from changing its initial offer, even if it wanted to modify that proposal. To do so would have caused the employer to lose face among its employees and the community as well. Boulwareism effectively precluded the employer from making a sincere effort and moving toward an agreement.[60]

---

58 *See* Robert P. Duvin, *The Duty To Bargain: Law In Search of Policy*, 64 Colum. L. Rev. 248 (1964).

59 NLRB v. General Electric, 418 F.2d 736 (2d Cir. 1969).

60 *Id.* Also, the message to employees was that the company was their true representative and the union was superfluous.

[2] *Per Se* Violations

In *NLRB v. Truitt Mfg. Co.*,[61] the Supreme Court used a *per se* approach to decide whether the duty to bargain included a duty to disclose information. In that case the employer offered a two and one-half cent an hour wage increase in negotiations for a new contract. The union pressed for a 10-cents-an-hour increase. The employer claimed that if it paid 10-cents an hour it would "break the company." In response, the union requested the employer's records and permission for its certified public accountant to examine the employer's books. The employer refused claiming the requested financial information was privileged from disclosure at the bargaining table and that the employer already had implemented a favorably competitive wage package. The Board found a violation and the Supreme Court agreed.

Though the Court in *Truitt* articulates a good faith rationale, it seems out of place where the record suggested that the company had an open mind and a sincere desire to reach agreement. Also, like the refusal to meet and confer, a refusal to supply information may make it impossible for the union to explore the employer's position and effectively perform its bargaining function. If collective bargaining is seen as reasoned, intelligent negotiations nourished by full and informed discussion, withholding information may be tantamount to removing uninformed items from the bargaining table. For this reason, the Board has treated the failure to supply relevant information in *per se* fashion.

The union must demonstrate the relevance of the information, which was not a problem in *Truitt* because the company made its ability to pay the pivotal issue in that case. In disclosure of information cases the relevancy standard, is the loose discovery standard—having something to do with the issue—rather than the stricter evidentiary standard.[62] While the showing of relevance is largely a case-by-case proposition, the Board, endorsed by the courts, will treat requests for wages and benefits information as presumptively relevant.[63] Financial data, on the other hand, may not always be relevant. For example, it would not be relevant simply because the employer says "my competitors are not paying any more than a .02 per cent increase and I refuse to pay more." In that case, unlike *Truitt*, there is no claim of inability to pay just unwillingness.

---

61 351 U.S. 149 (1956).

62 110 NLRB 856.

63 General Motors Corp., Inc. v. NLRB, 700 F.2d 1083, 1088.

Just as information gives the union a basis for negotiating intelligently, it also gives the union a basis for policing compliance with the collective bargaining agreement. The Supreme Court has also made it clear that the disclosure duty survives the negotiating process and has vitality during the administration of the Agreement. In *NLRB v. Acme Industrial Co.*,[64] the Court affirmed the Board's finding that the company violated its duty to bargain when it denied the union's request for information about the company's removal of certain machinery from the plant. The union had suspected that the removal constituted a breach of the agreement.

Relevance is not the only limitation on the duty to disclose information. This duty may also be qualified by legitimate employer concerns that militate against disclosure. In *Detroit Edison Co. v. NLRB*,[65] those concerns related to the confidentiality of employee test scores and the validity of tests. In that case, the union represented the operating and maintenance employees of an electric power public utility. The union filed a grievance against the utility for going outside the unit to fill six positions within a unit job classification. The contract provided for promotions within the bargaining unit based on seniority, unless the qualifications and abilities of applicants differed significantly. In the grievance, the union claimed that the testing procedure was unfair and by bypassing senior unit employees the company violated the collective bargaining agreement. The company denied the grievance, and the union took it to arbitration. Preparing for arbitration, the union requested materials related to the testing program for the relevant job classification. The company supplied the test validation study, scores without the examinees' names, sample questions, a detailed explanation of the scoring system, and it offered the scores with the names of employees who signed a waiver. The company refused to turn over test questions, answers, and applicants' scores, claiming a need to protect the integrity of the test and the privacy of the test-takers. The union rejected this offer as well as a later offer to give the question and answer sheets to a union selected psychologist, who would be obligated to preserve confidentiality. The Board held that this refusal to supply information violated the company's duty to bargain under Section 8(a)(5) and ordered it to turn over the test questions, answers, and individual test scores directly to the union under certain restrictions designed to protect the security of the tests. The Board found that the company's concerns about the security of the tests were outweighed by the union's interest in exploring the fairness of the company's promotion criteria. The Supreme Court refused to enforce

[64] 385 U.S. 432 (1967).

[65] 440 U.S. 301 (1979).

the order. The Court held that the Board abused its remedial discretion when it ordered the company to deliver the test battery and answer sheets directly to the union without adequate protection of the company's interest in the secrecy of the test. In reaching this conclusion the Court noted:

> A union's bare assertion that it needs information to process a grievance does not automatically oblige the employer to supply all the information in the manner requested. The duty to supply information under Section 8(a)(5) turns upon "the circumstances of the particular case," . . . and much the same may be said for the type of disclosure that will satisfy that duty.[66]

Regarding the duty to supply the actual tests of applicants, the company argued that even if the scores were relevant, the company's promise and the psychologists' ethical duty of confidentiality as well as the potential harm to the test-takers outweighed the union's need for the information. The Court agreed, holding that the company's conditional offer to disclose the scores only with the consent of the examinees was warranted. Importantly, the Court reiterated that the union's need for relevant information does not always predominate over other interests and cited cases where the union's interest yielded to employer concerns about harassment of employees,[67] privacy of employee information,[68] and competitive concerns.[69]

Unions, of course, have a reciprocal duty to supply information on the theory that both sides have an interest in engaging in intelligent discussion based on realistic bargaining positions. The move to common ground is facilitated through fully informed bargaining. The question is whether requested information has an impact on the employer's ability similar to the impact of the company's claim of financial vulnerability on the union in *Truitt*. For example, the union would have a duty upon request to disclose names where it claims in support of a wage increase demand that 15% of its members are on food stamps.[70] A similar obligation would probably not accompany the union's claim that all of the employer's competitors have given a 50-cents-per-hour wage increase to employees represented by the union.

---

66 *Id.* at 314-315.

67 Shell Oil Co. v. NLRB, 457 F.2d 615 (9th Cir. 1972).

68 United Aircraft Corp., 192 NLRB 382 (1971) (medical records).

69 Kroger Co. v. NLRB, 399 F.2d 455 (6th Cir. 1968) (operating data ratio).

70 *See* Local 13, Detroit Newspaper Printing & Graphic Communications Union v. NLRB (Oakland Press Co.), 598 F.2d 267 (D.C. Cir. 1979).

Another *per se* violation of 8(a)(5) is the unilateral change in existing wages, hours or terms and conditions of employment before the parties have reached an impasse in negotiations. The seminal case on this point is *NLRB v. Katz*,[71] where the employer and union were negotiating toward a collective bargaining agreement. The employer's sick leave, automatic wage increase and merit increase policies were among the items being considered. During the course of these negotiations and without notice or consultation, the employer unilaterally implemented a new sick leave policy, a new system of automatic wage increases, and awarded merit increases to 40% of the employees in the unit. Without making a finding of bad faith, the Board held that the employer's unilateral changes violated Section 8(a)(5). The employer challenged the Board's finding in the Second Circuit, arguing that unilateral actions alone could not be deemed to violate Section 8(a)(5) without a finding of lack of good faith, though they might be evidence on the issue of good faith. Though the Second Circuit agreed, the Supreme Court reversed reasoning as follows:

> The duty "to bargain collectively" enjoined by Section 8(a)(5) is defined by Section 8(d) as the duty to "meet . . . and confer in good faith with respect to wages, hours, and other terms and conditions of employment." Clearly, the duty thus defined may be violated without a general failure of subjective good faith; for there is no occasion to consider the issue of good faith if a party has refused even to negotiate *in fact* —"to meet . . . and confer" — about any of the mandatory subjects. [Footnote omitted.] A refusal to negotiate *in fact* as to any subject which is within Section 8(a), and about which the union seeks to negotiate, violates Section 8(a)(5) though the employer has every desire to reach agreement with the union upon an over-all collective agreement and earnestly and in all good faith bargains to that end. We hold that an employer's unilateral change in conditions of employment under negotiation is similarly a violation of Section 8(a)(5), for it is a circumvention of the duty to negotiate which frustrates the objectives of Section 8(a)(5) much as does a flat refusal. [Footnote omitted.][72]

The Court's discussion of each of the changes reflected a concern generally about their calamitous impact on the process of collective bargaining and the status of the union as representative. The granting of a more generous wage increase than the employer offered to the union amounted to a repudiation of the union, showing the employees that they

[71] 369 U.S. 736 (1962).

[72] *Id.* at 742-743.

were better off without the union. The effect of the change in sick leave policy was to disrupt the union's position as coordinator of competing interests within the union, some members being more likely to favor the change while others opposed it. The implementation of the merit increases without consultation with the union prevented it from policing the fairness of the employer's increases. Though the Court's concern might seemed to apply more persuasively where the employer unilaterally increases rather than decreases wages and benefits, the Board routinely holds that the latter as well as the former violate 8(a)(5).[73]

However, unilateral changes after impasse that implement proposals consistent with final offers made to the union do not violate Section 8(a)(5). The Board has described an impasse and its function in collective bargaining as follows:

> A genuine impasse in negotiations is synonymous with a deadlock: the parties have discussed a subject or subjects in good faith, and, despite their best efforts to achieve agreement with respect to such, neither party is willing to move from its respective positions. When such a deadlock is reached between the parties, the duty to bargain about the subject matter of the impasse merely becomes dormant until changed circumstances indicate that an agreement may be possible. Once a genuine impasse is reached, the parties can concurrently exert economic pressure on each other: the union can call for a strike; the employee can engage in a lockout, make unilateral changes in working conditions if they are consistent with the offers the union has rejected, or hire replacements to counter the loss of striking employees. Such economic pressure usually breaks the stalemate between the parties, changes the circumstances of the bargaining atmosphere, and revives the parties' duty to bargain.
>
> . . .
>
> Thus, a genuine impasse is akin to a hiatus in negotiations. In the overall ongoing process of collective bargaining, it is merely a point at which the parties cease to negotiate and often resort to forms of economic persuasion to establish the primacy of their negotiating position. [Footnotes omitted.][74]

---

[73] *See* George Schatzki, *The Employer's Unilateral Act—A* Per Se *Violation—Sometimes*, 44 Tex. L. Rev. 470, 503 (1966).

[74] Hi-Way Billboards, Inc., 206 NLRB 22, 23 (1973).

No impasse can exists where the employer has not offered the union the implemented changes or where the changes are more favorable than those offered to the union. But where the changes are in line with or no more favorable than those offered or approved prior to impasse, the employer has complied with the duty to sincerely seek agreement. The union can actually take credit for improvements even though they do not measure up to its proposals, the bargaining process can continue, and neither the process nor the union is disparaged.

To determine whether an impasse exists the Board considers a number of factors designed to measure whether bargaining has run its course including the following: number of meetings, length of meetings, period of negotiations, whether bargaining has been in good faith, whether the refusal to modify positions has developed over time or occurred at a recent meeting, whether either party has expressed a willingness to modify its position, whether a mediator has been called in (a sign of deadlock), the importance of the issues over which the parties disagree (the more important the issue the more likely an impasse), and the understanding of the parties regarding the state of negotiations.[75] Impasses are possible as to one but not all issues, triggering a continuing duty to bargain on other issues unless the issue precipitating the impasse is overriding enough to justify a finding of impasse as to all issues.[76] As the Board suggested in *Hi-Way Billboards*, impasses may be broken by the union's or employer's retreat or a change of conditions at the employer. The parties must then resume bargaining and refrain from making unilateral changes.

The factors determining the existence of an impasse permit considerable Board discretion in determining the existence of an impasse. For example, in *Bell Transit Co.*,[77] the Board found that an impasse existed because it decided to emphasize one factor over all others. In that case, the employer was a labor broker who hired, supervised and compensated drivers at the Union Carbide Institute, West Virginia facility. It was under pressure from its client to reduce costs. The employer and the union had only three meetings over two months. The only question holding up agreement was the size of the reduction of wages. There had been movement on the issue at each meeting, and the union submitted the employer's last proposal to its membership. Although the membership rejected the proposal by the

[75] *See* Robert A. Gorman, Basic Text on Labor Law: Unionization and Collective Bargaining 448-449 (West 1976).

[76] *Id.*

[77] 271 NLRB 1272 (1984).

required two-thirds vote, the union local president informed the company that it had submitted the employer's proposal to the regional office of the union and that its chances for approval were good. One week after the employer made the offer, and before the union regional office could respond, the employer implemented its last offer. The Board considered the pressure to reduce prices that the employer was receiving from its customer and held that an impasse had been reached despite the circumstances, because of the importance of the issue to the employer. The Board then indicated that it would stress the importance of the issue to the employer, at the expense of other traditional factors such as number of meetings and the understanding of the parties about the state of negotiations.[78]

An action taken by the employer before impasse is not a violation of Section 8(a)(5) unless it is a change in the status quo, which is dynamic rather than static. For example, an employer who has had a practice for the past 20 years of granting an automatic 5% across-the-board wage increase in July and does so, even though it is negotiating with the union in July on wages and other issues, has not violated Section 8(a)(5). The 5% increase is a part of the status quo, even though it changes the wages employees received at the onset of negotiations. Indeed, the employer violates Section 8(a)(5), if it refuses to grant the wage increase under these circumstances.[79]

Once a collective bargaining agreement has expired, the employer is "contractually" free to change wages, hours and working conditions. However, Section 8(a)(5) as interpreted in *Katz* substantially qualifies this freedom. Since the collective bargaining agreement has established the status quo, conceivably, every term of an expired bargaining agreement covering a mandatory subject of bargaining might be immune during negotiations from unilateral change before impasse. Employers have been permitted to unilaterally discontinue union shop and checkoff provisions but not superseniority for union members, the grievance procedure or contributions to a health and welfare fund.[80]

---

78 Ellen Dannin, *Legislative Intent and Impasse Resolution under the National Labor Relations Act: Does Law Matter?*, 15 Hofstra Lab. & Empl. L.J. 11 (1997).

79 *See* State Farm Mutual Insurance Co., 195 NLRB 871 (1972); NLRB v. Southern Coach & Body Co., 336 F.2d 214 (5th Cir. 1964); and Progress Bulletin Publishing Co., 182 NLRB 904 (1970), *modified per curiam*, 443 F.2d 1369 (9th Cir. 1971).

80 *See* Litton Financial Printing Div. v. NLRB, 501 U.S. 190 (1991) (explaining the Board's position on union shop and check-off obligations); Marine and Shipbuilding Workers v. NLRB, 320 F.2d 615 (3d Cir. 1963) (checkoff); NLRB v. Cone Mills Corp., 373 F.2d 595 (4th Cir. 1964) (union shop); Hilton-Davis Chem. Co., 185 NLRB 241 (1970) (employer may abandon the arbitration provision but not the grievance machinery).

Though rarely manifested, the union also has a duty to refrain from making unilateral changes before impasse. One of the few cases raising this issue was *New York Dist. Council No. 9, Painter v. NLRB.*[81] There, the employer and union had a collective bargaining agreement which provided that employees within the unit were to work seven hours a day, five days a week. Although the contract made no mention of any production quota, the tradition, known to all parties, was that journeyman painters completed an average of 11.5 rooms per week. At a union meeting, the union passed a resolution that no journeyman was to paint more than 10 rooms per week in order to improve health, safety, and work quality. Union members violating the resolution would be fined. In an order later enforced by the Second Circuit, the Board held that the union unilaterally reduced the hours of work without bargaining with the employer in violation of Section 8(b)(3).

[B]—Subjects of Collective Bargaining

Section 8(d) obligates the parties to bargain about wages, hours, and other terms and conditions of employment. Does that provision delimit the area of bargaining or simply exemplify the issues that are likely to be of immediate concern to the parties? The Court in *NLRB v. Wooster Division of Borg-Warner Corp.*,[82] interpreted the Act as erecting a three-tier structure governing the bargaining obligation. First, the subjects specified in Section 8(d) are *mandatory subjects.* The parties must bargain about those subjects in good faith, which involves the duty to disclose relevant information and refrain from pre-impasse unilateral changes. They have the freedom to insist to impasse upon their positions on these matters using economic weapons. Necessarily, agreement is permitted on mandatory subjects. Second, the parties may bargain over lawful subjects that are non-mandatory. They are known as *permissive subjects*; however, the parties have neither a duty to bargain nor the freedom to insist upon these subjects backed by economic weapons. However, agreement is permitted on these subjects. Third, *unlawful subjects* may not be submitted to bargaining. The parties have no duty to bargain and no freedom to bargain over unlawful subjects, and agreement on such subjects is not permitted.

Traditional mandatory subjects, such as wages, and unlawful subjects, such as a proposal to hire only union members in the absence of a pre-hire agreement, are easy to spot as mandatory and unlawful subjects of bargaining. But how should cases closer to the margin be decided? *Borg-Warner*

81 453 F.2d 783 (2d Cir. 1971), *cert. denied,* 408 U.S. 930 (1972).

82 356 U.S. 342 (1958).

raises this question. In that case, the United Autoworkers and the company engaged in collective bargaining after the International was certified as collective bargaining representative. During these negotiations, the employer insisted upon two items: a "ballot clause" requiring a pre-strike vote among the union membership on the company's last offer before the union could strike and a clause substituting the local union for the certified International union as the recognized employee representative. The Board and the Supreme Court held that the company's insistence on these clauses violated Section 8(a)(5) because neither clause was of a mandatory subject. The Court's test for distinguishing the mandatory subject (a no-strike clause) and non-mandatory subject (the ballot clause), though not well-developed, is: matters that "[regulate] the relations between the employer and the employees" rather than the employees and their union are mandatory subjects.[83] This statement of the test denies mandatory status to matters falling within the sovereignty of the other party, while reserving that status to matters of mutual concern to the parties.

The cases following *Borg-Warner* seem to support this restatement. For example, in *NLRB v. Detroit Resilient Floor Decorators Local Union No. 2265*,[84] the Sixth Circuit enforced a Board order, holding that the employer's contribution to an industry promotion fund was a non-mandatory subject of bargaining. It was outside of the employment relationship—concerned rather with the relationship among the employers contributing to the fund or the employer and consumers. By contrast, the price and availability of in-plant food services in *Ford Motor Co. (Chicago Stamping Plant) v. NLRB*,[85] the institution of polygraph testing to investigate vandalism of company property in *Medicenter v. Hotel & Restaurant Employees*,[86] and drug testing in *Johnson-Bateman Co. v. International*

[83] The Court also uses the *per se* approach on the rationale that an insistence on non-mandatory subjects as a condition for agreeing on statutory subjects is in effect a refusal to bargain on statutory subjects. Since this may not be the most intelligible rationale, it may be helpfully restated. The collective bargaining structure of the Act does not contemplate the use of economic weapons to control the internal affairs of the other party—those matters that relate to the other party's sovereignty as an entity. Only those matters of mutual concern to the employer and employees in relationship with each other were intended to be subjected to the full force of collective bargaining.

See Archibald Cox, *Labor Decisions of the Supreme Court at the October Term, 1957*, 44 Va. L. Rev. 1057 (1958) (generally criticizing the effort to draw precise overarching lines of demarcation between subjects of bargaining).

[84] 317 F.2d 269 (6th Cir. 1963).

[85] 441 U.S. 488 (1979).

[86] 221 NLRB 670 (1975).

Association of Machinists,[87] directly affected working conditions and were mandatory subjects.

A problem that quickly surfaces in trying to draw lines between various subjects of bargaining is how to decide those cases where the subject, although in the province of the other party, bears, perhaps tenuously, upon the relationship between the employer and employees. *Detroit Resilient Floor Decorators* is an example of this problem, since the success of the industry promotion fund may mean increased job security for the company's employees.

In *Fibreboard Paper Products Corp. v. NLRB*,[88] the leading case on this issue, the company and the union had a series of collective bargaining agreements. The union represented the maintenance employees. Toward the end of the most recent agreement, the employer decided that it could experience significant operational savings in the maintenance department by contracting out the maintenance work at its plant. During negotiations with the union for a new contract, the employer contracted with a maintenance company for the performance of maintenance services, a decision that was made without bargaining with the union. Whether this unilateral act was a violation turned on whether the subcontracting of maintenance work was a mandatory subject of bargaining. The Board answered this question affirmatively in a decision affirmed by the District of Columbia Circuit and the Supreme Court.

The Court looked at the importance and amenability of subcontracting as a collective bargaining issue and the cost concerns that underlay the employer's decision in arriving at its conclusion. It also viewed the subcontracting issue narrowly as whether "the replacement of employees in the existing bargaining unit with those of an independent contractor to do the same work under similar conditions of employment" is a mandatory subject of bargaining.[89] Because the subcontracting decision was a matter of immediate importance to both parties that could be successfully resolved through collective bargaining without intruding too much on the freedom of management to manage the business, the Court held that it was a mandatory decision.

Concerned about the potential breadth of the Court's decision, Justice Stewart wrote a concurring decision that has eclipsed the majority decision

---

87 295 NLRB 180 (1989).

88 379 U.S. 203 (1964).

89 *Id.* at 215.

in importance. Justice Stewart identified three categories of managerial decisions. First are those decisions that have a direct impact on employment such as the physical dimensions of the working environment, hours of work, layoffs, discharges, retirement and seniority systems. Such decisions have no entrepreneurial implications and are mandatory subjects. Second are decisions that indirectly and in an uncertain way affect job security. Examples are advertising expenditures, product design, manner of financing and sales programming. For Justice Stewart, the indirection and uncertainty of these decisions alone would render the subjects non-mandatory. Third are those decisions that directly imperil the job security of employees, but because they lie "at the core of entrepreneurial control," are non-mandatory subjects. Examples are investing in labor saving machinery and liquidating business assets or going out of business. Capsulizing the foregoing analysis, Justice Stewart said:

> If, as I think clear, the purpose of Section 8(d) is to describe a limited area subject to the duty of collective bargaining, those management decisions which are fundamental to the basic direction of a corporate enterprise or which impinge only indirectly upon employment security should be excluded from that area.[90]

While suggesting that an employer's subcontracting decisions are not generally mandatory subjects, Justice Stewart agreed with the majority that Fibreboard's decision to subcontract maintenance work was such a subject since it merely involved the substitution of one group of workers for another. He saw this decision as analogous to other questions of discharge and work assignment such as compulsory retirement, layoffs and work assignments that are mandatory subjects. Distinguishing the Fibreboard subcontracting decision Justice Stewart said:

> This kind of subcontracting falls short of such larger entrepreneurial questions as what shall be produced, how capital shall be invested in fixed assets, or what the basic scope of the enterprise shall be. In my view, the Court's decision in this case has nothing to do with whether any aspects of those larger issues could under any circumstances be considered subjects of compulsory collective bargaining under the present law.[91]

Fibreboard was the final authority on the classification of entrepreneurial decisions directly affecting employment until the Supreme Court decided

---

90 *Id.* at 223.

91 *Id.* at 225.

First National Maintenance Corp. v. NLRB[92] (*FNM*) 17 years later. *FNM* involved a maintenance contractor performing cleaning and maintenance services for commercial customers in the New York City area. Under the company's contractual arrangement with clients, the client paid actual labor costs and a fee. Because the fee paid by one client, a Brooklyn nursing home, was reduced by one-half, FNM decided to terminate the contract as not sufficiently profitable. During the period when FNM was deciding to terminate its contract with the nursing home, the union organized and became the certified representative of FNM's employees at the nursing home. After the union requested bargaining, the company terminated its contract with the nursing home and dismissed its employees without bargaining with the union about the decision or the effects of the decision on its employees. In a decision enforced by the Second Circuit, the Board held that the company had violated its duty to bargain about the decision to partially close its operations and the effects of the partial closing on its employees. Over a vigorous dissent by Justice Brennan joined by Justice Marshall, the Supreme Court reversed the holding on the question of decision bargaining. It did affirm the company's duty to engage in bargaining over the effects of the decision.

The Court, speaking through Justice Blackmun, explored the union's interest in participating in the decision to protect the job security of its members through offering concessions and other information that may forestall the decision. The Court thought that the union's rights to engage in effects bargaining and the 8(a)(3) protection against unlawfully motivated closures would adequately serve the union's interest. The Court saw management's more complex interest in unilaterally making the decision to be based on factors such as labor costs, the need for speed, flexibility, "and secrecy in meeting business opportunities and exigencies."[93]

Though the *FNM* Court adopted Stewart's three categories of managerial decisions, it decided upon an analytical approach that blended the Stewart and majority analyses in *Fibreboard.* Rather than making the entrepreneurial decision to partially close a non-mandatory subject of bargaining regardless of the amenability of the subject to bargaining, as Stewart would have done, the Court used the following test to determine the scope of bargaining in the category of entrepreneurial decisions that have a direct impact on employment: In order for such decisions to be mandatory subjects of bargaining, the benefits for labor relations must outweigh the burden upon

---

92 452 U.S. 666 (1981).

93 *Id.* at 682-683.

management's conduct of the business.[94] This statement of the test favors management sovereignty, since the test dictates that decision-bargaining be non-mandatory if the benefits to labor relations and burden to management decision-making are deemed to be roughly equal. This seems to place the *FNM* test closer to Stewart's than Warren's formulation in *Fibreboard.*

The Board has had some difficulty applying the *Fibreboard* and *FNM* precedents in Board cases. Three years after the *FNM* decision, the Board decided the *Otis Elevator* case[95] where the employer made a decision to discontinue part of its research and development operation and consolidate the remainder of its operations at a new facility. The four Board members agreed that this consolidation decision was not a mandatory subject of bargaining, but there was no majority rationale. Two Board members found that the test for distinguishing mandatory from non-mandatory decisions in the "entrepreneurial" category was "whether it turns upon a change in the nature or direction of the business, or turns upon labor costs" and not its effect on employees nor a union's ability to offer alternatives.[96] A concurring member established a two-step test: (1) A factor over which the union had control was a significant consideration in the employer's decision; and (2) the benefits for the collective bargaining process outweigh the burden on the business including extent of capital commitment, changes in operations, and the need for speed, flexibility and confidentiality.[97] The fourth member found that the duty depends on "whether the employer's decision is related to overall enterprise costs [and is] not limited specifically to labor costs."[98] Typically, following *Otis Elevator* the Board decided cases on the grounds that the results would be the same under any of the three tests.

Running into criticism at the Court of Appeals level for this "under any view" approach the Board in *Dubuque Packing* rejected *Otis Elevator* and announced a rule to be applied in relocation cases, the managerial decision involved in that case.[99] The Board considered the differences between the

---

94 *Id.* at 679.

95 269 NLRB 891 (1984).

96 *See id.,* decision of Donald L. Dotson, Chairman, Robert P. Hunter, Member.

97 *See id.,* decision of Member Dennis.

98 *See id.,* decision of Member Zimmerman. His broad definition of "amenability" encompassed situations where "union concession may substantially mitigate the concerns underlying the employer's decision, thereby convincing the employer to rescind its decision."

99 *See* Dubuque Packing, 303 NLRB 390 (1991), *enforced,* United Food & Commercial Workers, Local 150-A v. NLRB (Dubuque Packing Co.), 1 F.3d 24 (D.C. Cir. 1993), *cert. denied,* 511 U.S. 1138 (1994).

subcontracting in *Fibreboard* and the partial closure in *FNM* and concluded that the relocation of a plant was more like the *Fibreboard* subcontracting than the *FNM* partial closing. First, like the subcontracting employer in *Fibreboard* and unlike the employer partial closing in *FNM*, relocation involves the "replacement" of employees. Second, relocation is not like a decision whether to be in business at all as in *FNM*; the employer intends to be in business in a relocation case, the only question is where. Third, in relocation cases, the union may have substantial "control or authority" over the basis of the employer's decision—like costs in subcontracting. The new test: the General Counsel (GC) has the initial burden of showing that the employer's decision involved a relocation of unit work unaccompanied by a basic change in the nature of the operations. If the GC meets this burden, a prima facie case that the employer's decision is a mandatory subject has been made.[100] The employer may rebut this prima facie case by showing that the relocated work is significantly different from the work performed at the former plant or that the employer's decision involves a change in the scope of the enterprise. Alternatively, the employer can show: (1) labor cost (directly or indirectly) was not a factor in the decision, or (2) even if labor cost were a factor, "the union could not have offered labor cost concessions that could have changed the employer's decision to relocate."[101]

Once again, as in the dual motive cases,[102] the Board has used a rule of evidentiary procedure to bail it out of a difficult problem of balancing competing interests. The *Dubuque Packing* test tries to preserve an employer's entrepreneurial control, heeding Justice Stewart's admonitions in *Fibreboard.*[103] It also attempts to preserve a place for collective bargaining

[100] Like Justice Stewart in *Fibreboard*, the Board would find a decision involving a basic change in the scope of the enterprise to be non-mandatory.

[101] 303 NLRB 391 (1991). Importantly, the D.C. Circuit decision makes the union's willingness to offer concessions an important element of this futility defense.

[102] *See* Wright Line, 251 NLRB 1083 (1980), *enforced*, 662 F.2d 899 (1st Cir. 1981), *cert. denied*, 455 U.S. 989 (1982) *and* NLRB v. Transportation Management Corp., 462 U.S. 393 (1983).

[103] The D.C. Circuit described the Board's *Dubuque Packing* decision as involving three distinct layers of analysis. The first recognizes entrepreneurial decisions. The Court noted that the *Dubuque Packing* test permits employers to act unilaterally where relocation decisions involve:

> (1) "a basic change in the nature of the employer's operation," (2) "a change in the scope and direction of the enterprise," (3) situations in which "the work performed at the new location varies significantly from the work performed at the former plant," or (4) situations in which "the work performed at the former plant is to be discontinued entirely and not moved to the new location."

where that process has a good chance to work. In *Dubuque Packing*, the Board has also indicated a willingness to consider an employer's need for secrecy, speed and flexibility where it has a duty to bargain in entrepreneurial cases by giving those factors great weight in determining whether the parties have bargained to impasse.[104]

[C]—Multiemployer and Multiunion Bargaining

A substantial part of the organized American workforce is covered by multiemployer collective bargaining agreements.[105] This form of bargaining is particularly prevalent in the construction, longshore, clothing, coal mining, trucking and warehousing, and wholesale and retail industries. The First Circuit explained the attraction of multiemployer bargaining as follows:

> Multiemployer bargaining offers advantages to both management and labor. It enables smaller employers to bargain "on an equal basis with a large union" and avoid "the competitive disadvantages resulting from nonuniform contractual terms." . . . At the same time, it facilitates the development of industry-wide, worker benefit programs that employers otherwise might be unable to provide. More generally, multiemployer bargaining encourages both sides to adopt a flexible attitude during negotiations; as the Board explains, employers can make concessions "without fear that other employers will refuse to make similar concessions to achieve a competitive advantage," and a union can act similarly "without fear that the employees will be dissatisfied at not receiving the same benefits which the union might win from other employers." . . . Finally, by permitting the union and employers to concentrate their bargaining resources on the negotiation of a single contract, multiemployer bargaining enhances the efficiency and effectiveness of the collective bargaining process and thereby reduces industrial strife.[106]

---

1 F.3d at 30.

The second layer is subjective and the third is futility. Any of these can relieve the employer of the obligation to bargain about the decision.

104 The Worker Adjustment and Retraining Notification Act (WARN), 29 U.S.C. Section 2101-08 (1988), requires 60-days notice of a plant closing or mass layoff. The employer is not liable for notice under some circumstances, and WARN's provisions are enforceable in federal court by a union or affected employees. *See* United Food & Commercial Workers v. Brown Group, 517 U.S. 544 (1996).

105 *See* Charles D. Bonano Linen Service, Inc. v. NLRB, 454 U.S. 404 (1982).

106 Charles D. Bonano, 630 F.2d 25, 28 (1st Cir. 1980).

Despite its importance, the NLRA does not specifically address multiemployer bargaining. Section 9(b) of the Act authorizes the Board to decide whether a unit appropriate for collective bargaining shall be "the employer unit, craft unit, plant unit, or subdivision thereof."[107] It also addresses the significance of specific factors in unit determination, for example, professional and non-professional employees in the same unit, a previous unit determination, and guards and non-guards. Section 9(c)(5) also negates the extent of organization as a controlling factor in unit determination. However, Section 2(2) of the Act defines an "employer" as "any person acting as an agent of the employer," and Section 2(1) of the Act defines a "person" as "associations." The Board has held that the employer unit authorized by Section 9(b) of the Act includes the multiemployer unit.[108]

However, the Board does not direct an election initially in a multiemployer unit. Rather, such units are consensual, and once the union and employers agree, the unit is deemed appropriate.

A number of issues in multiemployer bargaining have involved formation and withdrawal from the unit. Inclusion in a multiemployer bargaining unit is marked by participation in multiemployer bargaining with an agreement to be bound.[109] The existence of a multiemployer bargaining unit with one unit of employees represented by the union, for example, production and maintenance workers, does not justify the extension of the multiemployer bargaining unit to include another unit of unconsenting employees such as clerical workers.[110] An employer may be part of a multiemployer bargaining unit for one unit of employees and a single employer bargaining unit for another unit of employees.[111]

Since multiemployer bargaining is a consensual relationship, withdrawal is permitted by one or more employers or the union with unequivocal notice before the onset of negotiations.[112] However, after negotiations begin,

---

[107] *See* Section 9(b), *supra* note 3.

[108] *See* Associated Shoe Industries of Southeastern Mass., Inc., 81 NLRB 224 (1949).

[109] Gorman, *supra* note 75, at 87-88.

[110] *See* NLRB v. Local 210, Teamsters (Dancker & Sellew, Inc.), 330 F.2d 46 (2d Cir. 1964).

[111] *See* Joseph E. Seagram & Sons, 101 NLRB 101 (1952).

[112] *See* Retail Associates, Inc., 120 NLRB 388 (1958) (unequivocal notice required) and Publishers' Ass'n of New York City v. NLRB, 364 F.2d 293 (2d Cir.), *cert. denied*, 385 U.S. 971 (1966) (union has equal withdrawal right). The union may withdraw from the entire multiemployer unit or from multiemployer bargaining with only one or more employers in the unit. Pacific Coast Ass'n of Pulp & Paper Mfrs., 163 NLRB 892 (1967).

Board rules seek to produce stability in the bargaining relationship by forbidding withdrawal from the multiemployer unit unless the other party consents or "unusual circumstances" exists. The Board has described its "unusual circumstances" doctrine as follows:

> [T]he Board has limited application of the term "unusual circumstances" to those cases in which the withdrawing employer has been faced with dire economic circumstances, i.e., circumstances in which the very existence of an employer as a viable business entity has ceased or is about to cease. Thus, the Board has held that an employer may withdraw from a multiemployer bargaining association after negotiations with the union have begun where the employer is subject to extreme economic difficulties which result in an arrangement under the bankruptcy laws; where the employer is faced with the imminent prospect of such adverse economic conditions as would require it to close its plant; or where the employer is faced with the prospect of being forced out of business for lack of qualified employees to do the job and the union refuses to assist the employer by providing replacements for the employees he lost. [Footnotes omitted.][113]

Because a bargaining impasse does not necessarily signal the end of the collective bargaining relationship, the Supreme Court held in *Charles D. Bonano Linen Service, Inc. v. NLRB*[114] that an impasse is not an "unusual circumstance" justifying withdrawal from the unit. The Court reasoned:

> [A]n impasse is not sufficiently destructive of group bargaining to justify unilateral withdrawal. As a recurring feature in the bargaining process, impasse is only a temporary deadlock or hiatus in negotiations "which in almost all cases is eventually broken either through a change of mind or the application of economic force." . . . Furthermore, an impasse may be "brought about intentionally by one or both parties as a device to further, rather than destroy, the bargaining process." Hence "there is little warrant for regarding an impasse as a rupture of the bargaining relation which leaves the parties free to go their own ways."[115]

Where a single large employer employs several units of employees represented by different unions, the unions may desire to coordinate their bargaining efforts. Unions have a right to engage in coordinated as

---

113 Hi-Way Billboards, Inc., 206 NLRB 22, 27-28 (1973).

114 454 U.S. 404 (1982).

115 454 U.S. 404, 412 (1982).

distinguished from consolidated or coalition bargaining. *General Electric v. NLRB,*[116] is an example of coordinated bargaining. General Electric (GE) employed almost 300,000 employees in 60 plants and 400 other facilities throughout the United States. More than 80 unions in approximately 150 bargaining units represented GE's employees. The International Union of Electrical, Radio and Machine Workers (IUE) represented about 80,000 of those employees. In an effort to increase the flow of information between the various unions and reduce the company's ability "to play one [union] off against the other," the union included representatives from seven other international unions representing GE employees on its negotiating committee. The company refused to bargain with this "mixed" negotiating committee. The Board, supported by the Second Circuit, held that the company's refusal to bargain violated Section 8(a)(5) of the Act. The reason is that Section 7, like Section 8(b)(1)(B), gives the parties the right to bargain through representatives of their own choosing.[117]

In order to avoid the obligation to deal with the other party's chosen representative, a party must show that a representative is "so infected with ill-will, usually personal, or conflict of interest as to make good-faith bargaining impractical."[118] The Court characterized this showing as a considerable burden. Acknowledging the "ill-will" exception, the Court in *General Electric* agreed with the Board that the overall policy of encouraging free selection of representatives made a *per se* rule banning mixed committees inappropriate.

On the other hand, the parties may agree to consolidate units for bargaining; but Section 8(b)(3) prevents unions from attempting to force employers into multi-unit bargaining through consolidated or coalition bargaining. The Oil, Chemical and Atomic Workers (OCAW) encountered this problem when they insisted that Shell Oil engage in multi-unit

---

116 412 F.2d 512 (2d Cir. 1969).

117 *See supra* § 4.1 for Section 7. Section 8(b)(1)(B) provides:

(b) It shall be an unfair labor practice for a labor organization or its agents—

(1) to restrain or coerce . . . (B) an employer in the selection of his representatives for the purposes of collective bargaining or the adjustment of grievances; . . . .

118 412 F.2d 512, 517 (1969). The Court cited and summarized the relevant cases as follows:

NLRB v. ILGWU, 274 F.2d 376 (3d Cir. 1960) (ex-union official added to employer committee to "put one over on the union"); Bausch & Lomb Optical Co., 108 NLRB 1555 (1954) (union established company in direct competition with employer); NLRB v. Kentucky Utilities Co., 182 F.2d 810 (6th Cir. 1950) (union negotiator had expressed great personal animosity towards employer).

412 F.2d 512, 517 (1969).

bargaining with 19 units of 6,000 employees over modifications to its benefits plans. The District of Columbia Circuit in *OCAW v. NLRB*[119] noted that forcing multi-unit bargaining upon an unconsenting employer would undermine the Board's exclusive jurisdiction over unit determination under the Act.

§ 7.5 Execution of the Agreement

Section 8(d) of the Act defines the duty to bargain to include the execution of a written contract of any agreement upon a party's request.[120]

The Act's concern for the status and effectiveness of the collective bargaining representative, seen in the general duty to bargain, the duty to refrain from making pre-impasse unilateral changes, and the duty to disclose information, is also manifested in the duty to sign and not to renege on agreements. Even before the explicit obligation of Section 8(d), the Supreme Court in *H.J. Heinz Co. v. NLRB*[121] held that the duty to bargain in good faith included the obligation to commit the agreement to writing. Adopting the Board's view of the importance of signing a contract to recognition of the union, harmonious labor relations, and memorializing the agreement, the Court explained:

> A business man who entered into negotiations with another for an agreement having numerous provisions, with the reservation that he would not reduce it to writing or sign it, could hardly be thought to have bargained in good faith. This is even more so in the case of an employer who, by his refusal to honor, with his signature, the agreement which he has made with a labor organization, discredits the organization, impairs the bargaining process and tends to frustrate the aim of the statute to secure industrial peace through collective bargaining.[122]

More recently, the Court has applied the explicit terms of Section 8(d) by finding that an employer member of a multiemployer association violated 8(a)(5) by seeking to withdraw from the association after an agreement had been reached and refusing to sign the agreement.[123]

---

119 486 F.2d 1266 (1973).

120 Section 8(d) of the Act provides in part:

> the execution of a written contract incorporating any agreement reached if requested by either party.

121 311 U.S. 514 (1941).

122 *Id.* at 526.

123 *See* NLRB v. Strong, 393 U.S. 357 (1969).

Reneging on agreements reached in the bargaining process is a milder form of the "refusal to execute" violation. In these cases the question is whether the repudiation of preexisting agreements indicates bad faith. The likelihood of a finding of bad faith is increased where the repudiation is unjustified.[124]

§ 7.6 Bargaining During the Term of the Agreement

Successful collective bargaining results in an agreement which orders the parties' relationship for some defined period. A typical agreement covers the full range of issues that are important to the parties such as union recognition and security, management rights, discrimination, wages and benefits, hours of work, holidays, vacation, seniority, discipline, grievance-arbitration, strikes and lockouts, safety concerns, and the duration and scope of the agreement.

For two major reasons, the parties' bargaining obligation does not end with the execution of the agreement. First, even where the agreement is comprehensive, questions may arise during the term of the agreement regarding the application of its provisions to specific situations. Second, because of the impossibility or impracticability of reducing to writing every issue that might arise during the term of the agreement, the parties may be called upon to deal with issues unaddressed contractually that emerge during the term of the agreement. What form does this mid-term obligation to bargain take?

[A]—Surviving Duties

The bargaining obligation defined in Section 8(d) includes the duty to negotiate any question arising under the collective bargaining agreement.[125] Frequently, such mid-term questions are addressed under the contractual grievance-arbitration procedure. For example, if an employer deprives a unit employee of a higher pay rate for temporary work in a higher job classification contrary to a contractual provision, the employee may file a grievance and, failing attempts to settle the grievance in earlier steps of the grievance procedure, proceed through the union to arbitration. As the Supreme Court noted in *United Steelworkers v. Warrior & Gulf Co.*, "The

---

[124] *See* Food Serv. Co., 202 NLRB 790 (1973) (where previous agreements were rescinded on advice of counsel based on legitimate business considerations). Questions sometimes arise concerning whether an agreement was actually reached and whether it was conditional upon the settlement of other contractual items.

[125] *See supra* note 49.

grievance procedure is, in other words, a part of the continuous collective bargaining process."[126]

Moreover, even though the compliance of the contracting parties with the duty to bargain in good faith has produced a collective bargaining agreement, other attributes of the duty to bargain retain vitality during the term of the agreement. For example, *National Labor Relations Board v. Acme Industrial Co.*[127] involved the duty to disclose information. In that case, the union discovered that the company was removing machinery from its plant and invoked contractual provisions barring the subcontracting of unit work and giving employees transfer rights. In processing the grievance, the union requested and the company denied information relevant to the removal of the equipment. Citing *Truitt*, the Board held that the company violated 8(a)(5) by depriving the union of information for the proper performance of its duties, in that case to intelligently evaluate the grievance. The Supreme Court upheld the Board's ruling, saying that "the duty to bargain unquestionably extends beyond the period of contract negotiations and applies to labor-management relations during the term of an agreement."

Some tension exists between the Board's enforcement of the parties' bargaining obligation during the term of the agreement and the parties' chosen dispute settlement mechanism, since both might involve an interpretation of the agreement. The legislative history of the 1947 amendments to the Act shows that Congress rejected an attempt to make any alleged violation of an agreement an unfair labor practice. That amendment would have given the Board ULP jurisdiction over all alleged breach of contract actions. The Supreme Court in *NLRB v. C&C Plywood*[128] said the following about Congress's rejection of the amendment:

> When Congress determined the Board should not have general jurisdiction over all alleged violations of collective bargaining agreements and that such matter should be placed within the jurisdiction of the courts [under Section 301 of the Labor Management Relations Act],[129] it was acting upon principle which this Court had already recognized:
>
> > "The Railway Labor Act, like the National Labor Relations Act, does not undertake governmental regulation of wages, hours, or working

---

126 363 U.S. 574, 581 (1960).

127 385 U.S. 432 (1967).

128 385 U.S. 421 (1967).

129 *See infra* Chapter 13, § 13.5.

> conditions. Instead it seeks to provide a means by which agreement may be reached with respect to them." [Citation omitted.]
>
> To have conferred upon the National Labor Relations Board generalized power to determine the rights of parties under all collective agreements would have been a step toward governmental regulation of the terms of those agreements. We view Congress' decision not to give the Board that broad power as a refusal to take this step. [Footnote omitted.][130]

This history makes it clear that Congress reserved garden variety breach of contract claims for the contractual dispute settlement mechanism rather than the Board.

The Seventh Circuit in *Acme Industrial* had refused to enforce the Board order requiring the company to disclose information regarding the removal of machinery, saying that the contractual arbitration procedure "foreclosed the Board from exercising its statutory power."[131] In reversing the Seventh Circuit and upholding the Board, the Supreme Court said:

> [W]hen [the Board] ordered the employer to furnish the requested information to the union, the Board was not making a binding construction of the labor contract. It was only acting upon the probability that the desired information was relevant, and that it would be of use to the union in carrying out its statutory duties and responsibilities. This discovery-type standard decided nothing about the merits of the union's contractual claims. When the respondent furnishes the requested information, it may appear that no subcontracting or work transfer has occurred, and, accordingly, that the grievances filed are without merit. On the other hand, even if it appears that such activities have taken place, an arbitrator might uphold the respondent's contention that no breach of the agreement occurred because no employees were laid off or reduced in grade within five days prior to the filing of any grievance. Such conclusions would clearly not be precluded by the Board's threshold determination concerning the potential relevance of the requested information. Thus, the assertion of jurisdiction by the Board in this case in no way threatens the power which the parties have given the arbitrator to make binding interpretations of the labor agreement.[132]

---

130 385 U.S. 421, 426 (1967).

131 *Id.* at 433.

132 *Id.* at 437-438.

The duty to refrain from making pre-impasse unilateral changes also survives during the term of the agreement. In *C&C Plywood*, the company unilaterally increased premium wages for a group of employees and refused to rescind the pay program during discussions with the union. The pivotal issue in the case was whether the contractual wage provision authorized the company to institute the wage program. In reading the provision, the Board concluded that it did not. The Ninth Circuit had agreed with the company that the issue as to the meaning of the wage provision placed the dispute before the courts under Section 301 rather than the Board. The Supreme Court disagreed. Noting the Board's lack of general jurisdiction over contractual violations, the Court said:

> But in this case the Board has not construed a labor agreement to determine the extent of the contractual rights which were given the union by the employer. It has not imposed its own view of what the terms and conditions of the labor agreement should be. It has done no more than merely enforce a statutory right which Congress considered necessary to allow labor and management to get on with the process of reaching fair terms and conditions of employment—"to provide a means by which agreement may be reached." The Board's interpretation went only so far as was necessary to determine that the union did not agree to give up these statutory safeguards. Thus, the Board, in necessarily construing a labor agreement to decide this unfair labor practice case, has not exceeded the jurisdiction laid out for it by Congress.[133]

[B]—Enforcement Jurisdiction

Since the alleged unilateral change in *C&C Plywood* may give rise to a statutory or contractual violation, nice jurisdictional questions arise concerning the jurisdictional relationship between the Board and contractual grievance-arbitration. The Supreme Court was confronted with such a case in *Carey v. Westinghouse Elec. Corp.*[134] where the union's claim of improperly assigned unit work might have breached the contract as well as Section 8(b)(4)(D) or 8(a)(5) or fallen within the Board's unit clarification jurisdiction. The Supreme Court compelled arbitration of the matter, even though it was subject to the Board's jurisdiction, citing the potential usefulness of arbitration in resolving the dispute and the Board's ability to defer or assert jurisdiction after the arbitrator's award.[135]

---

133 C&C Plywood, 385 U.S. at 428.

134 375 U.S. 261 (1964).

135 See generally the discussion on deferral, *infra* Chapter 13, § 13.5.

[C]—Mid-Term Modifications

Section 8(d) contains a number of procedural requirements that must precede termination or modification of the agreement.[136] These typically are triggered by the expiration of an existing agreement and require notice to the opposing party of a proposed modification of the agreement and notice to the Federal Mediation and Conciliation Service and comparable state agencies. That section also calls for a cooling off period for the suspension of strikes and lockouts.[137] Any party attempting a modification

---

[136] Section 8(d) provides in part:

Provided, That where there is in effect a collective-bargaining contract covering employees in an industry affecting commerce, the duty to bargain collectively shall also mean that no party to such contract shall terminate or modify such contract, unless the party desiring such termination or modification—

(1) serves a written notice upon the other party to the contract of the proposed termination or modification sixty days prior to the expiration date thereof, or in the event such contract contains no expiration date, sixty days prior to the time it is proposed to make such termination or modification;

(2) offers to meet and confer with the other party for the purpose of negotiating a new contract or a contract containing the proposed modifications;

(3) notifies the Federal Mediation and Conciliation Service within thirty days after such notice of the existence of a dispute, and simultaneously therewith notifies any State or Territorial agency established to mediate and conciliate disputes within the State or Territory where the dispute occurred, provided no agreement has been reached by that time; and

(4) continues in full force and effect, without resorting to strike or lock-out, all the terms and conditions of the existing contract for a period of sixty days after such notice is given or until the expiration date of such contract, whichever occurs later:

The duties imposed upon employers, employees, and labor organizations by paragraphs (2), (3), and (4) shall become inapplicable upon an intervening certification of the Board, under which the labor organization or individual, which is a party to the contract, has been superseded as or ceased to be the representative of the employees subject to the provisions of section 9(a), ...

[137] As indicated, *infra* Chapter 16, § 16.4, Section 8(d) removes protected status from employees engaging in a strike during any notice period. It also adds to the notice period for health care institutions as follows:

Whenever the collective bargaining involves employees of a health care institution, the provisions of this section 8(d) shall be modified as follows:

(A) The notice of section 8(d)(1) shall be ninety days; the notice of section 8(d)(3) shall be sixty days; and the contract period of section 8(d)(4) shall be ninety days.

(B) Where the bargaining is for an initial agreement following certification or recognition, at least thirty days' notice of the existence of a dispute shall be given by the labor organization to the agencies set forth in section 8(d)(3).

(C) After notice is given to the Federal Mediation and Conciliation Service under either

of the agreement without complying with these procedures violates the duty to bargain.

Attempts at mid-term modifications of the agreement that are not on the eve of expiration and negotiation of a successor agreement pose the most difficult legal problems. These take the form of efforts by one party, usually the union, to change an existing contractual provision or a party's, usually the employer's, unilateral change of an existing (though unwritten) practice. As a threshold matter, the employer has no duty to bargain about non-mandatory subjects, just as it has no such duty in the pre-contractual negotiation setting under *Borg-Warner.* The case making this point is *Allied Chemical and Alkali Workers v. Pittsburgh Plate Glass Co.*[138] In that case, the company sought to discontinue a negotiated health plan for retirees and substitute supplemental Medicare coverage. The union protested that this unilateral change constituted a violation of Section 8(a)(5). While the Board agreed, the Supreme Court considered the uncertain effects of retiree benefits on those of active employees and reversed, holding that retiree benefits are not mandatory subjects of bargaining.

The definition of the duty to bargain contained in Section 8(d) includes the following:

> the duties so imposed shall not be construed as requiring either party to discuss or agree to any modification of the terms and conditions contained in a contract for a fixed period, if such modification is to become effective before such terms and conditions can be reopened under the provisions of the contract.

Pittsburgh Plate Glass Co. demonstrates that the sanctity of the agreement's terms against mid-term modification applies only to mandatory subjects. As the Court notes: "The remedy for a unilateral mid-term modification of a permissive term lies in an action for breach of contract, . . . not in an unfair labor practice proceeding."[139]

---

clause (A) or (B) of this sentence, the Service shall promptly communicate with the parties and use its best efforts, by mediation and conciliation, to bring them to agreement. The parties shall participate fully and promptly in such meeting as may be undertaken by the Service for the purpose of aiding in a settlement of the dispute.

Section 8(g) tacks on a 10-day notice period before "engaging in any strike, picketing, or other concerted refusal to work at any health care institution."

138 404 U.S. 157 (1971).

139 *Id.* at 188.

As to mandatory subjects "contained in" in the agreement, Sections 8(a)(5) and 8(b)(3) prohibit any alteration during the term of the agreement without the consent of the other party.[140] Hence, the finding that a matter is "contained in" the agreement imposes a stricter constraint on the parties than the finding that it is not.[141] The question of what is "contained in" the agreement, therefore, is important to the parties' rights during the term of the agreement. In *Milwaukee Spring Div. of Illinois Coil Spring Co.*,[142] the Board considered whether the agreement should be broadly or narrowly interpreted to determine whether the agreement contained a provision preventing the employer from relocating its unionized Milwaukee Spring operations to its non-union McHenry facility during the term of the agreement. The union had argued that the company's relocation decision based upon labor costs at the Milwaukee Spring facility was a modification of the provision of the agreement setting wages at that facility. Narrowly interpreting the wage provision, the Board majority rejected that claim saying: "It is not for the Board, however, to create an implied work-preservation clause in every American labor agreement based on wage and benefits . . . provisions, and we expressly decline to do so."[143] The majority added that the onus was on the union to negotiate a work preservation provision. The dissent would have held that the company's relocation decision "was simply an attempt to modify the wage rate provisions in the contract, albeit indirectly," since it was motivated by the avoidance of wage rates at the Milwaukee Springs facility.[144]

Under the preceding language of Section 8(d) what does a party's duty to bargain over matters contained in the agreement entail? What about matters not contained in the agreement? What distinguishes the two? The Board's decision in *Jacobs Manufacturing Co.*,[145] offers the most definitive answers to these questions. In that case the employer and union executed a two-year contract with a provision allowing the subject of wages to be reopened after one year. The union invoked the reopener provision after

---

[140] *See* Oak Cliff-Golman Baking Co., 207 NLRB 1063 (1973), *enforced*, 505 F.2d 1302 (5th Cir. 1974), *cert. denied*, 423 U.S. 826 (1975).

[141] See discussion, *supra* note 140 and *infra* notes 142-147 and accompanying text, regarding the duty to bargain about mandatory subjects not contained in the agreement. Essentially, it is the duty to bargain to impasse enunciated in *Katz* that attaches to mandatory subjects not contained in the agreement.

[142] 268 NLRB 601 (D.C. Cir. 1984).

[143] *Id.* at 602.

[144] *Id.* at 611.

[145] 94 NLRB 1214 (1951).

one year. In addition to its demand for a wage increase, the union requested the employer's full funding of an existing group insurance program and the establishment of a pension plan for unit employees. Neither the insurance program nor pensions were mentioned in the agreement, though the parties had discussed the insurance program during contract negotiations. The employer refused to discuss the union's pension and insurance requests.

The issue was whether the subjects of insurance and pensions were "contained in" the contract within the meaning of Section 8(d). If they were, no duty to bargain existed. If they were not, the employer had a duty to bargain over these mandatory subjects. The disagreement among Board members over the definition of "contained in" reflected philosophical differences over collective bargaining policy. Members Houston and Styles held that "contained in" encompassed only those terms expressly written into the agreement, creating a duty to bargain over all other unwritten mandatory subjects. In their view, this reading encouraged flexibility in several ways: (1) it avoided a slowing down of the process by removing the pressure to pursue unimportant matters at the time of negotiations under the specter of later foreclosure should such matters become important, (2) it kept the door open for future discussion of unresolved issues, and (3) it recognized that not all important issues can be anticipated at the outset of negotiations.

Two other Board Members, Reynolds and Murdock, held that only the terms of the contract define the duty to bargain during the term. Neither party has a duty to bargain about terms not mentioned unless directed by some provision of the contract. This construction of the mid-term duty was thought necessary to advance stability in the workplace enabling employers to do long-term planning and employees to have job security. Permitting bargaining on unmentioned subjects would undermine stability by subjecting the agreement to continual alteration. Under this view, items not mentioned in the contract have been intentionally foregone or traded for other items and should remained settled. The duty to bargain during the term only means interpreting and administering the terms of the agreement through the grievance procedure.

Member Herzog cast the swing vote holding that items "fully discussed" or "consciously explored" were "contained in" the agreement. As to these items, there is no duty to bargain, agree or modify. Since the parties had discussed the insurance premium during negotiations, it was part of the agreement. On the other hand, the pension issue, not discussed during negotiations, had not been "fully discussed" or "consciously explored" and was not contained in the agreement. On that issue, the employer was obliged to bargain. This approach purported to strike a balance between stability and flexibility—not permitting either party to raise issues believed put to rest but allowing them to raise important matters not addressed at the time of bargaining.[146]

Even under *Jacobs*, the parties can avoid a duty to bargain about matter not contained in the agreement, such as the pensions in that case, by including a waiver known as a "zipper clause" in the agreement. Members Houston and Styles noted a zipper clause between the United Automobile Workers of America and General Motors to emphasize the point.[147]

But does such a waiver permit the employer to implement unilateral changes? Not if they are "contained in" the agreement, since such a modification without the consent of the other party would violate the duty to bargain as defined in Section 8(d). If they are not contained in the agreement, the answer is less clear. The Board construes waivers under a contextual approach. An examination of the contract, including interpretive arbitration awards, negotiating history, and past practices, must reveal a "clear and unequivocal waiver" of the employer's duty to refrain from making unilateral changes during the term of the agreement.[148]

Johnson-Bateman Co.[149] is a recent case that applies the Board's waiver doctrine. In that case, the company unilaterally adopted a mandatory alcohol

---

146 The Second Circuit in NLRB v. Jacobs Mfg. Co., 196 F.2d 680 (2d Cir. 1952), agreed with the Board majority that the company was obligated to bargain about the pension issue, which had not been discussed during negotiations. However, because the Board majority concluded that the company had no duty to bargain about the insurance program, the court did not pass upon the duty to bargain about matters discussed but not expressed in the agreement.

147 The noted zipper clause reads as follows:

> (154) The parties acknowledge that during the negotiations which resulted in this agreement, each had the unlimited right and opportunity to make demands and proposals with respect to any subject or matter not removed by law from the area of collective bargaining, and that the understandings and agreements arrived at by the parties after the exercise of that right and opportunity are set forth in this agreement. Therefore, the Corporation and the Union, for the life of this agreement, each voluntarily and unqualifiedly waives the right, and each agrees that the other shall not be obligated, to bargain collectively with respect to any subject or matter not specifically referred to or covered in this agreement, even though such subjects or matter may not have been within the knowledge or contemplation of either or both of the parties at the time that they negotiated or signed this agreement.

148 *See generally* Gorman, *supra* note 75, at 466-481.

149 295 NLRB 180 (1989).

and drug testing policy for all employees who were injured and required treatment. The union objected and filed a charge with the Board. After finding the drug testing policy a mandatory subject of bargaining the Board addressed the company's waiver argument. The company claimed that two contractual provisions, agreed to by the union, waived the right to bargain about the new drug testing policy. One provision reserved to management the right to "issue, enforce and change company rules" as well as all pre-contractual rights, privileges and prerogatives. A second gave management the right to discipline and discharge employees with just cause. A unilaterally promulgated extra-contractual work rule, whose validity was not in dispute, defined "just cause" to include "drinking or possessing any alcoholic beverages on company premises or on company time or reporting for work while under the influence of alcohol or drugs." The contract also contained a general zipper clause which read: "Except as provided herein this agreement resolves all the bargainable issues for the term hereof." The Board restated the general principle that waivers must be clear and unmistakable and found that the "management rights," "just cause," and "zipper" provisions were too general to be interpreted as waivers of the right to bargain about a change in the drug testing policy.

The provision that warranted the most discussion was the management rights clause. The Board said that its approach would be to evaluate bargaining history to determine whether the parties intended to relinquish the right to bargain where terms are general. In *Johnson-Bateman*, the Board found that the question of drug and alcohol testing was not "fully discussed or consciously explored" in bargaining and it was unwilling to jettison the right to bargain based on this history. While acknowledging the importance of arbitration decisions to understanding the meaning of contractual terms including the general waiver, the Board found that the awards cited by the company did not read the contract as containing a waiver of the right to bargain about drug and alcohol testing. The Board also examined past practice, but found that the union's acquiescence to other work rules did not constitute a waiver of the right to bargain about drug and alcohol testing.

[D]—The Bankruptcy Laws

The policy of stability in collective bargaining reflected in the mid-term bargaining rules of Section 8(d) conflicts with that of rehabilitating businesses under the federal bankruptcy laws. Specifically, the rule preventing the mid-term modification of terms and conditions contained in the contract is inconsistent with the power of a "debtor-in-possession" of a business to unilaterally reject an executory contract. The Supreme Court confronted this dilemma in *NLRB v. Bildisco & Bildisco*,[150] holding that a collective bargaining agreement was an executory contract that could be rejected under the Bankruptcy Code with the approval of the Bankruptcy Court. The debtor's required showing was "that the collective-bargaining agreement burdens the estate, and that after careful scrutiny, the equities balance in favor of rejecting the labor contract,"[151] a standard higher than the "business judgment" test normally applied to commercial contracts but lower that the highest possible standard. In addition to this intermediate standard, the Court required an effort to settle with the union upon a modification of the agreement. The Court also said that the debtor's unilateral rejection of the contract in that case was not an unfair labor practice, since the agreement was unenforceable from the date of the filing of the petition in bankruptcy.

Immediately following the decision, Congress amended the Bankruptcy Code by adding special provisions governing the rejection of collective bargaining agreements.[152] The amendment requires the debtor-in-possession, before seeking rejection of the collective bargaining agreement, to make a proposal to the union "for those necessary modifications in the employees benefits and protections that are necessary to permit the reorganization of the debtor and assures that all creditors, the debtor and all of the affected parties are treated fairly and equitably."[153] The proposal is to be accompanied by relevant information and good faith negotiations. Under the amendment, the Bankruptcy Court is to approve an application for rejection of a collective bargaining agreement only if the debtor made the proposal, the union refused to accept it without good cause, and the balance of the equities "clearly favor rejection of the agreement."[154] The Bankruptcy Court is responsible for scheduling a hearing on any application for rejection, issuing any necessary protective orders, authorizing interim changes to prevent irreparable harm to the businesses, and making a timely ruling on the debtor's application.[155] Both *Bildisco* and the Bankruptcy Code amendments exemplify the accommodations between policies reflected in the Act and other legislation.

---

150 465 U.S. 513 (1984).

151 *Id.* at 526.

152 *See* 11 U.S.C. § 1113.

153 11 U.S.C. § 1113(b)(1)(A).

154 11 U.S.C. § 1113(c).

155 11 U.S.C. § 1113(d) and (e).

§ 7.7 Remedies for Violations of the Duty to Bargain

In remedying unfair labor practices, Section 10(c) of the Act mandates that the Board "take such affirmative action including reinstatement of employees . . . as will effectuate the policies of the Act."[156] However, Supreme Court and Board decisions reveal severe limitations on the Board's ability to remedy breaches of the obligation to bargain in good faith.

In *H.K. Porter Co. v. NLRB*,[157] the parties had negotiated for eight years without an agreement because of what the Board found to be the employer's "bad faith" refusal to agree to the union's dues checkoff proposal. To remedy this violation, the Board ordered the employer to agree to the dues checkoff proposal. Finding that this order countered the policy of freedom of contract embedded in Section 8(d), the Supreme Court reversed. For the Court, the freedom of contract policy is manifested in the statute's intent to permit parties to benefit from their economic strength as indicated in *Insurance Agents International*.[158] The Court also noted the private nature of the bargaining process, where the government's role is supervisory—monitoring the bargaining procedures and the parties' approach to the process of bargaining—and not regulatory of the actual terms of the

---

156 Section 10(c) reads in part:

> The testimony taken by such member, agent, or agency or the Board shall be reduced to writing and filed with the Board. Thereafter, in its discretion, the Board upon notice may take further testimony or hear argument. If upon the preponderance of the testimony taken the Board shall be of the opinion that any person named in the complaint has engaged in or is engaging in any such unfair labor practice, then the Board shall state its findings of fact and shall issue and cause to be served on such person an order requiring such person to cease and desist from such unfair labor practice, and to take such affirmative action including reinstatement of employees with or without back pay, as will effectuate the policies of this Act: *Provided*, That where an order directs reinstatement of an employee, back pay may be required of the employer or labor organization, as the case may be, responsible for the discrimination suffered by him: *And provided further*, That in determining whether a complaint shall issue alleging a violation of section 8(a)(1) or section 8(a)(2), and in deciding such cases, the same regulations and rules of decision shall apply irrespective of whether or not the labor organization affected is affiliated with a labor organization national or international in scope. Such order may further require such person to make reports from time to time showing the extent to which it has complied with the order. If upon the preponderance of the testimony taken the Board shall not be of the opinion that the person named in the complaint has engaged in or is engaging in any such unfair labor practice, then the Board shall state its findings of fact and shall issue an order dismissing the said complaint.

157 397 U.S. 99 (1970).

158 *See supra* note 50.

contract. Given these limitations, the Court in *H.K. Porter* held that the appropriate remedy was a "cease and desist" order.

Although the available remedy under *H.K. Porter* is a mere slap on the wrist, there are other situations involving 8(a)(5) violations where the remedies are more concrete. For example, where an employee and union have actually agreed to bargaining agreement terms but one of the parties repudiates and refuses to sign, there is ample authority upholding the Board's power to order the document signed and the agreement honored.[159] Similarly, where the employer's unilateral act without bargaining has cost the employees money, restoration of the status quo may include back pay or, as in the *Fibreboard* subcontracting case, resumption of operations, reinstatement and back pay.[160]

But where the union is newly certified and the employer engages in surface bargaining or challenges the certification for the purpose of delay only, the remedy may be crucial to the continued support of the union and, thus, to continued bargaining. *Ex-Cell-O Corporation*[161] makes the point that a remedy that seeks to go beyond setting the future stage for bargaining by remedying the past effects of an employer's unlawful refusal must yield to the rationale of *H.K. Porter.* In *Ex-Cell-O*, the union won an election on October 22, 1964. The company filed objections, which were overruled by the Acting Regional Director. The Board reviewed that decision, which was affirmed on October 28, 1965. The company refused to bargain, committing a technical 8(a)(5) violation in order to secure judicial review of the representation case. The Trial Examiner commenced a hearing on the Section 8(a)(5) charge on June 1, 1966, and after the company unsuccessfully attempted to secure an injunction against the Regional Director and Trial Examiner, the latter issued an award that the Board ultimately affirmed on August 25, 1970. The Trial Examiner recommended a "make-whole" remedy that would have required the Board to construct the terms of a hypothetical agreement as a condition precedent to determining the compensation to which employee would be entitled. The Board majority rejected the "make-whole" remedy, saying that it would have required the employer to take responsibility for an agreement, albeit

---

159 *See, e.g.*, NLRB v. Strong Roofing & Insulating Co., 393 U.S. 357 (1969) (where the Court upheld the Board's authority to order an employer who untimely withdrew from a multiemployer bargaining association to sign the contract reached between the employer and the union, despite the employer's challenge based on *H.K. Porter*).

160 *See Fibreboard, supra* note 88.

161 185 NLRB 107 (1970).

hypothetical. Like the Court in *H.K. Porter* the Board majority in *Ex-Cell-O* acknowledged the inadequacy of the Board's remedial authority under Section 8(a)(5) but explained that it was incumbent upon Congress to correct the discrepancy.

Organized labor attempted to bring about legislative reform in this area of the statute in 1978. Unions lobbied for amendments that would: (a) give a make-whole remedy in certain refusal to bargain cases, (b) bar government contracts to employers who refuse to bargain, (c) and award double back pay to discriminatorily discharged employees. The legislation passed the House but failed in the Senate to a successful filibuster.

§ 7.8 Chapter Highlights

1. Once a collective bargaining representative has been certified, ordered, or voluntarily recognized, the employer has an obligation to bargain exclusively with that representative. (§§ 7.2, 7.3)

2. The duty to bargain in good faith involves substantive and procedural obligations that are analyzed using contextual and *per se* approaches. (§ 7.4[A])

3. The bargaining obligation only attaches to mandatory subjects of bargaining during negotiations as well as the term of the agreement. (§ 7.4[B])

4. Even though multiemployer and coordinated bargaining may be efficient ways of negotiating in the circumstances, the Act requires neither. Parties who voluntarily enter a multiemployer bargaining relationship incur legal obligations. (§ 7.4[C])

5. After successful bargaining has occurred, the parties are obligated to sign the agreement. (§ 7.5)

6. Even though an executed agreement orders the parties' relationship, the duty to bargain with its attendant obligations to supply information and refrain from making unilateral changes continues during the term of the agreement, unless altered by it. (§ 7.6)

7. Remedies for breach of the duty to bargain are limited. (§ 7.7)

CHAPTER 8
DURATION OF UNION'S STATUS AS BARGAINING REPRESENTATIVE

§ 8.1 Generally

Once a union achieves representative status by election or by voluntary recognition, the employer must recognize and bargain with it so long as that status is retained. Because industrial stability, a major policy goal of the labor laws,[1] is fostered by continuing bargaining relationships and infrequent changes of representative, the law gives substantial weight to the results of prior representation elections and interferes with bargaining relationships only in extraordinary cases. To foster industrial stability, the Board, with Supreme Court approval, has created a presumption that a person represented by a union continues to wish representation by that union absent strong proof to the contrary.

As this chapter will discuss, this "presumption of continued majority support" has major implications for successor employers and in cases where either the employer or employees wish to challenge the union's majority status.

§ 8.2 The Presumption of Continued Majority Status

[A]—Irrebuttable Presumptions

During certain time periods, a union is virtually impregnable to challenges to its majority status. During these time periods, a union is held to have an irrebuttable presumption of majority status.

[1] Certification Year

To permit collective bargaining to have a chance to work and to foster stability in labor relations, the Board, with Supreme Court approval, adopted a rule requiring that, absent unusual circumstances, an employer must recognize a union for the entire year following certification even if it has

---

[1] Section 1 of the National Labor Relations Act, as amended, sets forth a basic policy of the Act:

> Experience has proved that protection by law of the right of employees to organize and bargain collectively safeguards commerce from injury, impairment, or interruption, and promotes the flow of commerce by removing certain recognized sources of industrial strife and unrest, by encouraging practices fundamental to the friendly adjustment of industrial disputes arising out of differences as to wages, hours, or other working conditions, and by restoring equality of bargaining power between employers and employees.

29 U.S.C. § 151. As the Supreme Court has observed, "[t]he underlying purpose of this statute is industrial peace." Brooks v. NLRB, 348 U.S. 96, 103 (1954).

evidence of the union's loss of majority.[2] During this time period, the union is irrebuttably presumed to enjoy majority status. In *Brooks v. NLRB*,[3] the union won a representation election by a vote of 8 to 5 and, one week later, was certified. One day after the certification, 9 of the 13 employees provided the employer with a letter stating that they did not wish to be represented by the union. The employer then refused to bargain. Upholding the Board's irrebuttable presumption rule, the Supreme Court affirmed the finding that the employer had committed an unfair labor practice.

If the employer violates Section 8(a)(5)[4] by refusing to bargain in good faith during the certification year, the Board may remedy the violation by renewing or extending the certification year.[5] The basis for such an extension is that, once established, a collective bargaining relationship "must be permitted to exist and function for a reasonable period in which it can be given a fair chance to succeed."[6]

[2] Voluntarily Recognized Unions

Where a union has been voluntarily recognized by the employer without election,[7] a similar presumption of continued majority support is applied.

[2] Brooks v. NLRB, 348 U.S. 96 (1954). Unusual circumstances, in the Court's view, include a schism in the certified union, its becoming defunct, or a radical fluctuation in bargaining unit size in a short time period. The Board and courts do not take a broad view of the term "unusual circumstances." To do so could involve allowing the exception to engulf the rule. *See, e.g.*, NLRB v. Mr. B. IGA, Inc., 677 F.2d 32 (8th Cir. 1982) (three-year delay between representation election and certification during which a reduction in bargaining unit size from 19 to 3 persons occurred through the sale of 3 of 4 stores in the unit and fact that remaining 3 employees did not vote in original election held not to create "unusual circumstances" sufficient to justify refusal to bargain in certification year); Airport-Shuttle, 257 NLRB 955 (1981) ("disaffection" petition allegedly signed by majority of employees and union's failure to contact employer until 8 months after certification do not constitute "unusual circumstances"); Ajax Magnethermic Corp., 229 NLRB 317 (1977), *enforced*, 541 F.2d 1210 (6th Cir. 1979) (Board rejected employer's arguments that employee turnover and changes in "conditions" constituted unusual circumstances justifying withdrawal).

[3] Brooks v. NLRB, 348 U.S. 96, 98-104 (1954).

[4] 29 U.S.C. § 158(a)(5).

[5] *See, e.g.*, Glomac Plastics Inc. v. NLRB, 592 F.2d 94, 100-101 (2d Cir. 1979) (renewal of entire certification year).

[6] Franks Bros. Co. v. NLRB, 321 U.S. 702, 705 (1944).

[7] Voluntary recognition is considered by the Board and the courts to further the objectives of the national labor policy and is therefore generally encouraged. *See* NLRB v. Broadmoor Lumber Co., 578 F.2d 238, 241 (9th Cir. 1978); NLRB v. Broad Street Hosp. & Medical Center, 432 F.2d 302, 305 (3d Cir. 1971).

However, an employer has no duty to bargain with a union which does not represent a

In cases of voluntary recognition, however, the irrebuttable presumption of continued support continues only for a "reasonable period" of time after recognition rather than for the arbitrary period of one year. A reasonable period of time is defined by asking whether bargaining had a "fair chance to succeed."[8]

[3] Contract Bar

The Board has also established a virtually irrebuttable presumption of majority status which binds the employer for the period during which the collective bargaining agreement would bar an election petition.[9] This presumption is based on the Board's contract-bar rule which bars an election petition while a written contract is in effect. Since 1962, the Board has held that an election petition will be barred during the term of an agreement which extends for not more than three years or during the first three years of a contract of longer duration.[10] As the Supreme Court has noted, "[D]uring this time, an employer cannot use doubt about a union's majority as a defense to a refusal-to-bargain charge."[11]

---

majority of its employees and, in fact, bargaining with such a union may well be an unfair labor practice, since it may constitute company support for a minority union in violation of Section 8(a)(2) of the National Labor Relations Act. 29 U.S.C. § 158(a)(2); NLRB v. Book, 532 F.2d 877 (2d Cir.), *cert. denied*, 429 U.S. 920 (1976). There is, however, no duty for an employer to voluntarily recognize and it may insist on an election. Linden Lumber Div., Summer & Co. v. NLRB, 419 U.S. 301, 310 (1974).

[8] *See* Brennan's Cadillac, 231 NLRB 225, 227 (1977) (4 months constituted reasonable period where 8 bargaining sessions had allowed parties to fully explore all issues at bargaining table).

[9] *See* Pioneer Inn Ass'n v. NLRB, 578 F.2d 835, 838 (9th Cir. 1978) (employer may not refuse to abide by contract terms on basis of doubt as to majority status of union); Shamrock Dairy, Inc., 119 NLRB 998, 1002 (1957), *on remand*, 124 NLRB 494, 495-96 (1959), *enforced sub nom.* Local 310, Int'l Bhd. of Teamsters v. NLRB, 280 F.2d 665 (D.C. Cir.), *cert. denied*, 364 U.S. 892 (1960) (employer must recognize the union for at least the term of the contract); Hexton Furniture Co., 111 NLRB 342, 344 (1955) (during term of collective bargaining agreement, employer may not refuse to recognize or bargain with the union).

[10] General Cable Corp., 139 NLRB 1123, 1125 (1962).

[11] NLRB v. Burns Int'l Security Servs., Inc., 406 U.S. 272, 290 n.12 (1972) (citations omitted). The Board believes that it would be anomalous to allow an employer unilaterally to determine whether its employees wished to be represented by a union at a time when the Board would refuse to conduct an election for that purpose, even on petition of the employees. Hexton Furniture Co., 111 NLRB 342 (1955). The employer in *Hexton* withdrew union recognition after a majority of its employees signed forms cancelling their dues check-off authorizations. Since the collective bargaining agreement had one more year to run, any election or decertification petition would have been denied by the Board. The Board held

[B]—Rebuttable Presumptions

Once the certification year has expired, an incumbent union continues to enjoy a rebuttable presumption of continued majority status.[12] It is this presumption that requires an employer to recognize and continue to bargain with an incumbent union years and even decades after the original certification election at which the union was selected. The presumption applies even if there has been substantial or total turnover since the original certification election.[13] It is this presumption that prevents an employer from withdrawing recognition from the union and leads to issues of possible successorship when there is a change of employer ownership.

§ 8.3 Successorship

[A]—Generally

Changes in business ownership have become quite common in our modern economy. Where the acquired company has employees represented by a union, several issues arise. Federal policies in favor of industrial stability and employee rights in continued representation are balanced against business interests in the free transfer of capital. Determinations as to whether the acquiring company must assume the labor contract or must assume successor status for bargaining purposes will be important to setting the terms of the transaction. In some cases, they will determine whether the transaction occurs.

---

that it was an unfair labor practice for the employer unilaterally to decide the issue of representation when, under the contract-bar rule, the Board would refuse to redetermine the issue.

[12] *See* J. Ray McDermott & Co. v. NLRB, 571 F.2d 850, 858 (5th Cir.), *cert. denied,* 439 U.S. 893 (1978) ("the presumption is rebuttable and may be overcome by 'objective evidence' proffered by an employer"); NLRB v. Windham Community Memorial Hosp., 577 F.2d 805, 811 (2d Cir. 1978) ("[f]ollowing the expiration of the certification year, the presumption remains in effect but becomes rebuttable"); NLRB v. Frick Co., 423 F.2d 1327, 1330 (3d Cir. 1970) ("although a presumption of majority status continues *after* one year, it then becomes rebuttable") (emphasis in original); Celanese Corp., 95 NLRB 664 (1951) ("after the first year . . . the presumption is . . . *rebuttable* even in the absence of unusual circumstances") (emphasis in original). *Celanese Corp.* was cited with approval in Brooks v. NLRB, 348 U.S. 96 (1954).

[13] One of the bases for the NLRB's presumption that new employees support the union in the same ratio as did employees voting in the original election is that such employees already have had the advantage of union representation. *See, e.g.,* Thomas Indus, 255 NLRB 646 (1981), *modified,* 687 F.2d 863 (6th Cir. 1982).

[B]—The *Burns* Decision

The Supreme Court's decision in *NLRB v. Burns International Security Services, Inc.*,[14] resolved a number of important issues governing successorship. In that case, Burns Security replaced another employer, Wackenhut Company, in providing plant guard services for Lockheed Aircraft at an airport in California. When Burns began providing guard services, it employed 42 guards, 27 of whom had been employed by Wackenhut. Wackenhut employees at the location in question had recently elected the United Plant Guards Union as bargaining representative and the union had entered into a collective bargaining agreement with the employer.

Burns refused to honor the contract and refused to bargain with the union. The union filed charges and the Board, after finding the airport location to be an appropriate unit, held that the employer violated Section 8(a)(5) by refusing to recognize the union and by refusing to honor the collective bargaining agreement.

When the case reached the Supreme Court, the Court made three decisions that shaped the course of successorship law. First, the Court held that Burns was not required to honor the substantive terms of the collective bargaining agreement. Burns was not a party to the agreement. The Court noted that an employer considering taking over a struggling business might not be willing to do so if it were to be saddled with the old agreement and that this could impede the transfer of capital.[15]

---

[14] 406 U.S. 272 (1972).

[15] The general rule, then, is that an acquiring company, whether or not a successor for bargaining purposes, does not automatically assume the collective bargaining agreement of its predecessor. There are exceptions to this rule. For example, if the new employer s an *alter ego* of the predecessor in that it has essentially the same ownership, business purposes and controlling parties, it can be bound by the contract. *See, e.g.*, P.A. Hayes, Inc., 226 NLRB 230 (1976); Custom Mfg. Co., 259 NLRB 614 (1981); Haley & Haley v. NLRB, 880 F.2d 1147 (9th Cir. 1989). *See also* Howard Johnson Co. v. Hotel Employees, 417 U.S. 249, 259 n.5, (1974) ("alter ego is subject to all the legal and contractual obligations of the predecessor").

The new employer can also become bound by its predecessor's labor contract by assuming or adopting it. If the new employer applies the substantive terms of the labor contract and also consults with the union as representative, it may be found to have adopted it. *See, e.g.*, World Evangelism, 248 NLRB 909, *enforced*, 656 F.2d 1349 (9th Cir. 1981).

In the absence of evidence supporting one of these two exceptions, the new employer will not be bound by the predecessor's labor agreement even if it contained a successorship clause requiring that any purchaser assume the contract. In Howard Johnson Co. v. Hotel Employees, 417 U.S. 249, 258 n.3, however, the Supreme Court did suggest that a union

Second, the Court majority held that Burns was a successor employer and obliged to recognize and bargain with the union. There was continuity of the appropriate bargaining unit, continuity of operations in that employees were performing the same types of tasks in the same industry and, most importantly, continuity of workforce. Continuity of workforce occurs in the successorship situation when an employer hires a majority of *its* workforce from employees who had worked for its unionized predecessor.[16] In such a situation, the union is deemed the majority representative because the presumption of continued majority support is extended to presume that each of the employees previously employed by the predecessor would choose union representation at the successor employer.[17]

The third major element of the *Burns* decision has to do with the time when the duty to bargain arises in a successorship situation. The Court held that the duty to bargain does not generally begin until after a majority of the successor's workforce consists of former employees of the predecessor. This means that a company acquiring a unionized employer is generally free to set the initial terms at which it offers employment to prospective employees, whether they are from the predecessor or not.[18]

If the acquiring company then becomes a successor after hiring its workforce, it will already have had the opportunity to change terms and conditions from those in the prior contract and bargaining will begin from the newly implemented terms. The Court did note that the freedom to set

---

could seek federal court injunctive relief *prior to* the sale to enjoin a transaction that did not comply with the seller's promise to require the successor to be bound.

If the sale is structured as a stock transfer, however, the Board and courts could hold that there has been no change in the employer and that the acquiring owners step into the shoes of the selling owners in terms of contractual obligations and bargaining duties. *See* TKB International Corp., 240 NLRB 1082 (1979); Miami Foundry Corp., 252 NLRB 2 (1980), *enforced*, 682 F.2d 587 (6th Cir. 1982). The successorship issue could arise, however, if the substantial changes in operations demonstrate that the transaction was more than a mere substitution of one owner for another. *See* EPE, Inc. v. NLRB, 845 F.2d 483, 490 (4th Cir. 1988).

[16] The essential issue is what percentage of the acquiring employer's workforce had worked for the predecessor under union representation. Assume that the predecessor employed 100 persons in the bargaining unit but that the acquiring company intends to operate with only 50. If 26 of the 50 in its workforce had worked for the predecessor, it would be a successor because a majority of *its* workforce is presumed to support the union.

[17] Although an employer is not obliged to hire its predecessor's employees, it will violate Section 8(a)(3) if it fails to hire them because of their prior union affiliation. 406 U.S. at 280.

[18] 406 U.S. at 294.

initial terms unilaterally would not exist if the acquiring employer had made it perfectly clear that it planned to retain the predecessor's employees. In such a case, it would be necessary for the employer to give the union notice and an opportunity to bargain before setting terms of hire.

[C]—The *Fall River* Decision

In *Fall River Dyeing,*[19] the Supreme Court expanded and clarified the *Burns* rules. In *Fall River,* Sterlingwale, a unionized textile dyeing and finishing plant, laid off its employees in February, 1982, due to declining markets and went out of business in late summer, 1982. A former Sterlingwale officer and a former customer then formed Fall River and acquired Sterlingwale's plant, real property, equipment and some inventory. They began operations and hiring in September, 1982. Fall River initially intended to hire one full shift of workers (55 to 60) and then expand to two shifts if business permitted.

In October, 1982, the union formerly representing Sterlingwale employees requested recognition. Fall River refused. At the time, 18 of its 21 employees were former employees of Sterlingwale. By January, 1983, the company had reached its goal of one full shift. At that time, 36 of 55 were former Sterlingwale employees. Fall River continued to hire, reaching two full shifts in April, 1983. At that time, ex-Sterlingwale employees made up 52 or 53 of Fall River's 107 employees, slightly less than half.

The Board, upheld by the Supreme Court, held that Fall River had violated Section 8(a)(5) by refusing to bargain with the union and that the duty to bargain commenced in mid-January when Fall River had hired a substantial and representative complement of its workforce.

In reaching its decision, the Court held, first, that *Burns* is not limited to a situation where a union has been recently certified. The rebuttable presumption of continued majority status carries over despite a change in employers. Second, the Court upheld the Board's "substantial continuity" approach which asks whether the business of both employers is essentially the same, whether employees perform the same jobs in the same working conditions, and whether the new operation has the same production process and produces essentially the same product for the same customers.[20] The

[19] Fall River Dyeing & Finishing Corp. v. NLRB, 482 U.S. 27 (1987).

[20] Citing *inter alia Burns,* 406 U.S. at 280 n.4; Aircraft Magnesium, 265 NLRB 1344, 1345 (1982), *enforced,* 730 F.2d 767 (9th Cir. 1984).

approach focuses on whether employees will see their "job situations as essentially unaltered."[21]

Third, the Court held that the seven month hiatus between the end of Sterlingwale operations and the start-up of Fall River was not determinative of the successorship question. In the Court's view, existence of a hiatus is only one factor in the successorship analysis and can be outweighed by other evidence of substantial continuity between the companies. In addition, the Court viewed the hiatus from the perspective of employees and the union who were aware of the predecessor's efforts to maintain the plant while it looked for a buyer.

Fourth, and most important, the Court upheld the Board's "substantial and representative complement" rule for determining when the determination is to be made as to whether a majority of the new employer's workforce should be presumed to support the union. Under this rule, the determination is to be made when all the employer's job classifications have been filled or substantially filled, when it has hired a majority of the employees it intends to hire and when it has begun normal production. Under this rule, the proper time for measuring majority status in *Fall River* was in January, 1983, when Fall River had reached its initial goal of one shift of workers. At this time, 36 of its 55 workers were former Sterlingwale employees and the duty to bargain arose. In the Court's view, employees have a significant interest in being represented as soon as possible, especially during the vulnerable period of business transition.[22]

Finally, the Court also upheld the Board's "continuing demand" rule. Under this rule, the union's premature demand for recognition remained in effect until the employer had hired a substantial and representative component of its employees.

§ 8.4 Withdrawal of Recognition

[A]—The Test

Under the Board's withdrawal of recognition doctrine, an employer may "lawfully withdraw from negotiation . . . if it can show that the union had in fact lost its majority status at the time of refusal to bargain or that the

[21] Golden State Bottling Co. v. NLRB, 414 U.S. 168, 184 (1973).

[22] The substantial and representative complement rule applies to cases where the new employer has a start-up period in which it gradually builds up its operation and gradually hires employees.

refusal to bargain was grounded on a good faith doubt based on objective factors that the union continued to command majority support."[23] The employer's alleged good faith doubt must be raised in a context free of unfair labor practices which could have undermined the union's status as majority representative. If the employer's unlawful acts have caused any loss of majority, withdrawal of recognition will be unlawful.

Types of evidence brought forth by employers as allegedly objective facts to justify withdrawal of recognition include written and oral statements by employees repudiating the union,[24] filing of decertification petitions signed by a majority of employees,[25] and admissions by union officials that the union has lost its majority.[26]

The Board has generally required that such evidence unequivocally point to a rejection of the union while finding more ambiguous statements and indications insufficient to justify a refusal to bargain. Thus, evidence of employee turnover,[27] declining dues checkoff authorizations,[28] or employees crossing a picket line to return to work,[29] has been held insufficient to justify withdrawal.

In a strike situation in which the employer has hired permanent replacements, the Supreme Court held in *Curtin Matheson*[30] that the Board was

---

23 Harley Davidson Transp. Co., 273 NLRB 1531 (1985) (quoted and cited with approval in Fall River Dyeing & Finishing Corp. v. NLRB, 482 U.S. 27, n.8 (1987)). *See also* Pennco, Inc., 250 NLRB 716 (1980), *enforced*, 684 F.2d 340 (6th Cir.), *cert. denied*, 459 U.S. 994 (1982); Douglas E. Ray, *Withdrawal of Recognition from an Incumbent Union Under the National Labor Relations Act: An Appraisal*, 28 Vill. L. Rev. 869 (1983).

See Burroughs Corp., 180 NLRB 331, 332 (1960); Sky Wolf Sales, 470 F.2d 827, 830 (9th Cir. 1972) (employer that unlawfully assisted in circulation of decertification petition cannot assert good faith doubt).

24 *See, e.g.*, NLRB v. Sacramento Clinical Lab., 623 F.2d 110 (9th Cir. 1980); Frito-Lay, 151 NLRB 28 (1965) (verbal statement).

25 Dresser Industries, 264 NLRB 1088, 1089, n.7 (1982) (decertification petition not signed by majority of employees not sufficient, standing alone, for withdrawal).

26 *See, e.g.*, Upper Miss. Towing Corp., 264 NLRB 262 (1979). *Compare* Harvey's Wagon Wheel, Inc., 236 NLRB 1670 (1978), *enforced*, 640 F.2d 274 (D.C. Cir. 1980) (statement by union official that union "in trouble" too ambiguous).

27 *See* Physicians & Surgeons Comm. Hosp., 231 NLRB 512, 514 (1977).

28 *See* Servomation, Inc., 235 NLRB 974, 978 (1978).

29 *See* Garrett R.R. Car v. NLRB, 683 F.2d 731 (3d Cir. 1982) (failure to join strike and crossing picket line does not mean employee has abandoned union).

30 NLRB v. Curtin Matheson Scientific, Inc., 494 U.S. 775 (1990). *See generally*, Douglas E. Ray, *Withdrawal of Recognition After* Curtin Matheson: *A House Built Upon Sand*, 25 U.S.F.L. Rev. 265 (1991).

within its discretion to adopt no presumption whatsoever regarding the union sentiments of permanent replacements. To presume they supported the union could be counterfactual when they have crossed picket lines to take union jobs and the union seeks their ouster. On the other hand, if the Board presumed them to oppose the union, the employer could too easily avoid its duty to bargain by hiring sufficient permanent replacements to outnumber strikers.

Under this doctrine, the legality of the employer's withdrawal of recognition and refusal to bargain are then tested through lengthy unfair labor practice proceedings. The status of this test and its future enforcement are somewhat unclear in light of the Supreme Court's 1998 decision in *Allentown Mack Sales & Service, Inc. v. NLRB.*[31]

[B]—*Allentown Mack*

In *Allentown Mack,*[32] Mack Trucks, a unionized employer, sold its sales and service facility to Allentown Mack, which hired 32 parts and service employees, all of whom had worked for Mack Trucks and been represented by the Machinists Union. When the union demanded recognition, the new employer refused, claiming a good faith doubt as to the union's majority status. After prevailing in a poll which the union lost, the employer refused to bargain. The NLRB found that the employer lacked a good faith doubt and found unlawful both the poll and the subsequent withdrawal of recognition. The Supreme Court, after reviewing the evidence for itself, ruled that the employer had established a good faith doubt.

The Court majority, in an opinion by Justice Scalia, appeared to criticize the Board's past application of its good faith doubt test. It suggested that by insisting on a showing that at least half of bargaining unit employees had repudiated the union, the Board was requiring proof to a reasonable certainty that the union had lost its majority, not just good faith doubt.[33] Interpreting good faith doubt to require only the showing of a "reasonable uncertainty" as to majority status, the Court indicated that the Board should have given weight to anti-union statements made by employees in pre-employment interviews and to a complaint by an employee that the entire night shift (5 or 6 employees) opposed the union.[34]

---

[31] 118 S. Ct. 818 (1998).

[32] Allentown Mack Sales & Service, Inc. v. NLRB, 118 S. Ct. 818 (1998).

[33] 118 S. Ct. at 819.

[34] The Board's policy has been to disregard statements by employees about other employees' sentiments and to require statements of repudiation rather than mere disaffection. The Court rejected this approach. 118 S. Ct. at 824.

In light of *Allentown Mack,* the Board will have to rearticulate its test if it wishes to continue to make it difficult for employers to withdraw recognition. So long as the test is phrased in terms of good faith doubt, *Allentown Mack* authorizes reviewing courts to review the evidence to determine merely whether the employer has shown objective evidence sufficient to justify a reasonable uncertainty.

[C]—Polling

Sometimes an employer will seek to poll employees about their support for the union as a means of gathering evidence to support a withdrawal of recognition. The Board, however, will require the employer to show the same good faith doubt to justify a poll as it is required to show to justify a withdrawal of recognition.[35] This tends to discourage employer use of polls. The propriety of the Board's polling standard came before the Supreme Court in *Allentown Mack*[36] and the Court upheld the standard by a 5-4 margin. In addition, the employer must satisfy Board standards for ensuring that polling is not coercive and does not otherwise interfere with employee rights before polling employees on whether they wish to continue to be represented by the incumbent union.[37]

[D]—Consequences of an Unlawful Withdrawal of Recognition

An employer that unlawfully withdraws recognition violates Section 8(a)(5). It will be ordered to bargain with the union in good faith. In addition, an unfair labor practice finding against the employer can have other serious, although less obvious, consequences. While charges are pending, for example, it may be dangerous and potentially costly for an employer to change or adjust employee benefits. If the withdrawal of recognition and refusal to bargain are improper, it violates the duty "to bargain collectively" imposed by Section 8(a)(5) of the NLRA for an employer to institute changes regarding matters that are mandatory subjects of bargaining without first consulting the union that is the exclusive representative of its employees.[38] If recognition was withdrawn unlawfully

---

[35] *See* Montgomery Ward & Co., 210 NLRB 717 (1974); Texas Petrochemicals Corp., 296 NLRB at 1059-63 (1989). *See also* Joan Flynn, *A Triple Standard at the NLRB: Employer Challenges to an Incumbent Union,* 1991 Wisc. L. Rev. 653 (noting that same standard required for withdrawal of recognition, polling and obtaining an RM election).

[36] Allentown Mack Sales & Service, Inc. v. NLRB, 118 S. Ct. 818 (1998).

[37] *See* Retired Persons Pharmacy, 210 NLRB 443, 447, n.9 (1974), *enforced,* 519 F.2d 486 (2d Cir. 1975) (holding that rule of Struknes Constr. Co., 165 NLRB 1062 (1967), must be applied to such a poll).

[38] 29 U.S.C. § 158(a)(5). *See* NLRB v. Katz, 369 U.S. 736 (1962).

and the employer has changed benefits without bargaining, it can be ordered to restore them.[39] Further, the unlawful withdrawal can convert an economic strike into an unfair labor practice strike, possibly with expensive repercussions to the employer.[40]

Thus, if an employer has to adjust wages downward due to economic problems while the case is pending, or if it changes benefits or subcontracts unit work during this time period, it may have to compensate employees to make them whole. A careful employer might be well advised to avoid making any changes during the entire litigation period, possibly leaving it more constrained than it was during the time it recognized the union.[41]

§ 8.5 Decertification Elections

In 1947, Congress amended the Act to allow employees to file a petition requesting an election to decertify their union. Under Section 9(c)(1)(A)(ii) of the Act,[42] an employee or a group of employees may file a petition asserting that the labor organization certified by the NLRB or recognized by their employer as bargaining representative is no longer the representative of the majority. If the Board finds that a question of representation exists and if the petition is supported by a substantial number of employees, the Board will conduct an election.[43]

---

[39] In Fibreboard Paper Products Corp. v. NLRB, 379 U.S. 203 (1964), the Court recognized that an order restoring the status quo ante was within the NLRB's power in situations where the Board had found the employer to have refused to bargain over a mandatory subject of bargaining. *See also* Taurus Waste Disposal, Inc., 263 NLRB 309 (1982) (ordering employer who had unlawfully withdrawn recognition to make employees whole by paying all insurance, severance, and pension fund contributions as required by expired collective bargaining agreement which would have been paid but for employer's unilateral discontinuance of such payments, and to continue such payments until the employer negotiated in good faith with union to a new agreement or to impasse).

[40] *See, e.g.*, Whisper Soft Mills, 267 NLRB 813 (1983) (economic strike converted into unfair labor practice strike by unlawful withdrawal of recognition; strikers held entitled to reinstatement upon unconditional offer to return to work).

[41] During the period the employer recognizes the union it may make changes, provided it first gives the union notice and the opportunity to bargain and, if requested, negotiates to impasse, and provided that the matter is not covered in a current collective bargaining agreement. *See, e.g.*, NLRB v. Katz, 369 U.S. 736, 745 (1962); 29 U.S.C. § 158(d) (1988).

[42] 29 U.S.C. § 159(c)(1)(A)(ii).

[43] *See generally* Janice Bellace, *Union Decertification Under the NLRA*, 57 Chi.-Kent L. Rev. 643 (1981); Douglas E. Ray, *Industrial Stability and Decertification Elections: Need for Reform*, 1984 Ariz. St. L.J. 257.

There are only certain limited time periods during which decertification petitions may be properly filed. The "election-year bar" rule,[44] the "certification-year bar" doctrine[45] and the "contract-bar" doctrine substantially limit the availability of elections.

Under the contract-bar doctrine, a petition may not be filed while there is a collective bargaining agreement in effect except during a 30-day period which falls not more than 90 or less than 60 days before the contract's expiration date.[46] While petitions may be filed after the contract expires, the employer and union may enter into a new collective bargaining agreement effective on expiration of the old one. The new agreement will then bar petitions for its term. Thus, in many incumbent union situations, there will exist only a 30-day "window period" during which employees may petition.

The employer may not assist employees in preparing or filing decertification petitions. Such activity would be evidence of bad faith with regard to the employer's duty to bargain in good faith with the union as exclusive representative and would foreseeably interfere with the bargaining process.[47] If a decertification petition is "tainted" by unlawful employer assistance or interference, it can be dismissed.

---

[44] Section 9(c)(3) of the Act, 29 U.S.C. § 159(c)(3) (1982), provides in part that "No election shall be directed in any bargaining unit or any subdivision within which, in the preceding twelve-month period, a valid election shall have been held."

[45] Where a union wins an election, the Board, with Supreme Court approval, Brooks v. NLRB, 348 U.S. 96, 104 (1954), has ruled that the twelve-month period begins to run at certification rather than from the date of the election. These twelve months are referred to as the certification year, during which no petition may be filed. If the employer refused to bargain in good faith during this certification year, the Board sometimes extends the certification year as part of its remedy for the unfair labor practice. When the litigation is terminated, whether by Board order or by settlement, the certification year is extended "to embrace that time in which the employer has engaged in its refusal to bargain." Pride Ref. Inc., 224 NLRB 1353, 1354-55 (1976). *See also* Soule Glass & Glazing Co. v. NLRB, 652 F.2d 1055 (1st Cir. 1981).

[46] The Board's contract-bar rule bars an election petition while a contract is in effect up to a specified limit. Since 1962, the Board has held that an election petition will be barred during the term of an agreement which extends not more than three years or which is filed during the first three years of a contract of longer duration. General Cable Corp., 139 NLRB 1123, 1125 (1962).

[47] *See* Wahoo Packing Co., 161 NLRB 174 (1966).

§ 8.6 Employer Petition for Election

Under Section 9(c)(1)(B) of the Act,[48] an employer may file a petition for election after expiration of the certification year. Despite the seemingly obvious advantages of the election process over withdrawal of recognition, current Board policy does not encourage an employer to attempt to file an election petition rather than withdrawing recognition altogether. Rather, filing an election petition is made equally difficult. Since its 1966 decision in *United States Gypsum Co.*,[49] the Board has held that an employer petitioning for election where there is an incumbent union must: (1) establish the union's claim for continued recognition and (2) demonstrate by objective considerations that it has reasonable grounds for believing that the union has lost its majority status since certification. The decision is based on the notion that Congress, in enacting Section 9(c)(1)(B), did not intend to allow an employer, acting without good faith doubt of a union's majority status, to disrupt collective bargaining and frustrate industrial stability by repeatedly obtaining elections.[50] For this reason, the test for filing an election petition is almost identical to that applied for withdrawal of recognition.[51]

§ 8.7 Chapter Highlights

1. A union, once elected or recognized, is irrebuttably presumed to continue to represent a majority of the bargaining unit during the certification year or, in the case of voluntary recognition, for a reasonable period. The irrebuttable presumption of majority status also applies during the term of a collective bargaining agreement of up to three years. During these periods, neither the employer nor employees may challenge the majority status of the incumbent. (§ 8.2[A])

2. Once the certification year and/or contract expires, the union continues to enjoy a rebuttable presumption of majority status which is the basis for the employer's continuing duty to recognize and continue to bargain with the union. (§ 8.2[B])

---

48 29 U.S.C. § 159(c)(1)(B).

49 157 NLRB 652 (1966).

50 157 NLRB at 656.

51 *See generally* Joan Flynn, *A Triple Standard at the NLRB: Employer Challenges to an Incumbent Union*, 1991 Wisc. L. Rev. 653; Douglas E. Ray, *Withdrawal of Recognition from an Incumbent Union Under the National Labor Relations Act: An Appraisal*, 28 Vill. L. Rev. 869, 913-914 (1983).

3. An employer acquiring another employer is not required, with certain exceptions, to assume the collective bargaining agreement of its predecessor. If there is substantial continuity of business operations and working conditions, continuity of the appropriate bargaining unit, and continuity of workforce, the acquiring company can be labeled a "successor" and have a duty to recognize and bargain with the union which represented the predecessor's employees. Of these, continuity of workforce is most important. It occurs when a majority of the successor's bargaining unit workforce is made up of employees who formerly worked for the predecessor. The successorship doctrine represents an extension of the presumption of continued majority support. (§ 8.3)

4. Under the Board's withdrawal of recognition doctrine, an employer may withdraw from negotiations and withdraw recognition if it can show, in a context free of employer unfair labor practices, that either the union has in fact lost its majority status or that it has a good faith doubt based on objective factors that the union no longer represents a majority. The good faith test has been difficult to satisfy but its future application is uncertain in light of the Supreme Court's 1998 *Allentown Mack* decision. (§ 8.4)

5. An employer may conduct a poll to ascertain the union's majority status. To do so, however, it must satisfy the same good faith doubt test required to justify withdrawal of recognition. (§ 8.5)

6. Employees have the right to file a petition requesting a decertification election. The petition requires a showing of substantial interest and can be filed only during time periods when the Board will conduct elections. Employers may not lawfully assist employees in the filing of the petitions. (§ 8.5)

7. The employer, too, has been allowed to file a petition for an election to test the union's continued majority status. The petition must meet Board timing requirements and the employer must be able to show the same good faith doubt required for withdrawal of recognition. (§ 8.6)

CHAPTER 9
STRIKES

§ 9.1 Generally

The right to strike is statutorily protected and is considered a key element of a labor relations system designed to encourage productive and peaceful collective bargaining. It is the presence of effective weapons held in reserve by both sides that encourages negotiation and settlement within the statutory framework. Both the right to strike and the scope of employer activities allowed in response to a strike, however, are limited by a set of carefully worked out rules seemingly designed to keep economic weapons in check. The importance of understanding these rules cannot be overemphasized since the consequences for violations can be severe.

If a union strikes in violation of the recognized limits on the right to strike, the strike will be unprotected and strikers can be discharged with little or no recourse. If strikers engage in unprotected violence or sabotage, they can be fired as well. If the employer responds improperly to threats to strike or to the strike itself, it not only commits an unfair labor practice but it can lose the ability to hire permanent replacements for strikers, one of the most powerful weapons in its arsenal. Further, if the employer improperly discharges a striker or fails to recall a striker when it has a duty to do so, it can be ordered to reinstate and pay back pay.

§ 9.2 Statutory Notice Requirements

[A]—Generally

Section 8(d) was added to the Act in 1947. It provides in part that:

> where there is in effect a collective-bargaining contract covering employees in an industry affecting commerce, the duty to bargain collectively shall also mean that no party to such contract shall terminate or modify such contract, unless the party desiring such termination or modification—
>
> (1) serves a written notice upon the other party to the contract of the proposed termination or modification sixty days prior to the expiration date thereof, or in the event such contract contains no expiration date, sixty days prior to the time it is proposed to make such termination or modification;
>
> (2) offers to meet and confer with the other party for the purpose of negotiating a new contract or a contract containing the proposed modifications;

(3) notifies the Federal Mediation and Conciliation Service within thirty days after such notice of the existence of a dispute, and simultaneously therewith notifies any State or Territorial agency established to mediate and conciliate disputes within the State or Territory where the dispute occurred, provided no agreement has been reached by that time; and

(4) continues in full force and effect, without resorting to strike or lockout, all the terms and conditions of the existing contract for a period of sixty days after such notice is given or until the expiration date of such contract, whichever occurs later.[1]

A party (union or employer) desiring to terminate or modify a collective bargaining agreement must give notice and refrain from altering terms or conditions of employment or engaging in a strike or lockout to enforce the changes it proposes until after expiration of the statutory notice periods. A union may not strike prior to expiration of the notice period even if the collective bargaining agreement has already expired.[2]

Section 8(d) provides a strong sanction against unions and employees who fail to comply with its notice requirements. It provides:

Any employee who engages in a strike within any notice period specified in this subsection, or who engages in any strike within the appropriate period specified in subsection (g) of this section, shall lose his status as an employee of the employer engaged in the particular labor dispute, for the purposes of sections 8, 9, and 10 of this Act, as amended, but such loss of status for such employee shall terminate if and when he is reemployed by such employer.[3]

Thus, a striking employee may be fired if the union has failed to give the appropriate notices and wait the required time before commencing a strike. Because the striker will have lost his or her statutory status as an "employee," the Act will not provide protection.

Some types of strikes, however, have been ruled to be exempt from the notice requirements of Section 8(d). In its 1956 *Mastro Plastics Corp. v.*

---

1 29 U.S.C. § 158(d).

2 *See* Weathercraft Co. of Topeka, 276 NLRB 452 (1985), *enforced*, 832 F.2d 1229 (10th Cir. 1987). It should be noted that these restrictions on the right to strike do not apply to a newly recognized or certified union which has not been party to a prior collective bargaining agreement with the employer.

3 29 U.S.C. § 158(d).

NLRB[4] decision, the Supreme Court held that the requirements and time limits of Section 8(d) do not apply to strikes which are for the purpose of protesting employer unfair labor practices. Such strikes do not expose employees to loss of employee status whether no notice was given at all or whether a notice was given but the notice period had not yet run. In *Mastro Plastics*, the union struck one month after it had given the employer notice of its desire to negotiate new terms. The strike, which did not comply with the 60-day waiting period, was called to protest the discharge of a union supporter and the employer's provision of alleged unlawful assistance to another union seeking to displace the incumbent. The employer argued that, under the language of Section 8(d), "any employee who engages in a strike within the sixty-day period" lost his status as an employee and could be discharged. Justice Burton, writing for the majority, disagreed and adopted the argument of the National Labor Relations Board that the clause should be read in conjunction with the rest of Section 8. Under the analysis of the NLRB adopted by the Court, the Section 8(d) notice provisions apply only to strikes to "terminate or modify" the collective bargaining agreement and a strike to protest an unfair labor practice is not for the purpose of terminating or modifying the contract. The Court based its analysis in part on the statute's emphasis on freedom of concerted action and held that any limit on employees' right to strike to protest violations of Sections 7 and 8[5] must be explicit and clear.

It is not always clear, however, whether a strike is motivated by employer unfair labor practices or a desire to achieve economic goals. If the strike is found to be motivated by economic goals, the fact that employer unfair labor practices also exist will not excuse the union from providing timely notice and observing statutory waiting periods.[6]

Similarly, the Board and the courts have also held that Section 8(d) notice and waiting period requirements do not apply to strikes which protest dangerous working conditions. A one-time work stoppage of brief duration to protest abnormally dangerous working conditions will be presumed to be protected under the Act.[7]

---

[4] 350 U.S. 270 (1956).

[5] 29 U.S.C. §§ 157 and 158.

[6] *See* Puerto Rico Junior College, 265 NLRB 72 (1982).

[7] *See, e.g.*, NLRB v. McEver Engineering, Inc., 784 F.2d 634 (5th Cir. 1986) (employees working outdoors with electrical equipment on slick surface in rain refused to return to work; employer's discharge of all seven protesters held illegal). *See generally* NLRB v. Washington Aluminum Co., 370 U.S. 9 (1962) (employees leaving work in machine shop on grounds that shop was too cold to work in were engaged in protected concerted activity).

[B]—Health Care Industry Notice Requirements

As part of the 1974 National Labor Relations Act amendments to extend coverage to nonprofit hospitals, Congress established special notice periods that must be observed before employees of health care institutions[8] may strike or picket. The statute provides:

> Whenever the collective bargaining involves the employees of a health care institution, the provisions of this section shall be modified as follows:
>
> (A) The notice of section 8(d)(1) shall be ninety days; the notice of section 8(d)(3) shall be sixty days; and the contract period of section 8(d)(4) shall be ninety days.
>
> (B) Where the bargaining is for an initial agreement following certification or recognition, at least thirty days' notice of the existence of a dispute shall be given by the labor organization to the agencies set forth in section 8(d)(3).[9]

Thus, the Act requires a longer "cooling off" period for employees of health care institutions and imposes notice requirements on initial contract negotiations as well as negotiations involving modification of prior collective bargaining agreements.

In addition, Section 8(g) requires a union to give a health care institution a 10-day notice of its intent to strike or picket. Section 8(g) provides:

> A labor organization before engaging in any strike, picketing, or other concerted refusal to work at any health care institution shall, not less than ten days prior to such action, notify the institution in writing and the Federal Mediation and Conciliation Service of that intention, except that in the case of bargaining for an initial agreement following certification or recognition the notice required by this subsection shall not be given until the expiration of the period specified in clause (b) of the last sentence of section 8(d) of this Act subsection (D) of this section. The notice shall state the date and time that such action will commence. The notice, once given, may be extended by the written agreement of both parties.[10]

---

[8] Health care institutions are defined as including "any hospital, convalescent hospital, health maintenance organization, health clinic, nursing home, extended care facility, or other institution devoted to the care of sick, infirm or aged persons." 29 U.S.C. § 152.

[9] 29 U.S.C. §§ 158(d)(A) and (B).

[10] 29 U.S.C. § 158(g).

Since Section 8(g) applies to "any strike, picketing or other concerted refusal to work," it has been held to apply to sympathy striking and sympathy picketing. Unions seeking to honor picket lines of other unions at health care institutions must also give proper notice.[11]

Health care employees, too, can be discharged for engaging in a strike within the notice periods. Section 8(d) provides that an employee who engages in a strike within the notice periods of Section 8(d) or 8(g) shall lose his status as an employee. The Act does not, however, compel discharge.[12]

The *Mastro Plastics* rule[13] has been extended to the health care industry as well, and strikes to protest employer unfair labor practices have been held to be outside the notice and waiting period requirements of Sections 8(d) and 8(g).[14]

§ 9.3 No-Strike Clauses as a Limit on the Right to Strike

A union may waive employees' rights to strike by means of a no-strike clause, a contractual commitment not to strike during the term of the collective bargaining agreement. Strikes in violation of the contractual no-strike clause are generally held to be unprotected, exposing employees to the risk of discharge.[15] Because waiver of a statutory right, such as the right to strike, must be "clear and unmistakable,"[16] the Board will carefully review a no-strike clause before ruling that it waives the right to strike.[17]

Violation of a no-strike clause can also lead to lawsuits seeking injunctive relief, union liability for money damages, and issues concerning whether union officers can be disciplined.

The existence of a reopener clause in a collective bargaining agreement can also raise issues involving Section 8(d) notice periods and the extent

11 *See* Kaiser Foundation Hospitals, 268 NLRB 115 (1983), *enforced,* 746 F.2d 530 (9th Cir. 1984).

12 *See* Shelby County Health Care Corp. v. AFSCME, Local 1733, 967 F.2d 1091 (6th Cir. 1992) (employer can waive its ability to discipline or discharge noncomplying strikers).

13 *See supra* § 9.2[A].

14 *See, e.g.,* Pratt Institute, 288 NLRB 1122 (1988).

15 NLRB v. Sands Mfg. Co., 306 U.S. 332 (1939).

16 Metropolitan Edison Co. v. NLRB, 460 U.S. 693, 708 (1983).

17 *See* Yellow Freight Systems, 313 NLRB 309 (1993) (threat to discharge employees if they strike held unlawful where contract did not totally bar walkouts).

of a contract's no-strike clause. A reopener clause in a contract is often used where the parties wish the general stability of a two- or three-year contract but find themselves unable to agree over future application of a disputed term, most often wages. By use of a reopener, the parties can avoid a strike presently and agree to "reopen" the contract at a specified interim date for bargaining limited to the specific term. Although avoiding economic confrontation for the present, the parties' future bargaining over the disputed term may lead to a strike.

With regard to reopener strikes and the issue of statutory notice periods, the Supreme Court has held that, absent contractual restrictions, the National Labor Relations Act does not prohibit a union from striking during the term of a contract so long as Section 8(d)'s procedural requirements are satisfied. In *NLRB v. Lion Oil Co.*,[18] the Court upheld an NLRB ruling that the employer unlawfully discharged strikers who engaged in a union strike in support of timely invoked reopener bargaining, holding such strikers to be engaged in protected activity. It read the term "expiration date" in both Section 8(d)(1) and (4) as applying not only to contract expiration dates but also to any date that the parties fix in the contract as a period in which modifications may be made. The Court reasoned that if Congress contemplated a duty to bargain during reopener periods, then it must have intended to allow unions to retain "the strike threat which, together with 'the occasional strike itself, is the force depended upon to facilitate arriving at satisfactory settlements.' "[19] The Court observed that unions "would be wary of entering" into long-term agreements with reopener provisions if they could not strike during the contract term even where they had not expressly waived the right to strike.[20]

The *Lion Oil* Court expressly noted, however, that the collective bargaining agreement at issue lacked a no-strike clause, thus leaving open the issue of whether strikers engaged in a reopener strike would be protected if their union had agreed to a no-strike clause.

The NLRB, faced this issue in its 1989 *Hydrologics, Inc.*[21] decision, held that in the absence of a clear indication to the contrary, a no-strike clause will not prevent the union from striking over matters which are in the scope of and have been properly reopened under a reopener clause. In essence,

18 352 U.S. 282 (1957).

19 *Id.* at 291.

20 *Id.* at 289.

21 293 NLRB 1060 (1989).

the Board treats the contract as terminated as to those items covered by the reopener clause and assumes that the parties intended to reserve the freedom to use economic weapons in aid of bargaining over such items. In *Hydrologics*, the parties had a collective bargaining agreement effective from May 1, 1980 to May 1, 1982 which included a reopener clause providing that: "Either party may open the Agreement for changes in the Hourly Rate of Pay only by giving written notice to the other party of such intention no less than sixty (60) days, nor more than seventy-five (75) days, prior to May 1, 1981. Any changes in such hourly rates of pay shall not be effective prior to May 1, 1981." The contract also contained a no-strike provision providing that: "During the life of this Agreement the Union agrees that there shall be no strike, slowdown, or stay-in work stoppage or any other strike, and the Company agrees that there shall be no lockout of employees. It is understood and agreed that this Article shall not apply in the event of the Company's failure to apply an arbitration award."[22] On February 23, 1981, the union requested wage negotiations under the reopener and negotiations began March 26. On March 31, the union filed its Section 8(d)(3) notice. After bargaining reached impasse over wages, employees struck from May 11 until May 21. The employer responded with May 13 and May 20 telegrams stating it considered the strike to be in breach of the contract's no-strike provision and that it was rescinding the entire contract.

The Board found that the May 11 strike was protected, ruling that the employer had improperly rescinded and repudiated the contract by its May 13 telegram, thus unlawfully broadening the dispute and impeding settlement. For these reasons, the strike was deemed converted to an unfair labor practice strike on May 13, and the employer was ordered to reinstate all strikers who had not been permanently replaced by May 13. The union's acceptance of the May 20 offer was held binding on the employer. The key to this analysis is the Board's interpretation of the no-strike clause. On the issue of the intent of parties who include both reopener and broad no-strike clauses in their collective bargaining agreements, the Board noted that a no-strike clause generally applies "only during the term of the contract." The NLRB reasoned that:

> In the absence of language that the parties intend to include reopener strikes within their no-strike clause, parties intend to have the same economic weapons available in the reopener context as are available at the termination of their contract, at least with respect to proposals

22 293 NLRB at 1061 n.6.

encompassed within the reopening. This is so because, inter alia, during a reopening, a contract, at least as to reopened provisions, has been effectively terminated for a certain period.[23]

§ 9.4 Employer Interference with the Right to Strike

[A]—Generally

Because the right to strike is protected under Section 7 of the Act,[24] an employer which coerces or restrains employees or interferes with them in the exercise of the right to strike can violate Section 8(a)(1) of the National Labor Relations Act, as amended.[25] Any discrimination against strikers can also violate Section 8(a)(3).[26] Employers can violate employee rights by threatening to discharge employees who strike, by discharging employees for exercising the right to strike, by offering strikers inducements to abandon the strike, by discriminatorily denying or limiting payment of accrued benefits to strikers and by soliciting strikers to abandon the union. It is also unlawful to discriminate against former strikers who have returned to work.

[B]—Threats to Discharge or Replace Strikers

An employer may not legally discharge employees for engaging in a protected strike.[27] Thus, an employer may not legally threaten employees with discharge for striking.[28]

This issue is most frequently addressed in cases involving employer threats to permanently replace strikers. Because employers may legally replace strikers with permanent employees in an economic strike,[29] employers may sometimes legally address the issue[30] within the law. However, an employer lacks the right to permanently replace strikers if the strike is caused or prolonged by employer unfair labor practices. In such a case, a threat to permanently replace strikers constitutes an illegal threat.[31]

---

[23] *Id.* at 1060.

[24] 29 U.S.C. § 157.

[25] 29 U.S.C. § 158(a)(1).

[26] 29 U.S.C. § 158(a)(3).

[27] *See infra* § 9.4[C].

[28] *See, e.g.,* Gloversville Embossing Corp., 297 NLRB 182 (1989).

[29] NLRB v. MacKay Radio & Telegraph Co., 304 U.S. 333 (1938). *See infra* § 9.5.

[30] *See* Eagle Comtronics, Inc., 263 NLRB 515, 516 (1982); L.A. Water Treatment, Division of Chromalloy American Corp., 286 NLRB 868, 872 (1987) (employer may lawfully inform economic strikers they are subject to replacement).

[31] *See, e.g.,* Trumball Memorial Hospital, 288 NLRB 1429 (1988).

Further, even if an employer has the legal right to permanently replace strikers, it must be careful how it communicates the message. Replaced strikers remain "employees" under the Act[32] and are entitled to reinstatement when vacancies arise.[33] Thus, permanent replacement is not the same as discharge and an employer which implies that it is, violates the Act.

In *Ford Bros., Inc.*,[34] the Board held that letters telling economic strikers they would be permanently replaced if they did not return to work lawfully informed them they were subject to permanent replacement. A subsequent letter that informed permanently replaced strikers that they were "no longer employed" was, however, held to violate the Act because permanently replaced employees retain reinstatement rights. Similarly, telling employees the details of how they will be replaced can also lead to unfair labor practice charges if the messages threaten or coerce employees.[35]

[C]—Discharge of Strikers

Discharging a striking employee for his or her involvement in a protected strike violates Sections 8(a)(1)[36] and 8(a)(3)[37] of the Act.[38]

A frequently litigated issue is whether an employer's words to striking employees have the effect of a discharge. In *NLRB v. International Van Lines*,[39] the employer, which had not in fact hired permanent replacements, sent telegrams to strikers stating that "[f]or failure to report to work . . . you are being permanently replaced." The employer then refused to reinstate strikers who had unconditionally offered to return to work because of the false claim that the employer had hired permanent replacements. The Supreme Court held that the telegrams constituted unlawful discharges and that the strikers were entitled to reinstatement and back pay.

---

32 *See* 29 U.S.C. § 152(3).

33 *See infra* § 9.5.

34 294 NLRB 107 (1989).

35 *See* Child Development Council, 316 NLRB 1145 (1995) (telling union that strikers will be replaced in reverse order of seniority with most senior to be replaced first violates Act where union bargaining team made up of senior employees and no business justification existed for reversing order).

36 29 U.S.C. § 158(a)(1).

37 29 U.S.C. § 158(a)(3).

38 *See, e.g.*, NLRB v. Kaiser Steel Corp., 700 F.2d 575, 576-577 (9th Cir. 1983). *See infra* § 9.6 for a discussion of circumstances under which a striker may be discharged for strike violence.

39 409 U.S. 48 (1972).

In cases where the employer argues that its words and actions were too ambiguous to constitute a discharge, the Board and reviewing courts will ask whether the words and conduct would reasonably lead an employee to believe he or she was terminated.[40]

Thus, telling employees they "didn't work here anymore"[41] or telling permanently replaced employees "you are no longer employed . . ." and that accrued wages are enclosed "from your former employment with us"[42] can constitute a discharge.

[D]—*Erie Resistor* and Inducements to Return to Work

In conducting a "back to work" campaign and seeking to induce strikers to return to work, an employer might be tempted to offer them inducements to return. Not only can such inducements violate the employer's duty to bargain with the union, but they can violate Sections 8(a)(1) and 8(a)(3) as well.

In *NLRB v. Erie Resistor Corp.*,[43] the employer sought to continue operations during a strike with nonstrikers and replacements. Early in the strike, it promised replacements superseniority. Later in the strike, the employer announced that it would give nonstrikers, replacements and strikers who returned to work an additional 20-year's seniority added to a person's actual service for purposes of making layoffs under the seniority system. In response to unfair labor practice charges, the employer argued that its purpose was not discriminatory and that it was justified by an overriding business purpose. The Court stated that, "in view of the deference paid the strike weapon by the federal labor laws and the devastating consequences upon it which the Board found was and would be precipitated by respondent's inherently discriminatory super-seniority plan, we cannot say the Board erred in the balance which it struck here."[44]

[E]—Payment or Withholding of Benefits During a Strike

Because employees engaged in a strike are withholding their services, the employer is not generally required to pay them wages or benefits for

---

40 Pennypower Shopping News, Inc. v. NLRB, 726 F.2d 626, 629 (10th Cir. 1984) (issue "depends on the reasonable inferences that the employee could draw . . .").

41 NLRB v. Champ Corp., 913 F.3d 639 (9th Cir. 1990).

42 *See* L.A. Water Treatment, Div. of Chromalloy American Corp., 286 NLRB 868 (1987).

43 NLRB v. Erie Resistor Corp., 373 U.S. 221 (1963).

44 373 U.S. at 235. Superseniority is particularly destructive of employee rights because of its long-lasting impact. It can be an "offer you can't refuse."

the time they are on strike. The employer is not obliged to finance a strike against itself.[45] The issue of whether the employer can discontinue payment of accrued benefits to employees after the strike begins is more controversial and has been the subject of substantial amounts of litigation. Commonly arising issues include the failure to pay strikers' vacation benefits and discontinuance of sickness and accident payments to employees on disability leave when the strike begins.

The general test for determining whether an employer may discontinue or withhold benefits after a strike begins is analyzed under a test set forth by the Supreme Court in its 1967 decision in *NLRB v. Great Dane Trailers, Inc.*[46] In that case, the employer was charged with violating Sections 8(a)(3) and 8(a)(1) of the Act[47] when it denied payment of accrued vacation benefits to strikers.

Under the expired collective bargaining agreement, the employer agreed to pay specific vacation benefits to employees working a specific number of hours in the preceding year. In case of layoff, termination or quit, the contract entitled employees serving more than 60 days in the year to pro-rata shares of their vacation benefit. Benefits were to be paid on the Friday nearest July 1 of each year. The strike ran from May 16, 1963 until December 26, 1963.

During the strike, the employer continued to operate with nonstrikers, replacements and crossovers. It rejected the strikers' July 2 demand for accrued vacation pay, claiming that its duties under the contract had ceased. Soon after, it announced a new policy granting vacation pay to all employees who worked on July 1. This vacation pay was in the same amounts and subject to the same conditions called for in the expired contract. The Board held that the employer's actions violated Sections 8(a)(3) and (1) of the Act[48] because the employer discriminated in terms and conditions of employment which would discourage union membership and unlawfully interfered with protected activity. It directed the employer to pay accrued benefits to strikers. The Court of Appeals refused enforcement,[49] finding

---

[45] *See* E. L. Wiegand Div. v. NLRB, 650 F.2d 463, 468 (3rd Cir. 1981), *cert. denied*, 455 U.S. 939 (1982).

[46] 388 U.S. 26 (1967).

[47] 29 U.S.C. §§ 158(a)(3) and (1).

[48] *Id.*

[49] NLRB v. Great Dane Trailers, Inc., 363 F.2d 130 (5th Cir. 1966), *rev'd*, 388 U.S. 26 (1967).

no affirmative showing of unlawful motivation to discourage union membership or to interfere with the exercise of protected rights. The Court of Appeals asserted that the denial could have been motivated by cost-saving or other reasons.

The Supreme Court reversed, holding that once it is proven that an employer has engaged in discriminatory conduct which could have affected employee rights adversely, then the burden is on the employer to establish it was motivated by legitimate reasons. The Court held that where "inherently destructive" conduct is shown, a violation of Section 8(a)(3) can be proven without proof of improper motive even where the employer introduces evidence of a justification. Where the conduct has a "comparatively slight" adverse effect on employee rights, antiunion motivation must be proven if the employer has come forward with evidence of "legitimate and substantial business justifications for the conduct." The Court stated the test as follows:

> First, if it can reasonably be concluded that the employer's discriminatory conduct was "inherently destructive" of important employee rights, no proof of an antiunion motivation is needed and the Board can find an unfair labor practice even if the employer introduces evidence that the conduct was motivated by business considerations. Second, if the adverse effect of the discriminatory conduct on employee rights is "comparatively slight," an antiunion motivation must be proved to sustain the charge if the employer has come forward with evidence of legitimate and substantial business justifications for the conduct. Thus, in either situation, once it has been proved that the employer engaged in discriminatory conduct which could have adversely affected employee rights to some extent, the burden is upon the employer to establish that he was motivated by legitimate objectives since proof of motivation is most accessible to him.[50]

Because the employer had produced no evidence of a legitimate motive, the Court found it unnecessary to decide the degree to which the denial of vacation benefits affected employee rights. Since discriminatory conduct which had the potential to adversely affect employee rights had been proven and there was no evidence of a proper motive, the Section 8(a)(1) and (3) violations found by the Board were reinstated. In dissent, Justice Harlan, joined by Justice Stewart, argued that the Court had created a presumption of unlawful conduct and changed the burden of proving motive in Section 8(a)(3) cases.

---

[50] 388 U.S. at 34.

Under its 1987 *Texaco, Inc.*[51] decision, the Board applies *Great Dane*[52] to denial of benefits during a strike, including those cases involving vacations and holiday pay, using the following formula.

Under *Texaco*, the General Counsel bears the burden of proving at least some adverse effect of the benefit denial on employees' Section 7 rights. The General Counsel meets this burden by showing that the benefit was accrued, and that it was apparently withheld on the basis of a strike. The employer then must defend its action by showing that it had a legitimate and substantial business justification for terminating benefits, such as an explicit waiver by the union or reliance on a nondiscriminatory contract interpretation that is reasonable and arguably correct. If the employer establishes business justification, the Board may still find that the employer has committed an unfair labor practice if the conduct is demonstrated to be "inherently destructive" of important employee rights or motivated by antiunion intent. This test has been used in cases involving denial of vacation benefits[53] and denial of holiday pay.[54]

[F]—Treatment of Former Strikers

The employer's duty not to discriminate against strikers extends to how they are treated after they return to work. The employer may not discriminate against former strikers because of their strike activity. Thus, the employer may not discriminatorily fire or lay off former strikers[55] and it may not discriminate against them with regard to job assignments[56] or other benefits.[57] Such activities are illegal because they tend to interfere with

51 285 NLRB 241 (1987).

52 NLRB v. Great Dane Trailers, 388 U.S. 26 (1967).

53 *See, e.g.*, Noel Foods, 315 NLRB 905 (1994). (Requiring strikers to resign or return to work to receive accrued vacation pay held lawful where based on "reasonable and arguable correct" reading of collective bargaining agreement. Denial held not "inherently destructive" where non-strikers not treated differently.)

54 *See, e.g.*, Advertiser's Mfg. Co., 294 NLRB 740 (1989). It should be noted that past wages and benefits which have already accrued and which are already owed are not mandatory subjects of bargaining under Section 8(d). *See* R.E. Dietz Co., 311 NLRB 1259 (1993). Therefore, the employer may not extinguish its liability to strikers merely by bargaining to impasse on a modification and then implementing the change. Such bargaining would not constitute a legitimate and substantial business justification for denying accrued benefits to strikers. *See* Circuit Wise Inc., 309 NLRB 905 (1992).

55 *See* Midessa Construction Co., 290 NLRB 269 (1988) (layoff case).

56 *See* Seiler Tank Truck Service, Inc., 307 NLRB 1090 (1992) (job assignments).

57 *See* Suma Corp., 282 NLRB 667 (1987) (providing party for non-strikers).

and discourage employees' future exercise of their right to strike. The duty not to discriminate can extend to successor employers who fail to hire former participants in strikes against the predecessor employers.[58]

§ 9.5 Employer Countermeasures and Replacement Issues

[A]—Generally

An employer which decides to continue operations during a strike has a limited number of options available to it. It can continue operations with supervisors[59] or other non-bargaining unit employees who are willing to cross the picket line. This limited pool of workers is often not adequate to maintain production, however. In such cases, the employer may consider inviting strikers to return to work. As noted in Section 9.2 above, the employer may not threaten employees in making such offers[60] nor may it offer inducements.

The employer is allowed to hire temporary replacements, employees hired only for the duration of strike. The issue of whether it may hire permanent replacements is one of great difficulty. The permanent replacement option is the most powerful weapon in the employer's arsenal. It is subject to a number of legal limitations. If the employer has bargained in bad faith or responded improperly to the strike, it can lose the ability to permanently replace. If replaced strikers are denied reinstatement at the end of the strike, the employer can face substantial liability if it has not observed all legal requirements.

[B]—Temporary Replacements

The employer may hire employees to fill strikers' jobs for the duration of the strike. Such employees are generally referred to as "temporary replacements." The NLRB has ruled that the employer need not bargain with the union over the terms and conditions of employment to be offered temporary employees and suggested that such persons may be paid lesser benefits than the strikers they replace.[61]

---

58 *See* Southwest Merchandising Corp. v. NLRB, 53 F.3d 1334 (D.C. Cir. 1995).

59 Supervisors are not statutory "employees" and therefore do not have a protected right to join the strike by honoring the picket line. *See* Parker-Robb Chevrolet, Inc., 262 NLRB 402, *petition for review denied*, 711 F.2d 383 (D.C. Cir. 1983).

60 The employer can warn strikers they could be permanently replaced only if it has the legal right to permanently replace, often a contested issue. *See supra* § 9.4.

61 *See* Capitol-Husting Co., 252 NLRB 43, 45 (1980), *enforced*, 671 F.2d 237 (7th Cir. 1982); Goldsmith Motors Corp., 310 NLRB 1279 (1993) (temporary replacements for locked out employees).

Because strikers remain employees under the National Labor Relations Act, the employer which has hired temporary replacements must reinstate strikers who make unconditional application for reinstatement and must reinstate strikers at the conclusion of the strike.[62]

These reinstatement rights apply to all strikers who have not obtained "substantially equivalent employment."[63]

[C]—Permanent Replacements

In its 1938 *NLRB v. MacKay Radio & Telegraph Co.*[64] decision, the Supreme Court stated that, in order to keep their businesses operating during a strike, employers may hire permanent replacements for striking employees.[65]

Permanent replacement is a controversial issue that affects the balance of power at the bargaining table. It occurs when the employer offers permanent employment to a person hired to take the place of an employee on strike. When the striker offers to return to work at the end of the strike, the employer retains the replacement employee rather than immediately recalling the striker. Strikers remain employees with ultimate reinstatement rights when an appropriate vacancy arises. Although an employer may agree, as part of a strike settlement agreement, to release replacements and recall strikers, it is not legally compelled to do so if it has observed all legal standards for hiring permanent replacements.

The most important limit on the employer's ability to permanently replace strikers is that it may not do so in an unfair labor practice strike. A strike is labeled an unfair labor practice strike if it is caused or prolonged by an

---

62 *See* NLRB v. Fleetwood Trailer Co., Inc., 389 U.S. 375 (1967).

63 NLRB v. Fleetwood Trailer Co., Inc., 389 U.S. 375 at 381 (1967). The substantially equivalent employment reason for failing to reinstate is not easy to satisfy. The employer must show that the employee's new job has comparable wages, benefits, job assignments, working conditions and opportunities for advancement. *See, e.g.*, Lone Star Industries, Inc., 279 NLRB 550 (1986) and NLRB v. Oregon Steel Mills, 47 F.3d 1536 (9th Cir. 1995) (jobs paying less, requiring more travel or involving more difficult working conditions were not substantially equivalent).

64 304 U.S. 333, 345 (1938).

65 The issue was not directly before the Court and this rule constituted dictum. Since then, however, the rule has become a well-settled principle of labor law routinely noted in subsequent decisions. *See, e.g.*, Belknap, Inc. v. Hale, 463 U.S. 491, 500 (1983); NLRB v. Fleetwood Trailer Co., 389 U.S. 375, 379 (1967); NLRB v. Erie Resistor Corp., 373 U.S. 221, 225 (1963).

employer unfair labor practice.[66] Thus, not only must there have been an unfair labor practice but a causal relationship must be established as well. In determining the cause of a strike, the NLRB will look at whether employees are aware of the unfair labor practices, their reaction, the seriousness of the unlawful act and the relationship of the unfair labor practice to the bargaining disputes between the parties. The test looks to both subjective and objective considerations.

It should be noted that the employer's unfair labor practice need not be the sole cause of the strike. It need only be a contributing cause.[67]

In some cases, an unfair labor practice strike is established by showing that employees were aware of the employer's unlawful act and voted to strike in protest. In some such cases, testimony that union officials told bargaining unit members of the unlawful acts before employees voted to strike will be important.[68] It will also be relevant that strikers' picket signs and leaflets mention the unfair labor practice.[69] The fact that union officials declare a strike to be an unfair labor practice strike or that unfair labor practices were discussed before the strike vote will not always be determinative, however. The real issue is whether, under all the facts and circumstances, the unfair labor practice caused or prolonged the strike.[70]

---

[66] A strike to achieve economic objectives not caused in whole or in part by employer unfair labor practices is referred to as an "economic strike." The employer may hire permanent replacements in an economic strike.

[67] *See* Richmond Recording Corp. v. NLRB, 836 F.2d 289, 293 (7th Cir. 1987); NLRB v. Jarm Enter., Inc., 785 F.2d 195, 204 (7th Cir. 1986) ("The employer's unfair labor practice need not be the sole or even the major cause or aggravating factor of the strike; it need only be a contributing factor." (*quoting* NLRB v. Moore Business Forms, Inc., 574 F.2d 835, 840 (5th Cir. 1978))); Airport Parking Management v. NLRB, 720 F.2d 610, 614 (9th Cir. 1983) (collecting cases); Road Sprinkler Fitters Local 669 v. NLRB, 681 F.2d 11, 20 (D.C. Cir. 1982) ("contributing cause"); NLRB v. Cast Optics Corp., 458 F.2d 398, 407, *cert. denied*, 409 U.S. 850 (1972) ("if an unfair labor practice had anything to do with causing the strike, it was an unfair labor practice strike." (*quoting* General Drivers & Helpers Union, Local 662 v. NLRB, 302 F.2d 908, 911 (D.C. Cir. 1962), *cert. denied*, 371 U.S. 827 (1962))).

[68] *See, e.g.*, American Gypsum Co., 285 NLRB 100 (1987) (unlawful unilateral changes prior to impasse); Child Development Council, 316 NLRB 1145 (1995) (employer's illegal threat to replace senior strikers first discussed at strike vote meetings).

[69] *See* Fairhaven Properties, Inc., 314 NLRB 763 (1994). (Employees were advised before strike vote of what employer had done and told what an unfair labor practice strike was. Picket signs and leaflets bore messages consistent with unfair labor practice strike.)

[70] *See* Blue & White Cabs, 291 NLRB 1047 (1988) (strike found to be based on union's economic demands despite picket signs stating strike was unfair labor practice strike).

Often, timing provides crucial proof of a union's motive in striking. Where the strike follows immediately after an illegal act such as the discharge of a union supporter, the unfair labor practice is more likely to be found a precipitating factor.[71] A lapse of time between the unfair labor practice and the strike does not always mean that the strike cannot be an unfair labor practice strike, however. When other evidence establishes that the unfair labor practice contributed to causing the strike, the NLRB has found an unfair labor practice strike to occur despite lapses in time.[72]

Another important factor is the seriousness of the unfair labor practice at issue. Some unfair labor practices are serious enough to warrant finding an unfair labor practice strike even without proof of employee knowledge and reaction. Unfair labor practices such as unlawfully withdrawing recognition from a union[73] prolong a strike by removing the representative empowered to negotiate an end to the strike.[74]

Also relevant will be any relationship between the unfair labor practice and the issues which led to the strike. An employer's unlawful failure to provide information relevant to bargaining over an issue, for example, can cause an unfair labor practice strike if that issue was one which caused negotiations to reach impasse.[75]

Even if a strike is begun for economic objectives, its status can change and affect an employer's ability to hire subsequent permanent replacements. An employer unfair labor practice committed in the course of an economic strike which has the effect of aggravating or prolonging the strike can "convert" the strike to an unfair labor practice strike. In *NLRB v. Champ Corp.*,[76] the Court of Appeals for the Ninth Circuit held that a strike begun for economic objectives was converted to an unfair labor practice strike after the employer notified the union that certain strikers, including a bargaining committee member, would never be reinstalled or rehired. The

---

[71] *See, e.g.*, El San Juan Hotel, 289 NLRB 1453 (1988) (strike occurred three days after illegal discharge of union supporter).

[72] *See* R&H Coal Co., 309 NLRB 28 (1992) (strike 13 months after employer illegally changes wages without bargaining held unfair labor practice strike).

[73] *See, e.g.*, Brooks & Perkins, 282 NLRB 976 (1987) and Rose Printing Co., 289 NLRB 252 (1988).

[74] *See also* Gaywood Mfg. Co., 299 NLRB 697 (1990) (requiring resignation from union as condition to reinstatement); Hydrologics, Inc., 293 NLRB 1060 (1989) (unlawfully repudiating entire contract during lawful reopener strike).

[75] *See* North American Coal Corp., 289 NLRB 788 (1988).

[76] 913 F.2d 639 (9th Cir. 1990).

court held that such actions were serious enough to convert the strike even though picket sign language was not changed and the union did not protest the discharges at the bargaining table. When conversion occurs, as in *Champ Corp.*, it can limit the employer's ability to hire permanent replacements. Although replacements hired before the conversion may remain, any replacements hired after the conversion may not be retained in place of strikers who wish to return.

Limiting the employer's ability to hire permanent replacements to strikes not caused or prolonged by unfair labor practices has important consequences for our collective bargaining system. An employer may wish to hire permanent replacements in the event of a strike or it may wish to keep the possibility open to give it leverage at the bargaining table. In either event, it has a strong incentive to keep its behavior well within legal standards before and during any strike. It will be well advised to adhere to good faith bargaining before[77] and during a strike,[78] to provide the union with information needed for bargaining,[79] to avoid unfounded discharge and discipline of strikers,[80] and to meet its legal duties in a wide range of other areas including observance of the union's continuing status as exclusive bargaining representative.[81] Because the remedies available to the Board for an employer's failure to bargain in good faith are not strong, limiting the use of permanent replacements to economic strikes gives the employer an additional and powerful incentive to follow the rules of good faith bargaining which may help lead to agreement.

[D]—Status of Replacements as Permanent or Temporary

When an economic striker (or the union on his or her behalf) makes an unconditional offer to return to work, the employer must displace any temporary replacement in the striker's job but may refuse to immediately reinstate the striker if his or her position is occupied by a permanent replacement.

---

77 *See, e.g.*, American Meat Packing Corp., 301 NLRB 835 (1991) (take it or leave it attitude with expressed unwillingness to consider alternatives is illegal and causes strike to be unfair labor practice strike).

78 *See* Trumball Memorial Hospital, 288 NLRB 1429, 1470 (1988) (regressive bargaining after strike begins).

79 *See, e.g.*, NLRB v. Truitt Mfg. Co., 351 U.S. 149 (1956).

80 *See infra* § 9.6.

81 *See* Douglas E. Ray, *Withdrawal of Recognition After* Curtin Matheson: *A House Built Upon Sand*, 25 U.S.F. L. Rev. 265 (1991); S & F Enterprises, 312 NLRB 770 (1993) (requiring reinstatement of all strikers replaced after unlawful withdrawal of recognition).

To establish that replacement employees are permanent, the employer must show a mutual understanding between itself and the replacements that they are permanent.[82]

Replacement status will be determined in large part by the representations made by the employer at the time replacements are hired.[83] Thus, if the employer tells replacements that they are being hired for the duration of the strike, they are temporary employees who can be displaced by strikers. This is so even if the employer's subjective intent changes and it intends to regard them as permanent but has not yet communicated this intent to them.[84] In some cases, ambiguous statements to replacements about their status have not been sufficient to support permanent replacement status, especially in the absence of proof that replacement employees considered themselves permanent employees.[85]

The fact that an employer puts conditions on its offer of permanence does not necessarily make the replacement a non-permanent employee. Employers can advise replacements that they may be displaced by strikers in the event required by a union settlement or an NLRB order or settlement without rendering the offer non-permanent.[86]

In some cases, the issue of reinstatement will turn on whether the striker requests reinstatement before his or her position is filled by a permanent replacement. The NLRB generally holds that the striker's job is filled when the replacement accepts the employer's employment offer, even if the replacement has not yet started work.[87]

---

82 Hansen Bros., 279 NLRB 741 (1986), *enforced,* 812 F.2d 1443 (D.C. Cir. 1987).

83 *See* NLRB v. Murray Products, Inc., 584 F.2d 934 (9th Cir. 1978).

84 *Id.*

85 *Compare* NLRB v. Augusta Bakery Corp., 957 F.2d 1467 (7th Cir. 1992) (employer told replacements "if they worked out and did their job, they had a job;" held not permanent where evidence did not establish mutual understanding of permanent status) *and* Hansen Bros., 279 NLRB 741 (1986), *enforced,* 812 F.2d 1443 (D.C. Cir. 1987) (permanent status not established where employer told replacements he "wanted" to consider them permanent and "wanted" them to consider themselves permanent) *with* Gibson Greetings Inc. v. NLRB, 53 F.3d 385 (D.C. Cir. 1995) (employer not always required to use word permanent; post-hire statements can be used to establish permanent status).

86 *See* Belknap v. Hale, 463 U.S. 491, 503-504 (1983); Gibson Greetings v. NLRB, 53 F.3d 385 (D.C. Cir. 1995).

87 *See* Home Insulation Service, 255 NLRB 311, 312 n.9 (1981), *enforced mem.,* 665 F.2d 352 (11th Cir. 1981).

[E]—Status of Permanently Replaced Economic Strikers

Permanently replaced economic strikers remain employees under Section 2(3) of the National Labor Relations Act, as amended.[88] The replaced striker is placed on a preferential recall list while awaiting a vacancy. In addition, as an employee, a permanently replaced striker remains eligible to vote in any election to determine the union's continued majority status if the election is conducted within 12 months of the strike's commencement. Section 9(c)(3) of the Act states that "employees engaged in an economic strike who are not entitled to reinstatement shall be eligible to vote . . . in any election conducted within 12 months of the commencement of the strike."[89]

[F]—Reinstatement Rights of Permanently Replaced Strikers

Once an economic striker has been permanently replaced, he or she must unconditionally apply for reinstatement to be eligible. If there is a vacancy and the striker is qualified, he or she should be reinstated. If there is not a vacancy, the striker is placed on a preferential hiring list to await reinstatement as and when vacancies occur. If the striker obtains "substantially equivalent" employment, however, the employer no longer has a duty to recall the striker.

The first issue to be determined is whether there has been unconditional offer to return to work, made either by individual strikers or by the union on their behalf.[90] The employer may not put conditions or restrictions on the offers to return. It may not, for example, require individual requests if the union has made a blanket offer to return[91] or insist on individual interviews or other conditions that would delay reinstatement.[92]

The order of recall from the preferential recall list is a mandatory subject of bargaining. While seniority order may be the most common system, the employer may use other systems so long as it observes its bargaining

[88] 29 U.S.C. § 152(3).

[89] 29 U.S.C. § 159(c)(3).

[90] If the strikers' unconditional offers to return to work are received before the employer hires permanent replacements, it must reinstate the strikers rather than hiring replacements. *See* Clow Water Systems Co., 317 NLRB 126 (1995).

[91] *See* Marlene Indus. Corp. v. NLRB, 712 F.2d 1011 (6th Cir. 1983).

[92] *See* NLRB v. W. C. McQuaide, Inc., 552 F.2d 519 (3d Cir. 1977).

obligations and the system is applied consistently and does not discriminate based on union activity.[93]

Once an unreinstated economic striker has unconditionally offered to return to work, it becomes important to determine whether a vacancy exists. In *NLRB v. Fleetwood Trailer Co.*,[94] the Supreme Court stated:

> [t]he status of the striker as an employee continues until he has obtained "other regular and substantially equivalent employment" . . . . If and when a job for which the striker is qualified becomes available, he is entitled to an offer of reinstatement. The right can be defeated only if the employer can show "legitimate and substantial business justifications."[95] [96]

Disputes have arisen, however, over whether the employer has a duty to offer former economic strikers reinstatement to any opening for which they are qualified. In a 1991 decision, *Rose Printing Co.*,[97] the NLRB held that an employer could properly refuse to recall three bindery department employees off the record list and, instead, hire new persons for entry level general worker vacancies even though the former strikers were qualified for the general worker positions. The Board held that an employer's obligation to reinstate former economic strikers extends only to vacancies created by the departure of replacements from the strikers' former jobs and to vacancies in substantially equivalent jobs but not to any other job which a former striker is or may be qualified to perform.[98]

---

[93] *See* NLRB v. American Olean Tile Co., 826 F.2d 1496 (6th Cir. 1987) (order of reinstatement applications); Bio-Science Laboratories, 209 NLRB 796 (1974) (seniority in job classification); Lone Star Industries, 279 NLRB 550 (1986) (general rule).

[94] 389 U.S. 375, 381 (1967).

[95] Despite the apparent clarity of the language, "job for which the striker is qualified," disagreement has arisen over the range of jobs to which the striker is entitled to be reinstated. If the departure of a replacement leaves open the striker's former job, the issue is not controversial. The striker is to be reinstated. Similarly, if a vacancy occurs in a job which is "substantially equivalent" to that formerly held by the striker, he or she is to be reinstated to that job.

[96] The NLRB has been willing to take a somewhat broad view of what constitutes a "substantially equivalent" job for reinstatement purposes. *See, e.g.*, Fire Alert Co., 207 NLRB 885 (1973) (two senior strikers ordered reinstated to electronics assemblers positions where their former positions had been eliminated); Laidlaw Waste Systems, 313 NLRB 680 (1994) (ordering reinstatement to truck-driving jobs at another of employer's previously struck facilities 25 miles away from former jobs where duties, conditions and bargaining unit the same).

[97] 304 NLRB 1076 (1991).

[98] 304 NLRB at 1079.

Some courts of appeals have disagreed, relying on language in *Fleetwood Trailer* stating that "if and when a job for which the striker is qualified becomes available, he is entitled to an offer of reinstatement."[99]

Should the employer fail in its obligation to reinstate former strikers to vacancies, it can be directed to reinstate them with back pay. In addition, any subsequent strike in protest could easily be deemed an unfair labor practice strike.

The permanently replaced striker is entitled to full reinstatement, meaning reinstatement to the same or a substantially equivalent position as his or her prestrike job with the same seniority and benefits. The striker retains reinstatement rights until full reinstatement is achieved or he or she accepts substantially equivalent employment elsewhere. Upon the departure of a replacement, the employer must offer the position to the unreinstated striker whose position is now open rather than transferring another employee into the position.[100]

Once a striker is reinstated, he or she is entitled to restored seniority and benefits based on the striker's original hiring date. Reinstated senior strikers should retain their seniority priority in bidding and benefits over less senior employees whether they be replacements, cross-overs or other reinstated strikers.

The Supreme Court's *Fleetwood Trailer* decision[101] allows an employer to deny reinstatement to strikers for "legitimate and substantial business reasons." The burden of proof will be on the employer to show the existence of bona fide business justifications, such as needed changes in operations or downsizing, and that such business factors were not motivated by labor relations considerations.[102] The employer will have to show "actual reliance" on legitimate business reasons for failing to recall strikers.[103]

---

99 389 U.S. at 381. *See, e.g.*, NLRB v. American Olean Tile, 826 F.2d 1496, 1499, 1501 (6th Cir. 1987); Wright Tool Co. v. NLRB, 854 F.2d 812 (6th Cir. 1988). *See also* Arlington Hotel Co. v. NLRB, 785 F.2d 249 (8th Cir. 1986), *cert. denied*, 479 U.S. 914 (1986) (noting dispute).

100 *See* Nolan Systems, Inc., 268 NLRB 1248 (1984). If a striker has already been reinstated to a non-equivalent position, however, and his or her former position becomes vacant due to the departure of a replacement, the striker should be offered the former position when it becomes vacant. This permits full reinstatement.

101 NLRB v. Fleetwood Trailer Co., Inc., 389 U.S. 375, 378 (1967).

102 *See* Kurz-Kasch, Inc. v. NLRB, 865 F.2d 757, 760 (6th Cir. 1989).

103 *See* Chicago Tribune Co., 318 NLRB 920 (1995) (employer which operated short-

Finally, the employer may not prevent reinstatement by hiring replacements in numbers in excess of the number of employees on strike if its motive is to frustrate reinstatement or retaliate against employees for exercising the right to strike.[104]

[G]—Reinstatement Rights of Unfair Labor Practice Strikers

Unfair labor practice strikers have an absolute right to be reinstated to their former jobs upon making an unconditional offer to return to work. This is so even if replacements have been hired and is irrespective of whatever promises the employer may have made to replacements.[105] If an economic strike has been converted to an unfair labor practice strike, a striker's reinstatement rights will depend on the day he or she was replaced. If the striker was replaced while the strike was still an economic strike, the employer need not displace a permanent replacement to recall the striker. If, on the other hand, the striker was replaced after the strike was converted to an unfair labor practice strike, he or she is entitled immediately to displace the replacement.[106]

[H]—Suits by Displaced Replacements

In *Belknap v. Hale*,[107] the U.S. Supreme Court held that the Railway Labor Act does not preempt state law based lawsuits brought by discharged permanent replacements alleging breach of contract and misrepresentation. Thus, a permanent replacement who is displaced by a returning striker, whether due to a settlement agreement or NLRB order, may have a cause of action against the employer depending on the promises made and the availability of a cause of action under applicable state law. To avoid such problems, employers often advise replacements that their permanent status

---

handed and worked replacements at overtime rates violated law by failing to recall strikers to full-time vacancies where no proof of cost effectiveness of working replacements at overtime over recalling strikers to work at regular rates).

[104] *See* Outboard Marine Corp., 307 NLRB 1333 (1992) (hiring 234 replacements for 185 prestrike positions). Analysis will turn on the issue of motive. *Compare* Atlantic Creosoting Co., 242 NLRB 192 (1979) (replacement of 62 strikers with 80 laborers found to be without unlawful motive).

[105] *See* Mastro Plastics Corp. v. NLRB, 350 U.S. 270 (1956); Belknap v. Hale, 463 U.S. 491 (1983).

[106] *See, e.g.*, Hormigonera Del Toa, Inc., 311 NLRB 956 (1993) (replacement hired September 21 did not have to be displaced to make room for returning striker where strike not converted to unfair labor practice strike until September 23).

[107] 463 U.S. 491 (1983).

is subject to specific conditions such as NLRB settlement agreements, NLRB orders to reinstate strikers or strike settlement agreements.

§ 9.6 Unprotected Activity and the Strike

An unfortunate byproduct of some strikes, especially those in which the employer has hired replacements, is the outbreak of violence and other unprotected activity. When violence occurs and the employer responds, complex legal issues arise. Striking is an activity protected by statute. Discriminating against an employee for engaging in the right to strike violates Sections 8(a)(1) and 8(a)(3) of the Act.[108] On the other hand, some activities engaged in during a strike, such as violence, may be unprotected and leave an employee subject to lawful discipline or discharge. Other issues arise with regard to the power of state courts to limit or restrain picket line activity and the potential liability of labor organizations for tortious behavior engaged in by their members.

[A]—Discharge of Strikers for Misconduct

Although striking is a protected activity, a striker who engages in serious misconduct during the strike may go beyond the scope of protected activity and be subject to discharge by the employer. Discharges for strike-related violence involve difficult issues of proof and motive and the employer must have an "independent and adequate basis" unrelated to the protected strike activity for discharging or refusing to reinstate a striker.[109] If a discharge is found to be based on protected conduct, it will be a violation of Section 8(a)(1) and can expose the employer to liability for reinstatement and back pay. In addition, an unlawful discharge in the course of a strike can convert an economic strike into an unfair labor practice strike and eliminate the employer's ability to hire permanent replacements.

The standard of proof for determining the lawfulness of a discharge for misconduct is set forth in the Supreme Court's *NLRB v. Burnup & Sims Inc.*[110] decision. The Court stated:

> Section 8(a)(1) is violated if it is shown that the discharged employee was at the time engaged in a protected activity, that the employer knew it was such, that the basis of the discharge was an alleged act of

---

[108] 29 U.S.C. §§ 158(a)(1) and 158(a)(3).

[109] NLRB v. Fansteel Metallurgical Corp., 306 U.S. 240 (1939).

[110] 379 U.S. 21 (1964).

misconduct in the course of that activity, and that the employee was not, in fact, guilty of that misconduct.[111]

Burnup & Sims involved the discharge of two employees accused of threatening to dynamite company property. Although the employees were proven innocent, the employer sought to justify the discharge based on its honest belief in the truth of the accusation at the time of discharge. The Court held that good faith was not a defense if the alleged misconduct had not, in fact, occurred.

As the NLRB has developed the order of proof in strike misconduct cases, the Board's General Counsel has the ultimate burden of proving that the discharge or refusal to reinstate was illegally based on the striker's protected activity. The General Counsel must first establish that the striker was discharged or refused reinstatement for strike-related conduct. The burden will then shift to the employer to demonstrate "an honest belief" that the striker committed misconduct. To prove this, the employer must demonstrate "some specificity in the record, linking particular employees to particular allegations of misconduct."[112] If the employer demonstrates an honest belief, the General Counsel must establish either that the striker was not guilty of the misconduct in question or that the misconduct was not serious enough for discharge or denial of reinstatement.[113]

Acts of physical violence and serious property destruction are outside the protection of the Act and are often regarded as serious enough to justify discharge. As the Supreme Court stated in *NLRB v. Fansteel Metallurgical Corp.*:

> The employees had the right to strike but they had no license to commit acts of violence or to seize the employer's plant . . . . To justify such conduct because of the existence of the labor dispute or of an unfair labor practice would be to put a premium on resort to force instead of legal remedies and to subvert the principles of law and order which lie at the foundations of society.[114]

---

[111] 379 U.S. at 23.

[112] Axelson, Inc., 285 NLRB 862, 864 (1987); Beaird Industries, 311 NLRB 768 (1993). (Evidence placing strike captain near scene of incident not sufficient basis for good faith belief.)

[113] *See, e.g.*, Gem Urethane Corp., 284 NLRB 1349 (1987).

[114] 306 U.S. 240, 253 (1939).

Thus, employees who physically attack nonstrikers, replacements or supervisors are not engaged in protected activity and may be discharged.[115] With regard to verbal threats unaccompanied by physical acts, the NLRB applies the test developed in its 1984 *Clear Pine Mouldings, Inc.*[116] decision. The Board's test for determining whether conduct justifies discharge for a refusal to reinstate is:

> [W]hether the misconduct is such that, under the circumstances existing, it may reasonably tend to coerce or intimidate employees in the exercise of rights protected under the Act.[117]

In *Clear Pine*, strikers had threatened, but did not attack, a nonstriker in the context of a strike which had also included strikers swinging clubs at replacements, beating on vehicles and carrying baseball bats, ax handles and tire irons. The Board held that, in this context, some verbal abuse did not warrant protection and that an employer need not "countenance misconduct that amounts to intimidation and threats of bodily harm."[118]

The test is an objective one, asking whether the conduct would reasonably tend to coerce or intimidate an individual faced with such conduct in all the circumstances. It does not require proof that the conduct did, in fact, coerce or intimidate.[119]

The *Clear Pine* test is applied to nonverbal conduct of a threatening nature as well. Thus, in *Mohawk Liqueur Co.*,[120] the Board ruled that the employer could properly refuse to reinstate a striker who threw stones or pebbles at a job applicant's vehicle as the applicant drove across the picket line because such conduct "would reasonably tend to intimidate." Similarly, engaging in a high speed chase[121] or forcing a car off the road[122] can involve sufficient coercion to validate a discharge.

---

115 *See, e.g.*, Preterm, Inc., 273 NLRB 683 (1980).

116 268 NLRB 1044 (1984).

117 268 NLRB at 1046.

118 268 NLRB at 1046. *See also* Woodcraft Div., Georgia Craft Co., 275 NLRB 636 (1985) (threats by strikers outside employee's home and in front of employee's wife and child constituted serious misconduct justifying discharge); Alto-Shaam Inc., 307 NLRB 1466 (1992) (threat to nonstriker outside her home with child present); International Paper Co., 309 NLRB 31 (1992) (upholding discharge of striker for threatening to kill strike replacement).

119 *See* Keco Industries, 301 NLRB 303 (1991).

120 300 NLRB 1075 (1990).

121 Auburn Foundry Inc., 274 NLRB 1317 (1985).

122 Teamsters Local 162 v. NLRB, 782 F.2d 839 (9th Cir. 1986).

The *Clear Pine* Board recognized, however, that Congress must have intended to protect minor acts of misconduct when it provided for the right to strike.[123] Therefore, mere namecalling, even if profane in nature, is not likely to be an adequate cause for discharge if it is not accompanied by threats of violence or property damage.[124]

Destruction of property belonging to the employer or nonstrikers is unprotected and can also provide a basis for discharging or refusing to reinstate a striker.[125] Similarly, blocking access to a struck company's premises may be unprotected depending on the circumstances. The NLRB will look at the length and frequency of incidents in assessing their seriousness. A momentary blockage of an entrance to draw a truck driver's attention and peaceably deliver the picket's message may be protected conduct.[126] On the other hand, picketers must respect the rights of those who choose to cross the picket line and discharges have sometimes been upheld when picketers frequently block entrances for considerable periods of time.[127]

Messages contained on union picket signs or handbills may also make the picketing unprotected if they are designed to disparage the employer's reputation or product rather than to publicize the labor dispute. In *NLRB v. Electrical Workers, Local 1229 (Jefferson Standard),*[128] the Supreme Court found that a picket line handbill which attacked the quality of the employer's television broadcasts was unprotected and could subject picketers to discharge.[129] If employee communications are related to an ongoing labor dispute, however, they will be protected even if somewhat vitriolic.[130]

[B]—State Court Injunctions

Although the National Labor Relations Act generally preempts state law in the areas of labor representation and strikes, the Supreme Court permits

---

123 268 NLRB 1044, 1045.

124 *See* Longshoremen's Union, Local 6, 79 NLRB 1487 (1948).

125 *See* PBA Inc., 270 NLRB 998 (1984).

126 *See* Ornamental Ironwork Co., 295 NLRB 473 (1989).

127 *See* Tube Craft, Inc., 287 NLRB 491 (1987).

128 346 U.S. 464 (1953).

129 *See also* Sahara Datsun, 278 NLRB 1044 (1986), *enforced*, 811 F.2d 1317 (9th Cir. 1987) (statements to bank that employer falsified credit applications unprotected).

130 *See* El San Juan Hotel, 289 NLRB 1453 (1988) (leaflet concerning labor dispute which referred to bankruptcy trustee as "Robin Hood of the Rich" and "Dictator" and accused him of mismanagement protected).

parallel state regulation where there is a compelling state interest.[131] The Court allows states to regulate conduct "deeply rooted in local feeling and responsibility and of merely peripheral concern to the federal labor laws.[132]

Because states have a strong interest in preventing violence, state courts have been allowed to enjoin picketing involving violence or the threat of violence, mass picketing, obstructing public streets or plant entrances, and intimidation.[133] Such injunction will be governed by state law and may be subject to state statutory provisions setting forth particular proof standards that must be met.

Although injunctions must be carefully drawn so that they do not prohibit peaceful picketing, injunctions which enjoin acts of violence and limit the number of pickets and locations for picketing have generally avoided preemption problems.[134] If strike related violence and other unlawful acts continue after issuance of an injunction, the union may be exposed to significant penalties for criminal or civil contempt. In *United Mine Workers v. Bagwell*,[135] the Supreme Court reversed a Virginia Supreme Court ruling that a union could be held liable for $52,000,000 in court ordered civil contempt penalties for over 400 violations of an injunction against strike violence. The Court ruled that, in the circumstances, the fines were criminal sanctions and, given the magnitude of the fines, a trial by jury was required.

[C]—Civil Actions

Employees and employers may bring personal injury and property damage lawsuits for damages they have suffered during the labor dispute. Under *San Diego Building Trades v. Garmon*,[136] states are not preempted from granting "compensation for the consequences, as defined by the traditional law of torts, of conduct marked by violence and imminent threats to the public order." Suits can be brought against individual union members for their tortious acts and, sometimes, against their unions. To hold a union liable, the plaintiff generally must show that individual wrongdoers acted as agents of the union. If the claim is brought in federal court, there must

131 San Diego Building Trades v. Garmon, 359 U.S. 236 (1959).

132 359 U.S. at 243.

133 *See, e.g.*, McQuay, Inc. v. United Auto Workers, 245 Minn. 274, 72 N.W.2d 81 (1955), *aff'd*, 351 U.S. 959 (1956) (upholding state court jurisdiction to enjoin strike related violence).

134 *See, e.g.*, Ford v. Boeger, 362 F.2d 999 (8th Cir. 1966).

135 512 U.S. 821 (1994).

136 359 U.S. 236, 247 (1959).

be "clear proof" that the union approved of, actively participated in or knowingly tolerated the unlawful acts.[137]

Statements made in a labor dispute sometimes lead parties to consider an action for defamation. The Supreme Court has held that federal labor law does not preempt a state court libel action.[138] The Court has recognized, however, that federal labor law may protect "vehement, caustic and sometimes unpleasantly sharp attack,"[139] and that such immunity can be lost only if the speech is made with knowledge of its falsity or reckless disregard of whether it is true or false.[140] In practice, most statements made in a labor dispute will be considered protected speech.[141]

Parties considering filing suit in the context of a labor dispute should be aware that filing a frivolous lawsuit or maintaining a suit after it becomes clear that the suit lacks merit can itself be an unfair labor practice if the suit is brought or maintained to retaliate against strike activity.[142]

[D]—Unfair Labor Practice Charges Against the Union

Section 8(b)(1)(A)[143] makes it an unfair labor practices for a union to "restrain or coerce employees in the exercise of rights guaranteed under Section 7." Because Section 7 protects the right to refrain from engaging in concerted activities as well as the right to strike,[144] unions which engage in strike related violence, intimidation, reprisals or threats can be charged

---

137 *See, e.g.*, Kayser-Roth Corp. v. Textile Workers Union, 479 F.2d 524, 527-528 (6th Cir. 1973), *cert. denied*, 414 U.S. 976 (1973) (applying and interpreting Section 6 of Norris-LaGuardia Act); Yellow Bus Lines v. Teamsters Local 639, 883 F.2d 132 (D.C. Cir. 1989), *rev'd on other grounds on rehearing*, 913 F.2d 948 (1990), *cert. denied*, 501 U.S. 1222 (1991).

138 Linn v. United Plant Guard Workers, 383 U.S. 53 (1966).

139 383 U.S. at 62.

140 383 U.S. at 65.

141 *See, e.g.*, Yeager v. Teamsters, Local 20, 6 Ohio St. 3d 369, 453 N.E.2d 666 (1983) (picket signs describing officer of employer as "Little Hitler" using "Gestapo" tactics and operating "Nazi concentration camp" not basis for defamation claim against union).

142 *See* Bill Johnson's Restaurants, Inc. v. NLRB, 461 U.S. 731 (1983); H. W. Barss Co., 296 NLRB 1286 (1989) (filing $500,000 defamation suit against union and members for picket signs calling company and its president "scabs" violated NLRA because in retaliation for protected activity and baseless).

143 29 U.S.C. § 158(b)(1)(A).

144 29 U.S.C. § 157.

with unfair labor practices.[145] The Board has ruled that the prohibitions of Section 8(b)(1)(A) apply as well to violence against management, supervisors and others on the grounds that employees are likely to hear of such violence and be threatened by it.[146]

For a union to be held responsible for strike related violence, there must be proof that union officials authorized, participated in or ratified the violence. The presence of union agents on the picket line when misconduct occurs[147] or the union's failure to take steps to end the violence after it has knowledge of it[148] can be evidence supporting an unfair labor practice charge.

If a union continues to violate a Board cease and desist order after it has been enforced by a federal court of appeals, it can be held liable for contempt.[149]

When an unfair labor practice charge has been filed against a union for strike violence and the NLRB has issued a complaint, the NLRB may seek a federal court injunction against the union under Section 10(j) of the Act.[150] If injunctive relief is ordered, a union which continues to violate the injunction can be exposed to penalties for contempt.[151]

Because of possible delays in NLRB procedures and the limited remedies available from the NLRB, most employers attempt to deal with strike violence through state court actions for injunctive and civil relief. Criminal charges may be pursued as well.

---

[145] *See* NLRB v. Teamsters Local 639, 362 U.S. 274, 290 (1960); United Auto Workers Local 685 (T. B. Woods), 311 NLRB 1328 (1993) (mass picketing, thrown objects, videotaping nonstrikers, threats and assaults).

[146] *See* NLRB v. Union Nacional de Trabajadores, 540 F.2d 1 (1st Cir. 1976), *cert. denied,* 429 U.S. 1039 (1977) (assault on company president).

[147] *See* Teamsters Local 812 (Sound Distributing Co.), 307 NLRB 1267 (1992).

[148] Teamsters Local 783 (Coca-Cola Bottling), 160 NLRB 1776 (1966).

[149] *See* NLRB v. Teamsters Local 115, 800 F.2d 1136 (3d Cir. 1995), *cert. denied,* 517 U.S. 1133 (1996). (Union showed tolerance of continued violence when it was aware of continuing misconduct and took no steps to prevent it. Contempt finding upheld.)

[150] 29 U.S.C. § 160(j).

[151] *See* Squillacote v. Local 248, Meat & Allied Food Workers, 534 F.2d 735 (7th Cir. 1976) (affirming injunction in case involving violence, blocking ingress and egress and property damage).

§ 9.7 Unemployment Compensation and Strikes

Most states do not allow strikers to receive unemployment compensation benefits. In *New York Tel. Co. v. New York Dept. of Labor,*[152] however, the Supreme Court reviewed a New York statute that allowed payment of unemployment compensation benefits to strikers after an eight-week waiting period. The employer had attacked the statute on federal labor law preemption grounds arguing that it altered the balance of power in a strike situation by cushioning the economic impact on striking employees and making the strike more expensive for employers who fund payment of benefits through unemployment compensation taxes calculated under an experience rating system. The Court ruled, based on the legislative history of the Wagner Act, that Congress had not intended to preempt the states from making the policy choice to pay benefits to strikers.

§ 9.8 Chapter Highlights

1. A union must provide timely written notices to the employer and federal and state mediation agencies before striking. Failure to observe this requirement can leave strikers unprotected and subject to discharge. Section 8(d) applies to bargaining over termination or modification of an existing collective bargaining agreement. It does not apply to first contract situations where the union has just become the representative. Special provisions for health care institutions found in Section 8(g) do apply to bargaining for an initial certification or recognition as well as to continuing contracts. (§ 9.2)

2. The right to strike is protected under Section 7 of the Act. Employers may not threaten to discharge or discharge strikers nor may they offer inducements to abandon the strike or discriminatorily deny or limit payment of accrued benefits to strikers. (§ 9.4)

3. Where the employer engages in conduct "inherently destructive" of employee rights such as granting superseniority to replacements and crossovers, a violation of Section 8(a)(3) can be shown without proof of improper motive. For conduct with a lesser impact on employee rights, antiunion motivation must be shown if the employer shows evidence of a legitimate and substantial justification for its conduct. (§ 9.5)

4. An employer may continue operations during a strike by using supervisors and other non-bargaining unit personnel. It may also hire

152 440 U.S. 519 (1979).

temporary replacements, employees who work for the duration of the strike but who must be displaced when strikers, or the union on their behalf, request to return to work. (§ 9.5)

5. An employer may hire permanent replacements for strikers only if the strike was not caused or prolonged by employer unfair labor practices. Because an employer may not hire permanent replacements during an "unfair labor practice strike," it has a powerful incentive to ensure that its bargaining practices comply with statutory requirements. When the strike is over or when a striker requests to return to work, the employer is not required to immediately reinstate a permanently replaced economic striker. Rather, he or she is to be placed on a preferential recall list, eligible for reinstatement as vacancies arise. A permanently replaced striker remains an employee and retains reinstatement rights until full reinstatement is achieved or until he or she accepts substantially equivalent employment elsewhere. (§ 9.5)

6. Although striking is an activity protected by the National Labor Relations Act, some striker activities, such as physical violence or causing serious property damage, are outside the scope of the statute's protection. With regard to verbal threats, the NLRB's *Clear Pine Mouldings* test asks whether the misconduct may reasonably tend to coerce or intimidate employees in the exercise of their statutory rights. If the test is met, the misconduct is unprotected and the employer may lawfully discipline or discharge strikers engaging in such activities. The test is an objective one. (§ 9.6)

7. Because states have a strong interest in preventing violence, statute court jurisdiction to enjoin violence, mass picketing, intimidation and obstruction of streets or entrances is not preempted. State courts are also not preempted from handling civil actions for tortious acts stemming out of strikes including, under very narrow circumstances, defamation actions. (§ 9.6)

8. Section 8(b)(1) makes it an unfair labor practice for a union to restrain or coerce employees in the exercise of protected rights. Because Section 7 protects the right to refrain from engaging in protected activities, unions may not engage in violence, threats of violence or acts of intimidation against non-strikers and other employees. (§ 9.6)

9. Although states are not preempted from paying unemployment compensation benefits to strikers, most states disqualify strikers from receipt of benefits. (§ 9.7)

CHAPTER 10
LOCKOUTS

§ 10.1 Introduction

In a lockout, it is the employer that decides the timing of a work stoppage rather than the union. In essence, a lockout occurs when the employer shuts down its business and tells employees that they will not be able to return to work until the union and employer reach agreement in negotiations. Lockouts, although not common, raise a number of legal issues.[1]

§ 10.2 Statutory Notice Prerequisites and Contractual Limits

[A]—Section 8(d) Notice

Section 8(d) of the National Labor Relations Act,[2] as amended, provides that:

> where there is in effect a collective-bargaining contract covering employees in an industry affecting commerce, the duty to bargain collectively shall also mean that no party to such contract shall terminate or modify such contract, unless the party desiring such termination or modification—
>
> (1) serves a written notice upon the other party to the contract of the proposed termination or modification sixty days prior to the expiration date thereof, or in the event such contract contains no expiration date, sixty days prior to the time it is proposed to make such termination or modification;
>
> (2) offers to meet and confer with the other party for the purpose of negotiating a new contract or a contract containing the proposed modifications;
>
> (3) notifies the Federal Mediation and Conciliation Service within thirty days after such notice of the existence of a dispute, and simultaneously therewith notifies any State or Territorial agency established to mediate and conciliate disputes within the State or Territory where the dispute occurred, provided no agreement has been reached by that time; and

---

1 *See generally* James Baird, *Lockout Law: The Supreme Court and the NLRB*, 38 Geo. Wash. L. Rev. 396 (1970); Bernhardt, *Lockouts: An Analysis of Board and Court Decisions Since* Brown *and* American Ship, 57 Cornell L. Rev. 211 (1972); Walter E. Oberer, *Lockouts and the Law: The Impact of* American Ship Building *and* Brown Food, 51 Cornell L.Q. 193 (1966).

2 29 U.S.C. § 158(d).

(4) continues in full force and effect, without resorting to strike or lockout, all the terms and conditions of the existing contract for a period of sixty days after such notice is given or until the expiration date of such contract, whichever occurs later.

The duty to notify mediation services of a dispute under Sections 8(d)(3) and (4)[3] will rest on the employer if it is the initiating party. A failure to provide such notices can invalidate a lockout even if the union has filed notices. In *Bi-County Beverage Distributors*,[4] the Board held that, because the employer was the initiating party, its obligation to give pre-lockout notices was not satisfied when the union sent letters to state and federal mediation agencies indicating that the employer's association had reopened the collective bargaining agreement for negotiations. The lockout was held unlawful because the employer's letters of notice were not sent until two days after the lockout and did not constitute timely notice. Although the employer tried to argue that the shutdown was caused by lack of work, the Board found it had the purpose of bringing pressure on the union and it was, therefore, a lockout governed by the notice requirements of Section 8(d).

[B]—Contract Limitations

A lockout occurring during the course of a collective bargaining agreement can violate a no-strike/no-lockout clause of the type found in most labor agreements. Violations of no-lockout clauses generally can be grieved and arbitrated under the labor contract's grievance and arbitration procedures and can lead to substantial back pay liability.[5]

§ 10.3 Defensive and Offensive Lockouts

If an employer locks out employees in anticipation of a threatened union strike or as part of a multi-employer bargaining unit responding to a strike against one of its members, the strike is a "defensive" lockout. If the lockout is not of these types but is for the purpose of putting economic pressure on the union in support of the employer's bargaining position, it is an "offensive" lockout.

---

[3] 29 U.S.C. §§ 158(d)(3) and (4).

[4] 291 NLRB 466 (1988).

[5] *See, e.g.*, Hygrade Operators v. ILA Local 333, 945 F.2d 18 (2d Cir. 1991) (upholding arbitrator's award of $50,000 compensatory damages against tugboat operator which, anticipating a strike, had locked out employees two days before expiration of labor contract).

[A]—Defensive Lockouts

The NLRB has, for many years, held that an employer could lock out employees to prevent losses in the face of a threatened or imminent strike.[6] Similarly, lockouts have been sanctioned when designed to prevent sitdown strikes[7] or repeated quickie strikes.[8] If an employer operates a seasonal business and the union has threatened to strike during the busy season, a lockout which causes the work stoppage to occur before the busy season can be held to be defensive in nature.[9]

In 1957, the Supreme Court sanctioned a second type of defensive lockout. In *NLRB v. Truck Drivers Local Union No. 449 (Buffalo Linen),*[10] the union called a strike against one employer member of a multi-employer association of laundry companies. The association was bargaining with the union for a single collective bargaining agreement that would cover all companies in the association. The purpose of the "whipsaw strike" was to obtain a favorable agreement with the struck company because of the unfavorable competitive position in which the strike placed it and then continue to use the "whipsaw" tactic against other members in turn. In response, the nonstruck companies locked out their employees to maintain the strength of the multi-employer association. The Court held that the temporary lockout could be used lawfully in response to a union strike tactic that threatened the employers' interests in maintaining multi-employer bargaining.

In its 1965 *NLRB v. Brown* decision,[11] the Court further expanded an employer's rights in this area. In *Brown,* the union called a "whipsaw" strike against one member of a group of six retail food stores bargaining on a multi-employer basis. The other five stores locked out their employees but, unlike the *Buffalo Linen* employers, continued operations with temporary replacements. Although the NLRB had held that the use of replacements in this situation illegally interfered with the right to strike, the Supreme Court upheld the Court of Appeals' reversal of the Board. The Court upheld the use of temporary replacements on the basis that it was not more

---

6 *See* Quaker State Oil Refining Co., 121 NLRB 334 (1958).

7 Link-Belt Co., 26 NLRB 227 (1940).

8 International Shoe Co., 93 NLRB 907 (1951).

9 *See, e.g.,* Inter-Collegiate Press v. NLRB, 486 F.2d 837 (8th Cir. 1973); Betts Cadillac Olds, Inc., 96 NLRB 268 (1951).

10 353 U.S. 87 (1957).

11 380 U.S. 278 (1965).

destructive of employee rights nor more hostilely motivated than the lockout and was merely part of the employers' defensive efforts to preserve the multi-employer group. The Court noted that the struck employer was legally allowed to stay open for business through use of replacements and that if the employers who locked out their employees were forced to remain closed, the disparity could break up the multi-employer association.[12] Thus, in the view of the Court, the use of temporary replacements during the lockout was consistent with a legitimate business purpose.

Justice White dissented to the majority decision in *Brown*, arguing, among other things, that hiring temporary replacements while refusing work to union members violated Section 8(a)(3) which prohibits discrimination which discourages union membership,[13] and that it is "inherently destructive" of employee interests.[14]

[B]—Offensive Lockouts

The issue of whether a lockout can be characterized as "defensive" became far less important after the Supreme Court ruled, in its 1965 *American Ship Building Co. v. NLRB*[15] decision, that a temporary lockout for the purpose of putting economic pressure on the union does not necessarily violate Section 8(a)(1) or Section 8(a)(3) of the Act.

In *American Ship*, the employer, fearing a strike during the winter season when its shipyards would be most busy, gradually laid off most of its employees in the summer and fall, notifying each that the layoff was due to the unresolved labor dispute. The labor agreement had expired and negotiations were at impasse.

Although the Court might have been able to find the lockout to be a legal "defensive" lockout, it chose not to do so. Instead, the Court chose to resolve the legality of "the use of a temporary layoff of employees solely as a means to bring economic pressure to bear in support of the employer's bargaining position, after an impasse has been reached."[16] Overturning the Board's

---

12 The Court noted that the retail food industry is quite competitive and that a store temporarily closed during a lockout could lose long-term patrons to a struck store lawfully operating with replacements. This could cause one of the nonstruck association members to "bolt the group and come to terms with the Local, thus destroying the common front essential to multi-employer bargaining." 380 U.S. at 284.

13 380 U.S. 278, 297.

14 380 U.S. 278, 298.

15 380 U.S. 300 (1965).

16 380 U.S. at 308.

unfair labor practice finding, the Court found the lockout lawful. The Court carefully noted that this was not a case where the lockout had been used to injure the employee's bargaining representative, to evade the duty to bargain or to discipline employees for supporting the union.

Although such a lockout deprives the union of exclusive control of the timing and duration of work stoppages, the Court found that the right to strike did not carry with it the "right exclusively to determine the timing and duration of all work stoppages."[17] The Court found that the lockout was solely for the purpose of putting economic pressure on the union and held that it did not violate Section 8(a)(3) in the absence of evidence of a motive to discourage union membership or discriminate against union members. The Court noted that permanent replacement of strikers, unilateral imposition of terms at impasse or the refusal to make a concession that could end a strike all have a negative impact on strikers yet do not necessarily violate Section 8(a)(3).

The NLRB subsequently ruled that the *American Ship* decision "obliterated, as a matter of law, the line previously drawn by the Board between offensive and defensive lockouts . . . ."[18] Modern cases focus less on the labels, offensive or defensive, and more on the facts and circumstances of the bargaining and lockout.

§ 10.4 Good Faith Bargaining

A lockout is lawful only if the employer has engaged in good faith bargaining. Although *American Ship* involved a lockout occurring after the parties were at impasse, the Board has ruled that the absence of an impasse, although a factor to be considered, does not automatically render a lockout unlawful.[19] Instead, the Board focuses on the overall good faith and legality of the employer's pre-lockout actions. For example, a unilateral change in terms and conditions of employment can render a subsequent lockout unlawful. In *Association of D.C. Liquor Wholesalers*,[20] the employer waited until the twelfth negotiating session to propose a substantial wage cut, making its final offer and declaring impasse at the same meeting. It locked out employees the next day. The Board found the lockout illegal as part

[17] 380 U.S. at 310.

[18] Evening News Ass'n, 166 NLRB 219, 221 (1967).

[19] *See* Darling & Co., 171 NLRB 801 (1968), *enforced sub nom.* Lane v. NLRB, 418 F.2d 1208 (D.C. Cir. 1969).

[20] 292 NLRB 1234 (1989).

of an overall bad faith bargaining attempt "to abort the bargaining process through the false claim of impasse."[21] The employer's failure to give the union notice of the wage cut proposal combined with its failure to give the union time to consider and respond to the proposal were important to the decision.[22]

Similarly, failing to observe other good faith bargaining duties, such as providing relevant information to the union, can render a subsequent lockout unlawful. For example, in *Clemson Bros.*,[23] a lockout was illegal because the employer had violated its *Truitt* obligation[24] to provide requested information to verify its claims that the business was losing money and unable to provide greater wages.[25]

If a lockout is for the purpose of forcing agreement on a nonmandatory subject, this, too, is illegal. For example, a lockout in support of the employer's insistence on a change in the scope of the bargaining unit has been held unlawful,[26] as has a lockout in support of an employer's insistence on mail ratification of the employer's contract offer.[27]

§ 10.5 Replacement Issues

[A]—Generally

The issue of whether an employer which voluntarily locks out its employees can continue to operate with replacement workers is controversial. Although the Supreme Court and the Board have ruled that the employer may use temporary replacements in a lawful lockout, there are no cases indicating that permanent replacements may be used. This may explain, in part, why lockouts are not more common. An employer which waits for a strike has the additional bargaining leverage that comes with threatening or implementing permanent replacements. An employer that locks out lacks this leverage.

---

21 292 NLRB at 1236.

22 *See also* Union Terminal Warehouse, 286 NLRB 851 (1987) (preimpasse unilateral implementation of wage proposal renders subsequent lockout unlawful).

23 290 NLRB 944 (1988).

24 NLRB v. Truitt Mfg. Co., 351 U.S. 149 (1956).

25 *See also* Globe Business Furniture, 290 NLRB 841 (1988) (failure to provide insurance data needed to evaluate employer's proposal).

26 *See* Greensburg Coca-Cola Bottling Co., 311 NLRB 1022 (1993).

27 *See* Movers & Warehousemen's Ass'n, 224 NLRB 356 (1976), *enforced,* 550 F.2d 962 (4th Cir. 1977).

[B]—Temporary Replacements

[1] Defensive Lockouts

As noted above,[28] the Supreme Court's 1965 *NLRB v. Brown* ruling held that employers in a multi-employer bargaining situation may respond to a whipsaw strike against one of their members by locking out employees and hiring temporary replacements for the duration of the lockout. The Court reasoned that since the struck employer could stay open by hiring replacements, the other employers in the group need the same ability to stay open for business to maintain the effectiveness and integrity of the multi-employer group.

Subsequently, the Board and the courts have also authorized the hire of temporary replacements by employers engaging in other types of "defensive" lockouts such as the employer which locks out employees after it is threatened with a strike during its busy season.[29]

[2] Offensive Lockouts

While authorizing the employer's use of a lockout to bring economic pressure on the union in support of a legitimate bargaining position, the *American Ship* court[30] did not rule on the issue of whether replacements could be hired in an offensive lockout. It expressly reserved judgment on the question.[31] The NLRB reached the issue in its 1986 *Harter Equipment, Inc.*[32] ruling that an employer may use temporary replacements after a lawful lockout that is intended to put economic pressure on the union in support of legitimate bargaining demands. The Board found that such a use of temporary replacements was reasonably adapted to achievement of legitimate employer interests and had "only a comparatively slight adverse effect on protected employee rights."[33]

The issue was further explored by the Court of Appeals for the D.C. Circuit in *Boilermakers, Local 88 v. NLRB*.[34] That court accepted the

---

[28] *See supra* § 10.3[A].

[29] *See, e.g.*, Inter-Collegiate Press v. NLRB, 486 F.2d 837 (8th Cir. 1973).

[30] American Ship Bldg. Co. v. NLRB, 380 U.S. 300 (1965).

[31] 380 U.S. at 308 n.8.

[32] 280 NLRB 597 (1986), *enforced sub nom.* Local 825, IUOE v. NLRB, 829 F.2d 458 (3d Cir. 1987).

[33] 280 NLRB at 600. *Compare* Inland Trucking Co. v. NLRB, 440 F.2d 562, 565 (7th Cir. 1971) (characterizing use of replacements in bargaining lockout as "*per se*" unfair labor practice).

[34] 858 F.2d 756 (D.C. Cir. 1988).

NLRB's position that hiring temporary replacements in a lawful lockout was not conduct "inherently destructive" of employee rights. The court distinguished the case from *NLRB v. Erie Resistor Corp.*,[35] suggesting that use of temporary replacements did not have as destructive an impact on future bargaining. Rather, it compared use of temporary replacements in a bargaining lockout to the use of temporary replacements in a lockout designed to defend against a whipsaw strike which was authorized in *NLRB v. Brown.*[36] The court accepted the NLRB's categorization of the issue under *NLRB v. Great Dane Trailers*,[37] as one which "could have adversely affected employee rights to some extent."[38] *Great Dane* requires that the employer come forward with "legitimate and substantial business justifications" in cases involving "comparatively slight" impact on employee rights.[39] Applying this test, the court held that putting economic pressure on the union in support of legitimate bargaining demands was a legitimate business justification sufficient to justify the use of temporary replacements.

[3]—Limits on Use of Replacements

An employer may not hire temporary replacements for locked out employees if the lockout is not itself lawful.[40] At the conclusion of the lockout, bargaining unit employees must be returned with their seniority intact. They cannot be treated as temporary or new probationary hires.[41]

[C]—Permanent Replacements

As Professor Meltzer has observed, allowing use of permanent replacements in a lockout "might too easily become a device for union-busting, successfully disguised as an effort to protect the employer's bargaining position and his legitimate interest in maintaining operations."[42]

---

35 373 U.S. 221 (1963) (holding that grant of 20 years' superseniority to replacements and crossovers was inherently destructive of employee rights).

36 380 U.S. 278 (1965).

37 388 U.S. 26 (1967).

38 388 U.S. at 34.

39 380 U.S. at 34.

40 *See* Clemson Bros., 290 NLRB 944 (1988) (employer refusal to verify claims it could not pay rendered lockout unlawful; replacements not allowed).

41 *See* United Chrome Products, 288 NLRB 1176 (1988) (employer may not use lockout to destroy seniority rights).

42 Bernard Meltzer, *The Lockout Cases*, 1965 Sup. Ct. Rev. 87, 104. *See* Harter Equipment, Inc., 293 NLRB 647 (1989) (locked out employees cannot be permanently replaced).

§ 10.6 Lockouts and Union Majority Status

The use of temporary replacements for locked out workers should not affect the union's continuing majority status, no matter how long the lockout continues. In *Harter Equipment, Inc.*,[43] the employer hired temporary replacements for locked out employees in January, 1982. A decertification petition was later filed and the employer argued, at a 1986 hearing, that the locked out employees should not be allowed to vote. Finding that the locked out employees had not abandoned their jobs, the Board held that not only were they entitled to vote but that they were the only persons eligible to vote. The Board stated:

> It would be inconsistent with the Act and the decision in *Harter* to disenfranchise these employees. Had they been permanently replaced after they called an economic strike, their right to vote would have ended 1 year later or upon an affirmative act by them to end their employment. However, these employees are not strikers. Rather, the Employer locked out the bargaining unit in support of its bargaining demands and they were not, and could not lawfully be, permanently replaced.[44]

The Board held that all employees hired into unit jobs while the bargaining unit is locked out are necessarily temporary replacements and ineligible to vote no matter how long the lockout continues. Presumably, this ruling also means that an employer may not withdraw recognition based on the union sentiments of replacements for locked out employees. Because they are, by definition, temporary, their views do not matter.

§ 10.7 Unemployment Insurance Issues

The characterization of a labor stoppage as a strike or lockout can be important for purposes of eligibility for unemployment insurance payments under state law. Although most states prohibit strikers from collecting unemployment insurance benefits, a significant number allows locked out employees to receive benefits.[45]

Some states define the term "lockout" more expansively than does federal labor law and authorize unemployment benefits in labor stoppages which

---

[43] 293 NLRB 647 (1989).

[44] 293 NLRB 647, 647-648.

[45] *See* Stern, Lipsky & Hutchens, *Government Transfer Payments and Strike Activity: Reforming Public Policy*, Lab. L.J., Aug. 1990, at 505, 506 (reporting that 21 states authorize benefits to locked out employees).

labor law would characterize as strikes. Pennsylvania courts have held, for example, that a work stoppage occurring after the employer refuses to extend all terms of the expiring labor contract constitutes a constructive lockout for unemployment insurance purposes.[46] Other state courts have found a "lockout" for unemployment insurance purposes where the union's strike was precipitated by employer bargaining behavior which the courts felt left the union with no choice but to strike.[47] These cases apply state law and do not affect federal law definitions of strikes and lockouts.

§ 10.8 Chapter Highlights

1. A lockout occurs when the employer determines the timing of a labor stoppage and advises employees they may not return to work until contract settlement is reached. (§ 10.1)

2. The employer wishing to lock out its employees must insure that it has filed appropriate notices with mediation agencies as required by Section 8(d) if it is the initiating party. It must observe appropriate waiting periods. (§ 10.2)

3. A defensive lockout occurs where the employer is responding to a union threat to strike in the future or, as a member of a multi-employer bargaining unit, locks out in response to a whipsaw strike against one of the group's members. (§ 10.3[A])

4. An offensive lockout is a lockout designed to put economic pressure on the union. It is legal if it is the outcome of good faith bargaining and is in support of a legitimate bargaining position. (§§ 10.3 and 10.4)

5. An employer which lawfully locks out its employees may use temporary replacements (employees hired only for the duration of the lockout). This is true for both "defensive" and "offensive" lockouts. It may not hire replacements during an unlawful lockout nor may it hire permanent replacements for locked out employees. (§ 10.5)

6. Locked out employees retain their status as employees and retain their right to vote in any decertification election held to test the union's majority representative status. Any replacements hired for them are temporary replacements and are not eligible to vote in such an election. (§ 10.6)

---

[46] *See* Erie Forge & Steel Corp. v. Unemployment Comp. Bd., 400 Pa. 440, 163 A.2d 91 (1960); Hoffman v. Comm. Unemployment Bd., 524 Pa. 470, 574 A.2d 57 (1990).

[47] *See* Sunstar Foods, Inc. v. Uhlendorf, 310 N.W.2d 80 (Minn. 1981).

CHAPTER 11
SECONDARY BOYCOTTS

§ 11.1 Generally

Section 8(b)(4) of the National Labor Relations Act, as amended, provides in part that:

> It shall be an unfair labor practice for a labor organization or its agent—
>
> . . .
>
> (4)(i) to engage in, or to induce or encourage any individual employed by any person . . . to engage in, a strike or refusal . . . to . . . perform any services; or (ii) to threaten, coerce, or restrain any person engaged in commerce or in an industry affecting commerce, where in either case an object thereof is— . . . (B) forcing or requiring any person to cease using, selling, handling, transporting, or otherwise dealing in the products of any other . . . person . . . .[1]

Added in 1947, this "secondary boycott" provision has the effect of barring union picketing activity against all employers with which the union does not have a primary labor dispute. As Judge Learned Hand noted:

> The gravamen of a secondary boycott is that its sanctions bear, not upon the employer who alone is a party to the dispute, but upon some third party who has no concern in it. Its aim is to compel him to stop business with the employer in the hope that this will induce the employer to give in to his employees' demands.[2]

Under this section, a union having a dispute with an employer over the terms and conditions of employment offered its employees (the primary employer) must confine its picketing activity to that particular employer. It may not extend the labor dispute to other employers (secondary employers) in the hope that pressuring them to cease dealing with the primary employer will help it gain the upper hand in its primary dispute. Even if the union has other goals as well, the statute makes its picketing unlawful if "an object" is to pressure the secondary employer into ceasing to deal with the primary.[3] So long as even one of the union's objectives is to put pressure on the primary employer by influencing the secondary employer, the picketing can be found illegal. Violations can carry serious penalties,

---

1 29 U.S.C. § 158(b)(4).

2 IBEW Local 501 v. NLRB, 181 F.2d 34, 37 (2d Cir. 1950), *aff'd*, 341 U.S. 694 (1951).

3 29 U.S.C. § 158(b)(4). *See generally*, Lesnick, *The Gravamen of the Secondary Boycott*, 62 Colum. L. Rev. 1361 (1962).

including injunctive relief and monetary damages.[4] Charges and/or lawsuits can be brought by an injured neutral party, an injured primary employer or both.

Applying the statutory language has not proven easy. Difficult issues of policy and interpretation can arise in determining whether an employer is a protected neutral or, because of its ties to the primary employer, an "alter ego" or "ally" of the primary which can be lawfully picketed.[5] Other difficult issues can arise where the primary employer and neutral employers occupy the same site. Such problems can arise whether the primary employer is temporarily on the neutral employer's property ("ambulatory situs"),[6] both are on a site owned by another neutral ("common situs")[7] or the neutral is on the primary's property during a labor dispute.[8] In all these situations, the Board and the courts try to find ways to insulate the neutral employer and its employees from the labor dispute without impairing the union's right to picket the primary employer.[9]

§ 11.2 Primary Employer Status

Although the statute is designed to protect innocent third-party neutrals from labor disputes not of their own making, it is also intended to allow pressure to be put on the primary employer. The NLRB and the courts have defined the term "primary" employer to include both employers which share enough ownership and control to qualify as "alter egos," or a "single employer" and employers which have "ally status" because they aid the employer in resisting the strike by performing work that would have been performed by strikers.

[A]—Single Employers and Alter Egos

The NLRB and reviewing courts generally will look at common ownership, common management, interrelation of operations and common or central control of labor relations in determining whether separate entities constitute a single employer for secondary boycott purposes.[10]

---

[4] *See infra* § 11.8.

[5] *See infra* § 11.2.

[6] *See infra* § 11.4[A].

[7] *See infra* § 11.4[B].

[8] *See infra* § 11.5.

[9] *See* NLRB v. Denver Bldg. & Constr. Trades, 341 U.S. 675, 692 (1951) (Congress desired to preserve unions' right to pressure employers in primary disputes while "shielding unoffending employers and others from pressures in controversies not their own.").

[10] *See* Teamsters Local 50 (E.J. Dougherty Oil), 269 NLRB 170, 174 (1984).

The factors are considered together and all four need not be present. Where two entities have common ownership and control, have interrelated operations and common management, and there is centralized control of labor relations, they can be considered as a single employer and either may be lawfully picketed with regard to a labor dispute involving the other.[11]

In other cases, the same test has been used to determine whether a union may lawfully picket divisions, branches or commonly-owned subsidiaries. In two cases involving the Hearst Corporation,[12] the Board and reviewing courts held that operating divisions of a single corporation were to be considered separate and neutral entities for secondary boycott purposes if actual common control, especially in labor relations, was lacking.[13] It is "active, not potential control that is significant."[14]

[B]—Ally Status and Struck Work

A third-party employer which does work which, but for the strike, would have been done by employees of the struck employer may be lawfully picketed. Picketing at the premises of an employer performing such "struck work" is considered primary picketing because the employer doing struck work has become, in effect, an ally of the struck employer.

In the *Douds* case,[15] a federal court refused to issue an injunction against picketing at the premises of an employer which was performing drafting and design work previously performed by strikers. In that case, the union struck Ebasco, a firm which designed and drafted plans for industrial and utility installations. Ebasco had, in the past, subcontracted some work to an outside firm, Project. After the strike was called, Ebasco transferred more

[11] *See* Weinreb Management, 292 NLRB 428 (1989) (partnership owning and managing apartment buildings and partnership which provided maintenance and service to these buildings deemed single employer).

[12] L.A. Newsp. Guild, Local 69 (Hearst Corp.), 185 NLRB 303 (1970), *enforced,* 443 F.2d 1173, (9th Cir. 1971), *cert. denied,* 404 U.S. 1018 (1972); AFTRA, Wash. Balt. Local (Hearst Corp.), 185 NLRB 593 (1970), *enforced,* 462 F.2d 887 (D.C. Cir. 1972).

[13] *See also* IBEW Local 2208 (Simplex Wire), 285 NLRB 834 (1987) (Holding company was separate and neutral employer from one of its wholly-owned corporations where subsidiary chose its own employees and parent did not participate in labor negotiations of subsidiary. Picketing of parent's corporate office constituted unlawful secondary boycott.).

[14] United Mine Workers (Borch Mining Co.), 301 NLRB 897 (1991), *enforcement denied,* 955 F.2d 431 (6th Cir. 1992). *See generally* Siegel, *Conglomerates, Subsidiaries, Divisions and the Secondary Boycott,* 9 Ga. L. Rev. 329 (1975).

[15] Douds v. Metrop. Fed. Of Architects, Local 231, 75 F. Supp. 672 (S.D.N.Y. 1948).

work to Project, including some work already begun by Ebasco's employees. The union began picketing Project, and the NLRB Regional Director sought an injunction in federal court. After reviewing the legislative history of the secondary boycott provisions, the court determined that Project was not entitled to protection as a neutral because it had made itself a party and its conduct as an ally provoked the union's action. The court noted that Project employees "did work, which, but for the strike of Ebasco's employees, would have been done by Ebasco,"[16] and that this had the same effect as if Ebasco had hired strikebreakers to work on its premises. For these reasons, the court found that picketing at Project did not violate the secondary boycott laws.

Judge Learned Hand characterized the struck work doctrine as follows:

> One does not make oneself a party to the dispute with a primary employer by taking over the business that the strike has prevented him from doing. On the other hand if a secondary employer, knowing of the strike, not only accepts the customer of the primary employer but takes his pay, not from the customer but from the primary employer . . . [then he has] made common cause with the primary employer.[17]

Where the work previously done by strikers is not contracted for directly by the struck employer but, rather, is contracted for directly by third-party customers of the struck employer, the firm doing the work will be considered an ally and, therefore, a proper target for primary picketing only if the struck employer has set up and directed the arrangement.[18]

§ 11.3 *Denver Building Trades*

In *Denver Building & Construction Trades Council v. NLRB,*[19] the Supreme Court issued a decision that would set the tone for interpretation of Section 8(b)(4), especially in the construction industry. In that case, construction unions picketed a construction job site to protest the general

---

[16] 75 F. Supp. at 677.

[17] NLRB v. Local 459, IUE, 228 F.2d 553, 562 (2d Cir. 1995) (concurring opinion), *cert. denied,* 351 U.S. 962 (1956) (adopting *Douds* test).

[18] *See* Blackhawk Engraving Co. v. NLRB, 540 F.2d 1296, 1300-1301 (7th Cir. 1976) (union did not violate secondary boycott laws in picketing third-party printing firm where struck employer "orchestrated" arrangements whereby primary's customers used firm during strike). Levin, *"Wholly Unconcerned": The Scope and Meaning of the Ally Doctrine Under Section 8(b)(4) of the NLRA,* 119 W. Pa. L. Rev. 283 (1970).

[19] 341 U.S. 675 (1951).

contractor's decision to award the subcontract for electrical work to a subcontractor which did not use union labor. Picketers carried signs stating "This Job Unfair to Denver Building and Construction Trades." Because union employees refused to cross the picket line, the job was shut down until the general contractor removed the non-union subcontractor from the job. The Court found that forcing the contractor to terminate the subcontractor's contract was "an object" of the strike and that it, therefore, violated Section 8(b)(4). The Court indicated that picketing the general contractor over its labor relations with its own employees could be lawful but that this picketing was unlawful because it involved the employees of another employer, the subcontractor, and was thus "secondary."

§ 11.4 The Primary Employer on the Premises of a Neutral

[A]—Ambulatory Situs

When a primary employer is temporarily on the premises of a neutral employer, the union's right to picket the primary employer and the protection provided neutral employers by Section 8(b)(4) are in conflict. To recognize one is to restrict the other. This tension was recognized and resolved by the NLRB in its 1950 *Moore Dry Dock* decision,[20] a case that involved a ship temporarily tied up at a neutral's dock. Where a ship or truck or other movable work site is the primary presence which the union seeks to picket, it is often referred to as an "ambulatory" situs and the union's picketing will be governed by the *Moore Dry Dock* principles.

In *Moore Dry Dock*, the union picketed to protest use of a nonunion crew by the owners of the ship, Phopho, which was temporarily tied at the Moore Dry Dock for repairs and preparation. Having been denied access to Moore property, the union picketed outside the Moore Dry Dock entrance. Picket signs and letters sent to unions representing Moore employees emphasized that the dispute was limited to the Phopho and asked that no work be done on it. Although Moore employees continued to work on other ships, they ceased work on the Phopho. Moore filed Section 8(b)(4) charges.

In cases such as this where the situs of the dispute is temporarily located on the premises of a neutral employer, the Board held that the right of the union to picket at the site of its dispute must be balanced against the right of a secondary employer to be free from picketing concerning a controversy that does not involve it. Finding that both rights must be qualified, the Board

20 Sailors Union of the Pacific (Moore Dry Dock), 92 NLRB 547 (1950).

held that a union's picketing the premises of a secondary employer in such situations is primary (and, therefore, legal) if it meets the following test:

(a) the picketing is strictly limited to times when the situs of dispute is located on the secondary employer's premises;

(b) at the time of the picketing the primary employer is engaged in its normal business at the situs;

(c) the picketing is limited to places reasonably close to the location of the situs; and

(d) the picketing discloses clearly that the dispute is with the primary employer.[21]

The Board found that all four conditions had been met because preparing a ship for departure was part of the "normal business" of operating a ship. It therefore held that the picketing constituted lawful primary picketing.

All four of the *Moore Dry Dock* standards must be met for picketing to be lawful in an ambulatory situs situation. When they are, a union may lawfully picket even if its temporary picketing is inconvenient for the neutral employer as in the case of a union's picketing of the struck employer's delivery trucks while they are making deliveries.[22] If any of the four standards are not met, however, the picketing will be found unlawful.[23] The theme of *Moore Dry Dock* is that the picketing union must minimize the impact of its primary picketing on the neutral employer. For this reason, it may not continue to picket outside the premises of a neutral employer if it has been invited onto the premises to picket directly around the primary's truck.

---

21 92 NLRB at 549.

22 *See* Teamsters, Local No. 807 (Schulz Refrigerated Service, Inc.), 87 NLRB 502 (1949) (Employees of struck commercial trucking firm may picket around the trucks at pick-up and delivery points. Union may "picket between the headlights" to put economic pressure on primary.).

23 *See, e.g.,* Teamsters, Local 85 (Viking Delivery Service), 186 NLRB 462 (1970) (picketer wore sash stating "Picket" which did not disclose dispute was with delivery service); Teamsters, Local 776, 313 NLRB 1148 (1994) (union picketing unlawful because it occurred when struck employer's trucks not at site or when trucks were present but not operated by employees of struck employer).

[B]—Common Situs

[1] Generally

The *Moore Dry Dock* standards[24] have also been applied by the Board and the courts to situations in which the primary employer occupies a common work site with one or more neutral secondary employers. The union has a right to picket the primary employer at the work site but its picketing will be unlawful if it violates the *Moore Dry Dock* standards and its object is to disrupt a secondary employer's business in order to cause it to cease doing business with the primary employer.[25] A union which violates the *Moore Dry Dock* standards, for example, by picketing a common work site with signs that do not identify the primary employer, generally is presumed to have a secondary object.[26] The Board has held that picketing at a common situs in the construction industry will be governed by the *Moore Dry Dock* test even if the union's dispute is with the general contractor rather than with one of the subcontractors.[27]

[2] Reserved Gates

When neutrals and the primary employer and those doing business with them use the same gate or entrance to enter and leave a common work site, the union may lawfully picket the common entrance in order to get its message across to the work force of the primary employer and others doing business with it. This may cause unionized workers of neutral employers to refuse to cross the picket line even if the picket signs refer only to the primary employer. Other members of the public may refuse to cross as well.

To avoid such potential disruptions, neutral employers at a common site will often ask that a "reserved gate system" be set up. In such a system, entrances used by neutral employees and suppliers are physically separated

---

24 (a) The picketing is strictly limited to times when the situs of the dispute is located on the secondary employer's premises; (b) At the time of the picketing the primary employer is engaged in its normal business at the situs; (c) The picketing is limited to places reasonably close to the location of the situs; and (d) The picketing discloses clearly that the dispute is with the primary employer. 92 NLRB at 547.

25 The test remains one of whether there was illegal motive. *See, e.g.*, J.F. Hoff Elec. Co. v. NLRB, 642 F.2d 1266, 1269-1270 (D.C. Cir. 1980), *cert. denied,* 451 U.S. 918 (1981).

26 *See, e.g.*, Iron Workers Local 433 (United Steel), 293 NLRB 621 (1989).

27 *See* Bldg. & Constr. Trades of New Orleans (Markwell & Hartz), 155 NLRB 319 (1965), *enforced,* 387 F.2d 79 (5th Cir. 1967), *cert. denied,* 391 U.S. 914 (1968) (refusing to apply test of Local 761, IUE v. NLRB (General Electric), 366 U.S. 667 (1961), which governs picketing in the case of neutrals at a primary situs).

from the entrance used by the employer which is the primary target of the union's picketing. If a valid reserved gate system is established and maintained and the union continues to picket a gate used exclusively by neutrals, such union would not be limiting its picketing "to places reasonably close to the . . . situs" of its dispute with the primary employer. This violates the third *Moore Dry Dock* standard. If the union respects the reserved gate system and limits its picketing to the primary's separate gate, its actions will be presumptively legal.

A reserved gate system established by the owner or operator of the neutral work site will generally reserve one gate or entrance for the primary employer, its employees and suppliers. The primary employer, its employees and suppliers will be barred from using any other entrance to the property.

The gate reserved to the struck or primary employer will generally have a sign reading:

> This entrance is reserved exclusively for (primary), its employees and suppliers. All other persons are prohibited from using this entrance. (Primary), its employees and suppliers are prohibited from using any other entrance to these premises.

The other gates will generally have signs reading:

> (Primary), its employees and suppliers are prohibited from using this entrance.

Gates are generally policed to insure that employees and suppliers of the primary employer enter only through the assigned gate. Once the gate system is established, letters and telegrams are often sent to the union to insure that it is on notice of the restriction. Once the system is set up and the union is put on notice, the union must restrict its picketing to the gate reserved for the primary employer or face secondary boycott liability.

Once a reserved gate system is established, it must be policed and maintained to ensure that the primary employer, its employees and its suppliers do not use the gates reserved for use by neutrals. If a gate reserved for neutrals is used by the primary, depending on the extent of use, the reserved gate system may be regarded as destroyed.[28] If the gate system

---

[28] *Compare* IBEW Local 211 (Atlantic Cty Impr. Auth.), 277 NLRB 1041 (1985) (single delivery to primary at neutral gate is proof that system broken down) *with* OCAW Local 3-689, 307 NLRB 1031 (1992) (minimal use of neutral gate by employee of primary not

has broken down due to the primary's use of neutral gates, the union may lawfully picket the gates in question. If violations have tainted the neutral gate system, the employer may rehabilitate it by expanding its efforts to enforce limitations on the use of gates and notifying the union that the gates have been reestablished and will be enforced in the future.[29]

§ 11.5 A Neutral Employer on the Primary's Property

In the *General Electric* case,[30] the Supreme Court dealt with secondary boycott issues arising when a neutral employer is located on the property of the primary employer. In that case, General Electric plant employees went on strike. The thousand-acre plant was accessible only by means of five roadways designated as gates. The union representing G.E. employees picketed all five gates with picket signs reading: "LOCAL 761 ON STRIKE G.E. UNFAIR." The case involved the issue of whether it was unlawful for the union to picket Gate 3-A, a gate used by independent contractors performing various jobs on the G.E. site during the strike, including construction of new buildings, installation and repair of heating and ventilation equipment, retooling necessary to manufacturing changes and general maintenance work. Gate 3-A was posted with a sign stating: "GATE 3-A FOR EMPLOYEES OF CONTRACTORS ONLY G.E. EMPLOYEES USE OTHER GATES." The employer argued that the gate was used only by independent contractors and that the picketing violated Section 8(b)(4) because it was intended to enmesh neutrals in the dispute and induce neutral employees to refuse to work with an object of forcing their employers to cease doing business with G.E.

Although the NLRB had found a violation of the secondary boycott laws,[31] the Supreme Court did not agree. The Court noted, first, that Section 8(b)(4) is not to be literally construed and that a union is generally free to picket the primary employer even if it causes employees of neutral employers doing business with the primary to refuse to cross the picket line at the primary's place of business. The Court then reviewed Board precedent involving the drawing of lines designated to preserve the rights

---

sufficient to justify picketing) *and* IUOE Local 12 (Hensel Phelps Constr.), 284 NLRB 246 (1987) (occasional violation does not cause breakdown of system if system is diligently monitored).

[29] *See* NLRB v. Carpenters Local 1622, 786 F.2d 903 (9th Cir. 1986) (per curiam), *enforcing* 262 NLRB 1244, 1246 (1982).

[30] Local 761 IUE v. NLRB (General Electric), 366 U.S. 667 (1961).

[31] 123 NLRB 1547 (1959).

of unions to pressure primary employers while shielding neutral employers from the pressures of unrelated labor disputes.

The Court held that cases like this turn on the type of work being performed by contractors using the separate gate. The union may picket at gates used by employees, suppliers and customers of the struck employer. The union may also picket at gates used by independent contractors during work connected to the normal operations of the struck employer. The Court identified as "controlling considerations" whether the work is related to the normal operations of the struck employer and whether it is of the kind that would necessitate curtailing operations if done when the plant is engaged in regular operations. If the work is unrelated and would not require curtailment of operations, such as construction work on buildings, the union may not picket at gates reserved for contractors performing such tasks. If the work is related to normal operations or would have curtailed operations if not performed during a strike, the union may picket a gate reserved for employees of such contractor or contractors. The Court noted that Gate 3-A may have been a mixed-use gate used by employees of contractors who performed conventional maintenance work necessary to normal operations as well as by more neutral contractors. If there was mixed use, picketing would not violate Section 8(b)(4) and the Court remanded for findings on this matter.

Under this decision, a union may picket a gate being used by a contractor doing work on the struck employer's premises if the contractor is doing work necessary to help the employer continue operations in the face of the strike or work which enables the employer to lessen the economic impact of the strike by completing projects which would otherwise have curtailed production if not done during the strike. In effect, such contractors are almost "allies" of the employer in helping it resist the strike much as are employers doing "struck work."[32] If the contractor is doing work that is neither related to operations nor the type of work that would have curtailed operation, the union may not picket a gate specifically reserved for its use.[33]

The *General Electric* test is applied to cases where neutrals are working on the property of the primary employer. The Board does not apply it to

---

[32] *See supra* § 11.2[B].

[33] As noted above, a problem in G.E. was that the single gate for contractors seems to have been used by both "neutral" contractors and those whose work was related to continuing operations during the strike. In such a situation, the union may lawfully picket. *See generally,* Cantor, *Separate Gates, Related Work and Secondary Boycotts*, 27 Rutgers L. Rev. 613 (1974).

evaluate picketing at a common situs in the construction industry even when the dispute is with the general contractor, applying *Moore Dry Dock* instead.[34]

§ 11.6 Hot Cargo Clauses

The primary-secondary distinction developed for interpretation of Section 8(b)(4) is also important to understanding NLRA provisions dealing with the so-called "hot-cargo clause." An example of a hot cargo clause is a contract provision between a union and employers providing that employees do not have to handle products from a struck or non-union firm. The Supreme Court held in 1958 that such voluntary boycott clauses were not illegal and could be enforced in arbitration or court proceedings, although not by strike or economic pressure,[35] even though they required one party to cease doing business with another. Congress responded in 1959 by enacting Section 8(e)[36] which provides that it is an unfair labor practice for a labor organization and an employer to enter into a contract in which the employer agrees to "cease . . . from handling . . . any of the products of any other employer, or to cease doing business with any other person." Section 8(b)(4)(A) then provided it was an unfair labor practice for a union to coerce "any employer or self-employed person to . . . enter into any agreement which is prohibited by subsection 8(e). . . ."[37] Thus, it is illegal to enter into an agreement barred by Section 8(e) and a strike or any coercion to induce an employer to sign such a clause is an illegal secondary boycott under Section 8(b)(4).[38]

In essence, Section 8(e) prevents unions from accomplishing through contract that which Section 8(b)(4) prohibits them from accomplishing through other means. A contract provision by which a union induces one person from doing business with another generally violates Section 8(e) unless within the limitations discussed below.

---

[34] *See* Bldg. & Constr. Trades of New Orleans (Markwell & Hartz), 155 NLRB 319, 324-325 (1965), *enforced*, 387 F.2d 79 (5th Cir. 1967), *cert. denied*, 391 U.S. 914 (1968) (distinguishing *General Electric* on grounds that when the primary is on a construction site it is "but one of several employers operating on premises owned and operated by a third party").

[35] *See* Local 1976, Carpenters v. NLRB (Sand Door), 357 U.S. 93 (1958).

[36] 29 U.S.C. § 158(e). *See generally*, Theodore J. St. Antoine, *Secondary Boycotts and Hot Cargo: A Study in the Balance of Power*, 40 U. Det. L.J. 189 (1962).

[37] 29 U.S.C. § 158(b)(4)(A).

[38] Attempts to enforce such clauses through arbitration or court proceedings are also illegal. *See, e.g.*, IBEW Local 684, 246 NLRB 549 (1979).

[A]—Work Preservation Issues

A literal reading of Section 8(e) would prohibit every form of contract that requires the employer to stop doing business with another party. The Supreme Court has not gone so far, grafting the primary-secondary distinction of Section 8(b)(4) into hot cargo cases. A prime example is the Court's 1967 decision in *National Woodwork Manufacturers Association v. NLRB*.[39] In that case, a collective bargaining agreement between the Carpenters Union and Frouge, the general contractor on a Philadelphia housing project, bound the contractor to contract provisions governing the Philadelphia area contractors' association. That contract included a provision providing that "no member . . . will handle . . . any doors . . . which have been fitted prior to being furnished on the job. . . ." The Philadelphia project job specifications under which Frouge bid called for 3,600 doors but did not specify type. Frouge ordered premachined doors ready to hang rather than "blank" doors on which work site carpenters would have had to do mortising, routing and beveling to prepare the doors for knobs, hinges and hanging. When the doors arrived on the job site, the union ordered its members not to hang them. Frouge then withdrew the doors and replaced them with "blank" doors which were fitted and cut by job site carpenters. The National Woodwork Manufacturers Association filed charges alleging that the "will not handle" provision violated Section 8(e) and that the union violated Section 8(b)(4)(B) by forcing Frouge to stop using the products of the prefitted door manufacturers which was a member of the Association.

Upholding the NLRB's dismissal of the case, the Supreme Court held that Congress intended Sections (8)(e) and 8(b)(4)(B) to prohibit only "secondary objectives."[40]

The Court applied a test inquiring whether the union's objective was preservation of work for job site carpenters or whether the agreement and boycott "were tactically calculated to satisfy union objectives elsewhere."[41] In the words of the Court, "The touchstone is whether the agreement or its maintenance is addressed to the labor relations of the contracting

[39] 386 U.S. 612 (1967).

[40] 386 U.S. at 620. The Court reviewed legislative history. It further noted that Fibreboard Paper Products Corp. v. NLRB, 379 U.S. 203 (1964), requires parties to bargain over the contracting out of work previously performed by bargaining unit members and that it would be incongruous to invalidate under Section 8(e) clauses over which the parties may be required to bargain.

[41] 386 U.S. at 644.

employer vis-à-vis his own employees."[42] Under this test, the Court upheld the Board's finding that the objective of the provision was to preserve work traditionally performed by job site carpenters and therefore lawful.

A union can violate an otherwise valid work preservation clause by enforcing it against non-union products but not union products.[43] In *National Woodwork*, however, the Court noted that the union's maintenance of the provision did not violate Section 8(b)(4)(B) because the union refused to hang prefabricated doors whether or not they bore a union label and even refused to hang doors prefabricated off site by its own members.[44]

The issue of whether the union's object is work preservation becomes more difficult when changing technology has altered the nature of the work in question. This issue was addressed by the Supreme Court in two decisions involving a case brought against the International Longshoremen's Association.[45] The case involved the introduction of "containerization" to East Coast ports, a practice whereby employers used "container ships" designed to carry large containers of freight which could be attached directly to truck chassis and transported to and from the port. Use of these containers substantially cut the time a ship had to remain in port for loading and unloading. It also substantially cut the work available for longshoremen who had traditionally loaded and unloaded freight into and out of the holds of ships.

Rather than negotiating a "will not handle" clause of the type agreed to in *National Woodwork*, the union and employers negotiated a complicated set of "Rules on Containers." The negotiated rules provided that longshoremen were to be allowed to pack and unpack ("stuff and strip") containers on the pier if the loading of the containerized goods occurred within 50 miles of the port. This rule applied whether or not the work was actually necessary since the containers were already packed in most cases. In the alternative, employers could pay a $1,000 per container fee for violating the rules and not allowing on-pier re-packing or unpacking.

Case analysis turned on characterization of the work in question, the loading and unloading of containers within a 50-mile radius of the port. Charges were filed by trucking and warehouse companies which loaded and

---

[42] 386 U.S. at 645.

[43] This would be evidence of union objectives elsewhere other than work preservation.

[44] 386 U.S. at 646.

[45] *See* NLRB v. International Longshoremen's Ass'n, 447 U.S. 490 (1980) ("ILA I") and NLRB v. International Longshoremen's Ass'n, 473 U.S. 61 (1985) ("ILA II").

unloaded containers at off-port facilities. They characterized the work in question as the functional equivalent of loading the trailer of a truck, work which was not traditionally done by longshoremen. They therefore characterized the negotiated rules as unlawful "work acquisition" rather than work preservation.

A Supreme Court majority ultimately adopted the argument of the union; that the work was the functional equivalent of loading and unloading the hold of a ship and that the provisions therefore could represent lawful work preservation under *National Woodwork*. The Court held that:

> Elimination of work in the sense that it is made unnecessary by innovation is not of itself a reason to condemn work-preservation agreements under Sections 8(b)(4)(B) and 8(e); to the contrary, such elimination provides the very premise for such agreements.[46]

[B]—Right to Control Issues

Under a somewhat confusing limit on the work preservation doctrine, a union may not enforce an otherwise lawful work preservation clause if the primary employer does not have a "right to control" the assigned work in question. In *NLRB v. Enterprise Association*,[47] the Pipefitters Union entered into an agreement with an air conditioning contractor providing that threading and cutting of internal piping for climate control units being installed by the contractor would be performed on the job site by the contractor's union-represented employees. The contractor, Hudik, then received a subcontract from Austin, the general contractor, for installation of prefabricated climate control units with threading and cutting of internal piping already completed by the manufacturer. The union refused to install or handle the prefabricated units and the general contractor filed charges under Section 8(b)(4)(B).

The Supreme Court majority held that although the contract provision constituted lawful work preservation, it was an unlawful secondary boycott to enforce it under these circumstances. The Court majority reasoned that the union's objectives were not limited to influencing Hudik, the employer, but were also aimed at influencing Austin, the general contractor, which alone had the power to assign internal piping work. Because the union

---

46 473 U.S. 61, 80-81.

47 429 U.S. 507 (1977). *See generally*, Douglas L. Leslie, *Right to Control: A Study in Secondary Boycotts and Labor Antitrust*, 89 Harv. L. Rev. 904 (1976).

sought to influence the policies of another employer, the majority found the objectives of its economic pressure secondary.

Three justices dissented, arguing, among other things, that the purpose of both the contract provision and its enforcement was primary activity in protecting the work of the employer's own employees. They did not characterize Hudik, the employer, as a "neutral" in the dispute because it was still in a position to negotiate substitute protections even after entering the subcontract.

The "right to control" doctrine limits the enforcement of work-preservation oriented "will not handle" clauses. Its description and justification in *Enterprise Association* also demonstrates the marginal utility of the primary-secondary distinction as an analytical device in cases where traditional union interests are affected by more than one employer.

[C]—Subcontracting Clauses and Union Standards Clauses

A subcontracting clause which allows the employer to subcontract work only to employers having bargaining agreements with the union is illegal under Section 8(e). Even if such a "union signatory clause" relates to work that might validly be preserved under *National Woodwork*, it appears to be concerned with the labor relations of the potential subcontractor, making the potential subcontractor the primary employer. It fails the *National Woodwork* "union objectives elsewhere" test in that it is not limited to union concerns over protecting work at the contracting employer. The Board and the courts have, however, upheld clauses by which the employer agrees not to subcontract to any subcontractor providing less than the wages, benefits, hours and working conditions provided for in the union contract. The theory is that such a "union standards" clause has a primary objective in that it deters the employer from subcontracting merely to undercut contractual wage standards and thereby preserves jobs.[48]

[D]—Special Rules and Exemptions

Congress created special exceptions to the prohibitions of Section 8(e) for the clothing and apparel industry and for the construction industry. The garment industry proviso allows agreements by jobbers or manufacturers in the garment industry not to subcontract work to nonunion contractors. The proviso allows garment industry hot cargo clauses and also excludes the industry from the reach of Section 8(b)(4)(B) and other secondary

---

48 *See* Truck Drivers Union Local No. 413 v. NLRB, 334 F.2d 539 (D.C. Cir. 1964).

boycott provisions. Consequently, the union may strike for the purpose of securing an agreement requiring the employer not to contract work to nonunion shops.[49]

Under the less broad construction industry proviso, unions may negotiate agreements with construction employers not to subcontract job site work to nonunion contractors. A strike to obtain a hot cargo clause regarding the contracting or subcontracting of work to be done at the site of the construction is therefore lawful. It does not violate Section 8(b)(4)(A) because it is not a work stoppage to obtain an unlawful agreement. A work stoppage to obtain a hot cargo clause relating to work done off the job site, however, will violate Section 8(b)(4)(A) and may subject the union to a damages action under Section 303. Also, a strike to enforce a lawful construction industry hot cargo clause is unlawful under Section 8(b)(4)(B) where a union seeks to pressure the employer to sever relations with a nonunion contractor. Enforcement of a lawful job site clause may be accomplished through arbitration or other means, however.[50]

§ 11.7 Jurisdictional Disputes

Congress enacted Section 8(b)(4)(D)[51] in 1947 to deal with disputes arising over which specific union's members shall perform particular work for an employer. The provision makes it an unfair labor practice for a union to cause a strike or concerted refusal to handle goods to compel an employer to assign work to employees represented by a particular union instead of assigning it to employees represented by a different union. Without the provision, an employer would be vulnerable to a strike and picketing no matter which union was assigned the disputed work because the other might strike and picket.

If a union strikes or threatens to strike to obtain work, the employer or competing union can file a Section 8(b)(4)(D) charge. The NLRB Regional

---

[49] *See generally*, Danielson v. Joint Board, 494 F.2d 1230 (2d Cir. 1974).

[50] *See generally*, Northeastern Indiana Bldg. Trades, 148 NLRB 854 (1964), *enforcement denied on other grounds*, 352 F.2d 696 (D.C. Cir. 1965). *See also*, Connell Constr. Co. v. Plumbers and Steamfitters Union, Local 100, 421 U.S. 616 (1975) (Picketing to secure construction job site hot cargo clause not legal where union represented none of picketed contractor's employees. Purpose of proviso was to recognize union interest in eliminating need for union members to work beside nonunion employees at job site. Union in question represented no job site employees.). *But see* Woelke & Romero Framing, Inc. v. NLRB, 456 U.S. 645 (1982) (allowing broad construction industry clause not limited to job sites at which union and nonunion workers employed).

[51] 29 U.S.C. § 158(4)(D).

Director can then seek a federal court injunction under Section 10(l) if there is reasonable cause to believe a violation has occurred.

The Regional Office will then conduct a hearing under Section 10(k) of the Act with the record sent to the NLRB in Washington for a determination. If the Board finds reasonable cause to believe that the dispute is actually a jurisdictional dispute, it will issue a decision awarding the work to the union with the greater entitlement to it. If the losing union continues in its intent to strike, the Section 8(d)(4)(D) charge will be prosecuted based on the record made at the Section 10(k) hearing. If the winning union is not actually assigned the work, it may strike and picket without violating Section 8(b)(4)(D).[52]

§ 11.8 Remedies

Remedies for violation of the secondary boycott laws go far beyond the NLRB cease and desist orders issued in many unfair labor practice proceedings. The National Labor Relations Act, as amended, provides for both federal court injunctive relief and monetary damages in appropriate cases.

Section 10(l) of the Act,[53] provides that unfair labor practice charges alleging a violation of Section 8(b)(4)[54] are to be given priority treatment and investigation by the NLRB. If reasonable cause exists to believe the charge is true after such investigation, the officer or regional attorney to whom the matter is referred must seek "appropriate injunctive relief" in federal district court. The statute gives the federal court jurisdiction over such an action as well as power to "grant such injunctive relief or temporary restraining order as it deems just and proper." If the district court determines that there is "reasonable cause" to believe that unfair labor practices have occurred and that injunctive relief is "just and proper," it will issue an injunction.[55]

---

52 *See generally* NLRB v. Radio & Television Broadcast Engineers, Local 1212 (CBS), 364 U.S. 573 (1961) (holding that Board has statutory duty to determine, under Section 10(k), which union has better claim to the work). *See generally*, Mack A. Player, *Work Assignment Disputes Under Section 10(k): Putting the Substantive Cart Before the Procedural Horse*, 52 Tex. L. Rev. 417 (1974); 29 U.S.C. § 160(k).

53 29 U.S.C. § 160(l).

54 29 U.S.C. § 158(b)(4).

55 Gottfried v. Sheet Metal Workers, Local 80, 927 F.2d 926 (6th Cir. 1991) (setting forth appropriate considerations for injunction).

Section 303 of the Act,[56] provides a right to sue in any U.S. District Court for economic injuries suffered as a consequence of "any activity or conduct defined as an unfair labor practice in Section 8(b)(4). . . ." Suits may be brought by the primary employer as well as by injured neutral employers.[57] Plaintiff need not obtain a ruling from the NLRB establishing a Section 8(b)(4) violation to file suit or recover under Section 303.[58]

Plaintiffs under Section 303 must establish, by a preponderance of evidence, conduct which would violate Section 8(b)(4) and that they sustained losses "with reasonable certainty both as to fact and amount."[59] In *C&K Coal Co. v. United Mineworkers*,[60] five nonunion coal companies were awarded a total of over one million dollars from the international, district and locals of a union which had engaged in secondary activities against them in support of its strike against a unionized coal operators' association. Damages included awards for out-of-pocket expenses such as security guards and damages to property, lost profits from lost production and prejudgment interest.[61]

§ 11.9 Chapter Highlights

1. A secondary boycott occurs when the union seeks to put pressure on the primary employer (an employer with which it has a labor dispute) by inducing a neutral or secondary employer to stop handling the primary's products or stop doing business with the primary. The union may not, to accomplish this goal, induce individuals employed by the neutral to strike or refuse to perform services. Nor may it threaten or coerce any person (including a corporate or business entity "person") to achieve this purpose. Read Section 8(b)(4) carefully. Under its language, such activity is illegal if even "an object" is to pressure the secondary employer to cease to do business with the primary. (§ 11.1)

---

56 29 U.S.C. § 187.

57 *See* United Brick & Clay Workers v. Deena Artware, 198 F.2d 637 (6th Cir. 1952), *cert. denied,* 344 U.S. 897 (1952).

58 Int'l Longshoremen's & Warehousemen's Union v. Juneau Spruce Corp., 342 U.S. 237 (1952).

59 Eazor Exp., Inc. v. Teamsters, 520 F.2d 951 (3d Cir. 1975), *cert. denied,* 424 U.S. 935 (1976).

60 704 F.2d 690 (3d Cir. 1983).

61 *See also* Beelman Truck Co. v. Teamsters, Local 525, 33 F.3d 886 (7th Cir. 1994) (awarding damages of $138,500 for profits on hauling contracts lost due to union's unlawful picketing).

2. A union may picket the primary employer where it finds it. It may also picket employers which are "alter egos" or "allies" of the primary. Alter ego status turns on common ownership and control, especially common control of labor relation matters. Ally status can occur where an otherwise unrelated employer agrees to do "struck work" for the benefit of an employer whose employees are on strike. Struck work is work that, but for the strike, would have been done by strikers. (§ 11.2)

3. Where a union pickets an entire construction site with an object of forcing a construction general contractor to cease doing business with a subcontractor with which it has a labor dispute, it violates Section 8(b)(4). (§ 11.3)

4. When employees of a primary employer are temporarily working on the premises of a neutral employer, the union's right to picket the primary "where it finds it" must be balanced against the neutral employer's right to be free from picketing concerning labor disputes with which it is not involved. A union seeking to picket in such a situation must carefully minimize the impact on the neutral by picketing only under the four conditions set forth in *Moore Dry Dock*. This test applies to "ambulatory situs" picketing when union picketers seek to follow the primary employer's delivery truck to a neutral delivery site and picket at that site. (§ 11.4)

5. When the primary employer occupies a common work site with one or more neutral employers, the union may picket the primary employer at that site but it must observe the four standards of *Moore Dry Dock* to minimize the impact of the picketing on neutral employers. If the employers properly set up and enforce a reserved gate system, the *Moore Dry Dock* principles require that the union limit its picketing to the gate or entrance reserved for the primary employer. (§ 11.4)

6. When a neutral employer is working on the premises of a primary employer, such as an employer whose employees are on strike, a different rule is applied. A reserved gate may be used to insulate the neutral employer and its employees from picketing only if the neutral employer is not doing work related to the normal operations of the struck employer or of the kind that would necessitate curtailing operations if done when the plant was engaged in normal operations. Employers doing work related to normal operations or which would require shutting down the plant are seen to be helping the employer resist the strike and are treated like allies for site related picketing purposes. Any gate used by such employers or the primary employer may be picketed. (§ 11.5)

7. Under Section 8(e), a collective bargaining agreement provision can be an unlawful "hot cargo" clause if it requires the employer to cease handling the products of another employer or to cease doing business with any other person. The provision is not enforced literally and contract clauses having primary objectives, such as preservation of bargaining unit work, have been held lawful whether in the form of "will not handle" clauses or provisions limiting the employer's ability to subcontract. A union can render an otherwise valid work preservation or subcontracting clause invalid, however, by enforcing it in a way that reveals union objectives other than work preservation. This can occur, for example, if the union seeks to enforce the provision against non-union products but not against union products. (§ 11.6)

8. A union must take care to insure that a boycott campaign does not become an unlawful secondary boycott. Secondary boycott violations can expose unions to monetary damages under Section 303 of the Act as well as to injunctions and cease and desist orders. Damage awards can be significant. (§ 11.8)

CHAPTER 12
CONSUMER PICKETING AND HANDBILLING

§ 12.1 Generally

Another means by which unions can put economic pressure on an employer is by enlisting the aid of the consumer. If the employer with which the union has a labor dispute produces or distributes a consumer product, the union may wish to picket or handbill in front of stores selling the product to influence consumers. Such picketing or handbilling could be used to further a union's objectives in an organizational dispute or could be directed at products produced by a struck employer to increase strike pressures. In conducting such consumer-directed activity, unions must avoid violating Section 8(b)(4)(B) of the National Labor Relations Act, as amended, which makes it unlawful for a union "to threaten, coerce or restrain any person" with the object of "forcing or requiring any person to cease using, selling, handling or transporting or otherwise dealing in the products of another producer . . . or to cease doing business with any other person."[1] Should the union's picketing or handbilling be considered a secondary boycott, the union could face not only federal injunctive relief but also substantial financial liability under Section 303.[2]

An additional issue often addressed in consumer picketing and handbilling cases is that of access to private property. The Board and the courts will balance the Section 7 rights involved against the private property interests of the landowner.

§ 12.2 Product Picketing and *Tree Fruits*

The issue of whether a union can picket in front of a retail outlet and ask consumers to boycott a product produced by an employer with which the union has a labor dispute was resolved by the Supreme Court in a 1964 decision that has come to be known as the *Tree Fruits* decision.[3]

In that case, the union was on strike against 24 Yakima, Washington, fruit packers and warehousemen producing and distributing Washington State apples. The union placed pickets outside 46 Safeway grocery stores in Seattle, Washington. The picketers (usually two) picketed while wearing

---

1 29 U.S.C. § 158(b)(4)(B).

2 29 U.S.C. § 185. *See supra* § 11.8.

3 NLRB v. Fruit & Vegetable Packers & Warehousemen, Local 760 (Tree Fruits), 377, U.S. 58 (1964). (The struck firms were members of the Tree Fruits Labor Relations Committee, Inc., 377 U.S. at 60 n.2.) *See generally* Lee Modjeska, *The* Tree Fruits *Consumer Picketing Case — A Retrospective Analysis*, 53 U. Cin. L. Rev. 1005 (1984).

placards urging consumers not to purchase Washington State apples.[4] The union had advised picketers to patrol peacefully in front of consumer entrances and not to interfere with deliveries, pickups or employees' work. Picketers were told to stay away from delivery entrances. They arrived only after stores opened for business and left before stores closed. In addition, the union advised the stores by letter of these restrictions and that the picketing was only an appeal to customers not to buy Washington State apples.

The Supreme Court majority held that the picketing did not violate secondary boycott laws because it was confined to persuading customers not to buy the primary employer's product and did not threaten, coerce or restrain Safeway. Justices Harlan and Stewart dissented, differing with the majority as to Congress's intent and as to the impact such picketing could have on the neutral retailer.

Under *Tree Fruits,* a union may lawfully engage in consumer struck product picketing provided such picketing meets four safeguards. First, the picketing must be limited to times when potential customers are or can be present.[5] Second, it should be limited as to location; only consumer entrances should be picketed. Third, it must be targeted at consumers, not employees or delivery persons. Fourth, the message of such picketing must be limited to a request to refrain from buying the particular product in question. If the signs do not clearly identify the primary product and the primary employer, they might be perceived to be an unlawful call for a total boycott of the neutral retailer.[6]

§ 12.3 *Safeco* and Limits on Product Picketing

In his dissent to *Tree Fruits,* Justice Harlan criticized the majority opinion and noted that its rule would be even more questionable if a picketed retailer depended on sales of one product. He questioned whether an independent gas station owner which sold only the struck company's gasoline would feel less threatened by a picket sign that said, "Do not buy X gasoline" than it would by a sign which said, "Do not patronize this gas station."[7]

---

[4] The placards read: "To the Consumer: Non-Union Washington State apples are being sold at this store. Please do not purchase such apples. Thank you. Teamsters Local 760, Yakima, Washington." 377 U.S. at 60 n.3.

[5] *See* Millmen & Cabinet Makers, Local 550 (Steiner Lumber), 153 NLRB 1285 (1965) (picketing not limited to consumer hours can be illegal).

[6] *See* Meat Cutters, Local 248 (Milwaukee Indep. Meat Packers), 230 NLRB 189 (1977).

[7] 377 U.S. at 83.

That issue, the impact of product picketing on a retailer which is not a multiple article seller, was dealt with in the Court's 1980 *Safeco* decision.[8]

In *Safeco,* a union on strike against a title insurance company picketed Safeco headquarters as well as the offices of five small title companies which sold title insurance as well as searched titles. Over 90 percent of the title companies' revenues were derived from the sale of Safeco's title insurance policies.

The Supreme Court distinguished the case from *Tree Fruits* on the grounds that in *Tree Fruits,* successful picketing was perceived only to cause sales of the boycotted product to decline without necessarily harming the neutral. In *Safeco,* a consumer who wished to boycott the struck product had little choice but to boycott the neutral title company which would then be induced into severing its ties with the struck employer. Picketing which coerces a neutral into ceasing to do business with the primary employer constitutes an illegal secondary boycott.

For cases which arise between the relatively slight impact in *Tree Fruits* and the devastating impact suffered by the single product seller in *Safeco,* the Court asks whether such picketing is reasonably likely to threaten the neutral party with ruin or substantial loss. If it is, the picketing would constitute an unlawful secondary boycott. Thus, where the struck company's product makes up most of the picketed store's sales, consumer picketing will likely be unlawful.[9]

Other types of product picketing which have the effect of calling for a total boycott of the neutral retailer will also be unlawfully coercive. If, for example, the struck employer's product has lost its identity because it has been merged into the goods or products of the neutral, a consumer would have to boycott the neutral and its products to honor the union's request to boycott the struck product. Under what is sometimes referred to as the merged product doctrine, struck product picketing would be unlawfully coercive and violate Section 8(b)(4) under such circumstances.[10]

---

[8] NLRB v. Retail Store Employees, Local 1001 (Safeco Title Insurance Co.), 447 U.S. 607 (1980).

[9] *See, e.g.,* Teamsters Local 456 (Carvel Corp.), 273 NLRB 516 (1984) (consumer picketing of ice cream store unlawful).

[10] Imagine a union on strike against a bakery seeking a consumer boycott of the hamburger rolls used by a neutral fast food hamburger establishment. It is difficult to boycott the hamburger bun without refusing to buy the hamburger, pickles, onions and sauces which are usually packaged in the bun. *See* Teamsters, Local 327 (American Bread), 170 NLRB 91 (1968), *enforcement denied,* 411 F.2d 147 (6th Cir. 1969) (bread used in restaurant); Kroger Co. v. NLRB, 647 F.2d 634 (6th Cir. 1980) (paper bags used by grocery store).

§ 12.4 Handbilling

Handbills and other publicity have been increasingly used in recent years to communicate union messages about labor disputes and to ask for consumer boycotts. Although handbilling does not carry the same message to organized labor and the public as does organized patrolling with picket signs, picketing must be conducted under strict limits.[11] Handbilling is not so restricted. A proviso to Section 8(b)(4) specifically protects publicity "other than picketing."[12] Further, the Supreme Court has held that peaceful handbilling does not violate Section 8(b)(4) even when it calls for a total boycott of a neutral business.[13]

[A]—The Publicity Proviso

Congress amended Section 8(b)(4) in 1959 by adding what is known as the "publicity proviso." It provides:

> Provided, further, That for the purposes of this paragraph (4) only, nothing contained in such paragraph shall be construed to prohibit publicity, other than picketing, for the purpose of truthfully advising the public, including consumers and members of a labor organization, that a product or products are produced by an employer with whom the labor organization has a primary dispute and are distributed by another employer, as long as such publicity does not have an effect of inducing any individual employed by any person other than the primary employer in the course of his employment to refuse to pick up, deliver, or transport any goods, or not to perform any services, at the establishment of the employer engaged in such distribution.[14]

The proviso provides additional protection to "publicity, other than picketing." This can include handbills as well as newspapers, radio and television ads.[15] The proviso limits its protection to publicity about "a product or products" which "are produced" by a primary employer and are

---

[11] *See supra* § 12.2.

[12] 29 U.S.C. § 158(b)(4).

[13] Edward J. DeBartolo Corp. v. Florida Gulf Coast Bldg. & Constr. Trades & NLRB, 485 U.S. 568 (1988).

[14] 29 U.S.C. § 158(b)(4).

[15] If the union patrols or pickets while handing out handbills, however, it can lose the protection of the proviso. *See* Nashville Building Trades (Castner Knott Dry Goods), 188 NLRB 470 (1971) (handbilling while using picket signs that say "Please Read Handbills" is outside protection of proviso).

"distributed" by another employer. These words have not been interpreted literally. Warehouses, distributors and advertisers have been held to add value to the product furnished to retailers and have qualified as "producers" under the proviso.[16]

The Supreme Court interpreted the extent of the proviso's reach in its 1983 *DeBartolo I* decision.[17] In that case, the union had a primary labor dispute with a construction subcontractor, H.J. High Construction Company, which had been retained by the general contractor, H.J. Wilson Company, to construct a department store in a shopping mall owned by the Edward J. DeBartolo Corporation. The dispute concerned union allegations that High, the subcontractor, paid allegedly substandard wages and fringe benefits. The union sought to impose pressure by distributing handbills asking customers not to shop at any of the mall's stores "until the Mall's owner publicly promises that all construction at the Mall will be done using contractors who pay their employees fair wages and fringe benefits."[18] The handbills stated that the union did not seek to induce any person to cease work or to refuse to make deliveries.

The Supreme Court held that handbilling directed against the mall owner and tenants of the mall who had no business relationship with the builder went beyond the scope of the proviso. The Court agreed with the union that the handbilling was publicity other than picketing, that the appeal was truthful and that neither deliveries nor work was stopped. The Court also agreed with the union that, for purposes of the proviso, the storeowner having the store built and its builder shared a producer-distributor relationship and that Congress's use of the specific words "product" and "produced" did not limit the reach of the proviso. The Court held, however, that the proviso's protection did not extend to handbills calling for a boycott of other stores within the mall. These stores did not share a relationship with the builder and the union and did not "distribute" products of the primary employer.[19] The Court remanded the case for a determination of whether the handbilling violated the terms of Section 8(b)(4) and, if so, whether it was protected by the First Amendment.

---

16 *See* NLRB v. Servette, Inc., 377 U.S. 46, 56 (1964); Great Western Broadcasting Corp. v. NLRB, 356 F.2d 434 (9th Cir. 1966), *cert. denied,* 384 U.S. 1002 (1966).

17 Edward J. DeBartolo Corp. v. NLRB, 463 U.S. 147 (1983).

18 463 U.S. at 151 n.3.

19 463 U.S. at 155-157.

[B]—*DeBartolo II*

On remand, the NLRB ruled that the handbilling, which called for a total boycott of mall tenants, was coercive and violated Section 8(b)(4). The Court of Appeals for the Eleventh Circuit disagreed and the matter again reached the Supreme Court. In *DeBartolo II*,[20] the Court held that Section 8(b)(4)(B) did not prohibit peaceful handbilling in the case even though it called for a total boycott of all mall stores. The Court noted that prohibiting handbills could raise serious constitutional issues and found that Section 8(b)(4)(ii) was "open to a construction that obviates deciding whether a congressional prohibition of handbilling on the facts of this case would violate the First Amendment."[21] The Court held that handbilling such as that carried out in *DeBartolo* which involved no violence, picketing or patrolling and only an attempt to persuade persons not to shop at the mall did not "threaten, coerce or restrain any person" within the meaning of Section 8(b)(4)(ii). The Court noted that there was no coercive effect on customers of the mall because the handbilling was peaceful and merely sought to persuade. The Court further found that handbilling without picketing did not coerce secondary employers (the mall tenants) within the meaning of Section 8(b)(4). The Court distinguished the case from *Safeco*[22] on the grounds that picketing involves both conduct and communication and that handbills are much less effective than picketing.

DeBartolo II makes the publicity proviso less important in cases involving handbilling, newspaper, radio and television appeals and other forms of publicity other than picketing. Its protection may continue to be relevant only in cases where the publicity other than picketing is deemed coercive. Cases subsequent to *DeBartolo II* have demonstrated that the decision opens up new types of publicity tactics which enable a union to put economic pressure on neutral employers. In *Pet Inc.*,[23] the Board held that *DeBartolo II* permitted a union striking a corporation's subsidiary to call for a nationwide boycott of the products of Pet and all 27 of its divisions even if the divisions and subsidiaries were neutrals for purposes of Section 8(b)(4) so long as handbilling was done without violence, picketing or

[20] 485 U.S. 568 (1988). *See generally* Thomas C. Kohler, *Setting the Conditions for Self Rule: Unions, Associations, our First Amendment Discourse and the Problem of* DeBartolo, 1990 Wis. L. Rev. 149.

[21] 485 U.S. at 578.

[22] NLRB v. Retail Store Employees, Local 1001 (Safeco Title Insurance Co.), 447 U.S. 607 (1980).

[23] United Steelworkers (Pet Inc.), 288 NLRB 1190 (1988).

patrolling. The Sixth Circuit reached a similar result in its 1988 *Storer Communications* decision.[24] In that case, the Court found no violation where a union on strike against a television station notified businesses advertising on the station that they would be subjected to handbilling if they did not withdraw their advertising, and then handbilled in front of businesses that continued to advertise, urging consumers not to patronize the businesses.[25]

[C]—Threats to Handbill

Requests to store managers not to handle goods from primary employers and threats to handbill if the request is not complied with are governed by the Supreme Court's 1964 decision in *NLRB v. Servette, Inc.*[26] In that case, a union on strike against a wholesale food distributor requested managers of food stores not to handle goods from the distributor and threatened to pass out handbills if they did not comply. The Court held that the union did not violate Section 8(b)(4)(i) because it was not asking the managers to cease work. Rather, it was asking them to make a managerial decision on behalf of the store. The Court held further that the union's actions did not threaten, restrain or coerce the retailers under Section 8(b)(4)(ii). It held that a union may lawfully threaten to do what it legally is allowed to do and in this case, the handbilling would have been lawful under the publicity proviso.

§ 12.5 Access to Private Property for Consumer Picketing or Handbilling

Where a union seeks to conduct consumer picketing or handbilling on the private property of a store or business, the NLRB balances the private property interests of the store or business against the union's protected interest under tests developed in *NLRB v. Babcock & Wilcox Co.*[27] and *Lechmere, Inc. v. NLRB.*[28] A number of courts, however, have shown less

---

24 Storer Communications, Inc. v. NABET, 854 F.2d 144 (6th Cir. 1988).

25 Handbill messages protected under *DeBartolo II* may, however, lose their protection if the handbilling actually constitutes picketing. *See* Teamsters Local 917 (Industry City Associates), 307 NLRB 1419 (1992) (handbillers wearing poster-sized placards and patrolling are picketing).

26 377 U.S. 46 (1964).

27 351 U.S. 105 (1956).

28 502 U.S. 527 (1992). Since 1995, the Board has determined that the *Babcock & Wilcox* accommodation analysis should apply in nonorganizational settings. Its general rule is that an employer may prohibit nonemployees from gaining access to its private property to engage

willingness to recognize any exception to the rule for nonemployee access involving consumer boycott activities.[29] Similarly, the Board will allow nonemployee access on a disparate treatment rationale if the employer has allowed access for other types of distribution and handbilling; but some courts disagree.[30]

§ 12.6 Chapter Highlights

1. Struck product picketing and consumer handbilling allow a union to publicize its dispute with the primary employer and, if successful, put economic pressure on the primary employer. (§ 12.2)

2. A union may picket in front of a retail outlet with picket signs asking consumers to boycott a product produced by an employer with which the union has a labor dispute. The union may not, however, induce or encourage employees not to work or deliver and it must not threaten, coerce or restrain the retailer. Strict adherence to the *Tree Fruits* standards will be necessary to insure that product picketing is legal. (§ 12.2)

3. Product picketing will illegally restrain and coerce the neutral retailer if it calls for a total boycott of the retailer or if compliance by the consumer would threaten the retailer with ruin or substantial loss. (§ 12.3)

4. A threat to handbill is not unlawful if the handbilling itself would be legal. (§ 12.4[C])

5. Handbilling is not considered to be as coercive as picketing. Handbilling which calls for the total boycott of a business distributing a product produced by a primary employer can be protected by the publicity proviso

---

in consumer boycott activities. The Board has assumed, without deciding, that the *Lechmere* analysis allows an exception, permitting nonemployee access to private property if the union can establish that the employers are not reasonably accessible by other means. *See* Leslie Homes, Inc., 316 NLRB 123 (1995); Oakland Mall, 316 NLRB 1160 (1995) (consumer boycott handbilling).

[29] *See, e.g.*, NLRB v. Great Scot, Inc., 39 F.3d 678 (6th Cir. 1994) (consumer directed activity warrants less protection than organizational activity); Sparks Nugget, Inc. v. NLRB, 968 F.2d 991 (9th Cir. 1992) (refusing to apply inaccessibility exception to attempts to communicate with public).

[30] *See* Cleveland Real Estate Partners, 316 NLRB 158 (1995), *enforcement denied,* 95 F.3d 457 (6th Cir. 1996) (court overturns Board and allows mall to bar nonemployee handbillers despite history of access by charities). *Compare* Victory Markets, 322 NLRB 17 (1996) (boycott handbillers allowed access to mall property where wide range of charitable activity allowed).

of Section 8(b)(4). The producer-distributor relationship is broadly interpreted. Even if there is no producer-distributor relationship, *DeBartolo II* holds that consumer boycott handbilling of unrelated and neutral employers does not violate Section 8(b)(4) so long as there is no violence, picketing or patrolling. (§ 12.5)

CHAPTER 13
ENFORCEMENT OF THE COLLECTIVE BARGAINING AGREEMENT

§ 13.1 Introduction

While the collective bargaining agreement defines the rights and obligations of the employees, union and management, it is not self-enforcing. Like any other contract, the terms of the agreement are ultimately enforceable in the courts. However, virtually all collective bargaining agreements contain grievance-arbitration provisions that provide an alternative means of resolving disputes arising under the agreement.[1] The typical grievance-arbitration provision makes any alleged violation of the agreement subject to the grievance-arbitration procedure. The vast majority of grievances are settled informally in steps of the grievance procedure short of arbitration.

[A]—History of Arbitration Clauses

The standard clause found in the overwhelming majority of collective agreements goes back to World War II, when the War Labor Board enforced a "no-strike" "no-lockout" pledge by labor and management with a "*quid pro quo*" that government would decide finally the merits of all labor disputes affecting the war effort.[2] The War Labor Board at first attempted to do this on a case-by-case basis, even as to grievances requiring interpretations of existing contracts. The War Labor Board then decided, in the words of Former Disputes Director for the War Labor Board office in Detroit during the war, that it had neither the resources nor the inclination to be the final step in contractual grievance procedures.[3] Because of this, the War Labor Board fashioned a standard arbitration clause and ordered its insertion as the final step of the grievance procedure for any grievance that came to the board without an arbitration clause as the final step of the grievance procedure. The clause was to remain in those contracts for the duration of the war. At the beginning of the war, General Motors and the United Autoworkers were the only parties in the automobile industry that had an arbitration procedure, and such clauses were not the rule in other industries. Through the War Labor Board's involvement, arbitration clauses were inserted in the Ford and Chrysler contracts. By the end of the war, 85% of all collective bargaining agreements contained an arbitration clause. None

---

[1] *See* 1 Collective Negotiations and Agreements 8:3706 & 9:2521 (1997) (showing that "virtually all" of the approximately 140,000 collective agreements contain grievance arbitration provisions).

[2] *See* Calvin William Sharpe, *Introduction* to Symposium, *An Oral History of the National War Labor Board and Critical Issues in the Development of Modern Grievance Arbitration,* 39 Case W. Res. L. Rev. 505 (1988-1989).

[3] *Id.* at 511-513 n.20.

or very few of the parties took advantage of the end of the war emergency to terminate the arbitration provision.[4]

The reasons for the perpetuation of arbitration provisions are four characteristics of the arbitration proceeding. First, the informality of the hearing, the presentation of evidence, and the rendering of decision are particularly conducive to the settlement of labor relations disputes. Second, the arbitration process is less costly than litigation. Third, the neutrality of a third party is indispensable to the settlement of a dispute that the parties bilaterally have been unable to settle. Fourth, arbitration has a broader purpose beyond the immediate dispute of ventilating grievances and defusing potential employee unrest.[5]

[B]—The Role of the Courts

However, one question created by this system remained unanswered until the 1947 Taft-Hartley amendments to the National Labor Relations Act: if the grievance-arbitration provision settles disputes concerning other provisions of the agreements, what mechanism resolves disputes involving the grievance-arbitration procedure? The logical place to look for an answer to this question is the agreement itself.

The parties may have provided specifically in the agreement that breaches of the grievance-arbitration provision are subject to judicial challenge or the employees' right to strike. If the agreement is silent, the courts must enforce the grievance-arbitration provisions just as they would other contractual terms in the absence of an alternative settlement mechanism. In these cases, the question before the courts would be either one of arbitrability—did the parties agree to arbitrate the dispute contained in the grievance—or enforceability—should the award of the arbitrator be enforced.

Before Section 301 of the Labor Management Relations Act of 1947 (the Taft-Hartley amendment), a number of obstacles made enforcement of arbitration provisions uncertain. Primary among these was the uncertain

[4] Dennis R. Nolan and Roger I. Abrams, *American Labor Arbitration: The Maturing Years,* 35 Fla. L. Rev. 557, 568-577 (1983).

[5] See United Steelworkers of America v. American Mfg. Co., 363 U.S. 564 (1960); Roger I. Abrams, *The Nature of the Arbitral Process: Substantive Decision-Making in Labor Arbitration,* 551 U.C. Davis L. Rev. 551 (1981); Fran and Roger Abrams, *Arbitral Therapy,* 46 Rutgers L.J. 1751 (1994); Calvin William Sharpe, *From an Arbitrator's Point of View: The Art of Being a Good Advocate*, Disp. Resolution Journal (January 1995).

legal status of unions. In most states, unions were not legal entities having the capacity to sue or be sued. Moreover, only state courts had jurisdiction in contract enforcement cases involving arbitration provisions. Since state laws dealing with this issue varied from state-to-state, the enforceability of collective bargaining agreements and the rights and remedies available under them was hopelessly inconsistent. And even where federal courts took diversity jurisdiction, state substantive law, of course, was applied. Congress's antidote to these problems was Section 301.[6]

[1] *Textile Workers v. Lincoln Mills of Alabama* and the Developing Common Law

In *Textile Workers v. Lincoln Mills of Alabama*,[7] the Supreme Court took up the issue of how broadly to interpret Section 301. In that case, the Textile Workers Union and Lincoln Mills entered a collective bargaining agreement in 1953 to run from year to year. The agreement contained a no-strike clause and a grievance procedure providing for arbitration as the final step. Under this agreement, the union filed grievances relating to work loads and assignments. The grievances were processed to the final step—arbitration. The union requested arbitration, the employer refused, and the union filed suit in federal court to compel arbitration. First, the Court made it clear that Section 301 by its terms accomplished several improvements in the existing system. It cured the unions' common law problem of not being able to sue or be sued, putting them on a par with employers in Section 301(b). Second, it limited employee liability to the union's treasury and assets in Section 301(b), analogous to the treatment of a corporation. Third, Sections 301(c), (d) and (e) facilitated personal jurisdiction and service of process upon unions. Fourth, as interpreted by the Court in *Lincoln Mills*, Section 301 also solved the common law problem of hopeless inconsistency among state laws governing contract rights and remedies. The majority said that Section 301 not only conferred subject-matter jurisdiction but also directed the District Courts to develop a federal common law of labor agreements.

As exhaustively as one might examine Section 301 for language about rules to be applied in Section 301 cases, none is to be found. Indeed, Section 301 might have easily been read—and had been read by circuit courts before

---

6 *See* Archibald Cox, Derek Curtis Bok, Robert A. Gorman, and Matthew W. Finkin, Labor Law—Cases and Materials 724-726 (12th ed., Foundation) (1996); Textile Workers v. Lincoln Mills of Alabama, 353 U.S. 448 (1957).

7 353 U.S. 448 (1957).

the *Lincoln Mills* decision—as conferring only subject-matter jurisdiction. Such a reading would have left Section 301 as a jurisdictional statute without substantive rules to apply or would have left those rules to come from state law. This reading also would have created constitutional problems under Article III, Section 2, which limits federal jurisdiction to cases involving federal issues.[8]

The majority in *Lincoln Mills* states that the Article III limitation on judicial power is satisfied, since the federal courts will be deciding cases "arising under" Section 301(a). The substantive rules of Section 301 are to be fashioned from the policy of the national labor laws, borrowing from state rules where they are compatible with federal policy and absorbing them into the body of federal law governing collective agreements.

Justice Frankfurter criticized at length the majority's, in his words, "casting upon the federal courts, with no guides except 'judicial inventiveness' the task of applying a whole industrial code that is yet in the bosom of the judiciary."[9] There is a fundamental philosophical disagreement between Justice Douglas's writing for the majority and Justice Frankfurter's writing the dissent. This is based, perhaps, on the policy of industrial peace supporting the majority's reading or the proper approach to statutory interpretation. Justice Douglas is certainly far more pragmatic, less formalistic, in his reading of the statute than Justice Frankfurter. Justice Douglas's focus seems to be how best to serve the policy goals of the statute.

The majority seems to be responding not only to the need to avoid constitutional problems but also to the need for a set of substantive rules that could be consistently applied to labor agreements. The majority reads legislative history as mandating the consistent enforcement of collective bargaining agreements as the only way to assure the substitution of industrial peace for industrial strife. If collective bargaining agreements are not enforced, the parties have no incentive to agree. Industrial peace, of course, comes in the form of the no-strike promise. Since the *quid pro quo* for the "no-strike" promise is the promise to arbitrate, it must also be enforceable.

The substantive rule of contract enforcement announced in the *Lincoln Mills* case is that agreements to arbitrate can be specifically enforced. The

---

[8] Article III, Section 2 of the U.S. Constitution reads in part:

> The Judicial power shall extend to all cases, in law and equity, arising under this constitution, the laws of the United States . . . .

[9] 353 U.S. 448, 465 (Frankfurter J., dissenting).

Court announces this rule even though specific enforcement is a type of injunction and the Norris-LaGuardia Act essentially outlaws court injunctions in labor disputes. Norris-LaGuardia was passed to correct the abuse of the injunction in federal courts, where it had been used to eliminate work stoppages and other employee concerted activities. This abuse of federal court power had never been directed to "failure to arbitrate" and Norris-LaGuardia in its procedural section reflected a pro-arbitration congressional policy. So the Court did not consider Norris-LaGuardia an obstacle to its "specific enforcement" rule announced in *Lincoln Mills.*

[2] Other Cases

Following the *Lincoln Mills* decision the Supreme Court added substantially to the developing common law of collective agreements in several decisions by announcing a number of important rules. In *Dowd Box Co. v. Courtney,*[10] the Court held that actions could be brought under Section 301 in state or federal court. In *Local 174, Teamsters v. Lucas Flour Co.,*[11] the employer sued for damages in state court after the union struck to protest a discharge that was subject to arbitration where the contract contained no "no-strike" clause. The Court held that a state court deciding a case under Section 301 must apply the federal common law rather than state law. *Dowd Box* and *Lucas Flour* together create concurrent state and federal jurisdiction in Section 301 cases that preserves the scheme of federalism while assuring uniformity of enforcement.

The Court in *Lucas Flour* also announced the rule that an arbitration clause implies a promise not to strike about a dispute encompassed by the clause, even though the contract contains no "no-strike" clause. The implied promise not to strike was based largely on the policy of promoting arbitration as a means of resolving labor disputes. This is the same policy that led to the expansive reading of Section 301 and the "specific enforcement" rule of *Lincoln Mills.* In both cases, arbitration is seen as the *quid pro quo* for the "no-strike" promise. Not surprisingly, the scope of the implied promise is defined by the scope of the arbitration clause—no promise will be implied where the dispute is not subject to *binding* arbitration.

The developing common law spawned other substantive rules. In *John Wiley & Sons v. Livingston,*[12] where the successor employer merged with

[10] 368 U.S. 502 (1962).

[11] 369 U.S. 95 (1962).

[12] 376 U.S. 543 (1964).

the predecessor and fully carried over the predecessor's operations without any change, the Court held that a successor employer had a duty to arbitrate the union's grievance, even though it was the predecessor, and not the successor, who had contracted with the union. In *Smith v. Evening News Association*,[13] the Court held that individuals alleging individual injury from contract violations may bring Section 301 suits in spite of the arguable interpretation of that section as only permitting suits between employers and unions or unions and unions. Later in *Vaca v. Sipes*,[14] the Court held that in individual actions under Section 301, the grievance machinery must be exhausted (in the absence of a breach of the duty of fair representation) before the courts have jurisdiction to try alleged contract violations. The guiding principle in these cases is the encouragement of peaceful dispute resolution through arbitration.

§ 13.2 The *Steelworkers Trilogy*

[A]—*United Steelworkers of America v. American Manufacturing Co.*

The *Steelworkers Trilogy* contains the most important federal rules on the construction of arbitration clauses. These cases define the role of arbitration in American labor policy. In *United Steelworkers of America v. American Manufacturing Co.*,[15] the agreement between the company and the union had a standard arbitration clause submitting to the arbitrator all unresolved disputes between the parties "as to the meaning, interpretation and application of the provisions of the agreement." It also had a "no-strike" clause. The contractual clauses in dispute gave management the power to discharge or suspend employees "for cause" and obligated the company to re-employ and promote on the principle of seniority where ability and efficiency are equal. The grievant was rendered 25% partially disabled due to a work-related injury. His doctor's testimony to that effect was the basis of his worker's compensation claim settlement. Two weeks following the settlement, the union filed a grievance claiming that the employee was entitled to return to work because of the seniority provision. The employer refused to arbitrate and the union sued to compel arbitration under Section 301. The lower courts granted the company's motion for summary judgment because the grievant's workers compensation settlement was conclusive of his permanent partial disability and unequal ability to perform the job, making his seniority irrelevant. The Supreme Court reversed, holding that

[13] 371 U.S. 195 (1962).

[14] 386 U.S. 171 (1967).

[15] 363 U.S. 564 (1960).

the company must arbitrate grievances falling within the arbitration clause, regardless of how frivolous the claim.

The ruling in *American Manufacturing* had three justifications that spoke to the role of grievance-arbitration in the settlement of labor disputes. First, the *quid pro quo* between the "no-strike" clause and the arbitration agreement means that if the union must refrain from striking about arbitrable issues no matter what the employer does, the employer must arbitrate whatever dispute arises. Second, the mere airing of frivolous grievances may be therapeutic, reducing the tension in the workplace.[16] Third, the parties bargained for arbitration as a means of resolving disputes arising under the contract, and the courts should not undercut this bargain by usurping the role of the arbitrator under the guise of enforcing the agreement.

American Manufacturing does make it clear that the courts retain a role in enforcing agreements to arbitrate. Unless the parties have clearly indicated otherwise the courts decide the question of arbitrability—whether the resisting party has breached its promise to arbitrate a dispute. In *American Manufacturing*, where the company promised to arbitrate "any . . . grievances arising between the parties as to the meaning, interpretation and application of the agreement," the dispute was arbitrable. The employee's right to be rehired was a matter of interpreting and applying the seniority provision of the agreement.

[B]—*United Steelworkers of America v. Warrior Gulf Navigation Co.*

Does the pro-arbitration policy requiring the parties to arbitrate even frivolous claims go so far as to force the parties to arbitrate even when they have agreed not to arbitrate a particular dispute? The answer is "no" as long as the parties make clear their preferences on the point. A contrary result would place the policy favoring arbitration on a collision course with the policy favoring freedom of contract. Nonetheless, the strong policy favoring arbitration does find expression when the parties seek to limit the role of arbitration. *United Steelworkers of America v. Warrior & Gulf Navigation Co.*,[17] the second installment of the *Steelworkers Trilogy*, presented this set of facts. There, the union filed a grievance about the company's practice of subcontracting maintenance work formerly performed by unit employees, which caused the unit to shrink from 42 to 23

[16] *See* Fran and Roger Abrams, *supra* note 5.

[17] 363 U.S. 574 (1960).

employees. The arbitration clause of the agreement covered disputes about the "meaning and application of the Agreement, or . . . any local trouble of any kind . . . ." It also excluded from arbitration "matters which are strictly a function of management." In the union's suit to compel arbitration, the company argued that subcontracting as a function of management was excluded from arbitration rendering the dispute not arbitrable. The Court declined the invitation to decide whether subcontracting was a management function under the exclusion clause, because in doing so, it would be deciding the very question that the arbitrator would decide on the merits. A decision that subcontracting was not a management function would permit the arbitrator to decide the same issue on the merits, while a contrary decision would prevent the arbitrator from considering the merits.

While a clear exclusion of the grievance from arbitration will lead to a finding that it is not arbitrable, in *Warrior & Gulf*, the broad arbitration clause combined with the unclear exclusion created an ambiguity. The Court announced a presumption of arbitrability that is rebutted by "only the most forceful evidence of a purpose to exclude the claim from arbitration." Evidence of negotiating history may show that the parties intended to exclude the matter from arbitration.

The hardest distinction to understand in this area is that the question of arbitrability is different from the substantive issue. Consider the following hypothetical altering slightly the facts of *Warrior & Gulf.* A contract clearly both prohibits the employer from subcontracting and excludes contracting issues from arbitration. The employer then subcontracts maintenance work in clear violation of the contract. The dispute is not arbitrable. The union cannot secure a remedy through arbitration; rather, its only recourse for the contractual violation are through the courts or self-help. This distinction between questions of arbitrability and the merits suggests that the only relevant "forceful evidence" to clarify an ambiguity in a case like *Warrior & Gulf* must go to whether the parties intended to exclude subcontracting from arbitration, not whether they intended to outlaw it.

Whether the employer promised to arbitrate is an issue of substantive arbitrability. Issues of procedural arbitrability also arise, such as whether a grievance has been timely filed—filed in the proper form or against the correct party. Procedural arbitrability issues are decided by arbitrators rather than the courts for reasons related to administrative efficiency and the closeness of procedural and substantive issues.[18]

[18] *See* John Wiley & Sons v. Livingston, 376 U.S. 543 (1964).

[C]—*United Steelworkers of America v. Enterprise Wheel & Car Corp.*

The final chapter of the *Steelworkers Trilogy* is *United Steelworkers of America v. Enterprise Wheel & Car Corp.*[19] That case shows how the strong policy favoring arbitration as a means of settling labor disputes affects the standard of review of arbitration awards. In *Enterprise Wheel,* a group of employees was discharged for leaving their jobs to protest the discharge of a fellow employee. The company terminated the protesting employees. The union grieved the termination, and, when the employer would not arbitrate the grievances, sued to compel arbitration. The arbitrator reinstated the employees with back pay, despite the expiration of the agreement between the times of the discharges and arbitration award. The employer refused to comply with the award and the union sued for enforcement of the award. The Court of Appeals refused to enforce the award, because it disagreed with the arbitrator's decision to order back pay and reinstatement beyond the expiration of the agreement. The Supreme Court reversed, holding that it was improper for the Court of Appeals to refuse to enforce the agreement because of its disagreement with the arbitrator on the merits. Courts must apply a narrow scope of reviewing arbitration awards, determining only whether an award "draws its essence from the agreement."

The idea generally is that the parties have bargained for the arbitrator's reading of the agreement. The arbitrator is the parties' "contract reader" and the agreement will be enforced even if wrong, unless it is tainted by some procedural unfairness (fraud, corruption or bias), the arbitrator clearly exceeded her authority by contravening a clear provision of the agreement, or the award violates some explicit and well-defined public policy.[20]

§ 13.3 Public Policy Cases

Since the violation of public policy is one of the few grounds for refusing to enforce an arbitration award, the parameters of public policy and the determination of whether a violation exists are important enforcement questions and aspects of the common law of collective agreements.

[A]—*United Paperworkers International Union v. Misco*

Both questions as well as the analytical framework for deciding public policy issues were set forth in *United Paperworkers International Union*

[19] 363 U.S. 593 (1960).

[20] *See* Theodore J. St. Antoine, *Judicial Review of Labor Arbitration Awards,* 75 Mich. L. Rev. 1137 (1977).

v. Misco.[21] In *Misco*, a paper company discharged an employee for being in a car with a lit marijuana cigarette in an ashtray, citing a violation of its rule against having drugs on plant premises. The arbitrator upheld the grievance, holding that the company's proof of the grievant's presence in the back seat of a car with a marijuana cigarette burning in the front ashtray did not establish that the grievant had possessed or used marijuana on company premises. The District and Appellate Courts agreed that the award should be set aside as contrary to public policy because "it ran counter to general safety concerns that arise from the operation of dangerous machinery while under the influence of drugs, as well as to state criminal laws against drug possession."[22]

In reversing these decisions, the Supreme Court acknowledged the common law doctrine that a court may not enforce contracts that violate law or public policy, and noted the effect of this doctrine as an exception to arbitral finality. In public policy cases, a court is seen as a representative of the public's interest in circumscribing offending private agreements to which it is not a party. As contracts, collective bargaining agreements fall under the same judicial scrutiny. However, relying upon its earlier pronouncements in *W.R. Grace & Co. v. Rubber Workers*,[23] the Court said:

> a court's refusal to enforce an arbitrator's *interpretation* of such contracts is limited to situations where the contract as interpreted would violate "some explicit public policy" that is "well defined and dominant, and is to be ascertained 'by reference to the laws and legal precedents and not from general considerations of supposed public interests.' "[24]

In *Misco*, the Court found that the Court of Appeals had not reviewed law and legal precedent to identify a well-defined and dominant "policy against the operation of dangerous machinery while under the influence of drugs."[25] The Court also pointed to the absence of evidence showing that the grievant had actually used drugs in the workplace and that his reinstatement would violate the public policy identified by the Court of Appeals. Importantly, the Court made it clear that the factual inferences were to be drawn by the arbitrator as the parties' bargained-for factfinder rather than the court.

---

21 484 U.S. 29 (1987).

22 *Id.* at 35.

23 461 U.S. 757 (1983).

24 484 U.S. at 43 (emphasis in original).

25 *Id.*

[B]—The Progeny of *Misco* and *W.R. Grace*

The courts have found the *Misco* and *W.R. Grace* cases to be difficult to apply since the courts are being asked simultaneously to protect the jurisdiction traditionally enjoyed by arbitrators under the *Enterprise Wheel* standard and to protect the public interest in denying enforcement of private agreements that violate public policy. A few decisions are illustrative. In *Iowa Electric Light and Power Co. v. Local Union 204 of the International Brotherhood of Electrical Workers*,[26] the employer discharged a machinist who worked in a nuclear power plant who overrode a safety lock system in order to take an early lunch. The arbitrator upheld the employee's grievance and reinstated the employee. The District Court, affirmed by the Eighth Circuit Court of Appeals, denied enforcement of the award because it violated the well-defined and dominant public policy of strict adherence to safety rules by reinstating an employee who knowingly violated nuclear safety rules.

In *Stead Motors of Walnut Creek v. Automotive Machinists Lodge No. 1173*,[27] a Mercedes dealer discharged a mechanic for his repeated failure to properly tighten the lug nuts on the wheels of cars during repairs, a condition that created a safety problem. An arbitrator reinstated the mechanic, and the District Court vacated the arbitration award on the basis of California's public policy regarding automotive safety and maintenance. Ultimately, the Ninth Circuit Court of Appeals reversed the District Court holding that the public policy relied upon must "demonstrate that the policy . . . is one that specifically militates against the relief ordered by the arbitrator."[28]

In *Newsday Inc. v. Long Island Typographical Union, No. 915*,[29] the employer discharged an employee for repeated acts of unwanted touching of women co-workers constituting sexual harassment. The Second Circuit Court of Appeals vacated an arbitrator's award reinstating the employee. The court found a well-defined and dominant policy against sexual harassment in the workplace and the grievant's violation of that policy by engaging in the prohibited conduct.

By contrast, in *Chrysler Motors Corp. v. International Union, Allied Industrial Workers of America*,[30] the Seventh Circuit enforced the

[26] 834 F.2d 1424 (8th Cir. 1987).

[27] 886 F.2d 1200 (9th Cir. 1989), *cert denied,* 495 U.S. 946 (1990).

[28] 886 F.2d at 1212

[29] 915 F.2d 840 (2d Cir. 1990).

[30] 959 F.2d 685 (7th Cir. 1992), *cert. denied,* 113 S. Ct. 304 (1992).

arbitrator's award reinstating an employee discharged for repeated acts of sexual harassment. The court focused on whether the arbitrator's award reinstating the employee violated public policy and found no violation. In *Chrysler*, the arbitrator had discussed progressive discipline and determined that the employee could be rehabilitated.

What seems to explain these decisions that appear to be hopelessly in conflict is the trigger for the public policy inquiry by the reviewing court.[31] Where the court focuses on the conduct of the grievant, it is much more likely to vacate a reinstatement award as in *Iowa Electric* and *Newsday.*[32] On the other hand, where the court focuses on the award itself, it is more likely to enforce the award as in *Stead Motors* and *Chrysler.*[33] The latter approach seems more consistent with *Misco*'s pronouncements about deference to arbitral factfinding since it accords more respect to the arbitrator's findings regarding the future fitness of employees.

§ 13.4 Enforcing The No-Strike Clause

[A]—The Norris-LaGuardia Obstacle

Contractual remedies usually come in the form of damages and injunctions. The monetary remedy of damages poses no special problems in the enforcement of collective bargaining agreements since no relevant legislation makes such a remedy inappropriate in breach of contract cases. The use of the injunction as a judicial remedy in labor disputes, on the other hand, has been rendered improper by legislation.[34] The Norris-LaGuardia Act of 1932 outlawed the issuance by courts of injunctions in labor disputes.[35] This Act was prompted by the widespread perception that judges used injunctions to prevent the concerted activities of employees seeking to advance a range of legitimate employment concerns.[36] After Congress

---

[31] *See generally* Stephen L. Hayford and Anthony V. Sinicropi, *The Labor Contract And External Law: Revisiting The Arbitrator's Scope Of Authority*, 2 Journal of Dispute Resolution 249 (1993).

[32] *See also* Delta Air Lines v. Air Line Pilots Ass'n International, 861 F.2d 665 (11th Cir. 1988), *cert. denied,* 493 U.S. 871 (1989) (reversing the reinstatement of a pilot who was discharged for flying under the influence of alcohol).

[33] *See also* Interstate Brands Corp. v. Chauffeurs Local Union No. 135, 909 F.2d 885 (6th Cir. 1990), *cert denied,* 449 U.S. 905 (1991) (where the court upheld the reinstatement of an employee who was arrested for being under the influence of drugs or alcohol on his day off).

[34] 29 U.S.C. § 101 (1932).

[35] *See id.*

[36] *See* Frankfurter & Greene, The Labor Injunction 200 (1930), detailing the unsuitability

repositioned courts at the center of labor disputes through Section 301 of the Labor Management Relations Act of 1947 without amending the Norris-LaGuardia Act, questions arose concerning the continuing effect of Norris-LaGuardia. Before 1970, in several specific tests of the continuing effect of Norris-LaGuardia, the Supreme Court erased the statute as an obstacle to the issuance of injunctions. In *Virginian Railway Co. v. System Federation No. 40,*[37] the Court upheld the issuance of an injunction compelling the employer to bargain with the union under the Railway Labor Act of 1926. In *Graham v. Brotherhood of Locomotive Firemen & Enginemen,*[38] the Court upheld an injunction mandating the union's compliance with the duty of fair representation. The Court in *Brotherhood of R.R. Trainmen v. Chicago River & Ind. R. Co.,*[39] the Court upheld a court order enjoining a strike to reinforce grievances that were pending before the National Railroad Adjustment Board under the RLA. These cases featured competing legislation, the RLA and Norris-LaGuardia, and triggered the judicial inclination toward reconciling the terms of competing statutes where possible.

The Court had also upheld injunctions against refusals to arbitrate despite Norris-LaGuardia.[40] The anti-injunction provisions of Norris-LaGuardia were put to the severest test, however, when the question was whether the court could enjoin a strike in breach of contract.

[B]—*Boys Markets, Inc. v. Retail Clerks Union, Local 770*

Boys Markets, Inc. v. Retail Clerks Union, Local 770[41] presented precisely the issue of whether the anti-injunction provisions of the Norris-LaGuardia prevented a court from issuing an injunction against a strike in violation of an agreement enforceable under Section 301 of the Labor Management Relations Act. In that case, the union and employer had a collective bargaining agreement that contained a broad arbitration clause and a no-strike clause. A dispute arose after the employer's supervisors and other non-unit employees rearranged the merchandise in the frozen food

---

of courts to address the range of problems underlying labor disputes, the procedural unfairness characterizing the issuance and enforcement of labor injunctions, and the impact of labor injunctions on the prestige and legitimacy of the courts and ultimately the rule of law.

37 300 U.S. 515 (1937).

38 338 U.S. 232 (1949).

39 353 U.S. 30 (1957).

40 *See Lincoln Mills* and *The Steelworkers Trilogy, supra* notes 7, 15, 17 & 19.

41 398 U.S. 235 (1970).

cases of one of the employer's supermarkets. The union demanded that the cases be stripped and restocked by unit employees. When the employer refused to comply with the union's demand, the union struck and picketed the employer. After the union failed to respond to the employer's demand to terminate the work stoppage and invoke the grievance procedure, the employer sued for injunctive relief. Ultimately, the Supreme Court upheld the injunction against the strike. In finding that the Norris-LaGuardia Act must accommodate Section 301 of the LMRA, the Court found that Norris-LaGuardia's purpose of preventing courts from abusing injunctions was not implicated by enjoining the grievance strike. Rather, the Court was merely enforcing a dispute settlement system to which the union agreed, thus preserving the viability of grievance arbitration.

The Court was careful in *Boys Markets* to define the narrow scope of its holding. Injunctive relief against a strike is appropriate only under the following conditions: (1) the grievance is subject to a mandatory grievance-arbitration procedure under a collective bargaining agreement; (2) the employer is ordered to arbitrate as a condition of obtaining the injunction; (3) the contractual breach is occurring and will continue or is threatened and will be committed; (4) the breach will cause irreparable harm to the employer; and (5) the employer will suffer more from the denial of the injunction than will the union from the issuance.[42] The Court found that all of the conditions for the issuance of an injunction were present in *Boys Markets.*

[C]—*Buffalo Forge Co. v. United Steelworkers of America*

Buffalo Forge,[43] decided by the Supreme Court six years after *Boys Markets,* is an example of the impropriety of an injunction under the *Boys Markets* criteria. The company in *Buffalo Forge* operated three plants, and its production and maintenance and clerical and technical employees were in two separate bargaining units represented by different locals of the United Steelworkers. The clerical and technical employees struck the company during the course of negotiations over a first contract. The production and maintenance workers refused to cross the picket line established by its sister unit. The Supreme Court held that a *Boys Markets* injunction was inappropriate since the strike of the production and maintenance employees was not over an arbitrable grievance. Rather, it was a sympathy strike in support of the clerical and technical employees whose dispute with the company

---

42 398 U.S. 235, 253-254.

43 428 U.S. 397 (1976).

was not subject to the production and maintenance workers' grievance procedure. Unlike *Boys Markets*, the strike did not purport to evade the union's obligation to arbitrate contractual grievances.

[D]—Union and Member Liability Under No-Strike Clauses

Section 301(b) of the LMRA binds unions and employers to the acts of their agents, entitles unions to sue or be sued on behalf of their members, and insulates union members from individual liability by making judgments enforceable only against the organization as an entity and its assets.[44] The Supreme Court has ruled that individual union officers who may have "fomented, participated in and assisted" a strike in violation of a no-strike clause may not be held individually liable under Section 301(b).[45] Even wildcat strikers who engage in strikes that are unauthorized by the union cannot be held individually liable.[46]

---

[44] Section 301 reads:

Sec. 301. (a) Suits for violation of contracts between an employer and a labor organization representing employees in an industry affecting commerce as defined in the Act, or between any such labor organizations, may be brought in any district court of the United States having jurisdiction of the parties, without respect to the amount in controversy or without regard to the citizenship of the parties.

(b) Any labor organization which represents employees in an industry affecting commerce as defined in this Act and any employer whose activities affect commerce as defined in this Act shall be bound by the acts of its agents. Any such labor organization may sue or be sued as an entity and in behalf of the employees whom it represents in the courts of the United States. Any money judgment against a labor organization in a district court of the United States shall be enforceable only against the organization as an entity and against its assets, and shall not be enforceable against any individual member or his assets.

(c) For the purposes of actions and proceedings by or against labor organizations in the district courts of the United States, district courts shall be deemed to have jurisdiction of a labor organization (1) in the district in which such organization maintains its principal office, or (2) in any district in which its duly authorized officers or agents are engaged in representing or acting for employee members.

(d) The service of summons, subpoena, or other legal process of any court of the United States upon an officer or agent of a labor organization, in his capacity as such, shall constitute service upon the labor organization.

(e) For the purposes of this section, in determining whether any person is acting as an "agent" of another person so as to make such other person responsible for his acts, the question of whether the specific acts performed were actually authorized or subsequently ratified shall not be controlling.

[45] *See* Atkinson v. Sinclair Refining Co., 370 U.S. 238 (1962) (while the union could be held liable for the strike of 1,000 employees under the terms of a no-strike clause, 24 committeemen could not be held individually liable).

[46] *See* Complete Auto Transit Inc. v. Reis, 451 U.S. 401 (1981).

Section 301(e) of the LMRA provides that the factors of authorization and subsequent ratification are not controlling in determining whether an agency relationship exists.[47] The Court has held that common law principles of agency determine whether unions have vicarious liability for the actions of other unions.[48]

§ 13.5 The Arbitrator and the NLRB During the Term of the Agreement

The collective bargaining agreement gives the parties—the employees, union, and employer—a panoply of rights that are enforced typically through the grievance-arbitration provisions of the agreement. The Act, of course, similarly guarantees the parties a bundle of rights primarily set forth in Sections 7 and 8 of the statute. The NLRA specifically charges the Board with preventing "any person from engaging in any unfair labor practice."[49] Since the contract and the Act address the same audience, claims arising under either may well be cognizable under the other. For example, if the employer unilaterally changes a condition of employment that has been defined in the contract, the action may constitute both a breach of the contract and a violation of Section 8(a)(5) of the Act. Similarly, if the employer discharges an employee allegedly for engaging in union activity, a claim may appropriately be brought under the "just cause" provision of the agreement as well as Section 8(a)(3) of the Act. The deferral question involves the relationship between dispute resolution procedures under the contract and those contained in the Act. What should be the Board's posture when an unfair labor practice charge could have been, is being, or has already been, brought in the contractual forum?

The Board has developed a deferral doctrine to address this issue in a variety of contexts.[50] First, the Board is not absolved of its obligation to enforce the Act simply because an unfair labor practice charge might be

[47] Section 301(e), *supra* note 44.

[48] *See* Carbon Fuel Co. v. United Mine Workers, 444 U.S. 212 (1979) (the Court refused to hold the United Mine Workers or its District 17 liable for 48 wildcat strike by certain of the local unions within District 17 absent a showing that the District or UMWA adopted, encouraged or prolonged the strikes).

[49] 29 U.S.C. § 160(a) (1982).

[50] *See generally* Calvin William Sharpe, *NLRB Deferral to Grievance-Arbitration: A General Theory*, 48 Ohio St. L.J. 595 (1987). The word "deferral" is defined as the act of delaying or postponing and is an apt description of the Board's posture in many concurrent jurisdiction cases.

considered in another forum.[51] Second, the Labor Management Relations Act also makes it clear that the parties' chosen method of dispute settlement is desirable for the settlement of grievances.[52]

For these reasons, the question for the Board in deferral cases is when, not whether, it should consider the case. The Board's deferral procedures have attempted to strike a balance that allows it to conserve resources while meeting its obligation of guaranteeing the protection of party rights.

The least controversial deferral issue arises when the Charging Party simultaneously files a grievance under the contract and a ULP charge under the Act. Those situations are governed by *Dubo Manufacturing Corp.*[53] In that case, the union filed Section 8(a)(3) charges protesting the discharge of a number of employees while grievance arbitration was pending. Noting that the purposes of the Act would be effectuated if it deferred action on the complaint pending the completion of arbitration, the Board held that the statutory preference for contractual adjustment procedures made deferral appropriate. The Board regularly defers cases to a concurrent grievance proceedings under the *Dubo* rationale.[54]

When the Charging Party has filed a ULP charge but has not engaged the contractual grievance arbitration procedure, the issues are a bit less straightforward. The Board is willing to defer in this situation only if the grievance procedure is capable of adequately resolving the dispute. In *Collyer Insulated Wire*,[55] the Board articulated a number of factors to determine the ability of the grievance procedure to resolve the dispute. These involved the willingness of the parties to submit the matter to arbitration, the absence of hostility to employee statutory rights, the stability

---

51 Section 10(a) of the Act provides in part:

The Board is empowered as hereinafter provided, to prevent any person from engaging in any unfair labor practice . . . affecting commerce. This power shall not be affected by any other means of adjustment or prevention that has been or may be established by agreement, law, or otherwise . . . .

52 Section 203(d) of the LMRA says:

(d) Final adjustment by a method agreed upon by the parties is hereby declared to be the desirable method for settlement of grievance disputes arising over the application or interpretation of an existing collective-bargaining agreement. The Service is directed to make its conciliation and mediation services available in the settlement of such grievance disputes only as a last resort and in exceptional cases.

53 142 NLRB 431 (1963).

54 *See* Sharpe, *NLRB Deferral, supra* note 50, at 602.

55 192 NLRB 837 (1971).

of the bargaining relationship and the suitability of collective bargaining to resolve the dispute.[56]

The Board routinely *Collyerized* cases involving unilateral changes, such as subcontracting unit work, where the issue was whether the contract permitted the change. In these cases, the contractual and statutory issues were co-extensive and the Board benefitted from the arbitrator's reading of the contract. However, in cases involving individual rights such as an employee's claim of a discriminatory discharge, the Board's position proved inconsistent. One year after the *Collyer* decision, in *National Radio Co.*, the Board decided that it would defer in a case involving the discharge of a union president allegedly in violation of Section 8(a)(3).[57] Five years later, in *General American Transportation Corp.*, the Board distinguished cases alleging a violation of the duty to bargain and pivoting on contract interpretation from those charging violations of provisions protecting individual rights, choosing to defer in the former but not the latter.[58] In a 1984 case, *United Technologies Corp.*,[59] the Board decided to return to the earlier *National Radio* rule and defer when appropriate in both duty to bargain and individual rights cases. The Board reasoned as follows:

> It is fundamental to the concept of collective bargaining that the parties to a collective-bargaining agreement are bound by the terms of their contract. Where an employer and a union have voluntarily elected to create dispute resolution machinery culminating in final and binding arbitration, it is contrary to the basic principles of the Act for the Board to jump into the fray prior to an honest attempt by the parties to resolve their disputes through that machinery. For dispute resolution under the grievance-arbitration process is as much a part of collective bargaining as the act of negotiating the contract. In our view, the statutory purpose of encouraging the practice and procedure of collective bargaining is ill-served by permitting the parties to ignore their agreement and to petition the Board in the first instance for remedial relief.[60]

Perhaps the most controversial deferral issues arise after the contractual grievance arbitration procedure has run its course and the Board is asked

---

[56] *See id.* at 842.

[57] 198 NLRB 527 (1972).

[58] 228 NLRB 808 (1977).

[59] 268 NLRB 557 (1984).

[60] *Id.* at 559. The D.C. Circuit in Hammontree v. NLRB, 925 F.2d 1486 (D.C. Cir. 1991) (en banc), upheld the Board's application of its pre-arbitral deferral standards to individual rights cases.

to defer to the results of that process. For example, how should the Board treat a case where the discharged employee challenges a discharge for poor performance in arbitration solely on the grounds that performance was satisfactory? In the arbitration, the employer presents unrebutted evidence of a nonhostile union environment and convincing evidence of poor performance as the basis for discharge. The arbitrator denies the grievance without mentioning union activity, and upon losing in arbitration, the employee files a ULP charge claiming unlawful discrimination under Section 8(a)(3). The Board has vacillated on how to treat this kind of case.

In *Spielberg Manufacturing Co.*,[61] the Board decided that it would defer to arbitration awards if "the proceedings appear[ed] to have been fair and regular, all parties had agreed to be bound, and the decision of the arbitration panel [was] not clearly repugnant to the purposes and policies of the Act." This rule encouraged voluntary dispute settlement and preserved the arbitrator's conventional role, since the repugnancy standard did not require the arbitrator to decide the case as the Board would have decided it in order to receive deference. "Repugnancy" was held to mean "palpably wrong."[62]

In the poor performance discharge hypothetical the Board would defer under *Spielberg* since there was no deprivation of due process or fairness in the hearing, the parties had agreed to be bound, and discharge for cause is specifically permitted under the statute. However, under two cases decided after *Spielberg, Monsanto Chemical Co.*[63] and *Raytheon Co.*,[64] the Board altered the *Spielberg* approach to find deferral improper where the arbitrator has not considered the ULP. Since neither party raised the ULP issue and the arbitrator did not consider it, deferral would be improper under *Monsanto-Raytheon.*

After a period of broad swings regarding the amount of required consideration of the ULP claim, the Board decided *Olin Corp.*[65] In that case the Board held that the ULP need not have been expressly considered by the arbitrator as long as the statutory and contractual issues were factually

61 112 NLRB 1080 (1982).

62 International Harvester Co., 138 NLRB 923 (1962). The imprecision of the "clearly repugnant" standard led to inconsistency and judicial opposition to the Board's application of *Spielberg*. *See, e.g.*, Douglas Aircraft Co. v. NLRB, 609 F.2d 352 (1979) (Board should defer where the arbitrator's reasoning is susceptible to two interpretations—one permissible, one impermissible).

63 130 NLRB 1097 (1961).

64 140 NLRB 883 (1963).

65 268 NLRB 573 (1984).

parallel and the arbitrator had been presented with facts generally relevant to the statutory issue. Making the repugnancy standard more precise, the Board also explained that the necessary showing was that the award was "not susceptible to an interpretation consistent with the Act."[66] Finally, the Board assured a bias toward deferral in close cases by placing the burden of proving the inadequate scope of the hearing or the repugnance of the award on the party seeking a Board hearing. The *United Technologies* and *Olin* standards have resulted in more deferral to grievance-arbitration of ULP charges filed with the Board.[67]

§ 13.6 Chapter Highlights

1. The burgeoning of arbitration as the main enforcement mechanism of collective bargaining agreements can be traced to the War Labor Board of World War II. (§ 13.1[A])

2. The common law of the collective bargaining agreement started with a creative interpretation of Section 301 of the Act. (§ 13.1[B])

3. Arbitration became the centerpiece of labor dispute resolution in the legal context created by the *Steelworkers Trilogy*. (§ 13.2)

4. Though public policy challenges have threatened to undermine the finality of arbitration, it is a threat that has not been realized. (§ 13.3)

5. The enforcement of no-strike clauses through injunctive relief has further reinforced the preeminence of arbitration as the ultimate rights dispute settlement mechanism. (§ 13.4)

6. The Board has resolved the difficult issues of concurrent jurisdiction between the Board and arbitration through its deferral doctrine. (§ 13.5)

---

66 *Id.* at 577.

67 *See generally* Sharpe, *NLRB Deferral, supra* note 50.

CHAPTER 14
FEDERAL PREEMPTION OF STATE REGULATION

§ 14.1 Introduction

[A]—The Nature of the Problem

Preemption doctrine deals with the conflicts that arise between federal labor law and state laws and regulation. Where federal labor law is said to preempt state law, the state law in question, and in most instances the state institution that seeks to enforce it, must give way in favor of the federal scheme. The state laws that prompt preemption questions can take many forms. They may parallel the federal law, or supplement it, typically by providing remedies not available under federal law, or they may contradict it, by, for instance, prohibiting conduct deemed to be protected by the federal law. For example, a state statute might prohibit a union from picketing for recognition,[1] or it might provide remedies beyond those available under federal law when such picketing occurs.[2] The state statute might provide for payment of unemployment benefits to striking employees.[3] Or the conflict might be between federal law and the common law of tort or contract as in a breach of contract claim brought by a union member asserting that, in violation of the union constitution, he had been deprived of membership and hence employment.[4]

As a constitutional matter, Congress has the power to legislate exclusively in the area of labor relations by virtue of the Commerce Clause[5] and the Supremacy Clause.[6] The former gives Congress the power to "regulate Commerce . . . among the several States." The latter makes the Constitution and the laws enacted pursuant to it "the supreme Law of the Land . . . the Constitution or Laws of any State to the contrary notwithstanding." In other words, under the modern broad understanding of the Commerce Clause, Congress could, if it chose to, be the single source for all labor law. Its law would preempt all state or local regulation touching on labor relations.

Clearly, however, Congress has never chosen to exercise its power to the fullest extent. There are many state and local laws that explicitly apply to the workplace and others that have an impact on labor relations that would

[1] *See* Garner v. Teamsters Local 776, 346 U.S. 485 (1953).

[2] *See* San Diego Building Trades Council v. Garmon, 359 U.S. 236 (1959).

[3] *See* New York Tel. Co. v. New York State Dept. Of Labor, 440 U.S. 519 (1979).

[4] *See* Amalgamated Ass'n of Street, Elec. Ry. & Motor Coach Employees v. Lockridge, 403 U.S. 274 (1971); International Ass'n of Machinists v. Gonzales, 356 U.S. 617 (1958).

[5] U.S. Const. art. I, § 8.

[6] U.S. Const. art. VI.

have no force if Congress chose to occupy the field of labor relations exclusively. There are a number of reasons why Congress has not done so. Until the mid-1930s, the United States Supreme Court read the Commerce Clause narrowly and would not have upheld a congressional attempt to regulate labor relations fully, nor did the sentiment to do so exist in Congress. In the absence of comprehensive federal regulation, the states filled the gaps both with legislation regulating labor conditions and with the common law of contracts, torts, and criminal law. Nor could Congress have intended to turn over to the NLRB authority over the myriad of local issues that might involve employers, employees, and unions.[7]

Unfortunately, with few exceptions Congress has not been very helpful in delineating the extent to which federal law preempts state regulation.[8] Where it has failed explicitly to preempt state regulation, the courts have had to divine preemption rules.

[B]—Preemption Themes

The preemption decisions reflect a number of themes or guiding principles. Chief among them are avoidance of a conflict of substantive law and protection of the NLRB's primary jurisdiction, but in some of the cases additional themes emerge.

A principal concern in the preemption cases is to guard against a substantive conflict between state or local law and federal labor law. This

[7] The Senate Report on the Wagner Act noted: "Nor can the committee sanction the suggestion that the bill should prohibit fraud or violence by employees or labor unions. The bill is not a mere police court measure." S. Rep. No. 74-573, at 16 (1935); Allen-Bradley Local No. 1111 v. Wisconsin Employment Relations Bd., 315 U.S. 740 (1942).

[8] Indeed, the Supreme Court has described the statute as "Delphic" regarding preemption. International Ass'n of Machinists v. Gonzales, 356 U.S. 617, 619 (1958). There are, however, a few instances where the Act gives greater direction. Section 14(b), which was added as part of the 1947 Taft-Hartley Amendments permits states to regulate union security agreements otherwise governed by Section 8(a)(3). Section 14(c), enacted in the 1959 Landrum-Griffin Amendments to deal with the so-called "no-man's land" problem caused by the NLRB's decision to limit its jurisdiction short of its statutory authority on the basis of a minimum volume of business test and the Supreme Court's decision that state regulation was preempted in this area of voluntary relinquishment of Board authority, by extending to states the power to act where the Board has declined jurisdiction. A proviso which Congress added to Section 10(a) in 1947 authorizes the Board, under certain circumstances, to cede jurisdiction in a particular case to a state agency. The Board has never exercised its power under this last provision. Perhaps most important, while Title I of the LMRDA (Landrum-Griffin Act) creates various members rights vis-à-vis their union and enforceable in federal court, it also indicates in Section 103 that none of the rights conferred in Title I shall limit rights or remedies available to union members under state law.

occurs most obviously when a state law prohibits or restricts the exercise of a right protected by Section 7, but it can also occur where the state law imposes no such restriction on protected activity. For example, a state law might parallel federal labor law in prohibiting a certain activity, say secondary boycotts, but differ importantly in the remedies available to a party aggrieved by the prohibited conduct.[9] Or the nonfederal law might regulate activity that Congress chose to leave unregulated, thereby interfering with the balance of power between labor and management in any given situation.[10]

A second major theme is that of primary jurisdiction. This doctrine requires that when Congress has created an agency to administer a statute and has granted jurisdiction to that agency to adjudicate under the statute, no other branch of government can usurp the agency's role of being the court of first resort. Because of the NLRB's expertise and its sensitivity to the interests advanced by federal labor law, and in order to maintain a consistent and coherent body of law, the primary jurisdiction doctrine would require that parties turn first to the NLRB and not to other fora to resolve those disputes that involve federal labor law.

In addition to these two major themes or rationales for preemption, at times other themes have emerged with varying degrees of influence. Thus, in some instances, courts have looked at "how deeply rooted in local feeling and responsibility" or how "peripheral" to federal labor law the issue is. Also courts have looked at whether or not the state law at issue is one of general application or is one that specifically addresses labor relations, and whether a party will be left without a remedy if the state claim is preempted.

[C]—The Basic Preemption Rules

The Supreme Court has tried, with only mixed success, to lay down general rules of labor preemption and to avoid case-by-case litigation. While they are subject to various exceptions and modifications as we will see below, the Court has articulated three basic preemption rules. First, the *Garmon* rule states that the NLRA preempts state regulation of conduct that is protected or prohibited by the Act, or that is arguably protected or

[9] In Garner v. Teamsters Local 776, 346 U.S. 485, 498-99 (1953), Justice Jackson noted that "when two separate remedies are brought to bear on the same activity, a conflict is imminent."

[10] Lodge 76, International Ass'n of Machinists and Aerospace Workers v. Wisconsin Employment Relations Commission, 427 U.S. 132 (1976); Local 24, International Bhd. of Teamsters v. Oliver, 358 U.S. 283 (1959).

arguably prohibited by the Act. Second, the *Machinists* rule recognizes that the NLRA not only protects some conduct and prohibits other conduct, it also leaves open a field of economic conflict that Congress intended to keep unregulated. Consequently, state interference with this scheme impermissibly alters the balance of power that occurs under the "free play of economic forces" and is similarly preempted. Third, Section 301 of the NLRA provides for concurrent jurisdiction in state and federal courts to hear claims brought under collective bargaining agreements, and the Court has held that to promote uniformity in the interpretation of collective bargaining agreements, federal common law shall govern in Section 301 claims. Consequently, where a claim brought under state law requires an interpretation of a collective bargaining agreement, Section 301 preemption requires that the state claim be preempted.

§ 14.2 The *Garmon* Rule

[A]—Arguably Protected or Arguably Prohibited Conduct

In its original form, the NLRB regulated employer conduct through Section 8, which set out various unfair labor practices, but it did not similarly regulate union conduct. That gap was filled by the states, where courts had a long, though often criticized, history of involvement in labor disputes under the auspices of the common law and statute. When Congress in 1947 passed the Labor Management Relations Act (Taft-Hartley Act), it amended Section 8 by adding a Section 8(b) which specified prohibited union unfair labor practices. One consequence of this change was the increased incidence of preemption questions reaching the Supreme Court. Throughout the 1950s (and since) preemption cases appeared on the Court's docket. The most influential of these was *San Diego Building Trades Council v. Garmon.*[11]

Garmon arose out of union picketing for recognition and a union shop. A California Superior Court initially enjoined the picketing and awarded damages for the harm the picketing had done. After one trip to the United States Supreme Court, which vacated the California court's judgment, the California court set aside the judgment in accordance with the Supreme Court's ruling. The Supreme Court had not, however, reached the damages issue, and the California court sustained the damages award on remand. The Supreme Court granted certiorari again, this time to determine whether the California Court could award damages for harm caused by the picketing.

---

11 359 U.S. 236 (1959).

In reaching its holding and announcing the *Garmon* rule, the Court identified a number of underlying preemption principles. It stated its unwillingness to resolve preemption problems on the basis of a retrospective "ad hoc inquiry" into the particulars of each case in order to determine the nature and extent of the conflict between state and federal law and the harm caused by permitting a state judgment to stand, an inquiry that it believed courts were ill-equipped to make. Rather, it stated its preference for broad prospective categorical treatment of the preemption problem.[12]

The Court also identified the kinds of conflict that might occur between federal labor law and state law. The most obvious possible conflict is, of course, a conflict of substantive law. If, for instance, a state were to prohibit an activity that was protected by the NLRA, the conflict would be untenable. More controversially, the Court noted that even where state and federal law both prohibited the same activity, conflict requiring preemption may exist in the remedial schemes provided by federal and state law. Thus, by providing a remedy not available under federal labor law, state law may upset federal labor policy. Further, the Court noted that in addition to creating a federal law of labor relations, the NLRA created a specific body, the National Labor Relations Board, which has primary jurisdiction under the Act. Quoting from *Garner v. Teamsters Local 776*, one of its prior preemption decisions, the Court stated that: "Congress did not merely lay down a substantive rule of law to be enforced by any tribunal competent to apply law generally to the parties. It went on to confide primary interpretation and application of its rules to a specific and specially constituted tribunal and prescribed a particular procedure for investigation, complaint and notice, and hearing and decision . . . ."[13] Thus, even if the state's substantive law was in all other ways identical to the NLRA, the state action should be preempted in order to preserve the primary jurisdiction of the NLRA.[14]

Finally, the Court broke with prior precedent which had considered whether the relevant state law was directed specifically to labor relations or was a law of general application that only incidentally touched on labor

---

[12] *Garmon*, 359 U.S. at 242. In Amalgamated Association of Street Employees v. Lockridge, 403 U.S. 274, 290 (1971), the Court further stated that its preemption rule or rules must be "capable of relatively easy application, so that lower courts may largely police themselves in this regard."

[13] *Garmon*, 359 U.S. at 242 (*quoting* Garner v. Teamsters Local 776, 346 U.S. 485, 490 (1953)).

[14] *See* Amalgamated Association of Street Employees v. Lockridge, 403 U.S. 274, 292 (U.S. 1971).

relations. The Court said the focus of preemption analysis is properly "on the nature of the activities which the States have sought to regulate, rather than on the method of regulation adopted."[15] To hold otherwise would risk subjecting a course of conduct that was protected or otherwise regulated by the NLRA to potentially contradictory regulation so long as the relevant state law was of a general character, as, for example, its common law of contracts would be, rather than specifically related to labor relations.

The Court then stated its rule that when conduct which the state law purports to regulate is either protected by Section 7 of the Act or prohibited by Section 8, or if that conduct is arguably governed by Sections 7 or 8, state law must yield to the federal scheme.

[B]—Exceptions to the *Garmon* Rule

The Court noted two exceptions to the *Garmon* rule. Drawing on a number of its earlier decisions involving mass picketing and threats of violence in which the Court had held that state regulation was not preempted even though the conduct was also likely prohibited by Section 8, the Court stated that some state-regulated conduct involved "interests so deeply rooted in local feeling and responsibility," that it would not deem state regulation preempted absent express congressional direction.[16] In other words, does the state regulation fall within an area (regulation of labor relations excepted) that has historically been relegated to the states and which we associate with the exercise of state power. These cases typically involve conduct that amounts to a crime, an intentional tort, or both, where the state interest in regulation is strong and obvious.

The Court's second exception covered instances where the matter regulated by the state is of "merely peripheral concern" to federal labor

---

[15] *Garmon,* 359 U.S. at 243, 244.

[16] *Garmon,* 359 U.S. at 243-44. The Court cited United Automobile Workers v. Russell, 356 U.S. 634 (1958) (state court may enjoin picketing that is threatening and coercive and entails malicious interference with non-striking employee's lawful occupation); Youngdahl v. Rainfair, Inc., 355 U.S. 131 (1957) (state court may enjoin picketing that obstructs access to employer and that is threatening and coercive, but preemption doctrine bars that portion of the injunction that enjoined peaceful picketing); United Automobile Workers v. Wisconsin Employment Relations Bd., 351 U.S. 266 (1956) (state board may enjoin mass picketing, and coercive threats directed at non-striking employees); United Construction Workers v. Laburnum Constr. Corp., 347 U.S. 656 (1954) (state tort action brought by non-union construction company for union's agents' threats of violence against the company and its employees not preempted).

law,[17] In identifying this exception, the Court cited a case it had decided the previous term, *International Association of Machinists v. Gonzales,*[18] in which an expelled union member sued under California contract law for reinstatement of membership and for damages for loss of employment and physical and emotional suffering resulting from membership loss. In *Gonzales,* the Court acknowledged that the union's conduct might implicate Section 8(b)(2) of the NLRA, which prohibits a union from causing an employer to discriminate against an employee who has been deprived of membership in that union for any reason other than his failure to pay his initiation fee or periodic dues.[19] Nevertheless, the Court held that the state court's decision, ordering reinstatement and awarding damages, was not preempted. The Court reasoned that because union membership is a matter of contract law historically left to the states, because Gonzales did not allege an unfair labor practice or claim that the union had sought to cause employers to discriminate against him (his inability to obtain work was presumably instead the result of the union's failure to refer him for work), and because the state was providing remedies that would have been unavailable from the NLRB, the potential for conflict between California law and federal labor law was "too contingent" and remote to justify preemption. The *Garmon* Court's invocation of *Gonzales* initially seemed to suggest a broad exception from the *Garmon* rule for internal union matters. Twelve years later, however, the Court had the opportunity to reconsider both *Garmon* and *Gonzales,* and when it was through, it appeared that *Gonzales* had little, if any enduring relevance.

Amalgamated Association of Street Employees v. Lockridge[20] involved a contract action brought by a suspended union member against his union in Idaho state court. Lockridge claimed that the union had violated its constitution and general laws in determining that he was in arrears for dues and consequently suspending him. His suspension from membership, in turn, resulted in his discharge from employment pursuant to his union's security agreement with Lockridge's employer. If Lockridge's interpretation of the union's constitution and general laws was correct, the union would have violated Section 8(b)(2) by causing the employer to discriminate against him in violation of Section 8(a)(3). The trial court held, on the authority of *Gonzales*, that it had jurisdiction. It then concluded that there had been a contractual breach, ordered Lockridge's reinstatement in the

---

[17] *Garmon,* 359 U.S. at 243.

[18] 356 U.S. 617 (1958).

[19] See *infra* § 17.1[A] for a discussion of union security agreements.

[20] 403 U.S. 274 (1971).

union, and awarded him money damages. The United States Supreme Court rejected the Idaho court's reasoning. While it declined to overrule *Gonzales* expressly, choosing to distinguish the two cases, the Court greatly undermined the authority of *Gonzales.*[21] Its statement that "the full-blown rationale of *Gonzales* could not survive the rule of *Garmon,*" has narrowed the exception for state regulation of "internal union matters."[22]

[C]—Elaboration and Evolution of the *Garmon* Rule and its Exceptions

The *Lockridge* case was important for another reason in addition to its rejection of much of the reasoning of *Gonzales.* In *Garmon*, a bare five to four majority stated the broad *Garmon* rule that state regulation of conduct that was protected or arguably protected or was prohibited or arguably prohibited was preempted. In a concurring opinion joined by three other Justices, Justice Harlan reasoned that arguably protected conduct should be treated differently from prohibited or arguably prohibited conduct.[23]

The "threshold question" for preemption analysis was whether the conduct was or might be federally protected because states clearly could not regulate federally protected conduct. If the conduct was unprotected, as prohibited conduct would be, the Court must look further than to whether the NLRA regulated the conduct. As long as there was no conflict between a state's remedies and those afforded by the NLRA, the state action would not be preempted. To hold otherwise, he wrote, would leave states powerless to remedy various harms that did not fall within the prototypical exceptions of violent torts invoked by the *Garmon* majority. The broad *Garmon* rule was controversial and *Lockridge* provided an opportunity for the Court to reconsider Justice Harlan's argument. Throughout the 1960s, voices from the Court and within academia had criticized *Garmon,* and the year before *Lockridge* a call came "from within the Court, for reexamination and

---

[21] The Court noted that in *Gonzales* the issue of whether the union interfered with Gonzales's employment relationship by provoking his discharge was not present; the issue, instead, was simply one of construing the union constitution and rules. Consequently, the chances that the state court would implicate federal law principles in *Gonzales,* were "at best tangential and remote." Lockridge's claim, in contrast, turned on the proper interpretation of the union security clause in his collective bargaining agreement, a matter about which, the Court noted, "federal concern is pervasive and its regulation complex." *Id.* at 295-96.

[22] *Id.* at 295.

[23] San Diego Building Trades Council v. Garmon, 359 U.S. 236, 249 (Harlan, J., concurring).

narrowing of the preemption doctrine."[24] Instead, the *Lockridge* Court reaffirmed the *Garmon* rule and its rationale, once again in a five to four decision, this time with Justice Harlan writing for the majority.

This is not to say that the *Garmon* rule has endured without elaboration and modification. Indeed, the criticisms of the rule raised by Justice Harlan and others have played an important role in the subsequent history of the rule. Two important Supreme Court decisions, *Linn v. United Plant Guard Workers*[25] and *Farmer v. United Brotherhood of Carpenters,*[26] gave greater content to the *Garmon* exceptions and expanded them beyond instances of tortious assaults or threats.

Linn arose in the context of a drive to organize Pinkerton guards in Detroit. Linn, a Pinkerton manager, brought a defamation action under state law in federal district court alleging that the union, some of its officers, and a Pinkerton employee had circulated a defamatory leaflet. In addition to possibly being defamatory, distribution of the pamphlet might conceivably have violated Section 8(b)(1)(A)'s prohibition of union coercion or other restraint of the exercise of employees' Section 7 rights, although the Regional Director refused to issue a complaint after the Pinkerton National Detective Agency brought charges. Further, at the time, the NLRB followed the *Hollywood Ceramics* rule[27] under which the Board would set aside organization elections for material misrepresentations made at a time when there was no opportunity for the other side to respond and where there was a probability that the misrepresentation had a significant impact. The trial court dismissed the complaint on the authority of *Garmon,* and the Court of Appeals affirmed.

In *Farmer,* a union member who had incurred the anger of his local's officers claimed that the local discriminated against him in hiring hall referrals. He further claimed that local officers had subjected him to a course of outrageous conduct consisting of threats, ridicule, intimidation, and other verbal abuse causing him emotional and related bodily harm. The trial court dismissed the plaintiff's discrimination and breach of contract claims on

---

[24] *See* Howard Lesnick, *Preemption Reconsidered: The Apparent Reaffirmation of* Garmon, 72 Colum. L. Rev. 469, 470-71 & n.11 (1962) (discussing Taggart v. Weinacker's, Inc., 397 U.S. 223 (1970) and International Longshoremen's Ass'n Local 1416 v. Ariadne Shipping Co., 397 U.S. 195 (1970)).

[25] 383 U.S. 53 (1966).

[26] 430 U.S. 290 (1977).

[27] Hollywood Ceramics Co., 140 NLRB 221 (1962). For a discussion of this rule, see *supra* § 4.3[E][2].

preemption grounds. It allowed plaintiff to go forward with his intentional infliction of emotional distress claim. The jury returned a verdict for plaintiff, but, relying on *Garmon* and *Lockridge*, the appellate court reversed the judgment.

In both cases the Supreme Court reversed, holding that federal labor law did not completely preempt plaintiffs' claims. Taken together, the two cases set out a method for analyzing the preemption issue when a claim under state law purports to fall within the *Garmon* exceptions. What does the Court look for to determine whether to allow an exception from *Garmon*? First, is the underlying conduct unprotected? Here, we see the distinction that Justice Harlan drew in his concurrence between the protected and prohibited prongs of the *Garmon* rule reemerge. The Court appears more troubled by the prospect of state interference with protected conduct than with the prospects of state burdens on conduct which may also be prohibited by the NLRA. Second, is there an overriding state interest, one deeply rooted in local feeling and responsibility, in state regulation of the conduct in question, and/or is the regulated activity merely of peripheral concern to federal labor law? The Court's analyses in *Linn* and *Farmer* suggest these will often be coupled, the presence of one suggesting the presence of the other. Third, is there little risk that the state cause of action will interfere with the jurisdiction of the NLRB and with the effective administration of national labor policy? In answering this final question, the Court considers whether elements of the state claim and the unfair labor practice claim are different, whether the available remedies under the two schemes are different, and whether adjudication of the state claim is possible without regard to the merits of the underlying labor dispute.

In *Linn,* the Supreme Court held that the state defamation action was not preempted, or, more accurately, that it was not preempted as long as it met certain conditions described by the Court for the purpose of safeguarding federal labor policy. Writing for the majority, Justice Clark reasoned on the basis of the Board's practice of giving a wide berth to noncoercive speech in a representation campaign that the defamatory character of the speech and the state's interest in redressing that defamation would be a "merely peripheral concern of the [Act]."[28] He further concluded that a state's concern with preventing and redressing defamation was "deeply rooted in local feeling."[29] Finally, he reasoned that a state cause

[28] Linn v. United Plant Guard Workers, 383 U.S. 53, 61 (1966).

[29] *Id.* at 62.

of action for libel or defamation, limited to instances where the statement was made with knowledge that it was false or with reckless disregard to its truth or falsity, posed little danger of interference with the NLRB's jurisdiction or with the effective administration of national labor policy. Specifically, the Board's and the court's inquiries would focus on different aspects of the conduct. The Board would consider whether the leaflet was coercive or misleading to a degree and under circumstances requiring it to set aside the election. The court, on the other hand, would look to whether plaintiff could make out a prima facie case of defamation, but such elements of the tort as the harm to the plaintiff's reputation would not be relevant to the Board. He noted further that the Board was unable to give individual relief to Linn, which would, absent an opportunity to bring a state claim, leave any defamation that he suffered unremedied.[30]

While the Court held that the strong local interests in redressing defamation required that the state tort claim remain available in this context, it also reframed the tort to minimize the possibility that the availability of a defamation action would either inhibit the often free-wheeling debate characteristic of labor disputes or provide either side an additional economic weapon. Consequently, it held that libel or defamation actions in this context would escape preemption only so long as the defamation occurred with knowledge that the statements were false or with reckless disregard for their truth or falsity and the plaintiff could prove actual damages. The Court further suggested that excessive damages might require a different result regarding preemption.[31]

In *Farmer,* the Court similarly found that a state tort action alleging intentional infliction of emotional distress would, at least under some circumstances, escape federal preemption. The Court first noted that the sort of outrageous conduct which underlies the tort of intentional infliction of emotional distress (or as it is sometimes called "outrage") is not protected by the NLRA. It further noted the state's strong interest in protecting the emotional well-being of its citizens no less than their physical well-being or reputations. Finally, the Court concluded that with certain prophylactic constraints on the state claim, there was little risk of its interference with

[30] *Id.* at 63-64.

[31] *Id.* at 65-67. In applying the *Linn* standard, state and lower federal courts have not restricted its rule to the context of an organizational campaign (although such cases occur), and have, instead, read it to apply to any setting involving a labor dispute. *See* Beverly Hills Foodland v. Food & Commercial Workers Local 655, 39 F.3d 191, 194 (8th Cir. 1994) (holding *Linn* rule applies in context of union boycott of store, but affirming lower court's dismissal of claim on summary judgment).

federal labor policy. While the case arose in the context of a union member's assertion of hiring hall discrimination against him for reasons other than failure to pay union dues, which, if proven would constitute violations of Sections 8(b)(1)(A) and 8(b)(2), any NLRB proceeding would focus on whether local officials discriminated or threatened discrimination. Their statements and conduct would be considered for whatever evidence they brought to bear on those questions. Whether their statements and conduct were outrageous and caused severe emotional distress would be irrelevant to the Board's inquiry, and the Board would not be able to remedy such emotional distress. The state tort action, in turn, could be resolved without considering whether any unfair labor practice had occurred. Instead, the prima facie case required a showing that the defendant intentionally acted outrageously toward plaintiff and caused him severe emotional distress.[32]

As in *Linn,* the *Farmer* Court conditioned a finding of no preemption on a degree of federal control over the tort action. Specifically, the *Farmer* Court noted the strong possibility that the state action would get entangled with matters of exclusive federal interest if union discrimination regarding employment opportunities constituted the basis for the tort claim, although the outrageous *manner* in which it engaged in discrimination could be put in evidence with cautionary instructions from the court to disregard the fact of employment discrimination. The Court said, "it is essential that the state tort be either unrelated to employment discrimination or a function of the particularly abusive manner in which the discrimination is accomplished or threatened rather than a function of the actual or threatened discrimination itself."[33] Fearing, as in *Linn,* the misuse of the state tort action to thwart federal labor policy, the Court conditioned its availability on a definition of the tort that included outrageous conduct as an element, and it cautioned that it might reach a different result in a case involving "excessive" damages.[34]

Rounding out the Court's approach to *Garmon* preemption is its decision in *Sears, Roebuck and Co. v. San Diego County District Council of Carpenters.*[35] The Carpenters' Union peacefully picketed in Sears' parking lot to protest Sears' assignment of work to carpenters who had not been

[32] *Farmer,* 430 U.S. at 305.

[33] Because the record in *Farmer* indicated that no such distinction had occurred at trial, the Court did not reinstate the trial court's judgment, but remanded for appropriate proceedings instead. *Id.* at 306-07.

[34] *Id.*

[35] 436 U.S. 180 (1978).

hired through the union's hiring hall. The pickets refused Sears' request to leave its property. Sears then sought an injunction from the California Superior Court against the continuing trespass. While the trial court granted the injunction, the California Supreme Court concluded that the trespass action was preempted because the conduct was arguably either protected or prohibited.

Writing for the Court, Justice Stevens noted that the status of the picketing was ambiguous. It was arguably protected area standards picketing. However, it was also arguably prohibited under either Section 8(b)(4)(D)'s prohibition of picketing to force an assignment of work to a particular group of employees in a jurisdictional dispute, or under Section 8(b)(7)(C)'s regulation of recognitional picketing. He then separated the two prongs of the *Garmon* doctrine.[36] As to the arguably prohibited prong, his analysis followed *Linn* and *Farmer*. The state interest in preventing trespass was clearly strong, and this was traditionally an area within the purview of state power. He saw "no realistic risk of interference" with the NLRB's jurisdiction because the Board and a California court would focus their inquiries differently. The issue for the Board would be whether the Act had been violated, which would turn on the union's motives for picketing. The state claim would not turn on the purpose of the picketing but on its location—whether the pickets were trespassing on Sears' property. Thus, each body could adjudicate the issue before it without reference to the merits of the dispute before the other.

Justice Stevens stated that the arguably protected prong was more difficult because here the federal supremacy concerns were stronger, given the risk that the state might burden conduct that is actually protected by the NLRA. Moreover, in determining whether or not the conduct amounted to trespass, the California court would have to consider whether the Act gave the union the right to be on Sears' property, which might entail balancing the union's Section 7 rights against Sears' property rights, the same inquiry that the Board would have to make in deciding whether the union had a statutory right to picket there. Applying the primary jurisdiction rationale that repeatedly emerges in the preemption cases would almost certainly lead to the conclusion that the state action was preempted, since the NLRB and not a trial court should make the first determination of the proper balance between property and Section 7 rights. Nevertheless, the *Sears* Court concluded that the primary jurisdiction rationale evaporated in this case because it "justifies pre-emption only in situations in which an aggrieved

[36] *Id.* at 190.

party has a reasonable opportunity either to invoke the Board's jurisdiction himself or else to induce his adversary to do so."[37] Here, the union controlled access to the Board for a ruling on whether its conduct was protected despite the invasion of Sears' property. Only it could decide whether to file an unfair labor practice charge in response to Sears' request that the picketers leave, and it seemed counterintuitive and contrary to the goal of fostering industrial peace to encourage Sears to forgo recourse to the state courts in favor of forcible eviction of the picketers in the hope of provoking the filing of such a charge (and at the risk of provoking violence, instead). The Court concluded that the primary jurisdiction rationale is not a sufficient justification to preempt a state claim involving arguably protected conduct where a party who has a "fair opportunity" to present the protection issue to the Board fails to do so and the other party has no "acceptable" means to bring the question to the Board.[38]

§ 14.3 Regulation of Conduct that is Neither Protected Nor Prohibited: The *Machinists* Rule

[A]—Permitted Conduct

In addition to conduct protected by the NLRA and conduct that the Act explicitly prohibits, there is conduct that the Act neither protects nor prohibits. These "permitted activities"[39] include, among others, such union tactics as work slow-downs,[40] quickie strikes,[41] and concerted refusals to

[37] *Id.* at 201.

[38] *Id.* at 202-03, 207. The Court noted that removing this justification for preemption did not in and of itself resolve the preemption question, since preemption might still be appropriate if the risk was high that the state court would erroneously apply federal labor law and, consequently, interfere with protected conduct. In this instance, however, involving trespassory organizational activity or area standards picketing, the Court concluded that the general rule disfavored access to private property and the risk of erroneous interference with protected conduct was, therefore, not high enough to justify preemption under the circumstances. *Id.* at 203-07.

[39] The phrase is Archibald Cox's who writes: " 'Permitted activities' would be a better shorthand for this category of employee conduct because it may be—indeed is—protected against state, but not employer interference." *See* Archibald Cox, *Labor Law Preemption Revisited,* 85 Harv. L. Rev. 1337, 1346 (1972) (footnote omitted).

[40] *See* Elk Lumber Co., 91 NLRB 333, 336-39 (1950) (holding that work slow-down is unprotected). For a discussion of unprotected conduct and the loss of protection for concerted activity, see *infra* § 16.4.

[41] *See* International Union, UAW v. Wisconsin Employment Relations Bd., 336 U.S. 245 (1949).

work overtime[42] and such employer tactics as hiring permanent striker replacements in response to an economic strike,[43] and, under certain circumstances, engaging in an "offensive" or bargaining lockout.[44] This area of neither protected nor prohibited conduct is less appropriately described as a "gap" in the legislative scheme than as a deliberate decision for laissez faire regarding union and employer exercise of certain economic weapons. In the Supreme Court's words, this is an area deliberately left unregulated "to be controlled by the free play of economic forces."[45]

The Supreme Court first encountered the question of whether a state could regulate conduct that was neither protected nor prohibited by the NLRA in a 1949 decision: *Automobile Workers v. Wisconsin Employment Relations Board*,[46] a case generally known as the *Briggs-Stratton* case. There, the union adopted a plan of "quickie strikes," short unannounced strikes in order to pressure the employer during negotiations. Under the rule announced in that case, states were permitted to regulate conduct that the NLRA neither protected nor forbade.

[B]—Rejection of the *Briggs-Stratton* Rule

The *Briggs-Stratton* rule did not endure. In dictum, the *Garmon* majority intimated that the broad rule no longer governed.[47] The day before the Court heard argument in *Garmon,* it handed down its decision in *Local 24, International Brotherhood of Teamsters v. Oliver*,[48] a decision that pointed toward a new direction regarding state regulation of conduct that is neither protected or prohibited.

Oliver involved a multi-employer collective bargaining agreement entered into by a group of Teamster locals and motor carriers in twelve Midwestern states. Some drivers owned the trucks that they drove and leased

---

[42] *See* Lodge 76, International Ass'n of Machinists v. Wisconsin Employment Relations Bd., 427 U.S. 132 (1976).

[43] *See* NLRB v. Mackay Radio & Telegraph Co., 304 U.S. 333 (1938). For a discussion of *Mackay* and of employer economic weapons more generally, see *supra* § 9.5 and Chapter 10.

[44] *See* American Ship Building Co. v. NLRB, 380 U.S. 300 (1965).

[45] NLRB v. Nash-Finch Co., 404 U.S. 138, 144 (1971).

[46] 336 U.S. 245 (1949).

[47] San Diego Building Trades Council v. Garmon, 359 U.S. 236, 245 & n.4 (1959). The majority's comment provoked a spirited reaffirmation of *Briggs-Stratton* by Justice Harlan in his concurrence. *Id.* at 249, 253 (Harlan, J., concurring).

[48] 358 U.S. 283 (1959).

them to the carriers for whom they drove. Consequently, one article of the agreement set minimum rental and certain other lease terms for trucks that were leased to a carrier by an owner-operator of the truck to be driven by that owner for the carrier. One such owner-operator, Oliver, claimed that the minimum rental provision constituted illegal price-fixing, and he sought an injunction under Ohio antitrust law to prevent the parties to the agreement from giving effect to this provision. The state court granted the injunction.

It is hard to assimilate the provision in the bargaining agreement to a rule focused on whether the regulated conduct was protected or prohibited under the NLRA. Nothing in the Act prohibited the agreement. But neither can one say that the provision was protected by the Act, though it might be understood to be the product of protected activity, collective bargaining.

The union defended on the ground that the article was the "product of the exercise of federally sanctioned collective bargaining rights," and, therefore, exempt from forfeiture or alteration under state antitrust law. The Supreme Court accepted the union's argument that the purpose of the article was to prevent erosion of the negotiated wage by undercost rental fees and, therefore, was the product of bargaining over a mandatory subject of bargaining.[49] The Court also accepted the union's argument that application of Ohio antitrust law to the minimum lease terms article of the collective bargaining agreement would frustrate the congressional purpose of having parties bargain over the terms and conditions of employment and create "their own charter for the ordering of industrial relations." It thereby introduced the idea that the NLRA not only identifies protected and prohibited conduct, but also creates an area in which the parties are left free of government regulation, both federal and, therefore, necessarily local.[50]

In holding the state antitrust claim preempted, the *Oliver* court noted that the case did not involve a collective bargaining agreement that ran afoul of local health or safety regulations, areas of particular local interest.[51] This exception has been understood broadly to encompass state legislation that sets minimum terms of employment.[52]

---

[49] Justice Brennan wrote for the Court, "the point of the Article is obviously not price fixing but wages." *Id.* at 294.

[50] *Id.* at 295-96.

[51] *Id.* at 297.

[52] Metropolitan Life Ins. Co. v. Massachusetts, 471 U.S. 724 (1985) (Massachusetts statute that sets minimum mental health care benefits that must be provided under various insurance plans, including certain employee health care plans not preempted by either the NLRA or

The Court further articulated this notion that by not regulating the Act leaves some aspects of the relationship between unions and employers free of government intervention, and therefore free of state regulation as well as federal, in *Teamsters Union Local 20 v. Morton.*[53] In *Morton,* a union representing dump truck drivers orchestrated a boycott of their employer by its customers and suppliers during a strike. The employer sued the union in federal court alleging several violations of Section 303 of the LMRA,[54] and of Ohio common law. The trial court awarded damages for various violations of Section 303. It also held that in one instance, for which Morton sought recovery, no violation of federal law occurred because the union had peacefully persuaded the customer to cease doing business with the employer, instead of achieving that end through coercion, or by an appeal to the customer's employees. In that instance, however, it awarded damages for violation of Ohio law. The Supreme Court held that state law was preempted in this case. The Court's task was simplified by the existence of Section 303 which demonstrated that Congress had considered the extent to which it wanted to prohibit secondary boycott activity and legislated with specificity regarding the availability of damages for certain kinds of secondary boycott activity. That which Congress did not proscribe in Section 303, it meant to permit, and to permit a plaintiff to add to that provision's prohibitions with a pendent state law claim would undermine Congress's judgment about which economic weapons it wanted to leave available and which ones it wanted to outlaw.[55]

The Supreme Court elaborated on the *Morton* idea regarding state regulation of conduct that is neither protected nor prohibited, and overruled *Briggs-Stratton* in 1976 in its decision in *Machinists Lodge 76 v. Wisconsin Employment Relations Commission.*[56] After the lapse of a collective bargaining agreement during the course of protracted negotiations, the union and its members engaged in a concerted refusal to work overtime. In response, the employer first filed an unfair labor practice charge claiming a violation of Section 8(b)(3)'s duty to bargain in good faith. The Regional

---

ERISA (Employee Retirement Income Security Act of 1974)); Fort Halifax Packing Co., Inc. v. Coyne, 482 U.S. 1 (1987) (Maine statute that requires payment of severance pay in event of plant closing or certain plant relocations not preempted by either the NLRA or ERISA).

53 377 U.S. 252 (1964).

54 Section 303 permits suit in federal district court for damages suffered as a result of union violations of Section 8(b)(4), the Act's secondary boycott provisions.

55 Teamsters Local 20 v. Morton, 377 U.S. 252, 259-60 (1964).

56 427 U.S. 132 (1976).

Director dismissed the charge on the authority of *NLRB v. Insurance Agents*,[57] in which the Court held that the Board does not have the authority to weigh and select permissible economic weapons used in the course of bargaining.

Unsuccessful with its Section 8(b)(3) claim, the employer then filed an unfair labor practice charge with the Wisconsin Employment Relations Commission. The Commission declared the conduct an unfair labor practice under Wisconsin law and entered a cease and desist order, which was, in turn, enforced by the Wisconsin courts.

On certiorari, the United States Supreme Court identified a second line of preemption analysis separate from the *Garmon* approach. The focus in this second line of cases is on "whether Congress intended that the conduct involved be unregulated because left 'to be controlled by the free play of economic forces.' "[58] Relying on important articles by Professors Archibald Cox and Howard Lesnick, and drawing on a series of decisions in which the Court had cautioned the NLRB that it was not empowered to weigh and balance economic weapons used in the bargaining process,[59] the Court reasoned that the NLRA created, in addition to the categories of protected and prohibited conduct, a third area of "laissez-faire" where the contending economic forces (unions and employers) would draw on the strength of their bargaining skills and economic weapons without interference from government. The Court quoted Professor Lesnick's comment that "the state is not merely filling a gap when it outlaws what federal law fails to outlaw; it is denying one party to an economic contest a weapon that Congress meant him to have available."[60] The evil to be avoided by this prong of preemption doctrine was the possibility that the state would alter the balance of power in a particular labor conflict by putting its thumb on the scale, thereby subverting congressional intent that the matter be left free

[57] 361 U.S. 477 (1960). For a discussion of *Insurance Agents* and its place in the doctrine of good faith bargaining, see *supra* § 7.4.

[58] Machinists Lodge 76, 427 U.S. 132, 140 (1976) (*quoting* NLRB v. Nash Finch Co., 404 U.S. 138, 144 (1971)).

[59] These decisions include: American Ship Building Co. v. NLRB, 380 U.S. 300 (1965); NLRB v. Brown, 380 U.S. 278 (1965); NLRB v. Insurance Agents, 361 U.S. 477 (1960). For a discussion of these cases and of the issues relating to use of economic weapons, see *supra* §§ 7.4 and 10.3.

[60] *Machinists Lodge 76*, 427 U.S. at 141 & n.4 (*quoting* Howard Lesnick, *Preemption Reconsidered: The Apparent Reaffirmation of* Garmon, 72 Colum. L. Rev. 469, 478 (1972)). The Cox Article was Archibald Cox, *Labor Law Preemption Revisited*, 85 Harv. L. Rev. 1337, 1352 (1972).

of government intervention. Consequently, the Court overruled *Briggs-Stratton.*[61]

[C]—Application of the *Machinists* Rule

Courts have continued to apply the *Machinists* rule in holding that state and local laws that alter the balance of power between unions and employers are preempted. For example, the Supreme Court held, in *Golden State Transit Corp. v. City of Los Angeles,*[62] that the city council could not, without running afoul of *Machinists,* condition an extension of petitioner's taxicab franchise on its settling a strike with its workers by a prescribed date. Similarly, both federal and state courts have struck down on *Machinists* preemption grounds state and local efforts to prohibit the recruitment and use of striker replacements during strikes or lockouts.[63] And in *Cannon v. Edgar,*[64] a federal district court held that the Illinois Burial Rights Act, which required unionized cemeteries and their workers to include in their agreements a provision for establishing a pool of workers to be available during labor disputes to ensure no delay in burials where religiously mandated, was preempted under both *Garmon* and *Machinists.*

The Supreme Court has declined to find *Machinists* preemption in two cases that involved the payment or nonpayment of unemployment compensation benefits to striking workers, notwithstanding the effect that payment of benefits would have on the balance of power between employers and unions in a strike setting.[65] These cases, however, turned on the relationship

---

61 *Id.* at 151. In an important concurring opinion, and a necessary concurrence to supply a Court majority, Justice Powell, joined by Chief Justice Burger, argued that the *Machinists* rule should apply only to instances where state regulation seeks to alter the bargaining positions of employers or unions, and should not apply to "neutral" state regulation which has only an incidental effect on their relative bargaining strength. This argument that laws of general applicability should be analyzed differently than those that are directed at labor relations, which had been rejected in *Garmon,* was at the core of Professor Cox's proposal in his article *Labor Law Preemption Revisited.*

62 475 U.S. 608 (1986).

63 *See, e.g.,* Employers Ass'n v. Steelworkers, 803 F. Supp.1558 (D. Minn. 1992), *aff'd,* 32 F.3d 1297 (8th Cir. 1994) (Minnesota permanent striker replacement ban); Greater Boston Chamber of Commerce v. City of Boston, 778 F. Supp. 95 (D. Mass. 1991) (Boston ordinance prohibiting hiring of replacement workers during strike or lockout or recruiting or hiring them whenever likely to result in a threat to public safety); Midwest Motor Express v. Teamsters Local 120, 512 N.W.2d 881 (Minn. 1994) (striking down Minnesota statute).

64 825 F. Supp. 1349 (N.D. Ill. 1993).

65 New York Telephone Co. v. New York Dept. of Labor, 440 U.S. 519 (1979); Baker v. General Motors Corp., 478 U.S. 621 (1986).

between the NLRA and the nearly contemporaneously enacted Social Security Act, the Court's understanding from the legislative history of the two acts that Congress intended for the states to exercise control over the payment of unemployment compensation benefits, and its recognition that the state purpose was not to regulate labor relations. The Court has also read the *Teamsters v. Oliver* exception for local health and safety regulation rather broadly to find that state statutes setting minimum labor standards were not preempted in *Metropolitan Life Insurance Co. v. Massachusetts,*[66] and *Fort Halifax Packing Co., Inc. v. Coyne.*[67]

In one other important preemption decision, *Belknap v. Hale,*[68] a divided Supreme Court ruled that *Machinists* did not compel preemption of claims brought by "permanent" replacement workers who sued Belknap, their former employer, for misrepresentation and breach of contract after it agreed with the union to discharge them as part of the settlement of a strike. In *Belknap*, the employer advertised for and hired permanent replacements for striking workers. It made various assurances to the replacements that their positions would be permanent, including having them sign agreements identifying them as permanent employees. After a hearing on various unfair labor practice charges brought by the union, Belknap and the union engaged in settlement discussions that led to dismissal of the unfair labor practice charges and settlement of the strike. As part of the settlement, Belknap agreed to lay off replacement workers to make room for returning strikers. A Kentucky trial court granted summary judgment for Belknap, on preemption grounds, in the replacements' misrepresentation and breach of contract suit. The Kentucky Court of Appeals reversed.

At the Supreme Court, Belknap was joined by the NLRB and the AFL-CIO, both of which filed amicus briefs, in arguing the state claims should be preempted, though the three did not agree in their analyses. Belknap argued that both *Machinists* and *Garmon* governed.[69] Both Belknap and

---

66 471 U.S. 724 (1985) (Massachusetts statute that sets minimum mental health care benefits that must be provided under various insurance plans, including certain employee health care plans not preempted by either the NLRA or ERISA (Employee Retirement Income Security Act of 1974)).

67 482 U.S. 1 (1987) (Maine statute that requires payment of severance pay in event of plant closing or certain plant relocations not preempted by either the NLRA or ERISA).

68 463 U.S. 491 (1983).

69 Belknap was in the rather curious position of arguing regarding *Garmon* that because the strike might have been an unfair labor practice strike (a question left unanswered when the Regional Director dismissed the unfair labor practice charges pursuant to the strike settlement), the hiring of permanent replacements and their retention after the strike were

the AFL-CIO argued that allowing displaced permanent replacement workers to bring misrepresentation or breach of contract suits would upset the balance of power between employers and unions, although they predicted different effects. Belknap argued that the permanent replacement weapon would be impaired if employers were forced to make the jobs' "permanence" explicitly conditional (on the terms of a strike settlement and the prospect that the strike would be deemed an unfair labor practice strike requiring reinstatement of the strikers) or risk liability in state tort or contract actions brought by laid-off permanent replacement workers. The AFL-CIO argued that the prospect of civil liability for laying off replacement workers would undermine the chances of strike settlement. The majority, which clearly was distressed at the prospects of having to decide that the preemption doctrines shield fraud and other generally disagreeable behavior, and concerned that the replacement workers, who, notwithstanding their having signed agreements with the employer identifying by name the striker whom each was permanently replacing, the Court characterized as "innocent third parties,"[70] would be left without a remedy, concluded that allowing the suits would not have substantial impact on either the permanent replacement weapon or on strike settlement and the suits were not preempted.[71]

§ 14.4 Section 301 Preemption

This third branch of preemption doctrine arises out of principles relating to the resolution of disputes over purported breaches of the collective

---

arguably prohibited conduct. It further argued that, assuming the strike to be an unfair labor practice strike, allowing the state suits would place a burden on legally required conduct, thereby sending a confusing mixed message about legal obligations. The majority had little difficulty assimilating this case to the *Linn* and *Farmer* analysis, concluding that the state suits would not interfere with the jurisdiction of the Board (at least so long as the replacements did not seek and had no prospect of receiving a specific performance remedy), and fitting it into the *Garmon* exceptions. *Id.* at 507-12.

[70] *Id.* at 500. Given their knowledge of their role in the economic warfare between Belknap and its striking employees the adjective "innocent" seems misused. As one of my students remarked in a discussion of secondary boycotts and the ally doctrine: "If someone sticks his face in the middle of a strike to assist the employer, he should expect to get a bloody nose." I have always assumed that my student was speaking figuratively.

[71] For an insightful critique of *Belknap,* see Matthew W. Finkin, *Labor Policy and the Enervation of the Economic Strike,* 1990 U. Ill. L. Rev. 547, 549-56 (discussing, among other things, the "fundamental shift in the state law of individual employment," which went unnoticed by the Court, but serves as an important backdrop for the case, and the Court's dismissiveness of the Board's (admittedly wishy-washy) interpretation of the law of permanent replacements, and arguing that *Belknap* will seriously impair the ability of the parties to settle strikes).

bargaining agreement. Section 301 of the LMRA gives federal district courts jurisdiction to hear suits for violation of collective bargaining agreements.[72] In *Charles Dowd Box Co. v. Courtney*,[73] the Supreme Court concluded that state courts had concurrent jurisdiction over Section 301 claims. Previously, in *Textile Workers v. Lincoln Mills*,[74] the Court had held that the federal courts hearing Section 301 suits were to apply federal common law "fashion[ed] from the policy of our national labor laws."[75] Inevitably, after *Dowd Box* gave concurrent jurisdiction to state courts, the Court would face the question whether these state courts were to apply state law or federal common law when hearing Section 301 claims.

In *Teamsters v. Lucas Flour Co.*,[76] the Court held that, as in federal district courts, state courts were to apply federal common law, rather than potentially inconsistent local law, in Section 301 suits. The Court explained the need for uniformity in the following passage:

> The possibility that individual contract terms might have different meanings under state and federal law would inevitably exert a disruptive influence upon both the negotiation and administration of collective agreements. Because neither party could be certain of the rights which it had obtained or conceded, the process of negotiating an agreement would be made immeasurably more difficult by the necessity of trying to formulate contract provisions in such a way as to contain the same meaning under two or more systems of law which might someday be invoked in enforcing the contract. Once the collective bargain was made, the possibility of conflicting substantive interpretation under competing legal systems would tend to stimulate and prolong disputes as to its interpretation . . . [and] might substantially impede the parties' willingness to agree to contract terms providing for final arbitral or judicial resolution of disputes.[77]

This same concern, that the availability of inconsistent legal regimes would impede collective bargaining, is at the heart of Section 301 preemption. The Supreme Court first addressed this issue in *Allis-Chalmers Corp.*

---

[72] For a discussion of enforcement of the collective bargaining agreement, see *supra* Chapter 13.

[73] 368 U.S. 502 (1962).

[74] 353 U.S. 448 (1957).

[75] *Id.* at 456.

[76] 369 U.S. 95 (1962).

[77] *Id.* at 103-04 (footnote omitted).

v. Lueck,[78] a case involving a unionized employee's claim under Wisconsin law for bad-faith handling of an insurance claim. One of the benefits provided Lueck under the collective bargaining agreement with Allis-Chalmers was nonoccupational disability insurance. When Lueck was injured, he filed a claim under the policy, and though his claim was approved, he alleged that at Allis-Chalmers' request the insurer would periodically terminate payments and place various obstacles in his way in order to harass him. Avoiding the contract's grievance procedure, Lueck instead brought the potentially more lucrative tort action against his employer and insurance carrier. The trial court held that Lueck could only bring his claim under Section 301 because the bad-faith claim would be preempted. The Wisconsin Supreme Court reversed, reasoning that the bad-faith tort claim was distinct from any bad-faith breach-of-contract claim he might have. The United States Supreme Court disagreed. It concluded that the collective bargaining agreement created a duty of timely payments and good faith dealing in addition to specifying the benefits.[79] It further concluded that the state tort claim drew its existence and content from the contract and that the underlying duty could only be "ascertained from a consideration of the contract itself."[80] Because the state claim could not be determined without considering the meaning of the collective bargaining agreement, the Court held that Section 301 preempted the state bad-faith claim.[81]

The Supreme Court revisited the question of Section 301 preemption in 1988 in *Lingle v. Norge Div. Of Magic Chef, Inc.*[82] That case involved an employee who had been fired in retaliation for filing a worker's compensation claim. The collective bargaining agreement protected her from being fired without just cause. Her union grieved on her behalf, and ultimately the arbitrator ruled in her favor, ordering reinstatement and full back pay. At the same time, she sued in Illinois state court under the state's

---

[78] 471 U.S. 202 (1985).

[79] *Id.* at 213-16.

[80] *Id.* at 216 (*quoting* Hilker v. Western Automobile Ins. Co., 204 Wis. 1, 16 (1931)).

[81] *Id.* at 218-19. Because Lueck had not exhausted the contract's grievance procedure, his claim could not be converted into a Section 301 claim, which would have allowed him to go forward. Two years later, in Electrical Workers (IBEW) v. Hechler, 481 U.S. 851 (1987), the Court followed its *Lueck* analysis and held that Section 301 preempted a Florida tort claim which alleged that the union had breached its duty "to provide a union member with a safe workplace" resulting in her injuries. The Court held that the claim was preempted because any such duty arose under the contract and the existence and scope of such a duty could only be determined by construing the contract. *Id.* at 862.

[82] 486 U.S. 399 (1988).

worker's compensation law, which prohibits retaliatory discharge. After her case was removed to federal district court, the court dismissed her claim on the basis of *Allis-Chalmers,* and the Court of Appeals affirmed. The Supreme Court disagreed, holding that because plaintiff's claim arose independently of the collective bargaining agreement and could be resolved without interpreting the agreement—all that the state court needed to determine was that she was discharged and the employer's motive was retaliatory—Section 301 did not require preemption.[83]

While *Lingle* appeared to limit *Lueck,* it also reaffirmed its basic approach. In a context where states have increasingly sought to set minimum workplace standards and to provide some of the protections to their workers that might be otherwise available through collective bargaining, lower courts have invoked Section 301 preemption widely and often to deprive unionized workers of benefits that are available to their nonunionized counterparts. While the rationale for Section 301 preemption is to safeguard the collective bargaining and arbitration scheme, its consequence increasingly seems to be to undermine collective bargaining.[84]

§ 14.5 Chapter Highlights

1. When federal labor law preempts state law, the state law, and in most instances the state agency charged with enforcing it, must yield to federal law and the appropriate federal forum. (§ 14.1[A])

2. Labor preemption is almost wholly a judicial creation since Congress generally left the preemption question unaddressed. (§ 14.1[A])

3. The principal goals behind the labor exemption doctrine is to avoid a conflict of substantive law and to protect the NLRB's primary jurisdiction, but in some cases other values share the limelight with these two. (§ 14.1[B])

---

[83] *Id.* at 408-12. The Court noted that under circumstances where the state claim arises independently from the contract and, therefore, does not require resolution of contract issues, the state claim is not preempted even if resolution of each claim would require attention to precisely the same facts. *Id.* at 409-10.

[84] For further development of this criticism, *see generally,* Michael C. Harper, *Limiting Section 301 Preemption: Three Cheers for the Trilogy, Only One for* Lingle *and* Lueck, 66 Chi.-Kent L. Rev. 685 (1990); Katherine Van Wezel Stone, *The Legacy of Industrial Pluralism: The Tension Between Individual Employment Rights and the New Deal Collective Bargaining System,* 59 U. Chi. L. Rev. 575 (1992).

4. There are three basic kinds of labor preemption: *Garmon* Preemption; *Machinists* Preemption; and Section 301 Preemption. (§ 14.1[C])

5. The *Garmon* rule states that when a state law purports to regulate conduct which is either protected by Section 7 of the Act or prohibited by Section 8, or if that conduct is arguably governed by Sections 7 or 8, state law must yield to the federal scheme. (§ 14.2[A])

6. The Supreme Court has recognized exceptions to the *Garmon* rule where the state-regulated conduct involves "interests so deeply rooted in local feeling and responsibility" that it would not deem state regulation preempted absent express congressional direction, or is of "merely peripheral concern to federal labor law. These exceptions originally occurred in instances involving criminal or tortious assaultive behavior and questions of internal union matters, but the range of cases fitting the exception has since grown. (§ 14.2[B])

7. When one is trying to determine whether arguably prohibited conduct fits within the *Garmon* exceptions, one should ask: 1) Is there an overriding state interest, one deeply rooted in local feeling and responsibility, in state regulation of the conduct in question, and/or is the regulated activity merely of peripheral concern to federal labor law?; and 2) Is there little risk that the state cause of action will interfere with the jurisdiction of the NLRB and with the effective administration of national labor policy? In answering this final question, the Court considers whether elements of the state claim and the unfair labor practice claim are different, whether the available remedies under the two schemes are different, and whether adjudication of the state claim is possible without regard to the merits of the underlying labor dispute. (§ 14.2[C])

8. In *Linn* and *Farmer*, the Court held that while each fit within one or more *Garmon* exceptions, the state defamation and intentional infliction of emotional distress claims were partly preempted. In other words, the right to go forward with the state law claim was conditioned on a reframing of the state tort law to safeguard federal labor policy. (§ 14.2[C])

9. When one is trying to determine whether arguably protected conduct fits within the *Garmon* exceptions, one should ask: 1) Is there an overriding state interest, one deeply rooted in local feeling and responsibility, in state regulation of the conduct in question, and/or is the regulated activity merely of peripheral concern to federal labor law?; 2) Did the aggrieved party lack a reasonable opportunity to invoke the Board's jurisdiction or to induce

its adversary to do so, and if so, did the adversary have a fair opportunity to present the protection issue to the Board, but failed to do so?; and, apparently, 3) Is the risk of state interference with protected conduct low? (§ 14.2[C])

10. The *Machinists* rule requires that states not interfere with conduct that Congress intended neither to protect nor to prohibit, but to leave unregulated, instead "to be controlled by the free play of economic forces." This means that states may not intervene in labor disputes to put their thumb on the scale in favor of one party or the other by regulating the use of economic weapons. (§ 14.3)

11. There are fewer exceptional cases to the *Machinists* rule than there are to *Garmon,* but the Court has recognized the power of the states to regulate matters of health and safety by setting minimum labor standards. (§ 14.3[C])

12. Section 301 preemption requires that state claims that owe their existence to the collective bargaining agreement and cannot be adjudicated without interpreting the agreement be preempted in the interest of national uniformity in the law governing collective bargaining agreements. (§ 14.4)

CHAPTER 15
RECONCILING LABOR LAW AND THE ANTITRUST LAWS

§ 15.1 Introduction

The problem of reconciling labor law and antitrust law should be readily apparent. Antitrust law is intended to foster marketplace competition and to limit the aggregation of private economic power. Congress intended the Sherman Act as an antidote to cartels, trusts, and monopolies and to the anticompetitive effects of each. Federal labor law gives its blessing to at least one sort of anticompetitive behavior, the attempt by unions to control the labor market. The premise of the Wagner Act was that employees should be able to band together so that they would have greater power in the labor market than they would if they were all competing individually and against one another. Unions do not affect simply the labor market. Congress understood and accepted that combination of employees might have adverse effects on the price of products and services and on other participants in the market. Nor could the disruptive effects of strikes and boycotts on the product market have been lost on them.[1]

This chapter follows the doctrinal development of labor antitrust chronologically for the most part. It explains the major cases and describes the development of the statutory and nonstatutory labor exemptions.

§ 15.2 Labor Antitrust Jurisprudence Before the Norris-LaGuardia and Wagner Acts

Prompted by the growing concentration of industry, the rise of various corporate forms intended to allocate and control markets and to eliminate competition, concern over the consequences of monopolization for consumers and over some of the more notorious business methods by which some monopolies were achieved, Congress enacted the Sherman Act in 1890. Section 1 of the Act declared illegal "every contract, combination, in the form of trust or otherwise, or conspiracy, in restraint of trade or commerce among the several States."[2] Section 2 said that anyone "who shall monopolize, or attempt to monopolize, or combine or conspire with any other person or persons, to monopolize any part of the trade or commerce among the several States . . . shall be deemed guilty of a misdemeanor."[3]

---

[1] Douglas L. Leslie, *Principles of Labor Antitrust,* 66 Va. L. Rev. 1183, 1184-92 (1980); Randall Marks, *Labor and Antitrust: Striking a Balance Without Balancing,* 35 Am. U. L. Rev. 699, 714-18 (1986).

[2] 15 U.S.C. § 1 (1994).

[3] 15 U.S.C. § 2 (1994). In 1974 Congress amended the section, changing the crime from a misdemeanor to a felony.

There is no doubt that the framers of the law were thinking of industrial cartels and trusts and the danger they posed to smaller businesses. Nevertheless, in its early years, the Act was enforced against labor unions more often than it was against businesses. Courts interpreted it as reaching various secondary boycott activities, including consumer boycotts of employers placed on union "unfair lists" and refusals to handle struck goods. The Supreme Court approved of this application of the Sherman Act in the *Danbury Hatters* case,[4] where the Supreme Court held that the Act reached a union boycott of retailers who sold hats manufactured by an employer who had resisted unionization.

The *Danbury Hatters* case drew both criticism and active lobbying for its statutory undoing. When Congress passed the Clayton Act of 1914, which, among other things, created a private right of action for injunctive relief for anyone threatened with harm by a violation of the antitrust laws, it responded to union pressure and sought to limit the application of the antitrust laws to union activity. Section 6 stated that labor was "not a commodity or article of commerce," that labor organizations were not *per se* prohibited by the antitrust laws, and that neither did those laws prohibit unions from "lawfully carrying out" their "legitimate objectives."[5] Section 20 sought to prohibit the use of labor injunctions in cases of peaceful labor disputes and specified various activities that were not enjoinable. It further stated that the specified nonenjoinable conduct should not be considered violative of "any law of the United States."[6]

The Supreme Court gave these provisions a very narrow construction in *Duplex Printing Press Co. v. Deering*,[7] a secondary boycott case, where it emphasized Section 6's requirement that the union activity be "lawful" and "legitimate," and interpreted Section 20 to exclude secondary boycott activity from the lawful activity that it protected. Given the context of agitation to undo *Danbury Hatters* in which the Clayton Act became law, Justice Pitney's opinion for the Court required an incredible reading of the statute.

After *Duplex Printing,* the courts continued to apply the antitrust laws to union secondary boycott activity and to hot cargo agreements.[8] The

[4] Loewe v. Lawlor, 208 U.S. 274 (1908).

[5] 15 U.S.C. § 17 (1994).

[6] 29 U.S.C. § 52 (1994).

[7] 254 U.S. 443 (1921).

[8] *See, e.g.*, Bedford Cut Stone Co. v. Stone Cutters' Ass'n, 274 U.S. 37 (1927); United States v. Brims, 272 U.S. 549 (1926).

antitrust laws found application outside of the context of secondary boycotts as well. Thus, in a pair of decisions arising out of the same dispute, the Supreme Court held that whether primary picketing that shut down a coal operator violated the antitrust laws depended on whether it was instigated with a "local" motive—here, to resist a formerly organized company from breaching its contract with the union, locking out union members, and operating as a non-union company—or with the nonlocal intent "to stop the production of non-union coal and prevent its shipment to markets of other States . . . where it would by competition tend to reduce the price of the commodity and affect injuriously the maintenance of wages for union labor in competing mines."[9]

§ 15.3 *United States v. Hutcheson* and the Statutory Exemption

Continued frustration with labor law by injunction led to Congress's second effort to remove much of the injunction weapon from the federal judiciary, and to protect against ex parte proceedings where it did not take away the injunction power, by the Norris-LaGuardia Act. On its face, the Act said nothing about the extent to which the Sherman Act reached union restraints of trade.

In 1940, the Supreme Court took a different turn regarding labor antitrust—one that narrowed the realm of labor activity that would subject a union to antitrust liability. *Apex Hosiery v. Leader,*[10] involved a rather dramatic interference with trade. As a result of a protracted and violent sit-down strike in an attempt by a minority union to get a hosiery manufacturer to enter into a closed-shop agreement, for over three months the company's manufacturing operations were shut-down, and, for a portion of that time, its stocks of finished hosiery could not be shipped to fulfill orders. The question for the Court was whether this interference with trade was a "restraint of trade" within the meaning of the Sherman Act.

[9] UMW v. Coronado Coal Co. (Coronado I), 259 U.S. 344 (1922); Coronado Coal Co. v. UMW (Coronado II), 268 U.S. 295 (1925). The quoted language is from *Coronado II,* at 310. The decision, which to modern eyes looks quite silly and unworkable given the likelihood that a union would be acting from mixed local and nonlocal goals (although according to the Court that was not the case here, since it concluded that the union's goal was to destroy the mining operation), was grounded in the then current understanding that manufacturing or production were local, not matters of interstate commerce. *See* United States v. E.C. Knight Co., 156 U.S. 1, 12 (1895) (stating that "Commerce succeeds to manufacture, and is not a part of it"). For a discussion of the problems that beset the Court's approach, see Leslie, *Principles, supra* note 1, at 1193-95.

[10] 310 U.S. 469 (1940).

Writing for the majority, Justice Stone rejected the union's argument that Congress intended to exempt labor unions wholly from the reach of the Sherman Act.[11] But he also noted that the Court had never held that the Act applied to every union activity that interferes with trade, or, for that matter, to every interference with the transportation of goods beyond state lines. Turning to the legislative history and to an examination of the common law dealing with trade restrictions at the time of the Sherman Act's passage, he argued that the problem perceived by Congress was business combinations in an effort to suppress competition and to extract monopoly profits. In other words, the evil that Congress addressed was "restraint upon commercial competition in the marketing of goods or services."[12] By contrast, he wrote regarding the labor market:

> Since, in order to render a labor combination effective it must eliminate the competition from non-union made goods . . . an elimination of price competition based on differences in labor standards is the objective of any national labor organization. But this effect on competition has not been considered to be the kind of curtailment of price competition prohibited by the Sherman Act.[13]

Justice Stone did not speak of a labor immunity or exemption. As Professor Theodore St. Antoine points out, the Court "was careful to say . . . that this test did not vary depending on the nature of the alleged wrongdoer, whether union or management . . . the Sherman Act, as written, would simply not apply to a certain class of restraints."[14]

The following year, the Court took an abrupt turn in a new direction, abandoning the *Apex* approach of looking at whether the restraint was directed toward commercial competition or toward removing competition in the labor market. *United States v. Hutcheson*[15] was the product of Assistant Attorney General Thurman Arnold's decision to prosecute certain union "bad practices" aggressively under the Sherman Act. In that case, the losing side in a jurisdictional dispute, the Carpenters union at the

---

11 *Id.* at 487-89.

12 *Id.* at 495.

13 *Id.* at 503-4 (citations omitted).

14 Theodore J. St. Antoine, Connell: *Antitrust Law at the Expense of Labor Law,* 62 Va. L. Rev. 603, 606 (1976); *see also,* Archibald Cox, *Labor and the Antitrust Laws—A Preliminary Analysis,* 104 U. Pa. L. Rev. 252, 254-55, 262-64 (1955). For criticism of this view, see Michael H. Gottesman, *Union Summer: A Reawakened Interest in the Law of Labor?,* 1996 Sup. Ct. Rev. 285, 321-3 (1997).

15 312 U.S. 219 (1941).

Anheuser-Busch company, instigated a strike and a nationwide boycott of the company's beer in an effort to obtain the disputed work. The Court might have decided that the strike and boycott fell outside of the coverage of the Sherman Act on the authority of *Apex Hosiery,* as Justice Stone argued in his lonely concurrence.[16]

Instead, Justice Frankfurter wrote that whether or not a union's conduct constituted a violation of the Sherman Act could only be determined by "reading the Sherman Law and § 20 of the Clayton Act and the Norris-LaGuardia Act as a harmonizing text of outlawry of labor conduct."[17] Somewhat remarkably, Justice Frankfurter in looking at those statutes determined that the conduct protected from injunction by Section 20 of the Clayton Act taken together with, and thereby expanded by, Norris-LaGuardia was to be shielded from antitrust liability, also.[18] *Hutcheson* sets out the following condition: "So long as a union acts in its self-interest and does not combine with non-labor groups" peaceful conduct in the course of a labor dispute is not covered by the Sherman Act.[19]

Thus, the Court shifted the inquiry from the nature of the restraint to the character of the union's conduct: was it acting in its self-interest; had it combined with non-labor groups; was it peacefully engaged in a labor dispute. Because of its "interpretation" of the Sherman, Clayton, and Norris-LaGuardia Acts, the immunity that the Court created came to be called the "statutory exemption." As we will see below, this exemption is of limited use to unions because the ease with which the condition of unilateral conduct is lost.

In two cases, however, the Supreme Court has held that notwithstanding the unions' agreements with other parties, the statutory exemption survives. In *American Federation of Musicians v. Carroll,*[20] the musicians union's bylaws created a schedule of minimum prices that orchestra leaders could charge for one-time engagements ("club dates"), along with a minimum number of sidemen that they must employ. These prices reflected minimum

---

16 *Id.* at 237. Among commentators who argue that the Court's abandonment of the *Apex* approach was unfortunate are Professors Leslie and St. Antoine. *See* Leslie, *Principles, supra* note 1, at 1198-1200; St. Antoine, *supra* note 14, at 607.

17 *Hutcheson,* 312 U.S. at 231.

18 For evidence suggesting that Justice (then Professor) Frankfurter, the principal draftsman of the Norris-LaGuardia Act, had not always read the Act so expansively, see Archibald Cox, et al., Labor Law Cases and Materials 62-63 (and cited sources) (12th ed. 1996).

19 *Hutcheson,* 312 U.S. at 232.

20 391 U.S. 99 (1968).

prices for the sidemen and the leaders, along with a flat percentage to cover leader costs. Because the orchestra leaders were also union members, indeed they might be leaders for one club date and sidemen for the next, the union had the power to enforce its regulations. Yet, the orchestra leaders were also regarded as independent contractors and employers. The Court concluded that the price list escaped Sherman Act scrutiny because the orchestra leaders were "labor groups" and because the purpose of the price fixing was to protect the wage against erosion and to prevent price competition between the orchestra leaders and the sidemen.[21] In *H.A. Artists & Associates, Inc. v. Actors' Equity Association*,[22] the Court similarly analyzed the union's rule requiring its members to deal only with theatrical agents who had been licensed by the union.

§ 15.4 *Allen Bradley*: Union-Employer Collusion

Within a few years of *Hutcheson* the Court heard a case, *Allen Bradley Co. v. IBEW Local 3*,[23] in which it found that no exemption was available because of the collaboration between the union and employers in controlling the market for electrical contractors and electrical equipment manufacturers in New York City. Local 3 had aggressively campaigned to secure closed-shop agreements from most of the electrical contractors in New York City. It entered into agreements with these contractors obliging them to purchase electrical equipment only from manufacturers who had agreements with the Local. It similarly organized the manufacturers, and may have induced some of them with the promise of a sheltered market in New York City. It entered into an agreement with the manufacturers obliging them to sell equipment in New York City only to firms that employed Local 3 members. Through this arrangement, the union provided the contractors with control of the New York City market through its ability to exclude nonunion contractors. It provided the manufacturers a monopoly within the New York market by ensuring that its contractors would control that market and that they would only buy equipment from Local 3's manufacturers. The union was, of course, singularly well-situated to police this part of the agreement since its members knew whose equipment they installed. The manufacturers inflated the prices they charged within New York City, while the contractors

[21] *Id.* at 106. The Court said that whether the orchestra leaders were labor groups or not depended on whether there was "job or wage competition or some other economic interrelationship affecting legitimate union interests between the union members and the independent contractors."

[22] 451 U.S. 704 (1981).

[23] 325 U.S. 797 (1945).

rigged their construction bids. Presumably, the union, which had devised the scheme, took a share of the monopoly profits in the form of higher wages for its members.

Following the direction of *Hutcheson,* the Court said the union lost its immunity by combining with the contractors and manufacturers to control the market. Justice Black wrote, "we think Congress never intended that unions could, consistently with the Sherman Act, aid non-labor groups to create business monopolies and to control the marketing of goods and services."[24] The Court noted that the union could have acted alone to enforce a union boycott of goods and achieved the same result, at least from the union's vantage point, without violating the antitrust laws.[25]

While there was general agreement that the conduct described in *Allen Bradley* violated the antitrust laws, there was less agreement on the meaning and limits of that decision. A narrow reading would limit its holding to those instances where the union was involved in a sham agreement where the employers used the union to cover the employers' cartel behavior.[26] The Court's opinion in *Allen Bradley* suggested that the facts did not fit that theory, however.[27] Alternatively, Professor Meltzer has suggested that the Court's test is: did the combination "institute market restrictions essentially similar to those devised by businessmen even when they are free from union pressure," or, in other words, regardless of who initiated the combination, are "the restraints on the marketing of goods and services . . . of a kind that could have produced monopoly benefits for groups of employers . . . ."[28] This test is also troubling, however, because it leaves the permissible scope of multiemployer bargaining uncertain. Might, for instance, a group of employers, in the absence of a union, collude to set a ceiling on the price of one input, labor?[29] This would suggest that any

[24] *Id.* at 808.

[25] Professor Bernard Meltzer points out that Justice Black ignored the Supreme Court's antitrust jurisprudence relating to conscious parallelism in making this statement. Bernard D. Meltzer, *Labor Unions, Collective Bargaining, and the Antitrust Laws,* 32 U. Chi. L. Rev. 659, 672 & n.54 (1965).

[26] *See* Herbert N. Bernhardt, *The* Allen Bradley *Doctrine: An Accommodation of Conflicting Policies,* 110 U. Pa. L. Rev. 1094, 1099 (1962).

[27] *See* Meltzer, *supra* note 25, at 675-6 (criticizing this interpretation of *Allen Bradley*).

[28] *Id.* at 676.

[29] Would they run afoul of the antitrust laws if they did so? Because the Clayton Act in Section 6 states that labor is not a commodity, perhaps employers could do this. We return to this question below in the professional sports cases, *infra* § 15.7.

multiemployer bargaining, even over wages, would be vulnerable; but that hardly seems like a sensible reconciliation of labor and antitrust policy.

§ 15.5 *Pennington, Jewel Tea* and the Nonstatutory Exemption

Perhaps because of the incorporation into the Act of prohibitions on secondary boycotts in the 1947 Taft-Hartley amendments, thereby creating another avenue to contest union restraints on trade,[30] the Supreme Court did not decide another labor antitrust case for twenty years, when it split badly on two cases decided on the same day: *United Mine Workers v. Pennington,*[31] and *Local Union No. 189, Amalgamated Meat Cutters v. Jewel Tea Co.*[32] These two cases gave the Court another opportunity to consider the reach of the statutory exemption and the antitrust implications of multiemployer bargaining.

Pennington was the product of important changes in the coal mining industry. After World War II, coal operators faced the problem of oversupply of coal and the opportunity to mechanize portions of the production process by substituting machines for miners. Mechanization would, of course, mean significant job losses. In 1950, the United Mine Workers agreed with the large mine operators to stop resisting mechanization of the mines (as well as to various other concessions) in return for higher wages for the remaining miners, presumably to be funded by the productivity gains from mechanization, and changes favorable to the union and its members regarding the pension fund. The union and the operators also agreed that the union would "impose the terms of the 1950 agreement on all operators without regard to their ability to pay."[33] In the agreement and in subsequent amendments to it, they agreed to a variety of terms, including some that were not part of the case at the Supreme Court that were unquestionably intended to restrain competition in the product market and to injure the large operators' small competitors.[34]

---

[30] Recall how many of the antitrust cases arose in the context of secondary boycott activity, *Allen Bradley,* being just one of many.

[31] 381 U.S. 657 (1965).

[32] 381 U.S. 676 (1965).

[33] *Pennington,* 381 U.S. at 660.

[34] *Id.* at 660-61. They also agreed to lobby the Secretary of Labor to set a high minimum wage for employees of coal companies that sold coal to the Tennessee Valley Authority. This issue remained part of the case at the Supreme Court, which held that even if motivated by a desire to eliminate competition, such efforts to influence public officials were not subject to antitrust liability. *Pennington* is one of the two sources of the *Noerr-Pennington* doctrine to this effect.

The agreement to impose the same terms on the large operators' competitors can be understood in either of two ways. As the small operators would claim, it might have been pure predation—a scheme to crush the small operators by imposing costly terms on them, knowing that they would not have the capital to take advantage of the union's concessions regarding mechanization. There is obviously some evidence of predatory intent in some of the other anti-competitive terms to the agreement. Moreover, nothing else in the agreement seemed to address the problem of overproduction, and, indeed, to the extent that mechanization would lead to greater productivity, the problem would likely be exacerbated unless somebody's output—the smaller producers'—was diminished or eliminated. On the other hand, because of the large number of layoffs that were going to result from mechanization, the union and the large operators had reason to fear that a flood of unemployed miners would depress wages, giving a competitive advantage in the labor market to operators who were not parties to the agreement, and undermining the union wage. Thus, it some ways the UMW's behavior looked like an attempt, as Justice Stone had put it in *Apex,* to "eliminate . . . price competition based on differences in labor standards."

Pennington arose out of a claim brought by the trustees of the UMW's Welfare and Retirement Fund against the Phillips Brothers Coal Company for failure to make payments into the fund as required by bargaining agreements between Phillips and the UMW. The company filed a crossclaim against the union and the Fund trustees alleging the antitrust violations. At trial, Phillips won a judgment against the union, and the Sixth Circuit affirmed.

The Supreme Court split into three groups of three Justices each, as it also did in *Jewel Tea.* Justice White wrote the opinion of the Court in both cases, but in each he could only muster the support of two of his brethren for his analysis. Nevertheless, his opinion in each case came to be regarded as the prevailing view on the Court. In keeping with the doctrine developed in *Hutcheson* and *Allen Bradley,* Justice White looked first to see if the union had acted alone. Here, there was ample evidence that the union had acted in collaboration with the employers who were parties to the 1950 Wage Agreement and had agreed with them to impose the same wage demands on the small operators that it had negotiated with the large ones. Consequently, the union did not qualify for the statutory immunity. The *Hutcheson* and *Allen Bradley* decisions had stopped at that point, the immunity was won or lost on the basis of whether the union was acting unilaterally in its (or, actually, its members') interests.

Justice White indicated, however, that this was just a first step which only ended the inquiry if the union had been protected by the statutory immunity. There was, he contended, a need to harmonize more than the Sherman, Clayton, and Norris-LaGuardia Acts. In addition, the Court must harmonize antitrust law with national labor policy as expressed in the NLRA.[35] Here, Justice White pointed rather hazily to a second immunity.

Justice White acknowledged the appeal of the UMW's argument that the agreement related to wages which are at the core of mandatory subjects of bargaining, but he added that this alone did not mean that the agreement could flaunt the antitrust laws. The union, he wrote "forfeits its exemption from the antitrust laws when it is clearly shown that it has agreed with one set of employers to impose a certain wage scale on other bargaining units."[36] In an analysis that echoed the old distinction in *Coronado Coal* between "local" and more remote motives, he concluded that national labor policy failed to swing the balance in favor of antitrust immunity, because, he argued, the agreement offended principles of labor law, in addition to antitrust principles. Specifically, he adduced in the duty to bargain, a union duty not to "strait-jacket[]" itself in one negotiation regarding its bargaining with other employers. It was in the employers' interest for the union to agree to impose the same terms on their competitors, but not in the union's best interest or that of the competitors' employees.[37]

Jewel Tea also arose in the context of multiemployer bargaining. In 1957, seven locals of the Meat Cutters Union and 9,000 Chicago retailers of fresh meat (virtually all of the area retailers) negotiated a collective bargaining agreement that included the following provision: "Market operating hours shall be 9:00 a.m. to 6:00 p.m. Monday through Saturday, inclusive. No customer shall be served who comes into the market before or after the hours set forth above."[38] Prior contracts had included similar restrictions, and during the negotiations the unions resisted employer requests to relax this provision. Two retailers, Jewel Tea Company and National Tea Company, refused to sign the agreement, but under pressure of a strike vote Jewel Tea capitulated and signed an identical agreement. It then sued under the Sherman Act, claiming that the multiemployer group and the union had conspired to impose this provision. Jewel Tea argued that most of its stores were equipped to do self-service selling, that is, selling pre-packaged meat

[35] *Id.* at 665.

[36] *Id.*

[37] *Id.* at 665-69.

[38] *Jewel Tea,* 381 U.S. at 679-80.

during extended hours without requiring the butchers to do night work. The district court found no evidence of a conspiracy by the union and the other retailers to impose the marketing hour restrictions on Jewel Tea. It also found that, even in self-service markets, relaxation of the selling hours limitations would either require longer hours and night work, or would lead to butcher's work being assigned to nonbutchers. It ruled that the restrictions fell within the antitrust labor exemption.

The district court dismissed the suit, but the Court of Appeals reversed, without disturbing the court's factfinding. On certiorari the Supreme Court reversed the Seventh Circuit's ruling. The Court again divided into the same three groups as it did in *Pennington.*

Once again, Justice White concluded that the union was not exempt from antitrust scrutiny under the statutory immunity because of its bargaining agreement with Jewel Tea.[39] In other words, the Court had now clarified how limited the statutory immunity really was. It protected union pressure on an employer (so long as it met the *Hutcheson* requirements that it had not combined with non-labor groups and was acting in its best interest), but, remarkably, that immunity disappeared if the union realized its goals in a contract with the employer.

As in *Pennington,* Justice White next turned to the question of whether the interests of national labor policy outweigh those of the antitrust laws, thereby requiring that the union be immune from antitrust liability. The antitrust concerns were quite real. Unlike *Pennington,* where the contract provisions dealt with wages and eliminating wage competition, here the contract clause specifically addressed the product market by limiting the hours of service. It removed the opportunity for supermarkets like Jewel to differentiate themselves from their competitors by offering the convenience of purchasing meat after the work-day was over. Nevertheless, Justice White concluded that national labor policy interests outweighed the antitrust interests. The union and the district court had characterized the restrictions as directed toward mandatory subjects of bargaining: hours; work assignments; and whether butchers would have an increased workload at the end and beginning of each day to supply an adequate amount of prepackaged meat and to clean-up from the previous night. Justice White wrote that here the test of whether or not the union was entitled to this second immunity, was whether the hours of service clause was so "intimately related to wages, hours and working conditions that the unions' successful

[39] *Id.* at 688-89.

attempt to obtain that provision through bona fide, arm's-length bargaining in pursuit of their own labor union policies . . . falls within the protection of the national labor policy. . . ."[40]

Writing a single opinion dissenting in *Pennington* and concurring in the judgment in *Jewel Tea,* Justice Goldberg, joined by Justices Harlan and Stewart, argued that there was a clear congressional purpose to restrict judicial intervention in collective bargaining, which often happened under the umbrella of antitrust enforcement. Therefore, the Court should hold that "collective bargaining activity concerning mandatory subjects of bargaining under the Labor Act is not subject to the antitrust laws."[41] Justice Goldberg criticized Justice White for his apparent willingness to draw lines among different mandatory subjects of bargaining based on a "judicial determination of their importance to the worker," and to immunize some, but not all agreements dealing with mandatory subjects based on that assessment.[42] In that regard, he also criticized Justice White's implication that antitrust immunity would have been lost had the district court not found that night-marketing of meat in self-service markets would require either additional hours or additional work for the butchers or loss of jurisdiction over part of their work.[43] Here again, the Court echoes the distinction drawn in the older cases between local and nonlocal motive, and condemns any attempt by the union to address the consequences for its members in the smaller retail shops if the supermarkets sell meat in the evening.

Justice Douglas, who had essentially agreed with Justice White's approach in *Pennington* would have treated the multiemployer agreement setting the wage levels for their competitors as prima facie evidence of a conspiracy to restrain competition. Similarly, in *Jewel Tea* he would have treated the fact of the multiemployer agreement limiting selling hours, and the union's willingness to strike to impose that term on Jewel Tea as prima facie evidence of an antitrust violation.

---

[40] *Id.* at 689-90. Where a restriction on marketing hours is not the product of arm's-length bargaining, it is not immunized under the nonstatutory immunity. *See* Detroit Auto Dealers Ass'n v. FTC (Barnett Pontiac-Datsun), 955 F.2d 457 (6th Cir. 1992) (restrictions on automobile showroom hours).

[41] 381 U.S. at 710 (Goldberg, J., dissenting in part and concurring in part) (mem.) (footnote omitted).

[42] *Id.* at 727.

[43] *Id.* at 727-29. Justice White's analysis, he noted, reflected an overly circumscribed concept of mandatory subjects of bargaining.

Justice Goldberg's criticism of the balancing approach to determining antitrust immunity is quite telling.[44] As with any balancing test, Justice White's approach inserts an element of uncertainty into labor law. It does not accord the parties enough guidance to necessarily be able to predict whether their behavior will subject them to potential antitrust liability. Nor does it give adequate guidance to courts. Further, it projects the judiciary into the collective bargaining process to determine which union goals it will shelter and which ones it will leave vulnerable to antitrust liability. It turns the clock back to the pre-Norris-LaGuardia era.

One of the peculiarities of the *Pennington* decision is that while contract clauses like the 1950 Wage Agreement's in which the union promised to impose the same terms on the signing employer's competitors are subject to antitrust liability, the Board has held that most-favored-nations clauses are not, and are therefore mandatory subjects of bargaining.[45] Most-favored-nations clauses are contract provisions in which the union promises that should it enter into an agreement with one of the employer's competitors and grant the competitor more favorable terms, those terms will supplant the ones bargained-for in the collective bargaining agreement, giving the first employer the benefit of the second's bargain. While that provision does not literally bind the union to agree to no more favorable terms when negotiating with any other employer, there is reason to think that seldom will a union give a second employer more favorable terms, thereby triggering the most-favored-nation clause. Thus, while the contract looks like the union has bargained unit-by-unit and not tied its hands in future bargaining, the practical effect seems to be the same as in *Pennington.*

§ 15.6 *Connell Construction Company*: Further Light on the Nonstatutory Exemption?

Ten years after *Pennington* and *Jewel Tea,* the Court returned to the labor antitrust issue in *Connell Construction Co. v. Plumbers, Local 100.*[46] Connell was a general contractor in Dallas. It subcontracted out all of its plumbing and mechanical work and would take bids from both union and non-union subcontractors. Because it did none of its own plumbing and mechanical work, none of its employees were members of Local 100, although other construction unions did represent Connell employees.

---

44 For additional criticism of the Court's approach in these two cases see Leslie, *Principles, supra* note 1, at 1204-18; St. Antoine, *supra* note 14, at 608-16.

45 Dolly Madison Indus., 182 NLRB 1037 (1970).

46 421 U.S. 616 (1975).

Local 100 represented plumbing and mechanical workers in Dallas. It was a party to a multiemployer bargaining agreement with the Mechanical Contractors Association of Dallas. Included in that agreement was a most-favored-nations clause in which the union promised that should it agree to a more favorable contract term with any other employer, it would extend that term to all the Association members as well.

In November 1970, the union approached Connell, as it later did to other Dallas contractors, and asked it to agree to subcontract mechanical work only to employers that had a collective bargaining agreement with the union. The union was attempting to organize mechanical subcontractors from the "top-down," by creating pressure from the general contractors on the subcontractors to enter into agreements with the union. It simultaneously disclaimed any interest in representing Connell's employees. Upon Connell's refusal, the union stationed a picket at one of Connell's job sites, bringing work to a halt. Connell eventually signed the agreement under protest, but had, in the meantime, initiated a suit that ended up raising both state and federal antitrust claims in federal court.

The federal district court held that Connell's state antitrust claims were preempted. It further held that the subcontracting agreement was exempt from the federal antitrust laws because the construction industry proviso to Section 8(e) of the NLRA authorized such agreements.[47] The Fifth Circuit affirmed. On certiorari the Supreme Court agreed that the Texas antitrust claims were preempted, but it disagreed both with the district court's application of Section 8(e) and with its antitrust analysis.

Writing for the majority, Justice Powell concluded that the district court was mistaken and that the agreement was not permitted under Section 8(e). The union, therefore, could not raise Section 8(e) as a defense to the antitrust action. Turning to *Hutcheson*, he dismissed the statutory immunity because of the agreement between the union and Connell, a nonlabor entity. There is, however, a second immunity, he argued, a "nonstatutory exemption" which "has its source in the strong labor policy favoring the association of employees to eliminate competition over wages and working conditions."[48] Justice Powell derived this second immunity from the balancing

---

[47] Section 8(e) prohibits agreements between the union and the employer not to do business with any other person, but it also provides: "Provided, That nothing in this subsection shall apply to an agreement between a labor organization and an employer in the construction industry relating to the contracting or subcontracting of work to be done at the site of the construction, alteration, painting, or repair of a building, structure, or other work . . . ."

[48] *Connell*, 421 U.S. at 622.

of national labor policy and antitrust policy that he saw in *Pennington* and *Jewel Tea*.

Justice Powell then performed the requisite balancing in a manner that could only lead to the conclusion that the antitrust interests outweighed the labor policy interests. In doing this balancing, he considered "both actual and potential" anticompetitive effects of the agreement. He saw the agreement with Connell as an attempt to exclude nonunion contractors from the market "indiscriminately . . . even if their competitive advantages were not derived from substandard wages and working conditions but rather from more efficient operating methods."[49] Not surprisingly, he found that "[c]urtailment of competition based on efficiency" is not a goal of labor law, but that competition based on efficiency was valued by antitrust law.[50] This was not the only fault that Justice Powell found in the agreement, however. In a rather surprising turn in the analysis, he said that even though the multiemployer bargaining agreement between the union and the Mechanical Contractors Association had not been challenged in Connell's action, the Court would consider it to evaluate the effect of the union's agreement with Connell on the business market. Justice Powell noted that the multiemployer agreement contained a most-favored-nations clause, which guaranteed the members of the Association that the union would give no other subcontractor a competitive advantage over them. This, the Court noted, might extend to permissive subjects of bargaining. Coupled with the restrictions on subcontracting in the agreement with Connell, this would "eliminate competition on all subjects covered by the multiemployer agreement, even subjects unrelated to wages, hours, and working conditions."[51] As Professor St. Antoine points out, however, this problem was hypothetical; there was no evidence that there were any such provisions in the multiemployer agreement.[52]

This was not the only hypothetical mischief that Justice Powell saw in Local 100's conduct. As in *Allen Bradley,* the union could exploit the agreement with Connell, which prohibited subcontracting not merely to nonunion firms, but to firms that did not have a contract with Local 100, by exercising control over entry into the market. He wrote, "if the union thought the interests of its members would be served by having fewer subcontractors competing for the available work, it could refuse to sign

[49] *Id.* at 623.

[50] *Id.*

[51] *Id.* at 624.

[52] St. Antoine, *supra* note 14, at 618 n.68.

collective bargaining agreements with marginal firms . . . [or] it could exclude 'traveling' subcontractors."[53] Again, the harm to antitrust values is purely speculative. As the Court conceded, the record did not show that the union had any goal beyond organizing as many subcontractors as it could.

Justice Powell offered nothing as a counterweight on the labor policy side of the balance. Because Local 100 represented none of Connell's employees, "[t]he federal policy favoring collective bargaining . . . offer[ed] no shelter for the union's coercive action against Connell or its campaign to exclude nonunion firms from the subcontracting market."[54] Justice Powell offered no explanation why the countervailing labor policy interests did not include an interest in organizing employees (whether from the top down or otherwise). By adopting a stunted definition of federal labor policy, and by defining the market competition interests in highly speculative terms, Justice Powell insured that only one outcome was possible.

Finally, the union argued that even if its agreement was not authorized by the construction proviso to Section 8(e) and was not entitled to antitrust immunity, Section 303 of the LMRA provided the exclusive private remedy for violations of Section 8(e). Therefore, it argued, remedies under the antitrust laws, including treble damages should not be available. Writing in dissent, Justice Stewart interpreted the legislative history as supporting the union's position that the LMRA provided the exclusive remedy.[55] The majority disagreed with Justice Stewart's interpretation of the legislative history and concluded that even if it were true that Section 303 provided the exclusive private remedy for violations of Section 8(b)(4), which Congress had enacted in 1947, it did not for the separately adopted (in the 1959 Landrum-Griffin amendments) Section 8(e).[56]

In the aftermath of *Connell*, we are clearly left with two separate immunities. Confronted with a labor antitrust matter, one should look first to the statutory (*Hutcheson*) immunity. There, one should ask, is the union pursuing its self-interest in a labor dispute and has it refrained from combining with non-labor groups. Because all it takes is signing an agreement with the employer to combine with a non-labor group and lose the immunity, the statutory immunity will seldom be available.

---

[53] *Connell,* 421 U.S. at 624-25.

[54] *Id.* at 626.

[55] *Id.* at 638, 639-55 (Stewart, J., dissenting).

[56] *Id.* at 633-35.

Next, one should consider the nonstatutory immunity. This entails a balancing of the competing antitrust policies and labor policies, with all of the vagaries of a balancing approach. The cases suggest that where a predatory motive seems to underlie the restraints, as in *Pennington,* and the restraint has real product market effects a court will be hard-pressed to find the conduct immuned. It similarly appears that if the conduct violates labor law, as in *Connell* (or the Court's conception of it, as in *Pennington*), little if anything is left on the labor policy side of the scale to militate in favor of the nonstatutory immunity. Further, the mere fact that the restraints relate to mandatory subjects of bargaining will not be dispositive, although it militates in favor of finding the conduct immune. Nor will it be dispositive that the restraints are directed to the product market if they are "intimately related to wages, hours, and working conditions" and are the product of arm's-length bargaining by the union in pursuit of its own interests.

Finally, *Connell* suggests that in looking at product market restraints and evaluating the antitrust policy side of the balance, potential, as well as actual, market effects may be considered and that the labor policy side of the balance should be framed in terms of the policy of furthering collective bargaining.

§ 15.7 The Professional Sports Cases

In the typical labor market, combination has the consequence of driving labor costs up as unions eliminate wage competition. Professional sports, and some pockets of the entertainment industry, operate very differently. There, employers combine to counteract their tendency to compete for especially skilled athletes. They engage in multiemployer bargaining with the players' unions to set a master agreement that contains minimum terms above which individual players may negotiate. Through a variety of restraints on their inclination to bid against each other, employers organized as professional leagues dampen labor costs. These restraints have historically included various mechanisms to contain bidding for new players, such as football's and basketball's college draft, and to restrict the ability of established athletes from entertaining bids from many teams, through restrictions on free-agency.

Because of this anomaly, teams and leagues, rather than unions, appear in the role of defendant in these cases. These cases have provided occasion for the courts to consider to what extent the nonstatutory immunity protects employers and employers' groups, as well as unions. The Supreme Court confronted this question in *Brown v. Pro Football, Inc.*[57] In that case, after the collective bargaining agreement between the National Football League and its constituent clubs, and the National Football League Players' Association expired, the union and the league engaged in negotiations for a new contract. Under the old agreement, teams could negotiate individually with some number of players who had not made the regular player roster, but who practiced with the team and were available as substitutes for injured players. In the course of negotiations, the NFL proposed the creation of "developmental squads" of up to six players who did not make the team's regular roster, to be available, as in the past, as substitutes. Rather than negotiating on a player-by-player basis, the league proposed a salary of $1,000 a week for these players. When negotiations reached impasse, the league imposed its developmental squad plan.

A group of developmental squad players brought an antitrust action and obtained a judgment in their favor in the district court. The D.C. Circuit Court of Appeals reversed, holding that the nonstatutory immunity "waives antitrust liability for restraints on competition imposed through the collective bargaining process, so long as such restraints operate primarily in a labor market characterized by collective bargaining."[58] The Supreme Court affirmed, but on narrower grounds than those articulated by the D.C. Circuit. It held that because the employer's agreement to impose the "developmental squad" plan on the players after impasse grew immediately out of lawful multiemployer bargaining related to a mandatory subject of bargaining, and concerned only the parties to the bargaining relationship, the employers were entitled to the nonstatutory exemption.[59]

§ 15.8 Chapter Highlights

1. A labor union is entitled to immunity from the antitrust laws under the *Hutcheson,* or statutory, exemption if the "union acts in its self-interest and does not combine with non-labor groups" in the course of a labor dispute. (§ 15.3)

2. This statutory exemption is easily lost, however, and consequently, mostly protects a union's use of its economic weapons. If a union succeeds

[57] 518 U.S. 231 (1996). For discussions of *Brown,* see Michael H. Gottesman, *Union Summer: A Reawakened Interest in the Law of Labor?,* 1996 Sup. Ct. Rev. 285, 318-28 (1997); Douglas L. Leslie, *Essay:* Brown v. Pro Football, 82 Va. L. Rev. 629 (1996) (written prior to the Supreme Court decision in the case).

[58] Brown v. Pro Football, Inc., 50 F.3d 1041, 1056 (D.C. Cir. 1995).

[59] *Brown,* 518 U.S. at 249-50.

in persuading an employer to agree with its demands, the act of entering into an agreement with the employer (a non-labor group) extinguishes the exemption. (§§ 15.4-15.6)

3. A union may not act as either an enforcer or an instigator of an employer plan to restrain the product market to restrict entry by the employer's competitors, or to fix prices or to allocate customers. (§ 15.4)

4. In addition to the statutory exemption, the Court has recognized a non-statutory exemption which is a product of its efforts to harmonize the antitrust laws and federal labor law. Determining whether the exemption is available requires consideration of the antitrust policy interests and the labor policy interests at stake and a weighing and balancing of the two. (§§ 15.5-15.6)

CHAPTER 16
PROTECTING THE INDIVIDUAL IN A UNION AND NON-UNION ENVIRONMENT

§ 16.1 The Individual in Employment Generally

The legal protection afforded individuals varies depending upon whether the workplace is unionized or not unionized. In the public sector, non-union employees typically enjoy some protections under a range of federal, state, or local civil service laws.[1] However, in a private sector, non-union environment employment is governed by an at-will agreement.[2] The classical statement of the duration of an at-will employment relationship is that "an employer may discharge an employee for a good reason, a poor reason or no reason at all."[3]

Recent history has seen a drastic erosion of the employment-at-will doctrine through the incursion of statutory and common law developments. Statutes such as Title VII, the Age Discrimination in Employment Act, and the Americans With Disabilities Act shield individual employees from adverse employer actions based on specific motives. These motives are "poor reasons" that employers may not use to justify adverse action.

The Equal Employment Opportunity Commission enforces many of these protective statutes through its administrative apparatus or the courts.[4] Increasingly, arbitration agreements waive access to the courts in employment discrimination cases and mandate the use of an arbitration forum to adjudicate these claims.[5] In these cases typically the employee is responsible for her own representation.[6] The major shortcoming of many protective statutes is that they only isolate certain conduct, leaving employees vulnerable to a range of employer actions that are motivated by unfair rather than statutorily prohibited reasons.

On the other hand, in the unionized workplace, the collective bargaining agreement defines individual employee rights while the union enforces them. Since employees are concerned not only about specific kinds of discrimination but wages, hours and general terms and conditions of employment as well, collective agreements provide more comprehensive protection than do statutes. A "just cause" contractual provision protects employees not only from the kind of invidious discrimination outlawed by

---

[1] *See, e.g.*, 5 U.S.C. § 7513.

[2] *See* discussion in *supra* Chapter 3, § 3.2 regarding at-will employment.

[3] *See* Edward G. Budd Mfg. Co. v. NLRB, 138 F.2d 86 (3d Cir. 1943).

[4] *See* 42 U.S.C. § 2000e-5.

[5] *See* Gilmer v. Interstate/Johnson Lane Corp., 111 S. Ct. 1647 (1991).

[6] *See* Mei L. Bickner, Christine Ver Ploeg, and Charles Feigerbaum, *Developments In Employment Arbitration*, 52 Dispute Resolution Journal 8 (Jan. 1997).

Title VII, it also insulates employees from discipline and discharge for unfair reasons or using unfair procedures.

§ 16.2 The Individual in the Collective Setting

The distinction between individual rights and union enforcement under collective bargaining agreements gives rise to a tension that can undermine the comprehensive protection that employees expect. Because the union representative in the organized workplace negotiates with management exclusively on behalf of all employees in the bargaining unit,[7] individual rights may be sacrificed for collective reasons. Because of this potential tyranny of the majority,[8] individual employees have a right to fair representation under Section 301 of the Labor Management Relations Act and Section 8(b)(1)(A) of the National Labor Relation Act.

§ 16.3 The Duty of Fair Representation

This individual right to fair representation imposes a correlative union duty of fair representation (DFR), which was established by the Supreme Court in *Steele v. Louisville & Nashville R. Co.*[9] In that case, the Brotherhood of Locomotive Firemen and Engineers, an all-white union of locomotive firemen, excluded black firemen from membership in the union even though, as members of the unit, the union represented them as well as the white firemen. Without any notice to the black employees, the union in 1940 negotiated agreements with the 21 railroads designed to exclude all black employees from service as firemen and to reserve all of those positions for white men. An excluded black fireman sued on behalf of himself and others similarly situated. The Alabama Supreme Court held that the Railway Labor Act that granted exclusive status to the majority representative imposed no duty on the union to protect the rights of minorities from discrimination or unfair treatment. The United States Supreme Court rejected this holding, finding that the Railway Labor Act imposed upon the union "the duty to exercise fairly the power conferred upon it in [sic] behalf of all those for whom it acts, without hostile discrimination against them."[10] The Court ruled that the usual injunction and monetary remedies were appropriate for breach of the duty of fair representation.

---

[7] *See supra* Chapter 7, § 7.3 on exclusivity.

[8] *See* Emporium Capwell Co. v. Western Addition Community Organization, 420 U.S. 50 (1975).

[9] 323 U.S. 192 (1944).

[10] *Id.* at 203.

This DFR also applies to unions governed by the NLRA.[11] *J.I. Case,* the decision that had established the principles of exclusive representation and majority rule, created the necessity for the *Steele* decision later in the same term.[12] Under this scheme individuals and minority groups were no longer able to bargain on their own behalf. Their interests and bargaining power were subordinated to those of the majority. Individual advantages were contributed to the collective good. The DFR became one of the means of compensating individuals and minorities for this loss of bargaining power.

The DFR standard varies depending upon whether the union is engaged in contract-making or contract-administration and grievance processing. Negotiation establishes or changes the terms of an agreement that govern the rights and duties of employees and management. It precedes the making of a collective bargaining agreement and is directed toward writing and signing the document. Administration follows the making of the agreement and is directed toward enforcing and applying its terms, and grievance settlement occurs within the framework of the system of governing rules. Union business agents negotiate contracts, while shop stewards (often regular employees) administer agreements. Procedures for deciding upon appropriate demands, issue priority, and ratification are different from procedures for deciding what grievance to file and how to settle a grievance.[13] The agreement must accommodate competing demands of various interest groups within the union (multilateral) as well as competing interests of the employer and employees (bilateral) making for a complex package of provisions.[14] Since the union is acting like a legislature when it negotiates a contract, it needs a wide range of flexibility in this process. When a union administers the contract, it is acting more like an enforcement agency that must act within established rules, and it needs a much narrower range of flexibility when enforcing the terms of the agreement.

Ford v. Huffman,[15] which arose after World War II, is a negotiation case. In it Ford and the United Auto Workers agreed to give seniority credit for

[11] *See* Ford Motor Co. v. Huffman, 345 U.S. 330 (1953); NLRB v. Miranda Fuel Co., 140 NLRB 181 (1962).

[12] *See supra* Chapter 7, § 7.2.

[13] *See generally* Clyde W. Summers, *The Individual Employee's Rights Under The Collective Agreement: What Constitutes Fair Representation,* 126 U. Pa. L. Rev. 251 (1977).

[14] *See* Michael C. Harper and Ira Lupu, *Fair Representation as Equal Protection,* 98 Harv. L. Rev. 1212 (1985) (arguing that an equal protection model of "principled democracy" should define the limits of the union's DFR).

[15] *See supra* note 11.

military service to new employees who completed a probationary period of six months with the company. This system gave veterans who became new employees after the onset of this new policy an advantage over existing employees without military service. In a suit challenging the policy as discriminating on the basis of a factor not relevant to wages and working conditions and, therefore, violative of the DFR, the Court said that the union had the discretion to make reasonable distinctions among employees. The Court added that the union is entitled to a wide range of reasonableness in serving the unit and its discretion is limited only by the requirements of good faith and legitimate purpose.[16] In *Ford v. Huffman*, the seniority credit served the social policy of rewarding public service—a legitimate exercise of union discretion.

The Supreme Court in *Air Line Pilots Association, Int'l v. O'Neill*, recently reinforced the legislature analogy for unions negotiating agreements and held that agreements could be reviewed for rationality, the same as legislative action.[17] The Court found that the union had acted within the "wide range of reasonableness" even assuming that it accepted a settlement that on hindsight was worse than simply abandoning the strike.[18]

Vaca v. Sipes demonstrates the standard for measuring the union's DFR in grievance processing cases.[19] In that case, employee Benjamin Owens went on sick leave with high blood pressure. His condition improved and his family doctor approved his return to work. The company, Swift & Company's Kansas City Meat Packing Plant, did not permit Owens to return, based on the company doctor's diagnosis of the employee's blood pressure as too high. Owens was examined by another outside doctor, who approved his return to work; but when the company noticed Owens again at work, it terminated him. The union filed a grievance and processed it through the pre-arbitration steps. The company refused to settle, and the union paid for another medical examination by still another doctor to determine whether there was enough medical evidence of the employee's fitness for work to justify proceeding to arbitration. The union's medical report established that the employee was not medically fit to continue work, and the union voted to not take the employee's grievance to arbitration. Owens brought suit against the union in Missouri State Court and won a jury verdict which was affirmed by the Missouri Supreme Court.

---

[16] 345 U.S. 330, 338 (1953).

[17] 499 U.S. 65 (1991).

[18] *Id.* at 66.

[19] 386 U.S. 171 (1967).

The United States Supreme Court rejected the employee's claim in *Vaca* and announced the following rule:

> Before an employee can sue his employer under sec 301 of the Act for a simple breach of his employment contract, the employee must prove not only that he attempted to exhaust his contractual remedies, but that his attempt to exhaust them was frustrated by "arbitrary discriminatory, or . . . bad faith" conduct on the part of the union.[20]

The Court was concerned that employers and unions would not agree to grievance and arbitration procedures if unions could not settle grievances short of arbitration. If unions were forced to take all issues to arbitration, the increased burden to the arbitration procedure would prove too costly. If employees could routinely circumvent the contractual settlement procedure, employers' confidence in the union's authority would be undermined. Ultimately, the Court thought that grievants would not be harmed, if prearbitration settlements must be honest and in good faith.[21]

The Court in *Vaca* articulated a number of standards for measuring the DFR in processing grievances. The union's conduct should not be "arbitrary, discriminatory, or in bad faith."[22] The union may not "arbitrarily ignore a meritorious grievance or process it in a perfunctory fashion."[23] The union must act in good faith to settle grievances short of arbitration.[24] Similar complaints must be treated consistently, and the union must refrain from "patently wrongful conduct such as racial discrimination or personal hostility."[25]

The Court in *Vaca* also announced the following apportionment formula for liability and damages:

> The governing principle, then, is to apportion liability between the employer and the union according to the damage caused by the fault of each. Thus, damages attributable solely to the employer's breach of contract should not be charged to the union, but increases if any in those damages caused by the union's refusal to process the grievances should not be charged to the employer.[26]

---

[20] *Id.* at 203-204.

[21] *Id.* at 192.

[22] *Id.* at 190.

[23] *Id.* at 191.

[24] *Id.*

[25] *Id.* at 190.

[26] *Id.* at 197-198.

In *Bowen v. United States Postal Service*,[27] the Supreme Court relied upon this language to approve an apportionment scheme tolling damages to the employer as of a hypothetical arbitration date and charging the union from that date. Due to the inordinate delay in the Court's decision, the union bore the lion's share of the employee's damages.

Notwithstanding the theoretical liability of unions for breaches of the DFR, the standards in both the negotiating and contract administration contexts are sufficiently high as to make it difficult for individual employees to establish liability.[28] The Supreme Court has also solved the confusion regarding the statute of limitations to be applied in both the Section 301 suit against the employer and the DFR claim against the union by imposing a uniform limitations period of six months, borrowed from Section 10(b) of the NLRA.

§ 16.4 Section 7 of the National Labor Relations Act

One statutory limitation on the employment-at-will doctrine is the NLRA. Although Section 7 of the Act protects employees who seek union representation, its protection is broader. Section 7 also protects those employees who "engage in other concerted activity for the purpose of . . . other mutual aid or protection."[29]

The protection granted by Section 7 insulates employees from adverse employer actions such as discipline or discharge for exercising the rights conferred in that section."[30] An employer who takes an action against an employee based upon her exercise of Section 7 rights violates Section 8(a)(1) of the Act.[31]

---

[27] 459 U.S. 212 (1983).

[28] See, for example, Union News Co. v. Hildreth, 295 F.2d 658 (6th Cir. 1961), where the union, without incurring liability for a DFR breach, agreed to the conversion of a temporary layoff to a permanent one for dishonesty without any proof that the employee was involved in the misconduct.

[29] Section 7 reads as follows in part:

> Employees shall have the right to self-organization, to form, join, or assist labor organizations, to bargain collectively through representatives of their own choosing, and to engage in other concerted activities for the purpose of collective bargaining or other mutual aid or protection.

[30] NLRB v. Washington Aluminum Co., 370 U.S. 9 (1962) (discharge of employees who walked off their jobs to protest bitterly cold shop conditions violated Section 8(a)(1) of the Act).

[31] Section 8(a)(1) provides:

> (a) It shall be an unfair labor practice for an employer—

Section 7 protection is both broader than protection for union activity and limited by the existence of such activity. The provision protects both union activity and "other concerted activity for mutual aid and protection." Under this language, groups of employees who are not organized into a union are protected as long as their activity is for mutual aid and protection. In this sense, the protection is broader than union activity. However, if the employees in a given workplace select a union as their collective bargaining representative, they can no longer engage in certain concerted activity that would have been protected in the absence of a union.[32] The choice of union representation limits the scope of erstwhile protected concerted activity. Both organized and unorganized employees may lose Section 7 protection for certain conduct discussed below.

[A]—"Concerted" Activity

Though the language of Section 7 may appear to protect individual employees who are acting alone, the protection conferred by Section 7 protects only employees whose activity is concerted.[33] This is true even if the individual employee's activity is directed toward an issue that affects other employees. For example, if an employee in a non-union plant acting alone without consulting any fellow employees decides to complain to the plant manager about the poor lighting on the factory floor, the employer may fire the employee because of this complaint without violating Section 8(a)(1) of the Act. Though fellow employees may share the complainant's concern about the lighting, this activity is not concerted and, therefore, not protected under Section 7. On the other hand, if the employee had combined with one or more fellow employees in lodging the protest, the activity would have met the requirement of concert under Section 7.[34]

---

(1) to interfere with, restrain, coerce employees in the exercise of the rights guaranteed in section 7 . . . .

32 Examples of this point can be seen in J.I. Case Co. v. NLRB, 321 U.S. 332 (1944) (where the union's certification prevented the employer from contracting with individuals or small groups of employees rather than the union) and Emporium Capwell Co. v. Western Addition Community Organization, 420 U.S. 50 (1975) (where a small group of minority employees could not bypass the union and bargain with the employer about race discrimination issues).

33 *See generally,* Robert A. Gorman and Matthew W. Finkin, *The Individual and the Requirement of "Concert" Under the National Labor Relations Act,* 130 U. Pa. L. Rev. 286 (1981).

34 See generally *id.*, arguing against the distinction between one and two employees for a finding of "concert" where issues are of general concern to employees.

What sort of connection with one or more employees must an employee's activity have in order to be deemed concerted? A reasonable inference that other employees share the concern drawn solely from the subject matter of the activity is not enough.[35] However, if the activity of a lone employee is more concretely linked to the activity of one or more employees, the activity is concerted. For example, if the employee is acting as spokesperson for fellow employees or attempting to persuade fellow employees to raise the matter with the plant manager, the employee's activity is treated as an extension of the group or an indispensable first step to group activity.[36] The broadest reading of concerted activity so far condoned by the Supreme Court is contained in the "Interboro Doctrine," which holds that the assertion of a right grounded in a collective bargaining agreement is concerted activity."[37]

In *NLRB v. City Disposal Systems, Inc.*, the company discharged a truck driver when he refused to drive a truck that he reasonably and honestly believed to be unsafe. A collective bargaining agreement prohibited the employer from forcing an employee to drive an unsafe vehicle and insulated an employee who justifiably refused to do so. The Court held that the employee's invocation of a contractual right to refuse to drive a truck that he reasonably believed to be unsafe was concerted activity. The Court discerned a link between the individual refusal and the group process of collective bargaining that created the right, characterizing the rights assertion as a virtual reenactment of the group power that won the provision.[38]

---

[35] This broad notion of constructive concerted activity has been rejected by the Board. *See, e.g.*, Meyers Industries, Inc., 268 NLRB 493 (1984) (where the Board rejected the argument that an employee who refused to drive an unsafe truck and reported the employer to two state safety agencies was engaged in concerted activity because of the mutual interest of employees in the operation of safe equipment).

[36] *See* NLRB v. City Disposal Systems, Inc., 465 U.S. 822 (1984) (citing with approval cases where lone employees inducing group action or acting as group representatives are so linked to group activity as to be engaged in concerted activity).

[37] See *id.*, where an employee's assertion of a right to refuse to drive an unsafe truck was based on the following provision of a collective bargaining agreement: "the Employer shall not require employees to take out on the streets or highways any vehicle that is not in safe operating condition or equipped with safety appliances prescribed by law. It shall not be a violation of the Agreement where employees refuse to operate such equipment unless such refusal is unjustified."

[38] In adopting the "Interboro Doctrine," the *City Disposal Systems* majority noted the Board's distinguishing this doctrine from the broad constructive concerted activity argument in *Meyers*. Specifically embracing the *Meyers* decision, the dissent noted an explicit rejection of the broader doctrine.

[B]—Ends

In addition to the threshold requirement of concertedness, activity qualifying for Section 7 protection—also known as protected concerted activity—must be directed toward an appropriate purpose and carried out through appropriate means. As to purpose, Section 7 says that the activity must be directed toward "mutual aid and protection," a concept that can be more or less encompassing depending upon how broadly or narrowly interpreted.

In *Eastex, Inc. v. NLRB*,[39] the employer prevented employees from distributing a union newsletter with two paragraphs. One appealed to employees to write to state legislators and opposed incorporating a state's right-to-work law into the state's constitution, while the other noted the President's veto of a minimum wage increase and urged employees to register and vote to support candidates sympathetic to labor. The Supreme Court considered whether employee appeals were for mutual aid and protection under Section 7. The court broadly defined an appropriate purpose as one that bears immediately upon employee interest and found that the right-to-work clause related to union strength at the bargaining table and the minimum wage clause related to wage levels derived from collective bargaining.[40] While adopting this broad approach, the Court also acknowledged a limit under this definition—the "point [at which] the relationship becomes so attenuated that an activity cannot fairly be deemed to come within the 'mutual aid or protection' clause."[41] Though the scope of protected subject matter continues to be broad, a few cases have fallen outside its ambit. For example, in *Harrah's Lake Tahoe Resort Casino*,[42] the Board held that a baccarat dealer's distribution of a proposal for a leveraged buyout of the employer through the employee stock ownership plan to give the employees 50% ownership of the company did not advance the "employees' interests as employees but as entrepreneurs, owners and managers." Here, the Board acknowledged that the employee's plan related to the employees' interest in general but read the language in *Eastex* strictly to limit legitimate employee concerns under Section 7. In *NLRB v. Motorola, Inc.*,[43] employees opposed the company's implementation of a

[39] 437 U.S. 556 (1978).

[40] *Id.* at 569-570.

[41] *Id.* at 567-568.

[42] 307 NLRB 182 (1992).

[43] 991 F.2d 278 (5th Cir. 1993).

random drug testing policy and joined a civic organization that opposed such policies in general. The Fifth Circuit held that the relationship between employee efforts to solicit membership in the civic organization and employee interest in the company's drug testing policy was too attenuated to come within the "mutual aid and protection" language of Section 7.[44]

[C]—Means

Even when employee activity is concerted and properly directed to mutual aid and protection, it may be unprotected because of the way in which it is conducted. The leading case on this issue is *NLRB v. Local 1229, IBEW (Jefferson Standard Broadcasting Co.).*[45] In that case, nine technicians worked at a fledgling television station in Charlotte, North Carolina in 1949, and were represented by the International Brotherhood of Electrical Workers. The union and station had negotiated to impasse about the kind of arbitration provision to be contained in the new contract. After conventional picketing failed to generate sufficient pressure on the company at the bargaining table, the technicians commenced a campaign criticizing the quality of the station's programming. They passed out 5,000 handbills not only on the picket line, but in barber shops, restaurants and on buses stating that WBTV used stale piped-in programming rather than local programming such as sporting events offered by cities like New York, Boston, Philadelphia and Washington, because WBTV regarded Charlotte as a "second class city." The handbills were signed "WBTV TECHNICIANS." And, while it was conceded that the campaign was designed to bring pressure upon the company at the bargaining table, the handbills made no reference to the union, collective bargaining, or the labor dispute between the company and union. The company fired the technicians who participated in this campaign, and they filed a charge under Section 8(a)(1) of the Act. The Supreme Court held that this tactic breached the employees' duty of loyalty and was, therefore, not protected by Section 7.

Since the technicians in *Jefferson Standard* were engaged in concerted activity that was properly directed to a subject that bore immediately upon employee interests as employees, the employees' activity would have been

[44] *See* Local 174, UAW v. NLRB (Firestone Steel Prods. Co.), 645 F.2d 1151 (D.C. Cir. 1981) (where the Board, affirmed by the court, found that the union's leaflet on the day before an election urging employees to support the union's choice for Governor, Senator, and State Supreme Court Justices was a "political tract" and the employer's refusal to permit circulation was not a violation of Section 8(a)(1)).

[45] 346 U.S. 464 (1953).

protected if properly conducted. That case articulated the rule that employees could lose protection under Section 7 by engaging in concerted activity through improper means. *Jefferson Standard* did not create a framework for identifying improper means. Indeed, the Court's later decision in *NLRB v. Washington Aluminum Co.*,[46] created an issue regarding the extent to which conduct that would constitute cause for discharge in the absence of Section 7 is nonetheless protected by Section 7.[47] In *Washington Aluminum*,[48] the company fired seven non-union machinists who walked off the job to protest bitterly cold shop conditions. The Court rejected the argument, based on *Jefferson Standard*, that the employee walkout violated a plant rule forbidding employees from leaving work without the permission of the foreman and constituted cause for discharge. While acknowledging that Section 10(c) of the Act authorizes an employer to discharge employees for cause, the Court held that this authority does not extend to protected concerted activity under Section 7. While it is unclear after *Washington Aluminum* which means of engaging in concerted activity results in the loss of protection under Section 7, Professor Sharpe has proposed the following standard:

> Employees who engage in lawful concerted activity for a Section 7 purpose should not be deprived of protection unless the activity itself (the means) unreasonably threatens the long-term viability of the enterprise, labor-management relationship, or the employment relationship.[49]

§ 16.5 Chapter Highlights

1. The protection of individuals under national labor and employment policy varies widely depending upon whether one is part of a collective bargaining unit or not. Collective bargaining agreements offer a panoply of protections which depends upon the union for enforcement. (§§ 16.3 and 16.4)

2. The union's DFR gives it wide discretion in the treatment of its members, but draws the line at invidious or irrational distinctions. (§ 16.3)

---

[46] 370 U.S. 9 (1962).

[47] *See* Calvin William Sharpe, *"By Any Means Necessary"—Unprotected Conduct And Decisional Discretion Under The National Labor Relations Act*, 1999 Berkeley J. Emp. & Lab. L. (forthcoming). *See also* Elk Lumber, 91 NLRB 333 (1950).

[48] 370 U.S. 9 (1962).

[49] *See* Sharpe, *supra* note 47.

3. Though not widely appreciated, Section 7 of the NLRA affords protection to employees who act in concert, even when they are not represented by a union. (§ 16.4)

CHAPTER 17
NLRA REGULATION OF THE RELATIONSHIP BETWEEN THE INDIVIDUAL WORKER AND THE UNION

§ 17.1 Introduction

This section considers the ways in which the NLRA affects the relationship between the union and individual employees. It looks first at the sorts of agreements that a union may lawfully enter into with the employer that impose obligations of support on individual employees or that might tend to encourage union activity. It then turns to the question of union discipline of its members for violations of its rules.

This area involves a balancing, not always consciously, of collective rights against individual rights. Decisions that champion individual choice and voluntarism in the level or existence of one's union activity often do so at the expense of group strength and group goals, though clearly the NLRA was enacted with a vision of collective activity and collective strength. Decisions that champion the power of the group often sacrifice individual desires. The trend has been toward a greater solicitude for individual rights over collective ones.

§ 17.2 Membership and Union Security Agreements

[A]—Legal and Illegal Union Security Agreements

Union security agreements, provisions within collective bargaining agreements that require some level of participation in or support for a union as a condition of employment, come in a variety of forms, not all of them, lawful. In a closed-shop provision, the employer agrees to hire and retain union members exclusively. A provision of this sort gives a union considerable power over the employment relationship, since the union can both restrict access to jobs by limiting membership and can use its control over jobs either to enforce discipline or to punish disfavored members.

A union-shop provision differs from the closed shop by removing union membership as a precondition for employment. Instead, it allows a grace period, after which the employee must join the union in order to retain employment.

An agency-shop provision does not require conventional membership either as a precondition for employment or as a requirement after the passage of a grace period. It does, however, require that the employee pay for union services by paying an initiation fee and regular dues. The agency shop requires of those employees who opt not to become union "members," in the traditional sense of the word, a form of membership, "whittled down to its financial core."[1]

A maintenance of membership agreement imposes no obligations on employees who are not union members. It does require those employees who are members to remain members in good standing. Finally, a dues checkoff provision provides for payroll deduction of union dues, thereby sparing the union the work of collecting dues from its members.

Historically, unions sought a closed shop as a means to organize a particular workplace and to protect its position from defections or raiding unions. In the 19th and early 20th centuries, employees in many crafts had considerable control over the pace and the manner of their work, and unions enforced customary wage rates. In these crafts, compulsory union membership enabled the union to enforce customary or agreed upon work rules and rates against nonconforming members.[2] Union constitutions and bylaws provided for various fines and other penalties for such deviations, but they were only enforceable against union members.

Courts were typically far less enthusiastic about the closed shop than the unions were. In applying the lawful objectives/lawful means test in labor injunction cases, courts generally treated the closed shop as an unlawful objective.[3] The NLRA took a different approach, however. Section 8(3)[4] prohibited as an unfair labor practice employer discrimination in employment to encourage or discourage membership in a labor organization. Without more, Section 8(3) would have outlawed most union security devices. Recognizing this possibility, the framers of the Act included a proviso to Section 8(3) permitting the closed shop so long as the union had majority support and was not a company union. The proviso to Section 8(3) read:

> *Provided,* That nothing in this Act, or in any other statute of the United States, shall preclude an employer from making an agreement with a labor organization (not established, maintained, or assisted by any action defined in section 8 of this Act as an unfair labor practice) to require as a condition of employment membership therein if such labor organization is the representative of the employees as provided in section 9(a),

---

[1] NLRB v. General Motors Corp., 373 U.S. 734, 742 (1963).

[2] *See generally,* David Montgomery, Workers' Control in America: Studies in the History of Work, Technology and Labor Struggles 9-27 (1979).

[3] *See, e.g.,* Plant v. Woods, 176 Mass. 492 (1900).

[4] 29 U.S.C. § 158(3) (1994). This is the current Section 8(a)(3).

in the appropriate collective-bargaining unit covered by such agreement when made.

The NLRA's blessing of closed-shop agreements provoked much criticism of the evils of "compulsory unionism." When Congress returned to the question of labor relations in 1947, it used the Taft-Hartley Amendments to undo Section 8(3)'s green light for closed shops. Congress revised the proviso in the newly renumbered Section 8(a)(3) to prohibit the closed shop by providing a 30-day grace period for new hires to become union members before they would be subject to discharge for failing to be members of the union.[5] Under the revised proviso, union membership cannot be a prerequisite for hire, but a collective bargaining agreement can require that employees become members as soon as 30 days after hire.

Congress also added a second proviso limiting the circumstances under which an employer may discriminate against an employee because of her nonmembership or expulsion from a union. This second proviso stated:

> Provided further, That no employer shall justify any discrimination against an employee for non-membership in a labor organization (A) if he has reasonable grounds for believing that such membership was not available to the employee on the same terms and conditions generally applicable to other members, or (B) if he has reasonable grounds for believing that membership was denied or terminated for reasons other than the failure of the employee to tender the periodic dues and the initiation fees uniformly required as a condition of acquiring or retaining membership.[6]

In 1947, a number of unions still had whites-only provisions in their constitutions or otherwise discriminated on the basis of race. Also, union officers under closed-shop agreements were able to punish disfavored members by declaring that they were no longer members in good standing.

---

[5] Congress added the following language to the proviso after the phrase "as a condition of employment membership therein": "on or after the thirtieth day following the beginning of such employment or the effective date of such agreement, whichever is the later . . . ."

[6] Section 8(a)(3) as originally adopted in 1947 required that the union obtain authorization from the majority of the bargaining unit members before it entered into a union security agreement. Because that provision resulted in a large number of authorization elections, the vast majority of which resulted in authorization, in 1951 Congress shifted the burden onto unit members wishing to deauthorize the union and permitted unions to negotiate collective bargaining agreements containing lawful union security agreements without first obtaining authorization. Section 9(e) provides for such deauthorization elections.

The second proviso exempts employees who are victims of union discrimination from the operation of otherwise lawful union security provisions. It also limits the membership obligations that an employee must meet in order to be protected from discharge under a union security agreement. An employer may not, for instance, discharge pursuant to a union security agreement an employee who has been expelled from the union because of her dissidence on union affairs, her refusal to fulfill picket-line duty, or her unruliness at union meetings. All that the employee need do is tender her dues and initiation fee to ensure that she will not be discharged pursuant to the union security provision. In effect, this means that the most onerous lawful union security provision that a collective bargaining agreement may contain is an agency-shop provision, although agreements often speak in terms of the union-shop.[7]

In addition to the changes to Section 8(3), the Taft-Hartley Amendments added the present Section 8(b) which makes several union labor practices unlawful. Of particular relevance are Section 8(b)(1)(A) and Section 8(b)(2). Section 8(b)(1)(A) makes it an unfair labor practice for a labor organization to "restrain or coerce . . . employees in the exercise of the rights guaranteed under section 7."[8] The Taft-Hartley Congress had amended Section 7 to include among those rights the right to refrain from joining a union. Section 8(b)(2) makes it an unfair labor practice for a union:

> to cause or attempt to cause an employer to discriminate against an employee in violation of subsection (a)(3) or to discriminate against an employee with respect to whom membership in such organization has been denied or terminated on some ground other than his failure to tender the periodic dues and initiation fees uniformly required as a condition of acquiring or retaining membership.[9]

---

[7] NLRB v. Hershey Foods Corp., 513 F.2d 1083 (9th Cir. 1975). Initially, Section 8(a)(3) was understood to protect union-shop agreements. This assumption is evident in NLRB v. General Motors Corp., 373 U.S. 734 (1963), where the issue was whether it also protected agency-shop agreements, under which a unit employee need not become a member, but must tender periodic dues and an initiation fee. The Board had long taken the view that the proviso allowed an agency shop. *See* American Seating Co. 98 NLRB 800 (1952). The *General Motors* Court agreed with the Board's approach. Indeed, Justice White explained in that case that the only sort of "membership" that a union could require through a union-security agreement (even if on its face it appeared to be a union-shop agreement) was membership, "whittled down to its financial core." *General Motors Corp.*, 373 U.S. at 742.

[8] 29 U.S.C. § 158(b)(1) (1994).

[9] 29 U.S.C. § 158(b)(2) (1994).

Thus, it is an unfair labor practice for a union to make an employer, or attempt to make an employer, violate Section 8(a)(3).

[B]—State Right-to-Work Laws

Prior to Congress's enactment of the Taft-Hartley Amendments, a dozen states had enacted statutes or state constitutional provisions prohibiting all or certain union security agreements.[10] These "right-to-work" laws posed a potential question of federal preemption until Congress definitively resolved that question in the Taft-Hartley Amendments by eliminating the preemptive potential of federal labor law. Section 14(b), which Congress added in 1947 states: "Nothing in this Act shall be construed as authorizing the execution or application of agreements requiring membership in a labor organization as a condition of employment in any State or Territory in which such execution or application is prohibited by State or Territorial law."[11]

In *Retail Clerks Local 1625 v. Schermerhorn (Schermerhorn I)*,[12] the United States Supreme Court held that Section 14(b) empowered states to prohibit the agency shop, as well as the union shop. Currently, 21 states have right-to-work laws. These uniformly prohibit the union shop, and either explicitly outlaw the agency shop also, or have been interpreted to do so.

[C]—Dissenter's Rights: The *Beck* Decision

Must a bargaining unit member under a valid agency-shop agreement financially support all of a union's activities, notwithstanding strong personal objections? Section 19 of the Act provides that religiously-motivated conscientious objectors to unions may divert the funds they would have paid as fees and dues to certain charitable organizations.[13] More important, the Supreme Court in *Communication Workers of America v. Beck*,[14] held that union dissenters were only obliged to pay for their share of a union's collective bargaining activities.

Beck came in a line of cases mostly involving the right of dissenters under the Railway Labor Act.[15] Railroad and airline union security agreements

---

[10] In a series of cases decided after the Taft-Hartley Amendments, the Supreme Court rejected constitutional challenges to right-to-work laws in Nebraska, North Carolina, and Arizona. Lincoln Fed. Union 19129 v. Northwestern Iron & Metal Co., 335 U.S. 525 (1949); AF of L v. American Sash & Door Co., 335 U.S. 538 (1949).

[11] 29 U.S.C. § 164(b) (1994).

[12] 373 U.S. 746 (1963).

[13] 29 U.S.C. § 169 (1994).

[14] 487 U.S. 735 (1988).

[15] 45 U.S.C. §§ 151-88 (1994).

are governed by the RLA's Section 2 Eleventh, whose language is virtually identical to the relevant parts of Section 8(a)(3). The status of union security agreements under the two statutes has historically been quite different, however. Prior to 1951, when Congress amended Section 2 Eleventh with language largely lifted from the NLRA, the RLA prohibited union security agreements. The 1951 changes were apparently an attempt to bring the RLA's treatment of union security in line with the treatment under the NLRA as amended in 1947.

In a 1961 decision, *International Association of Machinists v. Street*,[16] the Court heard a First Amendment challenge to Section 2 Eleventh by employees who complained that they were compelled to pay fees and dues, a substantial portion of which funded political campaigns for candidates that they did not support and the propagation of political ideas that they did not hold. The Court avoided the Constitutional issue by construing Section 2 Eleventh to allow compelled payments to support collective bargaining, but not a union's political program. Based on its reading of the legislative history, the Court majority concluded that the purpose of Section 2 Eleventh was to resolve the free-rider problem of employees enjoying the benefits of collective bargaining and grievance adjustment without having to bear the costs. Thus, nonmember employees could be compelled to share the cost of collective bargaining and contract administration, but not other union expenses unrelated to those costs.[17] Two years later, the Court reiterated its holding in *Street*, and described the union expenses that could fairly be charged to nonmembers along with members as those "germane to collective bargaining."[18] In 1984, the Court returned to the meaning of Section 2 Eleventh in *Ellis v. Brotherhood of Railway, Airline and Steamship Clerks*,[19] further elaborating what kinds of expenditures were and were not taxable to dissenters. There, the Court stated that:

> [T]he test must be whether the challenged expenditures are necessarily or reasonably incurred for the purpose of performing the duties of an exclusive representative of the employees in dealing with the employer on labor-management issues. Under this standard, objecting employees may be compelled to pay their fair share of not only the direct costs of negotiating and administering a collective-bargaining contract and of settling grievances and disputes, but also the expenses of activities or

[16] 367 U.S. 740 (1961).

[17] *Id.* at 760-64.

[18] Railway Clerks v. Allen, 373 U.S. 113, 121 (1963).

[19] 466 U.S. 435 (1984).

> undertakings normally or reasonably employed to implement or effectuate the duties of the union as exclusive representative of the employees in the bargaining unit.[20]

Applying this test, the Court concluded that the costs of attending the union's national convention were properly charged to dissidents and that the costs of organizing employees outside of the collective bargaining unit was not.[21]

The Supreme Court finally encountered the question in the context of the NLRA in *Beck,* in which a group of dissidents argued that the use of their agency fees for the union's political purposes violated both Section 8(a)(3) and the Constitution. Plaintiffs won partial summary judgment, on constitutional grounds, in the district court, and the court was affirmed on statutory grounds by a divided panel of the Fourth Circuit and again by a divided Fourth Circuit sitting en banc. Once again, the Supreme Court avoided the Constitutional issue by interpreting the statute to permit extraction of agency fees from dissidents only for purposes related to collective bargaining. The Court's decision is troubling for a number of reasons. First, it resembles pre-Wagner Act decisions that evaluated the lawfulness of union conduct on the basis of whether or not its purpose was sufficiently "local."[22] More important, the Court ignored both the language of Section 8(a)(3) which speaks of assessing "uniform" dues and the legislative history of the 1947 Amendments, in favor of a construction of Congressional purpose which limits the purpose of Section 8(a)(3) to resolution of the free-rider problem, and which is derived not from the debates or reports, but from the Court's prior, criticized statement of the purpose of Section 2 Eleventh, which was enacted four years later.[23]

---

[20] *Id.* at 448.

[21] *Id.* at 448-52.

[22] A notable instance of this approach was the *Coronado Coal* cases. UMW v. Coronado Coal Co. (Coronado I), 259 U.S. 344 (1922); UMW v. Coronado Coal Co. (Coronado II), 268 U.S. 295 (1925). For a discussion of this approach and these cases, see *supra* § 15.2.

[23] For an illuminating discussion of the legislative history, one must turn to the dissents and the academic commentators. *See Beck,* 487 U.S. 735, 763, 770-80 (Blackmun, J., dissenting); Beck v. Communication Workers of America, 776 F.2d 1187, 1214, 1215-21 (Winter, C.J., dissenting); Kenneth G. Dau-Schmidt, *Union Security Agreements under the National Labor Relations Act: The Statute, the Constitution, and the Court's Opinion in* Beck, 27 Harv. J. on Legis. 51 (1990).

[D]—Union Hiring Halls

In certain industries where jobs are generally of short duration and are mobile rather than stationary and centralized, the union hiring hall serves an important role in bringing together employers and employees who would otherwise have trouble finding each other. The hiring hall is a particularly important institution in the construction industry, as well as in shipping where it supplies both seagoing crews and longshoremen to load and unload cargo. It also plays a lesser, but still important role, in the trucking industry. By one estimate, in 1979, 2,779 union locals in the United States, representing a total membership of over 2 million, operated hiring halls.[24]

The power over employment that the hiring hall gives to the hiring hall dispatcher and to other local officers naturally raises the specter of potential abuse either to reward or assist favorites or to punish political rivals. More systematically, a union local might use its hiring hall to create the equivalent of a closed shop. Misuse of the hiring hall's control over job referral might violate either or both Section 8(b)(1)(A)'s prohibition of union interference with Section 7 rights or Section 8(b)(2)'s prohibition of union conduct, causing an employer to discriminate in violation of Section 8(a)(3).[25]

This power led the Board in the 1950s to regard the hiring hall as an especially dangerous institution. In *Mountain Pacific Chapter of the Associated General Contractors, Inc.*,[26] the Board held that an exclusive hiring hall agreement, one where the employer or employers agree to hire only employees referred by the hiring hall, inherently and unlawfully encouraged union membership in violation of Section 8(b)(2), unless the agreement provides: 1) that the selection of applicants will be nondiscriminatory and the hall will not favor union members; 2) that the employer retains the right to reject any applicant; and 3) that the hiring hall post prominently the procedures governing the hall.[27]

The Supreme Court soon rejected this *per se* approach toward assessing the behavior of hiring halls. In *Local 357, International Brotherhood of*

---

[24] Barbara J. Fick, *Political Abuse of Hiring Halls: Comparative Treatment Under the NLRA and the LMRDA*, 9 Indus. Rel. L.J. 339, 343 (1987).

[25] If the hiring hall does not have an exclusive agreement with the employer, generally Section 8(b)(2) is not considered applicable since the employee had another avenue toward employment and only Section 8(b)(1)(A) remains. If the hiring hall has an exclusive agreement, both provisions may be applicable. *Id.* at 353-54.

[26] 119 NLRB 883 (1957).

[27] *Id.* at 894-97.

Teamsters v. NLRB,[28] the Court acknowledged that the hiring hall might by its very existence encourage union membership, but so, the Court noted, might the union by its existence and successes. The Court held that at least where the hiring hall agreement contains an antidiscrimination provision, the Board may not infer a violation, but must find actual discrimination before finding that the union has committed an unfair labor practice.[29]

Notwithstanding *Teamsters Local 357*, Board practice is to place the burden on the union to show that the hiring hall is not discriminating in its referrals. It will permit a variety of bases for preferences in referrals including seniority and proficiency testing. The Board permits hiring halls to charge non-union members a reasonable referral fee to offset their portion of the hall's operating costs.

[E]—Bargaining Agreement Terms that Favor Union Officers

There are a number of ways in which unions might seek different treatment of stewards and other local officials. For instance, they will often bargain for the employer's agreement to allow the steward to conduct union business, such as attending to grievances, on company time. Because it is important that those union officers who deal with the day-to-day administration of the collective bargaining agreement be present in the workplace and because of the need for continuity in that role, it is common for unions to seek superseniority provisions for union officials (there are obviously also less benign reasons why they might seek such provisions). Such agreements, on their face, would appear to violate Sections 8(a)(3) and 8(b)(2) of the Act by discriminating regarding terms of employment to encourage union participation. In *Dairylea Cooperative*,[30] the NLRB permitted such grants of superseniority for stewards, but it limited their permissible reach to seniority for purpose of layoff and recall. The premise was to help ensure stability in the administration of the bargaining agreement and in the relationship between the union and the employer by making it less likely that a steward would face layoff.[31] Where superseniority

---

28 365 U.S. 667 (1961).

29 *Id.* at 676-77.

30 219 NLRB 656 (1975), *enforced sub nom.* NLRB v. Milk Drivers & Dairy Employees, Local 338, 531 F.2d 1162 (2d Cir. 1976).

31 The Board noted that superseniority "furthers the effective administration of bargaining agreements on the plant level by encouraging the continued presence of the steward on the job. It thereby not only serves a legitimate statutory purpose but also redounds . . . to the benefit of all unit employees." *Id.* at 658.

applied to such benefits as priority in route and shift selection or vacation time, its grant to union officers did nothing to promote stability in the bargaining relationship or to ensure that stewards were available in the workplace for grievance adjustment, but instead rewarded union officers for their level of involvement in the union by discriminating among employees regarding work benefits. The Board, therefore, indicated that while superseniority clauses limited to layoff and recall are presumptively lawful, those that on their face extend beyond layoff and recall are presumptively unlawful, subject to a showing by the party urging their legality that they serve a legitimate statutory purpose.[32]

In *Gulton Electro-Voice, Inc.*,[33] the Board considered which union officials a lawful grant of superseniority could include. There, it concluded that a grant of superseniority to union officials who were not involved in the adjustment of grievances or other duties that require their presence on the shop floor (in that case, the recording secretary and the financial secretary-treasurer) violated Section 8(b)(2).

§ 17.3 NLRA Regulation of Union Discipline

As noted above, Section 8(b)(1)(A) makes it an unfair labor practice for a union to restrain or coerce employees in the exercise of their Section 7 rights. Among those Section 7 rights is the right to refrain from concerted activity. This means that the Act protects an employee's right not to strike as much as her right to strike. Section 8(b)(1)(A)'s prohibition is subject to a proviso, however, stating "[t]hat this paragraph shall not impair the right of a labor organization to prescribe its own rules with respect to the acquisition or retention of membership therein."[34] The cases discussed in this section revolve around the question of when may a union apply its own rules to members notwithstanding their tendency to burden or interfere with the employees' exercise of Section 7 rights.

An important starting point in this area is *NLRB v. Allis-Chalmers Manufacturing Co.*,[35] which involved union discipline of members who had

---

32 *Id.* at 658-59. The Board has similarly found that shift-protection clauses for shift stewards are analogously presumptively lawful. *See, e.g.*, Auto Workers Local 561 (Scovill, Inc.), 266 NLRB 952, 953 n.9 (1983).

33 266 NLRB 406 (1983), *enforced sub nom.* Electrical Workers IUE Local 900 v. NLRB, 727 F.2d 1184 (D.C. Cir. 1984).

34 29 U.S.C. § 158(b)(1) (1994).

35 388 U.S. 175 (1967).

crossed a union picket line to return to work during an authorized strike. Two union locals involved in the strike imposed fines on the strikebreakers, and when some employees refused to pay, one local brought suit in state court for their collection. Allis-Chalmers filed an unfair labor practice charge, but the Board held that the imposition of the fines came within the proviso. A panel of the Seventh Circuit agreed, but, sitting en banc, the Court withdrew the panel decision and ruled that the locals had violated Section 8(b)(1)(A).

A divided Supreme Court rejected the Seventh Circuit's analysis and reversed the judgment. At least where fines were not "unreasonably large," the majority found no inconsistency between a union's imposition of fines on strikebreaking members or enforcement of those fines in state courts and Section 8(b)(1)(A).[36]

The majority emphasized the collective rights of union members. Justice Brennan reasoned that a core premise of national labor policy was that the selection of a union as their representative by the majority of employees "extinguishes the individual employee's power to order his own relations with his employer and creates a power vested in the chosen representative to act in the interests of all employees."[37] To fulfill this role, unions depend on the power to strike and to discipline members who break ranks during a strike. An examination of the legislative history of the Taft-Hartley Amendments, Justice Brennan argued, bolstered the view that Congress did not intend the 1947 amendments to interfere with internal union affairs. Nor could the majority imagine that when Congress did explicitly regulate aspects of internal union affairs in the Landrum-Griffin Amendments in 1959, it had "preceded the . . . amendments with an even more pervasive regulation of the internal affairs of unions."[38]

The majority also rejected the argument that the proviso permitted the union to expel, but not fine, strikebreaking members. It noted that where union membership is valuable a fine is a lesser disciplinary measure, and surely if a union can take the more draconian step of expulsion from membership it can also impose gentler discipline. Where the union is weak and membership has less value, the relative burdens of expulsion and a fine

---

[36] The Court reserved the question of whether some fines might be so unreasonable as to be coercive. It returned to that question in NLRB v. Boeing Co., 412 U.S. 67 (1973), where it decided that the Board had no authority to determine whether the amount assessed was reasonable.

[37] *Allis-Chalmers,* 388 U.S. at 180.

[38] *Id.* at 183.

might be quite different from the instance where expulsion represents a significant loss. Yet, the Court noted, "it is just such weak unions for which the power to execute union decisions taken for the benefit of all employees is most critical to effective discharge of its statutory function."[39]

In a series of subsequent cases, the Supreme Court refined the picture of permissible discipline within the proviso to Section 8(b)(1)(A). The occasion for discipline in *NLRB v. Industrial Union of Marine Workers,*[40] the Court's next encounter with the proviso, was a union member's failure to exhaust internal union remedies in a dispute with his local president before filing an unfair labor practice charge against the union. In response to this evasion of the union's remedial scheme, the union expelled the union member, who then filed an unfair labor practice charge challenging the expulsion. The Court contrasted the grounds for discipline in *Allis-Chalmers,* strikebreaking where a legitimate union interest of solidarity was implicated, with the union's exhaustion requirement which did not forward similarly strong union interests. Moreover, it identified a strong countervailing public policy consideration: uninhibited access to the NLRB, which it concluded outweighed the union's interest in enforcing its internal dispute resolution procedures.[41] Consistent with *Marine Workers,* a union may not discipline a member for filing unfair labor practice charges or testifying before the Board.[42] The Board has treated discipline for filing decertification petitions, or otherwise challenging a union's majority status, somewhat differently. Although access to Board proceedings are at issue in these cases also, the Board has recognized that a union has a legitimate interest in self-defense that justifies expulsion, if not imposition of fines, in such cases.[43]

One year after *Marine Workers,* the Supreme Court more fully articulated a standard for determining whether union discipline violates Section 8(b)(1)(A) or falls within the protection of the proviso. *Scofield v. NLRB*[44]

[39] *Id.* at 184.

[40] 391 U.S. 418 (1968).

[41] *Id.* at 423-24.

[42] *See, e.g.,* Auto Workers Local 2017 (Federal Mogul Corp.), 283 NLRB 799 (1987) (violation to reprimand members for filing unfair labor practice charge); Automotive Salesmen's Ass'n (Spitler-Demmer, Inc.), 184 NLRB 608 (1970) (fine imposed after member testified at unfair labor practice hearing).

[43] *See* Teamsters Local 165 (Goodyear Tire & Rubber Co.), 211 NLRB 707 (1974); International Molders Local 125 (Blackhawk Tanning Co.), 178 NLRB 208 (1969), *enforced,* 442 F.2d 92 (1971).

[44] 394 U.S. 423 (1969).

involved a longstanding union rule intended to protect piece-rate workers at the Wisconsin Motor Corporation from either speed-ups or an erosion of the piece-rate if workers were encouraged to work at maximum speed. The rule set a ceiling on members' daily wages. On those days when a member's piece-rate earnings exceeded the ceiling, the member would bank the excess for days when his earnings fell short of the ceiling. When the union determined that some members had violated the rule, it imposed fines and a year's suspension of union membership on the offending members. When the members refused to pay, the union brought a contract action in the state court to enforce its rule.

The Supreme Court set out a four-part test to determine whether enforcement of union discipline violates Section 8(b)(1)(A). Under the test stated in *Scofield,* a union may enforce a rule if it: 1) is "properly adopted"; 2) "reflects a legitimate union interest"; 3) "impairs no policy Congress has imbedded in the labor laws"; and 4) "is reasonably enforced against union members who are free to leave the union and escape the rule."[45] Applying this test to the instant case, the Court determined that the union had not committed an unfair labor practice.

Applying the *Scofield* test, the Board and the Circuit Courts have found that union discipline imposed for such things as a refusal to strike in violation of a no-strike clause in the collective bargaining agreement,[46] and a refusal to honor a picket line that violated Section 8(b)(4)'s prohibition of secondary boycotts[47] or one that violated Section 8(b)(7)'s prohibition of certain recognitional picketing[48] all violated Section 8(b)(1)(A).

Despite hints in *Allis-Chalmers, Marine Workers,* and *Scofield* that the Court would only allow a union to impose "reasonable" fines, when the Supreme Court eventually confronted the issue of the reasonableness of a union's fines in *NLRB v. Boeing Co.,*[49] the Court concluded that the NLRB properly ruled that Section 8(b)(1)(A) does not empower it to evaluate the reasonableness or unreasonableness of union fines. As the Court noted, its ruling did not leave unions free to impose any fine whatsoever, without

---

[45] *Id.* at 430.

[46] Marble Polishers Local 24 (Bemco Maintenance Corp.), 305 NLRB 943 (1991), *enforced,* 969 F.2d 1043 (2d Cir. 1992) (mem.); Glaziers Local 1162 (Tusco Glass, Inc.), 177 NLRB 393 (1969).

[47] Longshoremen's Local 30, 223 NLRB 1257, *enforced,* 549 F.2d 698 (9th Cir. 1977).

[48] Retail Clerks Local 1179, 211 NLRB 84 (1974), *enforced,* 526 F.2d 142 (9th Cir. 1975).

[49] 412 U.S. 67, 74-8 (1973).

regard to size and commensurableness with the occasion for discipline. The Court pointed out that state courts, called upon to enforce union fines as a matter of state contract law, may, consistent with contract principles and the law of voluntary associations, adjudicate the issue. And, as it further noted, in practice, state courts have not been shy about exercising this authority.[50]

As Professor David Abraham has noted, *Allis-Chalmers* contained an "Achilles heel" for unions insofar as it applied only to current union members.[51] Left unaddressed by *Allis-Chalmers* were the circumstances under which a union member might relinquish membership in order to avoid discipline for strikebreaking.

In *NLRB v. Granite State Joint Board, Textile Workers Union Local 1209*,[52] the Court encountered a case where the disciplined employees resigned from the union after having had participated in two votes authorizing the strike (and fines for strikebreaking members), but before crossing the picket line to return to work. Writing for the Court, Justice Douglas reasoned that because neither the union's constitution nor bylaws limited the right of members to resign, members had an unlimited right to resign, even mid-strike, and imposition of fines violated Section 8(b)(1)(A). The following year, in *Booster Lodge 405, Machinists v. NLRB*,[53] the Court held that a union constitution in prohibiting members from abandoning any strike authorized by the membership had not limited its members resignation rights and had not bound its members in any way regarding post-resignation behavior.

Finally, in *Pattern Makers' League of North America v. NLRB*,[54] the Court heard a case involving an explicit and unambiguous union constitutional provision that prohibited resignation during a strike or lockout or when either was imminent. The Board had found that locals of the Pattern Makers' League violated Section 8(b)(1)(A) when they refused to accept

50 *Id.* at 74.

51 David Abraham, *Individual Autonomy and Collective Empowerment in Labor Law: Union Membership Resignation and Strikebreaking in the New Economy,* 63 N.Y.U. L. Rev. 1268, 1308 (1988). In addition to Abraham's powerful critique of *Pattern Makers' League v. NLRB* and of the tendency to favor individual autonomy over solidarity and collective power in recent labor law decisions, see also Note, *Section 8(b)(1)(A) from* Allis-Chalmers *to* Pattern Makers' League*: A Case Study in Judicial Legislation,* 74 Cal. L. Rev. 1409 (1986).

52 409 U.S. 213 (1972).

53 412 U.S. 84 (1973).

54 473 U.S. 95 (1985).

members' resignations and imposed sanctions on those members for returning to work during a strike.

In an opinion replete with references to the deference due to the Board, the Court in a five to four decision held that the Board's interpretation of the statute was reasonable.[55] The majority rejected the union's arguments that both the express language of the proviso and the legislative history of the Act show that Congress did not intend to interfere with union rules restricting resignation of membership, and that the question should be governed by state law as are similar questions regarding other voluntary associations. It also dismissed Justice Blackmun's arguments made in dissent that the Board's rule would impair the right to strike and that it devalues the resigning members' promises, voluntarily entered into and relied upon by striking members, not to break ranks. Instead, the Court invoked notions of individual autonomy and voluntary unionism in upholding the Board's decision.

§ 17.4 Chapter Highlights

1. Prior to 1947, the NLRA permitted unions and employers to negotiate closed-shop agreements. The Taft-Hartley Amendments prohibited the closed shop by adding to Section 8(3), which became Section 8(a)(3), language that created a grace period of at least 30 days before a new employee can be required to become a union member under a lawful union security agreement. (§ 17.2[A])

2. A proviso that Congress added to Section 8(a)(3) in the 1947 amendments limits those instances where an employer may discriminate against an employee for nonmembership in a union to those instances where nonmembership was the consequence of failure to tender an initiation fee and periodic dues uniformly required of members and membership was available to the employee on the same terms as it is generally available to other members. While it is commonly said that the Act permits a union shop, the proviso limits the obligations of membership to "its financial core," thereby making an agency shop, where employees need not become members but must pay dues and fees in support of the union's collective bargaining activity, the strongest form of union security agreement permitted under the Act. (§ 17.2[A])

3. The Taft-Hartley Amendments also added Section 8(b)(2), which prohibits union efforts to cause an employer to discriminate on the basis

---

[55] *Id.* at 100.

of union membership except as permitted in Section 8(a)(3), and Section 14(b) which insulates state right-to-work laws from the preemptive effects of the NLRA. (§§ 17.2[A] and [B])

4. Under the *Beck* decision, the Supreme Court extended to unions covered under the NLRA its doctrine regarding dissenter rights developed under the Railway Labor Act. Consequently, even under a valid agency-shop agreement, a nonmember can only be compelled to pay that portion of her dues that pays for expenditures that are germane to collective bargaining and contract administration. (§ 17.2[C])

5. Although a union hiring hall may enhance the reputation of a union, thereby encouraging membership, and although a hiring hall gives a union considerable control over employment and the opportunity for abuse, hiring halls that operate under an exclusive agreement with employers are not *per se* violative of either Section 8(b)(1)(A) or Section 8(b)(2). Unions violate one or both sections, however, if they operate their hiring halls discriminatorily. (§ 17.2[D])

6. A union may discipline member strikebreakers by expelling them from the union, or by imposing fines on them, but a union may not restrict the power of its members to avoid such discipline by giving up their membership, even during a strike that the resigning members voted to authorize. (§ 17.3)

7. In general, the test of whether union discipline that does not affect the employment relationship is permissible under the proviso to Section 8(b)(1)(A) even though it might otherwise be viewed as coercing or restraining an employee's exercise of her Section 7 rights is: 1) was the rule "properly adopted"; 2) does it serve a "legitimate union interest"; 3) does it impair no policy of federal labor law; 4) is it "reasonably enforced against . . . members who are free to leave the union and escape the rule." (§ 17.3)

TABLE OF CASES

[References are to page numbers]

A

B

C

D

E

F

G

H

I

J

K

L

M

N

O

P

Q

R

S

T

U

V

W

Y

Z

INDEX

PUBLISHER'S INDEXING STAFF

Peter Kendrick	Indexing Manager
Joseph Schneider	Index Editor

Linda Alpert	Freelance Indexer

INDEX

[References are to page numbers.]

A

[References are to page numbers.]

B

[References are to page numbers.]

[References are to page numbers.]

D

[References are to page numbers.]

[References are to page numbers.]

[References are to page numbers.]

[References are to page numbers.]

[References are to page numbers.]

[References are to page numbers.]

[References are to page numbers.]

[References are to page numbers.]

T

[References are to page numbers.]

U

W

Z